STRENGTHS AND CHALLENGES OF NEW IMMIGRANT FAMILIES

STRENGTHS AND CHALLENGES OF NEW IMMIGRANT FAMILIES

Implications for Research, Education, Policy, and Service

EDITED BY
ROCHELLE L. DALLA, JOHN DEFRAIN,
JULIE JOHNSON, AND DOUGLAS A. ABBOTT

LEXINGTON BOOKS
A Division of Rowman & Littlefield Publishers, Inc.
Lanham • Boulder • New York • Toronto • Plymouth, UK

LEXINGTON BOOKS
A division of Rowman & Littlefield Publishers, Inc.
A wholly owned subsidiary of The Rowman & Littlefield Publishing Group, Inc.
4501 Forbes Boulevard, Suite 200
Lanham, MD 20706

Estover Road
Plymouth PL6 7PY
United Kingdom

British Library Cataloguing in Publication Information Available

Library of Congress Cataloging-in-Publication Data

Strengths and challenges of new immigrant families : implications for research, education,
policy, and service / edited by Rochelle L. Dalla . . . [et al.].
   p. cm.
 Includes bibliographical references and index.
 ISBN-13: 978-0-7391-1456-8 (cloth : alk. paper)
 ISBN-10: 0-7391-1456-5 (cloth : alk. paper)
 ISBN-13: 978-0-7391-3060-5 (electronic)
 ISBN-10: 0-7391-3060-9 (electronic)
 1. Immigrant families. 2. Family social work. 3. Family policy. 4. Family. I. Dalla,
Rochelle L.
 HQ519.S77 2009
 306.85086'912—dc22   2008024522

Printed in the United States of America

♾ ™ The paper used in this publication meets the minimum requirements of American
National Standard for Information Sciences—Permanence of Paper for Printed Library
Materials, ANSI/NISO Z39.48-1992.

CONTENTS

Introduction

ROCHELLE L. DALLA, JOHN DeFRAIN, JULIE JOHNSON,
AND DOUGLAS A. ABBOTT

IMMIGRATION. How can a single word evoke such emotionally charged and intense reactions? On the one hand, passion and compassion; on the other, anger and even rage. Although we cannot answer this question definitively, we do know that the general public obtains most information and knowledge about *immigration* through media snippets, newspaper headlines, and CNN highlights. Unfortunately, the majority of these accounts are negatively slanted and often politically motivated.

In fact, in this 2008 election year, much attention has focused on immigration issues—political hot buttons—including "the problem" of America's porous borders, the provision of so-called amnesty for undocumented residents, and English-only legislation. Many of these issues have, not surprisingly, spurred demonstrations and protests across the country. Often missing from the dialogue, however, is a discussion of the *strengths* of immigrant newcomers—the abilities and positive characteristics they bring as individuals and families to our country, and how these contribute to the agency, growth, and vitality of America. This book was created as a means of contributing to the ongoing dialogue on immigration in this country.

The initial idea to create a book about *Strengths and Challenges of New Immigrant Families* surfaced nearly four years ago. In the fall of 2004, Drs. John DeFrain, Julie Johnson, Doug Abbott, and I were the guest editors for a special edition of *Great Plains Research* (see DeFrain, Dalla, Abbott &

Johnson, 2004) which focused exclusively on the *strengths and challenges* of new immigrant families in the Great Plains (i.e., the high plateau region in central North America that stretches from northeastern Canada to southern Texas—an area of approximately 1,200,000 square miles). Our intent from the outset was transparent; we wanted to move the discussion of immigration, generally speaking, and of immigrant families specifically, to include *how* and *in what ways* new immigrants to America (those arriving within the past thirty years) have changed the social and geocultural landscape of this country in positive, beneficial, and valuable ways. We wanted the *assets* of new immigrant families—their capacities for resilience, for learning, for growth, and for adaptation—to be evident to the reader, in addition to the clear generalization of how these attributes contribute to the host country. Despite the geographic focus of the special edition of *Great Plains Research*, the response to our call for manuscripts was impressive.

Manuscripts were submitted from colleagues in academia, as well as policy advocates and human-service providers. They described working with immigrant families arriving in the Great Plains from nearly every corner of the globe. Limited only by space constraints, the final product was a compilation of ten separate articles that, collectively, began an open and rich dialogue about new immigrant families living beyond the borders of the Great Plains—those residing across the entire nation from coastal seaports and urban gateway cities, to isolated rural areas in low-lying southern states and the midwestern prairies and western plains. It was through this discussion that this book was conceived.

There is much to consider when one assumes the editorial responsibilities for the creation of a book—from structural and functional issues (i.e., size, page limitations, primary audience) to abstract and conceptual possibilities (e.g., To what extent will new discoveries be made in our understanding of the strengths and resilience of new immigrants? To what extent will these new discoveries contribute to future scholarship, intervention strategies, and policy initiatives?). In discussing these issues, we made an important decision that helped to form the foundation for this book: The focus would not only be on the *strengths* of immigrant families, but additionally, we concluded that the *implications* of these strengths for families, communities, and the culture as a whole needed to be made explicit. This book, it was hoped, would provide a springboard from which to answer the *application* and *what now* questions for those who work with immigrant families in a variety of capacities—from academicians and researchers, to educators and human-service providers.

Our call for papers was distributed extensively, reaching every region of the country, and received with considerable enthusiasm. Similar to the *Great Plains Research Special Edition* Call, we received manuscripts from members of the academic community representing a variety of fields and disciplines, and also from human-service providers and policy advocates. Manuscripts were diverse in content and scope, and written to convey strengths and challenges of new immigrant families in America through a *variety of means*, including qualitative and quantitative research, theoretical and discussion pieces, and personal essays. As the editors, our primary task was to read, reread, review, and digest each manuscript, with careful and deliberate consideration to the *contribution* each would make to the book, to the literature base, and to a larger understanding of immigrant family strengths and challenges. In addition to our own study of the articles presented, we created an editorial board—an international group of colleagues that literally spanned the globe. These astute advisers provided us with additional content knowledge and practically oriented expertise and understanding. The editorial board members served as reviewers; each manuscript was blind-reviewed by at least two individuals whose own work and experience positioned them to add additional insight into the potential contribution of each manuscript. Editorial board members' feedback and helpful suggestions, in conjunction with our own analyses, allowed for final selection of nineteen articles to be included in this publication.

However, given the extensive range of topics covered, populations described, and strategic foci (e.g., basic research versus programmatic intervention), arranging the final manuscripts into a coherent whole proved more complex than earlier imagined. Over the course of several weeks, Dr. DeFrain and I read, and then reread, each of the articles. Our task was to perform a content analysis, in a manner of speaking, that would result in a table of contents complete with labels and headings, which would reveal a natural, logical, and overarching structure to the diversity of manuscripts before us. We assumed, inaccurately, that our two tables of contents would look quite similar; this, however, was not the case. We quickly determined that several different individuals charged with the same task would each devise a host of varied, yet completely defensible and *accurate* organizational structures.

Rather than becoming discouraged, we viewed this minor impasse as an opportunity for greater exploration and discussion. Together, the four editors met as a group with the goal of explicating themes of convergence between the two tables of contents, and further, to examine in greater depth potential similarities among the articles that may have been over-looked. From this discussion, a new table of contents emerged including four overarching sections comprised of four or five chapters in each. The authors of each chapter pose a number of significant questions, provide new insights for working with immigrant families, and reveal significant strengths of immigrant newcomers that often go unnoticed.

In the first section, for instance, "How Immigration Changes Immi-grants and How Immigrants Change America," the authors address critical issues such as:

- How the measures, research designs, and analytic strategies used to examine the dual-cultural adaptation processes of acculturation and enculturation, have *not* kept pace with the theoretical literature (Knight, Jacobson, Gonzalez, Roosa, and Saenz);
- Psychosocial adaptation among Cambodian adult refugees in Massachusetts who experienced the brutality of the Khmer Rouge (Nou);
- The range of diversity (both within and between) immigrant groups, and the implications of such for policy and service (Trask, Brady, Qiu, and Radnai-Griffin); and
- How cross-cultural competence among family scholars and practitioners includes awareness of one's own ethnic/racial identity on multiple levels, including knowledge about the identity negotiations of new immigrant families and sensitivity to the meaning of white ethnic identity for immigrants (Blume and De Reus).

In the second section, "Marriages and Families," a host of additional critical issues are addressed including:

- The changes in both marriage and family life attributed to the process of immigration to America, as experienced by Indian immigrants (Abbott and Moulik Gupta);
- How cultural values and practices inform our understanding of strong marriages among Latinos (Skogrand, Hatch, and Singh);
- Processes of maintaining strength and resilience in the face of diversity, across multi-generational Hmong and Somali families (Detzner, Şenyürekli, Yang, and Sheikh);
- Bereavement and the grief process related to the immigration experience and loss of the home country (Miller and González); and

- Career development and employment transitions among immigrant women (Yakushko).

The third section of the book, "Parents and Children," is comprised of six chapters. In each, significant factors relevant for understanding parent-child relationships across the life-course are explored. These include the following:

- Challenges and barriers to childcare faced by African immigrant parents (Amarapurkar and Hogan);
- Cultural dilemmas and child rearing practices and decisions experienced by immigrant Asian Indian parents (Londhe);
- Intergenerational differences in acculturation and family conflict among Korean immigrant parents and adolescents (Hofstetter, Usita, Hovell, Irvin, Martinez-Donate, Jung, Park, Paik, Zakarian, and Lee);
- Experiences of the "Lost Boys" (and girls) of Sudan displaced by the Sudanese war and relocated in Michigan (Luster, Johnson, and Bates);
- Relationships between migrant adult children and their parents who remain in the home country (Panda and Sanders); and
- Family dynamics created by co-residence among Chinese immigrants and their adult children in the United States (Xie and Xia).

The fourth and final section of this book, "Community and Programmatic Issues," focuses exclusively on community-level structures and processes, and intervention-based strategies influencing new immigrants' adaptation to life in America. The chapters pose significant questions for consideration, and raise critical points for discussion, such as:

- Predictors of satisfaction among newly arrived and long-term residents of a rural, Midwestern community following rapid influx of immigrants (Potter, Cantarero, and Boren);
- The extent to which immigrant families' food security, housing, and social support are impacted by state and community context (Greder, Cook, Garasky, Sano, and Randall);
- A new theoretical model regarding factors which can precipitate and diffuse stress experienced by immigrant parents (Radina, Wilson, and Hennon); and

- Strategies for achieving full cultural competency and responsiveness among organizations serving Spanish-speaking immigrant Latinos (Uttal).

Despite the complexities involved in creating and editing a book on the *Strengths and Challenges of New Immigrant Families* in the United States and focusing specifically on *implications* for continued scholarship and service, this project was a labor of love from its inception. The authors have impressed us with their passion for working with new immigrant families, with their interdisciplinary expertise, and with their commitment to seeing this book to fruition. We believe we have been successful in achieving our original intent: To create a book that honors the remarkable *attributes* of new immigrant families that do, and will continue, to shape, mold, and influence this country, their new homeland, in positive and beneficial ways.

References

DeFrain, J., Dalla, R. L., Abbott, D. A., & Johnson, J. (2004). New immigrants in the Great Plains: Strengths and challenges. *Great Plains Research: A Journal of Natural and Social Sciences, 14*(2), 163–368.

HOW IMMIGRATION CHANGES IMMIGRANTS AND HOW IMMIGRANTS CHANGE AMERICA I

An Evaluation of the Psychological Research on Acculturation and Enculturation Processes among Recently Immigrating Populations

1

GEORGE P. KNIGHT, RYAN P. JACOBSON, NANCY A. GONZALES, MARK W. ROOSA, AND DELIA S. SAENZ

Abstract

This chapter describes the dual-cultural adaptation processes of acculturation and enculturation among recent immigrant populations. Based upon a critical review of the available measures of these processes; we conclude that these measures, the research designs in which they have been used, and the analytical strategies that researchers have utilized have generally not kept pace with the richness of the theoretical literature. This is particularly the case with regard to acculturation and enculturation being multi-axial and multidimensional processes of change. Finally, we provide suggestions for researchers interested in furthering our understanding of these processes of dual-cultural adaptation.

Keywords: Immigrant Families, Acculturation, Mixed Cultural Families, Dual-Cultural Adaptation, Enculturation

Address all correspondence to Dr. George P. Knight, Department of Psychology, Arizona State University, Box 871104, Tempe, AZ 85287-1104. Phone: 480-965-2590. E-mail: george.knight@asu.edu.

T HE RACIAL AND ETHNIC MAKEUP of the United States is rapidly changing (U.S. Census Bureau, 2002). These demographic changes are partly a function of substantial immigration with approximately 12 percent of the current U.S. population being foreign born (U.S. Census Bureau, 2004). These demographic shifts present a host of challenges for public policy makers, psychological research, and for the immigrants themselves. Immigrants, who usually are ethnic minorities, face the dual cultural adaptations required to be functioning members of their ethnic groups, and at the same time of mainstream U.S. society. They must adapt to the expectations of their ethnic cultures (i.e., become enculturated) while simultaneously adapting to a host culture (i.e., become acculturated) that may have different rules, different values, and a different language from their culture of origin. These dual adaptation demands can be quite challenging, presenting substantial risks for mental health problems, poor academic performance, and other negative life outcomes. Clearly, a better understanding of the processes of dual–cultural adaptation is critical from a public health and public policy perspective (Gonzales, Knight, Birman & Sirolli, 2004) if social scientists are to adequately respond to the challenges presented by rapidly changing U.S. demographics. In this chapter, we focus on measurement of cultural adaptation processes. Through a critical analysis of item content, scoring procedures, and the manner in which existing measures have been used, our intent is to stimulate necessary methodological advances in this important research field. In our analysis we focus on the ability of current measures to assess the processes of acculturation and enculturation among ethnic groups with a recent and continuing history of immigration to the United States; we discuss key limitations of these measures and the ways in which they have been used, and we offer suggestions for overcoming these limitations.

Acculturation, Enculturation, and Dual-Cultural Adaptation

Based upon recent advances in theoretical perspectives on acculturation and enculturation at the level of the individual immigrant (e.g., Berry, 2003; Gonzales, Knight, Morgan-Lopez, Saenz & Sirolli, 2002; Nguyen, Messe & Stollak, 1999; Tsai, Chentsova-Dutton & Wong, 2002), we define acculturation and enculturation as processes of cultural adaptation that produce changes in a wide array of psychosocial dimensions, including behaviors, knowledge, beliefs, attitudes, values, and self-concept broadly conceived (Gonzales et al., 2002). Acculturation is a process of adaptation to the mainstream or host culture, while enculturation is a process of adaptation to the ethnic culture. These adaptations occur through developmental and socialization processes in the home and broader community. Moreover, these adaptations unfold over time and throughout the lifespan of ethnic minority individuals who have been in the United States for several generations, as well as those who have recently immigrated. We believe that changes in knowledge, behaviors, attitudes/beliefs, and values based upon these socialization experiences become internalized in the form of social identities (i.e., an ethnic identity and a mainstream identity) that, along with other social identities, form the basis of self-concept. Ethnic and mainstream identities include the degree to which the individual sees herself or himself as a member of an ethnic group and/or the majority, and like other social identities, have a broader influence by providing the cognitive/mental structures used to organize knowledge and understanding of relevant cultural phenomena. Further, the self-concept may include multiple social identities that collectively reflect varying levels of congruence, and sometimes competing, attitudes, expectations, and values.

Changes produced by these socialization processes are likely to be dependent upon the developmental state of the individual. That is, enculturation and acculturation processes during early childhood may be manifested in changes in relatively simple behaviors (e.g., native language/English language use and proficiency, parent-directed ethnic/mainstream social interactions) and knowledge (e.g., customary ethnic/mainstream traditions and celebrations). During adolescence and young adulthood, enculturation and acculturation processes may be manifested in changes in awareness of more complex volitional social behaviors represented as preferences (e.g., self-chosen preferences to speak native language/English and to interact with ethnic/mainstream persons, or self-directed identity achievement) and internalized values (e.g., familism). Since enculturation and acculturation experiences provide direction for these broadly defined developmental and socialization processes, it is necessary to use developmentally appropriate measures to assess these processes of change.

The developmental state of an individual may also influence the general rate at which acculturative and enculturative changes occur and the social spheres that are most salient as sources of cultural influence. For example, relative to their parents, immigrant children often experience more rapid rates of acculturation and associated changes in their mainstream social identities, because they attend U.S. schools and have extended daily interactions with mainstream peers and teachers (Portes & Rumbaut, 1996; Szapocznik & Kurtines, 1993). Adolescents, relative to younger children, may have a more highly developed mainstream social identity, because they are more apt to be influenced by their peers and broader community influences, and because of increased involvement in social groups outside the home (Ying, Coombs & Lee, 1999). Parents, on the other hand, have greater abilities to structure their own enculturative and acculturative experiences. Some immigrant parents may limit their own involvement in or be excluded from mainstream social settings, and experience much slower rates of acculturation and much less development of their mainstream social identity. Differential rates of cultural adaptation among family members may lead to disparities in values and expectations *within* the family that cause difficulties for families (Szapocznik & Kurtines, 1980), particularly during developmental transitions around adolescence.

Measures of Acculturation and Enculturation

In this chapter, we examined thirty-seven measures of acculturation, enculturation, and ethnic identity that have been used in research focused on major U.S. immigrant groups. Our analysis is based upon three key features of these measures: the ability to assess enculturative as well as acculturative axis constructs; the ability to assess multiple psychosocial dimensions; and the likely developmental period in which the measure may be able to detect acculturative and enculturative changes in the psychosocial dimensions measured. The first two criteria, psychosocial dimensionality and multiple axes of change, are central to a number of recent theoretical contributions (e.g., Berry, 2003; Gonzales et al., 2002; Nguyen et al., 1999; Tsai et al., 2002). The third criterion, developmental relevance, is an extension of the concept of psychosocial dimensionality and reflects our speculations regarding the developmental periods over which changes in specific psychosocial dimensions are most likely. Consideration of these assumptions in measurement will play an important role in stimulating future advancements in research on acculturation and enculturation.

Table 1.1 presents the framework of psychosocial dimensions used in our analysis, including a definition of each category, an example item, and the most relevant developmental periods. Table 1.2 presents an overview of our analyses of the measures with respect to each of the three theoretical considerations, including results for all dimensional subcategories. In

Table 1.1. Definition (Example) of Each Psychological Dimension Used in the Item Coding

Dimensions	Developmental Relevance	Definition [Example]
Knowledge		**Items assess knowledge of facts, behaviors, and practices associated with a given culture.**
Facts	Early Childhood	Knowledge of current and historical facts relevant to a given culture [e.g., "How well do you know American national heroes?" —Zea et al. (2003)].
Behaviors and Practices	Early Childhood	Knowledge of appropriate behaviors and practices within a given culture. [e.g., "I am familiar with Chinese cultural practices and customs." —Tsai et al. (2000)].
Behaviors		**Items assess simple behaviors, general aspects of lifestyle and abilities, and complex social behaviors.**
Simple Behaviors	Early Childhood	Engaging in a behavior or the general likelihood of engaging in a behavior without invoking personal volition [e.g., "How frequently do you eat Vietnamese food?" —Nguyen & von Eye (2002)].
Lifestyles, Exposure, and Abilities	Early Childhood	General features of a person's daily life or their past and/or present exposure to general cultural influences [e.g., "My contact with Mexico has been . . . "—Cuellar et al. (1995)].
Complex Behaviors	Late Childhood/ Early Adolescence	Presence of personal volition, refers to behaviors in very specific social contexts, and/or refers to active involvement in a specific social activity [e.g., "Whenever possible, I try to speak my Chinese language with my Chinese friends." —Kwan & Sodowsky (1997)].
Attitudes and Beliefs		**Items assess the endorsement of culturally relevant attitudes, beliefs, and/or preferences.**
Context-dependent	Late Childhood/ Early Adolescence	Individual's attitude, belief, or preference in a specific social situation or context [e.g., "What is your food preference at home?" —Suinn et al. (1987)].
General	Adolescence/ Young Adulthood	General and/or enduring attitude or belief [e.g., "Which culture and way of life do you believe is responsible for the social problems (such as poverty, teenage pregnancies, and gangs) found in some Mexican-American communities?" —Mendoza (1989)].
Values	Adolescence/ Young Adulthood	**Items assess the endorsement of culturally relevant values [e.g., "Personal achievements are the most important things in life." —Knight, Gonzales, et al. (2006)].**
The Self		**Items assess culturally relevant aspects of the self-concept and/or identity.**
Cultural/ Ethnic Label	Early Childhood	Individual's choice of cultural or ethnic label [e.g., "How do you identify yourself?" —Cuellar et al. (1980)].

(continues)

Table 1.1. *(continued)*

Dimensions	Developmental Relevance	Definition [Example]
Cultural/Ethnic Exploration	Late Childhood/ Early Adolescence	Active involvement in the development of a cultural or ethnic identity [e.g., "In order to learn more about my ethnic background, I have often talked to other people about my ethnic group." —Phinney (1992)].
Cultural Pride	Adolescence/ Young Adulthood	Pride an individual feels for their group [e.g., "Members of my ethnic group do not have much to be proud of." —Barry (2002)].
Belonging	Adolescence/ Young Adulthood	Extent to which an individual feels that they belong to their group [e.g., " I feel that I am part of Russian culture." —Birman & Trickett (2001)].
Identity	Adolescence/ Young Adulthood	Extent to which a cultural or ethnic label represents who they are [e.g., " I have a strong sense of being Asian." —Barry (2002)].
Centrality of Culture	Adolescence/ Young Adulthood	Centrality or importance to the self of being part of a culture or engaging in behaviors, endorsing beliefs, or holding values reflective of a given culture [e.g., " Being a member of my culture of origin plays an important part in my life." —Zea et al. (2003)].

analyzing the measures, the second author conducted the primary coding of measures while the first author coded a random selection of 20 percent of the measures to allow for an examination of reliability. Agreement regarding primary psychosocial categorization was achieved for 95.3 percent of the items. Agreement regarding dimensional subcategories was achieved for 90.6 percent of the items.

Multiple Axes of Change

Numerous theorists have suggested that acculturative and enculturative processes are separable, each representing a distinct axis of cultural change (e.g., Berry, 2003; Gonzales et al., 2002; Ryder, Alden & Paulhus, 2000) such that simultaneously high, simultaneously low, or quite different levels of adaptation to both mainstream and ethnic cultures are possible. We analyzed the uni- versus dual-axis focus of each measure through examination of item content and scoring procedures. For example, the Acculturation Rating Scale for Mexican Americans II (ARSMA II: Cuellar, Arnold & Maldonado, 1995) contains items that assess both acculturative and enculturative processes in separate items, producing separate scales for Mexican Orientation and Anglo Orientation. However, a final overall *acculturation*

Table 1.2. Percentage of Items across Axes, Dimensions, and Stages of Developmental Relevance

Author/Inventory	Total Items	Axes			Knowledge		Behaviors			Attitudes & Beliefs		Values	The Self						Developmental Relevance			
		Acculturation	Enculturation	Uni-axial	Facts	Beliefs and Practices	Simple Behaviors	Lifestyle, Exposure, and Abilities	Complex Behaviors	Context-Dependent	General		Self-Label	Cultural/Ethnic Exploration	Pride	Belonging	Identity	Centrality of Culture	Early Childhood	Late Childhood	Early Adolescence	Adolescence/Young Adulthood
Uni-Axial Measures																						
Barry (2001)	29	13.8	13.8	31.0			10.3	13.8	41.4	13.8	3.5	3.5				13.8			24.1	55.2		20.7
Barry (2002)	40		100						30.0		20.0	22.5		2.5	15.0		2.5	5.0		35.0		65.0
Bernal & Knight (1991)	136	21.3	58.1	5.1	14.7		15.4	22.8	26.5	10.3		1.5	0.7		0.7				53.6	36.8		2.2
Burnam et al. (1987)	26			100			42.3	42.3	7.7	3.9			3.9						88.5	11.5		
Cuellar et al. (1980)	20		5.0	95.0			10.0	45.0	5.0	15.0	10.0	5.0	5.0		5.0		5.0		60.0	20.0		20.0
Deyo et al. (1985)	4			100				75.0			25.0								75.0			25.0
Franco (1983)	10			100				70.0		20.0			10.0						80.0	20.0		
Garcia & Lega (1979)	8		100		50.0		25.0	25.0											100			
Kim et al. (1999)	36		100									100										100
Kwan & Sodowsky (1997)	35		100				5.7	11.4	37.1		22.9	5.7		2.9			5.7	8.6	17.1	40.0		42.9
Marin et al. (1987)	12			100			50.0	16.7	8.3	16.7	8.3								66.7	25.0		8.3
Martinez et al. (1984)	30		100				10.0	86.7		3.3									96.7	3.3		
Mendoza (1989)	29			100	3.5		51.7	17.2	3.5	3.5	10.4				3.5		3.5	3.5	72.4	6.9		20.7
Montgomery (1992)	30	33.3	33.3	33.3				16.7	3.3	60.0	16.7		3.3						20.0	63.3		16.7
Norris et al. (1996)	4			100			75.0		25.0										75.0	25.0		
Phinney (1992)	23			100			17.4	8.7	4.4		13.0		4.4	17.4	13.0	8.7		13.0	30.4	21.8		47.8
Ramirez (1983)	66	9.1	25.8	34.8			13.6	83.3		3.0									97.0	3.0		
Suinn et al. (1987)	26	7.7	11.5	80.8			11.5	34.6		19.2	3.9	7.7	3.9		3.8	7.7	7.7		50.0	19.2		30.8
Szapocznik et al. (1978)	24			100			33.3	12.5	12.5	41.7									45.8	54.2		
Tropp et al. (1999)	10			100	10.0		40.0				10.0				10.0	30.0			10.0	40.0		50.0

(continues)

Table 1.2. *(continued)*

Measure	n																	
Tsai & Curbow (2001)	26	23.1	73.1	3.8								29.4	35.3		23.5	15.4	23.1	61.5
Umana-Taylor et al. (2004)	17		100			11.8										11.8	29.4	58.8
Unger et al. (2002)	8			100		25.0	12.5	25.0	12.5				12.5			37.5	37.5	25.0
Wallen et al. (2002)	4			100			25.0	25.0	25.0							25.0	50.0	25.0
Wolfe et al. (2001)	18	66.7	33.3				11.1			16.7	72.2						11.1	88.9
Multi-Axial Measures																		
Birman & Trickett (2001)	50	50.0	50.0			32.0	40.0					8.0	8.0	8.0	4.0	72.0		28.0
Chung et al. (2004)	45	66.7	33.3		6.7	40.0	6.7		20.0			6.7	6.7	6.7		60.0	20.0	20.0
Cuellar et al. (1995) Scale 1	30	43.0	57.0			13.3	36.7	6.7	30.0					13.3		50.0	36.7	13.3
Felix-Ortiz et al. (1994)	35	20.0	48.6	28.6	22.9	2.9	17.1	5.7	20.0	17.1	14.3					42.9	25.7	31.4
Knight, Gonzales et al. (2006)	63	36.5	63.5							7.9	92.1							100
Marin & Gamba (1996)	24	50.0	50.0			41.7	50.0	8.3								91.7	8.3	
Nguyen & von Eye (2002)	50	50.0	50.0			36.0	8.0		8.0	12.0	24.0			4.0	8.0	44.0	8.0	48.0
Oetting & Beauvais (1991)	12	50.0	50.0			16.7	50.0	33.3								66.7	33.3	
Stephenson (2000)	32	50.0	50.0		3.1	34.4	15.6	9.4	15.6				9.4			65.6	25.0	9.4
Szapocznik et al. (1980)	33	36.4	36.4	27.3		36.4			100								100	
Tsai et al. (2000)	77	49.4	49.4	1.3	2.6	44.2	24.7	5.2	2.6	6.5		6.5	3.9	2.6	1.3	71.4	7.8	20.8
Zea et al. (2003)	42	50.0	50.0		28.6	42.9						9.5	4.8	9.5	4.8	71.4		28.6

Note: Within-measure percentages do not always sum to 100 percent across coding categories as the classification of some items is unclear. Unclear items are included in the total item counts for each measure, but are excluded from the subcategory percentage breakdowns.

score is calculated by subtracting the Mexican Orientation score from the Anglo Orientation score. Hence, the scoring system generates two scores (Mexican Orientation and Anglo Orientation) that represent a dual-axial process and a single score (acculturation) that represents a uni-axial process. In stark contrast, the original version of this measure (the ARSMA: Cuellar, Harris & Jasso, 1980) includes almost exclusively uni-axial items and produces only an acculturation score.

In our analyses, we classified a measure as dual-axial only if the items and scoring procedures retained a distinction between these two forms of cultural change. Based on these criteria, twenty-five (68 percent) are uni-axial (listed first in table 1.1). Seven of the uni-axial measures include items that have the potential to assess both axes, but the scoring procedures subvert this distinction. Twelve (32 percent) of the measures are dual-axial and allow for separate assessments of acculturation and enculturation, although even several of these measures include a few uni-axial items that pit acculturative responses against enculturative responses within the context of these items.

Multiple Psychosocial Dimensions of Change

While most recent theoretical approaches acknowledge the importance of a multidimensional approach, consensus regarding the relevant psychosocial dimensions has not been established. Examples of some of the proposed dimensions include knowledge of cultural facts, communication styles, affiliation preferences, daily habits, participation in cultural activities, language use and preference, beliefs, attitudes, values, cognitive styles, personality, self-concept, and ethnic or cultural identity (Berry, 1980; Félix-Ortiz, Newcomb & Myers, 1994; Marin, 1992; Ryder et al., 2000; Zane & Mak, 2003). To accommodate this diversity, we created a framework that relies upon five general psychosocial dimensions that can be impacted by cultural change. These dimensions are knowledge, behaviors, attitudes and beliefs, values, and the self. Subcategories reflect different aspects of these general psychosocial dimensions.

While our categorization system simply focuses on the psychosocial dimension implied by particular items, it does not necessarily reflect a comprehensive range of psychosocial dimensions that could be impacted by these processes of change. We do not claim that all items included within a dimensional subcategory are equally precise. Measures of acculturation and enculturation assess cultural *knowledge* primarily within two subcategories, knowledge of *facts* and knowledge of *behaviors and practices* (table 1.1). Nine (24 percent) measures in our review contain at least one item that assesses cultural knowledge. The average proportion of knowledge items within these nine measures is relatively small (18 percent) and the majority of these (90 percent) assess knowledge of *facts*.

Behaviors are assessed by current measures in three general ways (table 1.1). Items assessing *simple behaviors* focus on the frequency of engaging in specific behaviors that may be typical in a given culture. These items assess the frequency or likelihood of engaging in a particular behavior and do not invoke the presence of personal volition. *Lifestyles, exposure*, and *abilities* items capture features of a person's daily life, past and present exposure to cultural influences, and/or basic abilities and capacities relevant to participation in a particular culture. These items do not make explicit reference to individual behaviors, but behavioral contexts are implied by references to features of the community, objects in the home, participation in cultural celebrations, generational status, or language ability. More *complex behaviors* are assessed by items that focus on very specific social behaviors or on cultural influences on cognitive style with an emphasis on personal volition. Thirty-four measures (92 percent), and 60 percent of the items on these measures, contain items that assess some aspect of behavior (table 1.2). However, a substantial portion (33 percent) of these items focus on language use. The largest subcategory of behavioral items was *lifestyles, exposure*, and *abilities* (47 percent), followed by *simple behaviors* (35 percent) and *complex behaviors* (18 percent).

Attitudes and *beliefs* items are subcategorized into those that assess *context-dependent* versus *general* attitudes and beliefs (table 1.1). Context-dependent attitude/belief items assess an individual's attitude or preference in a particular social situation or context. General items assess more enduring, context-independent, attitudes and beliefs. Twenty-nine measures (78 percent, table 1.2) contain at least one item that assesses attitudes and beliefs, and constitute 21 percent of the items in these measures. Sixty-two percent of the attitude/belief items were considered *context-dependent* and 38 percent were *general*. Items assessing attitudes toward language (i.e., general or context-dependent preferences for a specific language) were also prevalent, making up 28 percent of the total attitude/belief items.

Values items (table 1.1) ask about general adherence to a culture's value system or specific values reflective of a given culture. Eleven measures (30 percent, table 1.2) have at least one item that assesses values. Twenty-nine percent of the items in these measures assess adherence to values.

The *self* dimension includes six categories (table 1.1): *cultural self-labeling* items ask the respondent only to assign to themselves a cultural or ethnic label; *cultural/ethnic exploration* items assess the extent to which a person thinks about or explores the meaning of their culture/ethnicity; *cultural/ ethnic pride* items assess the pride felt for one's cultural group or attitudes directed toward aspects of group membership; *belonging* items assess the sense of belonging to or fit when interacting with members of a cultural group; *identity* items assess the extent to which a person feels identified with a particular cultural or ethnic group; and *centrality* items assess the degree to which engaging in cultural behaviors or practices, endorsing culturally specific attitudes/beliefs, or holding certain core cultural values is important to the person's sense of self. Within this framework, we distinguish between items that reflect a simple choice of cultural label and those that assess the extent to which that label adequately represents their identity. Twenty-one measures (57 percent, table 1.2) contain items assessing some aspect of the self and constitute 27 percent of the items in these measures. Items assessing aspects of the self are distributed across subcategories as follows: 5 percent assess *self-labeling*, 9 percent assess *cultural/ethnic exploration*, 28 percent assess *cultural pride*, 21 percent assess *belonging*, 20 percent assess *identity*, and 17 percent assess *centrality*.

A majority of the measures (68 percent) assess three or fewer of the five general dimensions. Further, many of the measures that include items assessing four or five dimensions include too few items to assess all of these dimensions adequately. Finally, twelve (32 percent) of the measures had a third or more of the items focusing disproportionally on language-related (behaviors, abilities, and/or attitudes) items.

Linkage between Psychological Dimensions and Development

One advantage of differentiating the psychological dimensions assessed in these measures is that changes in these different psychological dimensions are likely to occur during quite different developmental periods. For example, the ability to abstract rules from consistent behavioral guidance provided by parents requires a level of cognitive ability that may not be available until late childhood or adolescence. If so, then it is likely that the internalization of culturally related values does not occur in an efficient manner until late childhood or early adolescence. Further, changes in certain psychosocial dimensions (e.g., knowledge and/or behaviors) may create the potential for changes in others (e.g., attitudes/beliefs, values, self).

We have speculatively linked each psychosocial dimension to a potentially relevant developmental period (i.e., early childhood, late childhood/ early adolescence, adolescence/young adulthood). This linkage is intended to be suggestive for future research, rather than an absolute guide for measure selection. Further, it is likely that there will be some degree of change in each psychosocial dimension outside the developmental periods we identify as most relevant. Additionally, acculturative and enculturative changes across psychosocial dimensions may not mirror a normative developmental progression for individuals who immigrate to the United States later in their lives (after developing an established sense of self and identity elsewhere). Despite this complexity, developmental relevance should play a significant role in measure selection. Please note that the assignment of items to developmental periods is based solely on the underlying psychosocial dimension implied by the item. Word choice and phrasing complexity of individual items may not necessarily be appropriate for the developmental period we have assigned.

The early childhood category was assigned to dimensions that do not clearly reflect personal volition or self-involvement (i.e., behavioral frequency rather than preference). The late childhood/early adolescence categorization was assigned to dimensions characterized by items indicating a moderate to high degree of personal volition and self-involvement and that are more central to the emerging differentiation of distinct social identities. The presence of contextual or situational explanations for responses to some of these items is a factor that limited them from assessing even more developmentally sophisticated changes. For example, items reflecting context-dependent preferences (e.g., preferred language *at home*) were included in the late childhood/early adolescence category, while general preference items (e.g., preferred language) were included in the adolescence/young adulthood category. The adolescence/young adulthood categorization was assigned to psychosocial dimensions that reflect central features of the self-concept and are essential to the development of fully differentiated social identities. Changes within these dimensions are likely to influence a particularly broad range of individual outcomes and are also likely to be dependent on earlier and less developmentally sophisticated changes. The presence of self-involvement and personal volition are key indicators of these developmentally sophisticated changes. Thirty-two (86 percent, table 1.2) measures focus at least 50 percent of their items at a single developmental level. Perhaps more importantly, twenty (54 percent) measures include at least one item representing each level of developmental sophistication.

Limitations Associated with the Use of These Measures of Acculturation and Enculturation

The empirical research examining the process of acculturation and enculturation has progressed slowly in part because of three major limitations associated with the research strategies utilized. First, theory has suggested that it is important to measure the dual-axial nature of cultural adaptation separately along a number of dimensions (e.g., Berry, Trimble & Olmedo, 1986; Cuellar et al., 1995) in order to identify levels of biculturalism in individuals. In fact, the majority of the studies reported in the literature have measured acculturation along a continuum representing the culture of origin at one extreme and the host culture at the other extreme (Gonzales et al., 2002). Even among studies that specifically set out to examine the effects of biculturalism, most assumed that bicultural individuals simply fall at some midway point on a scale ranging from not acculturated to highly acculturated (for a notable exception, see Félix-Ortiz & Newcomb, 1995). Our review of the measures presented above is clearly consistent with this interpretation of the current state of the literature.

Second, despite widespread agreement in the theoretical literature regarding the multidimensional nature of acculturation and enculturation (i.e., adaptation in terms of knowledge, behaviors, attitudes, beliefs, values, the self-concept, and identity), the majority of studies assess a narrow range of behavioral indicators, often only focused on language skills or affiliation with ethnic or mainstream peers (Gonzales et al., 2002). By attending primarily to language or affiliation patterns, we may be missing other important aspects of acculturation. Even when multiple dimensions are assessed, the scoring procedures often ignore the multidimensional nature by combining all dimensions into a single index. Furthermore, there have been few attempts to ensure that the dimensions assessed are selected based upon the developmental status of the participants sampled. For example, measures such as the ARSMA II are often used in adolescent and young adult samples, even though the limited longitudinal evidence available (Knight, Vargas-Chanes, Cota-Robles, Losoya, Chassin & Lee, 2006) indicates that the psychological dimensions assessed by this measure do not change significantly during these developmental periods. Once again our review of the measures of acculturation and enculturation is consistent with this interpretation of the literature.

The preponderance of language and/or affiliation measures and the underrepresentation of other dimensions (particularly values and self-concept dimensions) may result in skewed assessments and a limited understanding of how acculturation and enculturation processes relate to mental health and other significant outcomes associated with adaptation processes. The various dimensions of culture change do not necessarily change at the same pace and may change during quite different developmental periods. For example, Knight, Vargas-Chanes, et al. (2006) identified trajectories of change in ethnic/mainstream affiliation preferences, ethnic affirmation and belonging, and ethnic identity achievement among older adolescents, but not in language use. Nor is it likely that acculturative and enculturative changes in these domains impact youths' mental health, academic, and life outcomes in the same manner (Cuellar, Nyberg, Maldonado & Roberts, 1997). For example, Félix-Ortiz and Newcomb (1995) demonstrated differential effects of discrete dimensions of acculturation depending on the type of drug use and gender. Certain components were associated with increased drug use (e.g., defensive Latino activism), whereas others were associated with decreased drug use (e.g., traditional family role expectations). A more complete investigation of the multiple psychological dimensions that change as a result of acculturation and enculturation processes is sorely needed.

Measurement of these processes is also likely to benefit from identification of other potentially relevant psychosocial dimensions outside of currently used frameworks. For example, recent theory and research focused on cultural influences on cognition suggests that cognitive style may be a dimension impacted during acculturative and enculturative processes. Nisbett, Peng, Choi, and Norenzayan (2001) provided a review of research suggesting that East Asians and members of the mainstream U.S. culture differ markedly in their cognitive styles, and that these different cognitive styles result in quite different inferences regarding the cause of real-world events. Emotional style may be another culturally variable dimension that may be impacted by acculturation and enculturation. For example, research has demonstrated ethnic variation in the reported duration and intensity of particular emotion states (Scherer & Wallbott, 1994) and the reported frequency of experiencing particular emotions (Kitayama, Markus & Kurokawa, 2000). If these differences are socialized, then investigations of emotional style and cognitive style within a multidimensional framework may help to provide a more complete understanding of the complex relationships between psychological development, cultural influences, and the significance of cultural changes for the individual.

Third, and perhaps most unfortunately, there have been very few actual assessments of *changes* associated with this dual-cultural adaptation. There have been only three longitudinal studies that we are aware of that have analyzed change over time at the level of the individual. Phinney and Chavira (1992) demonstrate developmental progression in stages of ethnic identity over a three-year period for a very small, non-representative sample of older adolescents from several ethnic groups. French, Seidman, Allen, and Aber (2006) demonstrated developmental changes in group esteem and exploration dimensions of ethnic identity development among adolescents from several ethnic groups. Finally, Knight et al. (2006) demonstrated changes in affiliation preferences and ethnic identity achievement, but not language use, in a sample of older Mexican American adolescents. Hence, although acculturation and enculturation represent processes of change, the literature (with the exception of these three studies) is based upon cross-sectional comparisons (or studies using some other proxy for change such as generational status) and there is a dearth of studies that have actually examined changes in culturally related knowledge, behaviors, attitudes, expectations, values, and social identities over time. Given the tremendous variability in immigrant populations with regard to how many generations their families have been in the United States, how long recently immigrating persons have been in the United States, their reasons for immigration, and the ethnic qualities of the communities in which they live, it is likely that cross-sectional differences confound developmental and background differences in ways that make interpretation of results problematic at best. For example, cross-sectional comparisons of affirmation/belonging and ethnic identity achievement among adolescents and young adults has sometimes been based upon comparisons of high school and college students (e.g., Phinney, 1992). Clearly it is very unlikely that college and high school students are equally representative of the young adults in these ethnic groups. Researchers have relied upon proxies, and relatively indirect evidence, for change that may or may not accurately portray the underlying developmental processes.

Recommendations

It is essential that we address these limitations by investigating the processes of dual-cultural adaptation among immigrant populations longitudinally, and by using assessments that identify changes over time in psychological constructs that reflect the influence of both acculturative and enculturative processes. This requires that researchers selectively examine psychological dimensions appropriate for the developmental status of participants throughout the longitudinal research plan. It is particularly important that we investigate longitudinal changes across life transitions that may involve changes in the degree of contact with, or influence of the ethnic and mainstream community, such as when a child or young adolescent is transitioning from a neighborhood school to a more diverse middle/junior high school. Further, these longitudinal research plans will raise additional difficulties for researchers.

Perhaps foremost among these associated demands, researchers must sample the ethnic population being investigated more broadly. Much of the past research on children has assessed acculturation in a single school or school district representing a narrow proportion of a larger community. Studies of adults most often sample college students or other highly select subsets of the populations. These convenience samples have rarely had more than a fraction of the diversity that exists within the broader ethnic populations. For example, much of this research has sampled only inner-city participants. Further, many of the studies have included only English-speaking participants, even when the broader population includes a substantial proportion of individuals that are not fluent in English or for whom English is a second and less comfortable language. Although some elements of the theories of acculturation and enculturation may be investigated in less than fully diverse and representative samples, a more complete and accurate empirical understanding of these processes will require representative samples.

In addition to this general call for greater sample diversity in acculturation/enculturation research, we recommend that researchers pay careful attention to the issue of sample diversity when choosing analytic plans. As an example, a method of analysis that has gained popularity in recent years involves either categorization (often by arbitrary cut points) or empirical classification of participants into theoretically proposed acculturation *types* based upon responses to a series of items. The most common of these classification systems proposes that there are four acculturation types: assimilation, separation, integration, and marginalization (e.g., Berry, 1980). We suggest that this analytic technique is inappropriate for the vast majority of research projects due to limitations in sample diversity. For example, underrepresentation of separated and marginalized individuals is highly likely in most samples, unless very costly strategic efforts are employed to include such persons. That is, enlisting marginalized and separated individuals into the research endeavor is likely to be difficult simply because they are not psychologically connected to the mainstream culture from which most research efforts originate. Indeed, in one of the relatively better attempts to categorize participants, Coatsworth, Maldonado-Molina, Pantin, and Szapocznik (2005) identified only one marginalized participant and 13 separated participants in a sample of 315 Hispanic adolescents, using criteria that were much less arbitrary than most such attempts. With less than fully diverse and fully representative samples, arbitrary or empirically derived cut points for acculturation categories are very likely inaccurate and misleading. Until category cut points have been validated on fully representative research samples, we recommend that researchers avoid such categorization approaches and concentrate on generating valid continuous dual-axial and multidimensional assessments of acculturation/enculturation.

Furthermore, we need to attend more carefully to the specific cultural experiences of individuals within different groups. Although the general processes of acculturation and enculturation may be the same for individuals across different cultural groups, the specific content that must be measured to assess these changes is highly likely to vary cross-culturally. Hence, we need to move away from sampling strategies that treat all Latino subgroups and all Asian American subgroups as though they are the same. We need to understand and respect that subgroups may experience different ethnic socialization, and that these subgroups might exist within different social contexts and may experience quite different acculturative experiences.

To examine longitudinal changes that occur at specific developmental times, it may be necessary to conduct analyses at the level of the individual psychological dimension or on a composite of a few dimensions rather than on some composite of scores across all dimensions. Given the limitations in the psychological dimensions assessed in most measures and the absence of evidence of actual change associated with enculturation and acculturation, the lack of consideration of the concordance between the individual's developmental status and the developmental relevance of the psychological dimensions assessed has gone unnoticed. The items that have been classified as assessing knowledge and simple behaviors may be more characteristic of enculturative and acculturative changes among young children. The items that have been classified as assessing attitudes, values, and self-concept may be more characteristic of changes occurring during later adolescence and adulthood. If the participants are older adolescents and adults, it may be less meaningful to look for changes in dimensions that reflect simple experiences and behaviors (e.g., specific food consumption, interactions with other ethnic peers, or language use). Indeed, older adolescents (Knight, Vargas-Chanes, et al., 2006) demonstrated changes in attitudes and goals (i.e., affirmation/belonging and ethnic identity achievement) but not simple behaviors (i.e., language use). If participants are young children it may not be meaningful to look for changes in responses that are developmentally beyond them (e.g., ethnic identity achievement). Further, some research questions may be better addressed by the analysis of selective dimensions while other research questions may be better suited to the use of a composite of a broad range of developmentally relevant dimensions.

In addition, researchers need to develop techniques to assess the more significant types of indicators of participants' levels of acculturative and enculturative status. Specifically, we need strategies for assessing the degree of centrality of one's ethnic identity and one's mainstream identity to one's broader self-concept. Identifying the relative centrality of these two social identities to individual's self-concepts could well provide a useful snapshot of cultural orientation among older adolescents and adults. Further, examining changes in this relative centrality over time associated with exposure to acculturation and enculturation experiences may provide the quintessential assessment of the processes of dual-cultural adaptation.

This chapter has focused mainly on our review of extant measures and recommendations for conducting empirical research on acculturation and enculturation. However, many researchers are really focused upon other research topics and simply want to measure acculturation and enculturation to examine some of the diversity within their samples. For example, is the relation between parent-child conflict and child distress moderated by the child's (or parent's) level of acculturation? Our recommendations for these researchers are really little different from those noted above. These researchers need to assess the acculturative and enculturative status of participants using measures that accurately identify participants' connections to the mainstream and ethnic groups (i.e., use measures that are dual-axial), across multiple dimensions that are appropriate indicators of cultural orientation given the developmental state of the participants. Additionally, these researchers need to sample broadly enough so that there is diversity on the dimensions of interest within their samples. Research on the dual-cultural adaptation processes, as well as on the roles these processes play in healthy development, should advance more rapidly once researchers become more aware of the measurement issues involved and make more informed design and analysis decisions.

Acknowledgments

Preparation of this manuscript was supported, in part, by the National Institute of Mental Health (grant # 5-R01-MH68920).

References

Barry, D. T. (2001). The development of a new scale for measuring acculturation: The East Asian Acculturation Measure (EAAM). *Journal of Immigrant Health*, *3*(4), 193–197.

Barry, D. T. (2002). An ethnic identity scale for East Asian immigrants. *Journal of Immigrant Health, 4*(2), 87–94.

Bernal, M. B., & Knight, G. P. (1991). *Ethnic Identity Questionnaire.* Unpublished manuscript, Arizona State University.

Berry, J. W. (1980). Acculturation as varieties of adaptation. In A. M. Padilla (Ed.), *Acculturation: Theory, models and some new findings* (pp. 9–23). Boulder, CO: Westview Press.

Berry, J. W. (2003). Conceptual approaches to acculturation. In K. M. Chun, P. B. Organista & G. Marin (Eds.), *Acculturation: Advances in theory, measurement and applied research* (pp. 17–37). Washington, DC: American Psychological Association.

Berry, J. W., Trimble, J. E., & Olmedo, E. L. (1986). Assessment of acculturation. In W. J. Lonner & J. W. Berry (Eds.), *Field methods in cross-cultural research* (pp. 291–324). Beverly Hills, CA: Sage.

Birman, D., & Trickett, E. J. (2001). Cultural transitions in first-generation immigrants: Acculturation of Soviet refugee adolescents and parents. *Journal of Cross-Cultural Psychology, 32*(4), 456–477.

Burnam, M. A., Telles, C. A., Karno, M., Hough, R. L., & Escobar, J. I. (1987). Measurement of acculturation in a community population of Mexican Americans. *Hispanic Journal of Behavioral Sciences, 9*(2), 105–130.

Chung, R. H. G., Kim, B. S. K., & Abreu, J. M. (2004). Asian American Multidimensional Acculturation Scale: Development, factor analysis, reliability, and validity. *Cultural Diversity and Ethnic Minority Psychology, 10*(1), 66–80.

Coatsworth, J. D., Maldonado-Molina, M., Pantin, H., & Szapocznik, J. (2005). A person-centered and ecological investigation of acculturation strategies in Hispanic immigrant youth. *Journal of Community Psychology, 33*(2), 157–174.

Cuellar, I., Arnold, B., & Maldonado, R. (1995). Acculturation Rating Scale for Mexican Americans-II: A revision of the original ARSMA scale. *Hispanic Journal of Behavioral Sciences, 17*(3), 275–304.

Cuellar, I., Harris, L. C., & Jasso, R. (1980). An acculturation scale for Mexican American normal and clinical populations. *Hispanic Journal of Behavioral Sciences, 2*, 199–217.

Cuellar, I., Nyberg, B., Maldonado, R. E., & Roberts, R. E. (1997). Ethnic identity and acculturation in a young adult Mexican origin populations. *Journal of Consulting and Clinical Psychology, 25*(6), 535–549.

Deyo, R. A., Diehl, A. K., Hazuda, H., & Stern, M. P. (1985). A simple language-based acculturation scale for Mexican Americans: Validation and application to health care research. *American Journal of Public Health, 75*(1), 51–55.

Félix-Ortiz, M., & Newcomb, M. D. (1995). Cultural identity and drug use among Latino and Latina adolescents. In G. J. Botvin, S. Schinke & M. A. Orlandi (Eds.), *Drug abuse prevention with multiethnic youth* (pp. 147–165). Thousand Oaks, CA: Sage.

Félix-Ortiz, M., Newcomb, M. D., & Myers, H. (1994). A multidimensional scale of cultural identity for Latino and Latina adolescents. *Hispanic Journal of Behavioral Sciences, 16*(2), 99–115.

Franco, J. N. (1983). An acculturation scale for Mexican-American children. *The Journal of General Psychology, 108*, 175–181.

French, S. E., Seidman, E., Allen, L., & Aber, J. L. (2006). The development of ethnic identity during adolescence. *Developmental Psychology, 42*(1), 1–10.

Garcia, M., & Lega, L. I. (1979). Development of a Cuban ethnic identity questionnaire. *Hispanic Journal of Behavioral Sciences, 1*(3), 247–261.

Gonzales, N. A., Knight, G. P., Birman, D., & Sirolli, A. A. (2004). Acculturation and enculturation among Latino youths. In K. I. Maton, C. J. Schellenbach, B. J. Leadbeater & A. L. Solarz (Eds.), *Investing in children, youth, families, and communities: Strengths-based research and policy* (pp. 285–302). Washington, DC: American Psychological Association.

Gonzales, N. A., Knight, G. P., Morgan-Lopez, A., Saenz, D., & Sirolli, A. (2002). Acculturation and the mental health of Latino youths: An integration and critique of the literature. In J. M. Contreras, K. A. Kerns & A. M. Neal-Barnett (Eds.), *Latino children and families in the United States: Current research and future directions* (pp. 45–74). Westport, CT: Praeger.

Kim, B. S. K., Atkinson, D. R., & Yang, P. H. (1999). The Asian Values Scale: Development, factor analysis, validation, and reliability. *Journal of Counseling Psychology, 46*(3), 342–352.

Kitayama, S., Markus, H., & Kurokawa, M. (2000). Culture, emotion, and well-being: Good feelings in Japan and the United States. *Cognition and Emotion, 14*(1), 93–124.

Knight, G. P., Gonzales, N. A., Saenz, D. S., German, M., Deardorff, J., & Updegraff, K. (2006). The Mexican American Cultural Values Scale for adolescents and adults. Manuscript in preparation.

Knight, G. P., Vargas-Chanes, D., Cota-Robles, S. L., Losoya, S., Chassin, L., & Lee, J. M. (2006). Acculturation and enculturation trajectories among Mexican Americans juvenile delinquents. Manuscript under review.

Kwan, K. K., & Sodowsky, G. R. (1997). Internal and external ethnic identity and their correlates: A study of Chinese American immigrants. *Journal of Multicultural Counseling & Development, 25*(1), 51–67.

Marin, G. (1992). Issues in the measurement of acculturation among Hispanics. In K. F. Geisenger (Ed.), *Psychological testing of Hispanics* (pp. 235–251). Washington, DC: American Psychological Association.

Marin, G., & Gamba, R. J. (1996). A new measurement of acculturation for Hispanics: The bidimensional acculturation scale for Hispanics BAS. *Hispanic Journal of Behavioral Sciences, 18*, 297–316.

Marin, G., Sabogal, F., Marin, B. V., & Otero-Sabogal, R. (1987). Development of a short acculturation scale for Hispanics. *Hispanic Journal of Behavioral Sciences, 9*, 183–205.

Martinez, R., Norman, R. D., & Delaney, H. D. (1984). A children's Hispanic background scale. *Hispanic Journal of Behavioral Sciences, 6*, 103–112.

Mendoza, R. H. (1989). An empirical scale to measure type and degree of acculturation in Mexican-American adolescents and adults. *Journal of Cross-Cultural Psychology, 20*, 372–385.

Montgomery, G. T. (1992). Comfort with acculturation status among students from South Texas. *Hispanic Journal of Behavioral Sciences, 14*(2), 201–223.

Nisbett, R. E., Peng, K., Choi, I., & Norenzayan, A. (2001). Culture and systems of thought: Holistic versus analytic cognition. *Psychological Review, 108*(2), 291–310.

Nguyen, H. H., Messe, L. A., & Stollak, G. E. (1999). Toward a more complex understanding of acculturation and adjustment: Cultural involvements and psychosocial functioning in Vietnamese youth. *Journal of Cross-Cultural Psychology, 30*, 5–31.

Nguyen, H. H., & von Eye, A. (2002). The Acculturation Scale for Vietnamese Adolescents (ASVA): A bidimensional perspective. *International Journal of Behavioral Development, 26*(3), 202–213.

Norris, A. E., Ford, K., & Bova, C. A. (1996). Psychometrics of a brief acculturation scale for Hispanics in a probability sample of urban Hispanic adolescents and adults. *Hispanic Journal of Behavioral Sciences, 18*, 29–38.

Oetting, E. R., & Beauvais, F. (1991). Orthogonal cultural identification theory: The cultural identification of minority adolescents. *The International Journal of the Addictions, 25*(5A & 6A), 655–685.

Phinney, J. S. (1992). The Multigroup Ethnic Identity Measure: A new scale for use with diverse groups. *Journal of Adolescent Research, 7*(2), 156–176.

Phinney, J. S., & Chavira, V. (1992). Ethnic identity and self-esteem: An exploratory longitudinal study. *Journal of Adolescence, 15*, 271–281.

Portes, A., & Rumbaut, R. G. (1996). *Immigrant American: A Portrait.* (2nd ed.). Berkeley: University of California Press.

Ramirez, M. (1983). *Psychology of the Americas: Mestizo perspectives on personality and mental health.* New York: Pergamon.

Ryder, A. G., Alden, L. E., & Paulhus, D. L. (2000). Is acculturation unidimensional or bidimensional? A head-to-head comparison in the prediction of personality, self-identity, and adjustment. *Journal of Personality and Social Psychology, 79*(1), 49–64.

Scherer, K., & Wallbott, H. (1994). Evidence for universality and cultural variation in differential emotion response patterning. *Journal of Personality and Social Psychology, 66*(2), 310–328.

Stephenson, M. (2000). Development and validation of the Stephenson Multigroup Acculturation Scale (SMAS). *Psychological Assessment, 12*, 77–88.

Suinn, R. M., Rickard-Figueroa, K., Lew, S., & Vigil, P. (1987). The Suinn-Lew Asian Self-Identity Acculturation Scales: An initial report. *Educational and Psychological Measurement, 47*, 401–407.

Szapocznik, J., & Kurtines, W. M. (1980). Acculturation, biculturalism and adjustment among Cuban Americans. In A. M. Padilla (Ed.), *Acculturation: Theory, models, and some new findings* (pp. 139–159). Boulder, CO: Westview Press.

Szapocznik, J., & Kurtines, W. M. (1993). Family psychology and cultural diversity: Opportunities for theory, research and application. *American Psychologist, 48,* 400–407.

Szapocznik, J., Kurtines, W. M., & Fernandez, T. (1980). Bicultural involvement and adjustment in Hispanic-American youths. *International Journal of Intercultural Relations, 4,* 353–365.

Szapocznik, J., Scopetta, M. A., & Kurtines, W. M. (1978). Theory and measurement of acculturation. *Interamerican Journal of Psychology, 12,* 113–130.

Tropp, L. P., Erkut, S., Garcia Coll, C., Alarcon, O., & Vasquez Garcia, H. A. (1999). Psychological acculturation: Development of a new measure for Puerto Ricans on the U.S. mainland. *Educational and Psychological Measurement, 59,* 351–367.

Tsai, G., & Curbow, B. (2001). The development and validation of the Taiwanese Ethnic Identity Scale (TEIS): A "derived etic" approach. *Journal of Immigrant Health, 3*(4), 199–212.

Tsai, J. L., Chentsova-Dutton, Y., & Wong, Y. (2002). Why and how researchers should study ethnic identity, acculturation, and cultural orientation. In G. C. N. Hall & S. Okazaki (Eds.), *Asian American psychology: The science of lives in context* (pp. 41–65). Washington, DC: American Psychological Association.

Tsai, J. L., Ying, Y., & Lee, P.A. (2000). The meaning of "being Chinese" and "being American": Variation among young adults. *Journal of Cross-Cultural Psychology, 31*(3), 302–322.

Umaña-Taylor, A. J., Yazedjian, A., & Bámaca-Gómez, M. (2004). Developing the Ethnic Identity Scale using Eriksonian and social identity perspectives. *Identity: An International Journal of Theory and Research, 4*(1), 9–38.

Unger, J. B., Gallaher, P., Shakib, S., Ritt-Olson, A., Palmer, P. H., & Johnson, C. A. (2002). The AHIMSA Acculturation Scale: A new measure of acculturation for adolescents in a multicultural society. *Journal of Early Adolescence, 22*(3), 225–251.

U.S. Census Bureau. (2002). Census 2000, Public Law 94-171 Summary file: Tables for race and ethnic distribution in the United States. EEO Visions, Inc.: Bethesda, MD. www.eeoc.gov/stats/census/majorgroups/US/US_states.html

U.S. Census Bureau. (2004). U.S. Census Immigration Statistics: Population Division, Immigrations Statistics Staff. Maintained by Information & Research Services Internet Staff, U.S. Census: Washington, DC. www.census.gov/population/www/socdemo/foreign.html

Wallen, G. R., Feldman, R. H., & Anliker, J. (2002). Measuring acculturation among Central American women with the use of a brief language scale. *Journal of Immigrant Health, 4*(2), 95–102.

Wolfe, M. M., Yang, P. H., Wong, E. C., & Atkinson, D. R. (2001). Design and development of the European American values scale for Asian Americans. *Cultural Diversity and Ethnic Minority Psychology, 7*(3), 274–283.

Ying, Y., Coombs, M., & Lee, P. A. (1999). Family intergenerational relationship of Asian American adolescents. *Cultural Diversity and Ethnic Minority Psychology, 5*(4), 350–363.

Zane, N., & Mak, W. (2003). Major approaches to the measurement of acculturation among ethnic minority populations: A content analysis and an alternative empirical strategy. In K. Chun, P. Organista & M. Gerardo (Eds.), *Acculturation: Advances in theory, measurement, and applied research* (pp. 39–60). Washington, DC: American Psychological Association.

Zea, M. C., Asner-Self, K. K., Birman, D., & Buki, L. P. (2003). The Abbreviated Multidimensional Acculturation Scale: Empirical validation with two Latino/Latina samples. *Cultural Diversity and Ethnic Minority Psychology, 9*(2), 107–126.

About the Authors

Nancy A. Gonzales, Ph.D., is a professor in the Department of Psychology, Arizona State University, Tempe, AZ 85287-1104. E-mail: nancy.gonzales@asu.edu.

Ryan P. Jacobson, M.A., is a doctoral student in the Department of Psychology, Arizona State University, Tempe, AZ 85287-1104. E-mail: ryan.jacobson@asu.edu.

George P. Knight, Ph.D., is a professor in the Department of Psychology, Arizona State University, Tempe, AZ 85287-1104. Phone: 480-965-2590. E-mail: george.knight@asu.edu.

Mark W. Roosa, Ph.D., is a professor in the School of Social and Family Dynamics, Arizona State University, Tempe, AZ 85287-3701. E-mail: mark.roosa@asu.edu.

Delia S. Saenz, Ph.D., is an associate professor in the Department of Psychology, Arizona State University, Tempe, AZ 85287-1104. E-mail: delia.saenz@asu.edu.

A Sociological Analysis of the Psychosocial Adaptation of Khmer Refugees in Massachusetts

2

LEAKHENA NOU

Abstract

This paper uses a sociological stress process model to examine psychosocial adaptation among Cambodian adult refugees (N = 80) in Massachusetts. An assessment of the mental well-being of Cambodian refugees in the United States thirty-three years after experiencing the brutality of the Khmer Rouge (1975–1979) was conducted. A quota sample of nonclinical respondents for the study was recruited from three communities in Massachusetts. Four stepwise regression models were used to predict the respondents' total Brief Symptoms Inventory (BSI) to indicate their level of psychosocial adaptation. The subdimensions of psychological and somatic symptoms for BSI were also examined. Comparisons of multivariate models predicting each of the dependent variables showed that daily hassles and unresolved post-traumatic stress disorder (PTSD) symptoms were significantly related to poor overall BSI scores and psychological and somatic symptoms. Specific results, social policy recommendations, and directions for future research are discussed.

Keywords: Cambodian Refugees, Psychosocial Adaptation, Post-Traumatic Stress Disorder.

THIS STUDY EXPLORES the psychosocial adaptational patterns of adult Cambodian refugees in Massachusetts thirty-three years after resettlement. Cambodians in Massachusetts and those in other parts of the Cambodian diaspora have had repeated exposure to numerous pre- and post-migration stressors prior to resettlement in the United States. The stressors reflect the suffering Cambodian refugees endured under the Khmer Rouge regime (1975–1979). The purpose of the study was to determine the extent to which specific pre- and post-migration stressors interfere with people's ability to adjust successfully to life in the United States after experiences with genocide. The violation of human rights, loss of social status, and being uprooted from one's homeland and removed from cultural familiarity highlight the extreme stressors refugees bring to their new environment. Some literature sources have noted that Cambodian refugees are particularly at risk of developing serious mental health problems due to pre-migration stressors such as war and genocide, the escape process, and the refugee camp experience; and post-migration stressors such as learning a new language, adjusting to new roles, learning new skills, and entering mainstream vocational or educational programs (Carlson & Rosser-Hogan, 1993; Chung, 2001; Nicholson, 1999).

Most Cambodians in the United States today arrived under the auspices of the 1980 Refugee Act and its subsequent resettlement program. During that period approximately 157,500 Cambodians entered the United States under three immigration categories: refugees, immigrants, and humanitarian and public interest parolees (Zucker & Zucker, 1992; Refugee Reports, cited in Chan, 2004). The estimated number of Cambodians in the United States could, in fact, be underreported, partly as a result of a fear and distrust of formal institutions, which could prevent people from participating in the census. Based on census statistics reported by the Institute for Asian American Studies (IAAS) at the University of Massachusetts, Boston, Asian Americans are the fastest growing racial group in Massachusetts, having grown by nearly 68 percent since 1990 (IAAS, 2004). The same study shows that as a subgroup, Cambodians comprised 8.3 percent of all Asian ethnic groups in the state, and had the lowest annual incomes ($25,000 or lower) of all Asian groups. Indians and Chinese were found to have substantially higher rates of educational achievement (as measured by their rate of obtaining college, graduate, or professional degrees) than Cambodians and Vietnamese (IAAS, 2004).

The lower economic status and lack of education are only two difficulties faced by Cambodian Americans. This research focuses on a theoretical Khmer psychosocial adaptation process model of the stress–health relationship between four domains in order to investigate challenges encountered by Cambodian refugees in the assimilation process. The first domain includes social-structural context factors, including gender, age, social status, and employment status. The second domain focuses on individuals' exposure to and experience with current stressors, specifically negative life events and daily hassles. The haunting memories of previously unresolved post-traumatic stress disorder (PTSD) symptoms stemming from the Khmer Rouge period and current access to social support will act as mediators of the stress–health dynamic in the third domain. Finally, the fourth domain examines the effects of structural, stressor, and mediator variables to predict the mental well-being (i.e., total Brief Symptoms Inventory [BSI] and psychological and somatic symptoms) of Cambodian Americans. One major implication of this model is that failure to overcome life adversities could influence individuals' adjustment and assimilation in the host nation as a result of the inadequate levels of social support found there.

Theoretical Model

The theoretical model for the present study was first formulated in the author's doctoral dissertation (Nou, 2002). A version of the same model (see figure 2.1) for this study explored the ways in which stressors negatively affect Cambodian genocide survivors in Massachusetts. Conceptualization of the stress process model is adapted from the work of renowned stress scholars (Pearlin, 1989; Pearlin, Lieberman, Menaghan & Mullan, 1981). The arrows connecting the domains indicate hypothesized relationships

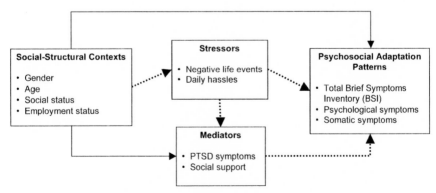

Figure 2.1.   The Khmer Psychosocial Adaptation Process Model

between the three domains (social-structural contexts, stressors, and media-tors) and the psychosocial adaptational domain. The dashed lines represent major causal pathways.

The social-structural contexts domain is hypothesized to affect the psychosocial adaptation of Cambodian refugees in three ways. First, indi-viduals' exposure to and experience with stressors, to a certain extent, are regulated and directed by the larger social orders of society and the statuses that people occupy within them (social-structural contexts → stressors). In particular, the social characteristics of people, such as gender, age, so-cial status, and employment status will influence the types and degrees of stressors they experience. Second, the social-structural domain triggers suppressed traumatic memories of the past and/or affecting the current availability of social support (social-structural contexts → mediators). Third, social-structural contexts directly influence psychosocial outcomes (social-structural contexts → mental health outcomes).

Research literature has documented that, because of predominant social relationships and inequalities, those suffering from stress are likely to be female rather than male (Menaghan, 1990; Milkie & Thoits, 1993), older rather than younger (Marshall, Schell, Berthold & Chun, 2005), of lower status rather than higher status (Menaghan, 1990; Mirowsky & Ross, 1989; Turner & Lloyd, 1999) and unemployed rather than em-ployed (Lie, Sveaass & Eilertsen, 2004; Uba & Chung, 1991). Exposure to stressors can be especially detrimental to mental health and well-being under these conditions. Harmful stressors are consequential of negative life events or persistent, daily hassles. "Negative life events" refers to the undesirable, life-altering experiences that require people to readjust their lives to accommodate the new social environment (Holmes & Rahe, 1967). *Daily hassles* refers to the predictable (such as pollution) or un-predictable (such as misplacing things), cumulative circumstances that affect people negatively on a daily basis. These hassles are often beyond the individual's control (such as bad weather conditions, traffic jams, and poor economy) (Kanner, Coyne, Schaefer & Lazarus, 1981). Repeated exposure to stressors without the use of positive coping strategies and social support can be catastrophic to people's physical or mental health (Gruen, Folkman & Lazarus, 1988; Lazarus, 1981; Lin, Dean & Ensel, 1981; Nicholl & Thompson, 2004).

Mediators of stress are usually called upon to illuminate why people have particular responses to stressors (mediators → mental health out-comes). The model points out that negative life events and daily hassles (stressors) affect psychosocial adaptational patterns by triggering lingering

PTSD symptoms. Social support serves to moderate the impact of traumatic negative life events and daily hassles by helping individuals cope with stress, and thus lowering their level of psychological dysfunction (Bjork & Tambs, 1995; Thoits, 1995). Hence, social support is defined as a form of social capital that people can access through their social network during stressful times.

In summary, outcome variables (i.e., total BSI score and its subdimensions of psychological and somatic symptoms) are expected to be directly influenced by the social-structural context variables (i.e., gender, age, social status, and employment status) and people's exposure to the stressor variables (i.e., life events and daily hassles). People's responses to stressors are also determined by certain social-structural contexts or roles that permit access to resources and opportunities (i.e., mediators) in society and social relations. These resources and opportunities enable individuals to combat life stressors.

Method

Participants
Respondents were all refugees from Cambodia who resided in the cities of Lowell, Lynn, or Revere, Massachusetts. These three cities were chosen as designated research sites because of their large concentrations of Cambodian residents. All respondents were survivors of the Khmer Rouge genocide (1975–1979). They were selected through a nonrandom and nonclinical sample based on the participants' convenience, and recruited through grassroots contact in the Cambodian communities. Data collection took place from January 2004 until April 2005. Participants were recruited through a combination of techniques, including contacts with community leaders, telephone calls, informal focus groups, a community forum, and use of Khmer media and radio-broadcast outlets. Back-up respondents to replace those who withdrew from the study were recruited as well, as logistical challenges (e.g., severe snowstorms) occurred in the field during data collection. Unexpected, blizzard-like conditions discouraged many individuals from participating in the study.

Procedures
The survey instruments were administered in community facilities familiar to respondents in each of the three cities. These were a health center in Lowell, a family center in Lynn, and a Buddhist temple in Revere. At each

survey session, respondents were given oral instructions on the purpose of the study, asked to read the information sheet about the study before agreeing to participate, and provided with the option of withdrawing from the study if they felt uncomfortable.

On average, the younger respondents usually spent between forty-five minutes to one hour to complete the thirty-two-page survey package. Older respondents, on the other hand, especially those in their sixties, needed two to four hours to complete the entire questionnaire package. They were especially careful to ask for clarification when they did not fully understand a question, thus prolonging the process of completing the survey. Many of these older respondents had little or no experience filling out research questionnaires that required them to relate sensitive information from their past and present. Special attention from the research team focused on assisting these respondents with the survey package. Two sessions involving older respondents exceeded our estimate of four hours per survey session; these two sessions lasted six hours each. The principal investigator and a research assistant were available to answer questions until each respondent completed the entire survey package, regardless of the time commitment required. Detailed information about the research methodologies employed (e.g., the use of an evaluative criterion for the translation of research materials, fielding and pretesting the questionnaire and research package, and data cleaning) is available by contacting the researcher directly and/or by referring to her previously published works.

Instruments

BRIEF SYMPTOM INVENTORY (BSI). The Brief Symptom Inventory (BSI) was chosen to measure psychosocial adaptation. It is a self-report questionnaire of psychological and somatic symptoms. The fifty-three-item BSI (Derogatis & Melisaratos, 1983) is a shortened version derived from the original Symptom Checklist-90 (SCL-90) (Derogatis, 1977). Subjects were asked, "How much are you distressed by . . . ?" followed by a listing of the fifty-three items on the BSI. Each item is rated on a five-point scale of distress, ranging from 0 (*none at all*) to 4 (*extremely*). One additional item (item 54, "Feeling the need to show off about yourself") was included in the BSI at the suggestion of pretest participants.

DEMOGRAPHIC QUESTIONNAIRE. The demographic questionnaire is composed of two major sections. The first section asks respondents to share information on the major structural variables under study, such as gender (60 percent males; 40 percent females); age (55 percent 30–39; 32.5 percent 40–49; 10 percent 50–59; and 2.5 percent 60–69); social status (35 percent lower status; 65 percent higher status); and employment status (73.75 percent employed full-time; 26.25 percent unemployed). Other relevant information is related to refugee status; such information includes length of stay in the refugee camp, year of arrival in the United States, and personal and family background before the Khmer Rouge genocide. Part two of the demographic section explores respondents' personal educational attainment and financial situation in the United States.

SOCIAL READJUSTMENT RATING SCALE (SRRS). The Holmes and Rahe (1967) Social Readjustment Rating Scale (SRRS) was used to measure negative life events. This forty-three-item life events inventory combines information about diverse life events (e.g., "Change in residence to a worse residence") into one overall measurement of recent stress exposure. The Life Events Questionnaire is a revised version of the SRRS with twenty-two culturally relevant items and was structured to follow a *yes/no* response format. One open-ended item was also included to provide respondents with the opportunity to indicate personal undesirable life changes not mentioned in the events list. A response of *no* to the stimulus item received a 0, while a *yes* received a recode of 1. Summing the total number of life events experienced by our Khmer adult population produced the Life Events Questionnaire score.

HASSLES SCALE. The Hassles Scale was developed by Kanner, Coyne, Schaefer, and Lazarus (1981) as a way to assess different areas of daily stress such as work, health, family, friends, the environment, practical considerations, and chance occurrences. The items tap into a variety of everyday concerns such as the misplacement or loss of personal items, deteriorating physical health, lack of family time, concerns related to finances, and pollution. The cumulative severity score for daily hassles was calculated by tallying the three-point severity ratings on 117 hassle items; totals ranged from 0 to 351 (117 hassle items × 0 to 3 points per item). Our respondents averaged approximately forty-four daily hassles per month.

IMPACT OF EVENT SCALE-REVISED. PTSD is measured by the Impact of Event Scale-Revised (IES-Revised). This scale was designed by Weiss and Marmar in 1997 to correspond to the PTSD criteria in the *Diagnostic and Statistical Manual of Mental Disorders* (DSM-IV). While the original IES tapped only two of the four criteria (intrusion and avoidance) highlighted for PTSD in the DSM-IV, the IES-R also included hyperarousal as a sub-scale (e.g., anger and irritability, and heightened startle response). All four criteria have cultural relevance to the Cambodian population. The IES-R was designed to assess a respondent's subjective distressing experiences with twenty-two life events. Adding to the original, fifteen-item IES, the IES-R includes seven new items. Six of these tap hyperarousal symptoms (e.g., difficulty concentrating, hypervigilance), and the seventh, an intrusion item, involves recurring flashbacks and dissociative feelings (Weiss & Marmar, 1997).

For this study, scale items asked respondents to use a traumatic event within the past two weeks as a point of reference. Some sample scale items included: "Any reminder brought back feelings about it," "Found myself acting or feeling as though I was back at that time," "Reminders of it caused me to have physical reactions, such as sweating, trouble breathing, nausea, or a pounding heart."

SOCIAL SUPPORT SCALE. The scale used in this study was adapted from the Instrumental-Expressive Social-Support Scale developed to measure types of instrumental and expressive social support (Ensel & Woelfel, 1986). The five items for this study reflected a variety of interpersonal re-lationships and included, for example, "Not seeing enough of people who are close to you" and "No one to depend on." The choices include 5 (*most or all of the time*), 4 (*occasionally or a moderate amount of the time*), 3 (*some or a little of the time*), 2 (*rarely*), and 1 (*never*).

Results
For descriptive results see table 2.1.

Analytic Procedure for the Multivariate Results
The multivariate relationships indicated in table 2.2 show the effect of each of the dependent variables after controlling for the effects of all other independent variables. In this sense, table 2.2 illustrates the real impact of each of the variables. Regression coefficients indicate the effect of a one-unit change in the independent variable on the dependent variable as they hold the effects of the other independent variables constant. Four equations for each of the four regression models tested the effects of the predictor variables, including social-structural contexts (i.e., gender, age, social status, and employment status), stressors (i.e., negative life events and daily hassles), and mediators (PTSD symptoms and social support) as

Table 2.1. Descriptive Statistics

Variable Name	N	Mean/Percentage	Standard Deviation	Unstandardized Cronbach's α (number of items in parentheses)	Standardized Cronbach's α
Gender	80	Males = 60.0% Females = 40.0%	—	—	—
Age	80	30–39 = 55.0% 40–49 = 32.5% 50–59 = 10.0% 60–69 = 2.5%	—	—	—
Social status	80	Lower class = 35.0% Higher class = 65.0%	—	—	—
Employment status	80	Unemployed = 26.25% Employed = 73.75%	—	—	—
Negative Life Events	78	3.68	2.510	.655 (20)	.664
Daily Hassles	80	43.60	35.425	.975 (116)	.975
PTSD symptoms	80	26.88	19.330	.960 (22)	.960
Social support	80	11.31	4.440	.686 (5)	.684
Brief Symptoms Inventory	80	44.41	36.030	.974 (54)	.974
Psychological symptoms	80	6.85	7.050	.908 (9)	.909
Somatic symptoms	80	6.00	2.236	.632 (4)	.659

Table 2.2. Standardized OLS Regression Coefficients for Estimations of Brief Symptoms Inventory (BSI), (N = 78)

	Structural Model	Stressor Model	PTSD Symptoms Model	Social Support Model
Gender	.036	.052	.064	.037
Age	.156	.095	–.018	.023
Social status	–.031	–.049	–.140	–.127
Employment status	.110	.144	.120	.152*
Negative life events		.247*	.135	.113
Daily hassles		.471***	.244**	.201*
PTSD symptoms			.595***	.554***
Social Support				.205*
Adjusted R²	.000	.329	.585	.616
Model F	.519	7.288***	16.535***	16.472***

Notes: *p < .05, **p < .01, ***p < .001

they affect psychosocial adaptation (total score of BSI symptoms and its subdimensions). Four regression equations were estimated and modeled for each dependent variable. The four models are labeled according to the independent variables examined: the structural model (age, gender, social status, and employment status), stressor model (negative life events and daily hassles), PTSD symptoms model (PTSD symptoms), and social support model (social support).

Standardized Ordinary Least Squares (OLS) Regression for Estimation of BSI

Model results for the BSI reported no significance for the structural variables, whereas negative life events ($b = .247$, $p < .05$) and daily hassles ($b = .471$, $p < .001$) were significant. A comparison of Beta coefficients indicates that daily hassles are a better predictor of total symptoms than are negative life events. A significant correlation between daily hassles ($b = .244$, $p < .05$) and PTSD symptoms ($b = .595$, $p < .001$) was found in the third model. This finding shows that when PTSD symptoms were introduced, the impact of daily hassles decreased, implying the more powerful lingering effects of PTSD. In the fourth model, daily hassles ($b = .201$, $p < .05$) and PTSD symptoms ($b = .554$, $p < .001$) retained their significance from the third model when social support was introduced. Once again, PTSD symptoms outweighed daily hassles in the effect on total BSI symptoms.

Counterintuitively, social support was positively associated with increased BSI symptoms. This surprising correlation suggests that social support is counterproductive to Cambodian refugees' psychological well-being, calling into question the usefulness of many traditional Western sources of social support. One possible explanation for this finding is that some individuals have little trust for members of their own community and outsiders, and as a result, any support offered becomes of questionable value. In the adult Cambodian refugee population, this lack of trust stems from life under the Khmer Rouge regime. In order to escape execution, many individuals were forced to reveal the personal identities of family, friends, and neighbors who supposedly had Western training or imperialist backgrounds. Therefore, extensive social networks became a dangerous source of vulnerability rather than a source of comfort and assistance in times of need. The only structural variable found to be significant was employment status, as indicated in the fourth model.

Discussion

The Khmer Psychosocial Adaptation Model suggests that the BSI, along with its subdimensions of psychological and somatic symptoms, is a strong measure of current adjustment and adaptational patterns for adult Cambodian American refugees. The model shows that the difficulties this refugee population experiences depend on the degree and intensity of their negative life events combined with their current experiences with daily hassles; the severity of these combined difficulties can be exacerbated by lingering PTSD symptoms.

Social-contextual factors had very little predictive power for the total BSI scores and psychological symptoms, except that when social support was factored into the regression equation, employment status increased BSI symptoms. This finding indicates that working people experience more stress than unemployed people, especially if they have to balance work and family life. Only the structural variables of age and social status are significantly related to somatic symptoms. Many older Cambodian refugees and those from lower-class backgrounds are less likely to fully utilize their health/mental healthcare coverage, a state that leads to increased somatic manifestations. The initial reporting of somatic complaints to Western healthcare providers is consistent with the cultural value of *saving face* rather than admitting to psychological problems, and preferring to keep personal matters private.

The mainstream stress literature (Menaghan, 1990; Pearlin, Lieberman, Menaghan, & Mullan 1981) frequently suggests that gender and lower status place people at greater risk for mental health symptoms. This theory was not supported by the current study, in which neither gender nor lower social status was significantly related to total BSI and its subdimensions' scores. Perhaps the stressful impact of structural variables such as gender and social status is simply less powerful than the impact of negative life events and daily hassles, which significantly increase total BSI scores and somatic symptoms, but not psychological symptoms. This finding highlights the fact that all Cambodians within a certain age range, regardless of their socioeconomic backgrounds, were affected by the atrocities committed by the Khmer Rouge.

The stepwise regression analyses suggest an interesting elaboration of the model processes regarding stressors (i.e., negative life events and daily hassles) and PTSD symptoms. The stressful impact of negative life events and daily hassles appears to be reduced when PTSD enters the regression equation. It is as if past serious traumas interfere with the adaptations refugees must make to meet the complex demands of their current life circumstances. It is the resulting stress of being less able to deal with daily hassles that finally makes the negative impact of extreme PTSD clear. Negative life events combined with difficult life histories make adjusting especially challenging, reflecting the reality that Cambodian refugees are still haunted by memories of the Khmer Rouge.

The findings in this study are consistent with research conducted by Blair (2000), who found that risk factors (such as experiencing a greater number of war traumas and resettlement stressors during the past year) increased the levels of PTSD and depression among Cambodian adult refugees in Utah. According to Blair, current stressors such as anxiety about the future in the United States and financial worries were significantly associated with PTSD and depression. Blair's data also indicated that the effects of these disorders are not always immediately apparent, but that they can have long-term and chronic consequences. Similar to Blair's study, the Khmer Psychosocial Adaptation Model raises important considerations in the analysis of Cambodian mental well-being for future research. For example, respondents who developed mild psychosomatic symptoms resulting from the stressors of negative life events and daily hassles without physical/mental healthcare intervention increased their preexisting PTSD symptoms. Individuals with symptoms of PTSD or any other mentally related symptoms (such as anxiety and depression) may be less capable of adapting to life in the host country, and consequently may experience more chronic stress. Future research is needed to examine demographic and environmental risk factors associated with unique Cambodian manifestations of mental health sequelae in greater depth.

Limitations of the Study
The cross-sectional approach and small sample size of the current study precludes complete statistical validation of results for specific endorsement of symptoms. Future research with a much larger sample of various Cambodian American communities is needed in order to validate symptomatic results for comparison purposes.

Policy Recommendations
Policy recommendations based on this research include general recommendations of how funding could be spent to alleviate the health/mental health conditions of Cambodians, as well as specific suggestions for ad-

dressing the major aspects of the study's findings (helping people reduce their daily hassles, increase their functioning, and improve their mental and physical health).

General Recommendations

A critical emphasis for social and healthcare policy makers is to fund mid- to long-term needs analyses of the health/mental health circumstances of Cambodian American refugee communities. This funding should also include a clinical research component, preferably one that is academically based, to consider psychosocial factors embedded in the current Western healthcare system and the healthcare providers who serve Cambodian American refugees.

Social scientists working alongside medical and social/human services professionals should collect data on relevant sociodemographics. These would include previous hospitalization or diagnosed illnesses, household income and family background prior to the Khmer Rouge, and mul- tifaceted issues such as personal experience with torture and witnessed execution. Such data would shed light on patterns of health behaviors and negative health consequences. The systematic studies conducted should focus on longitudinal and cross-sectional data. These technical investiga- tive efforts must be done in collaboration with successful Western health- care clinics in combination with traditional Cambodian health practices. Healthcare providers are urged to take a compassionate approach when attempting to heal the wounds and silent suffering of the Cambodians.

A second critical recommendation for policy makers is that they as- sist Cambodians in strengthening family relationships, focusing particu- larly on their cohesion, hardiness, and functioning. One effective way to strengthen relationships among family members is to address issues sur- rounding intergenerational and intercultural conflicts. Miscommunication between survivors and their children is often the source of the problem. The limited education and English-language ability of many older Cambo- dian refugees is another common source of intercultural tension that needs to be addressed (Nou, 2006).

A third issue for policy makers to address is helping Cambodian com- munities reestablish a sense of trust in the larger community. The lack of trust between and among Cambodians as being destructive to social har- mony was raised by respondents in the qualitative portion of this study. Buddhism is of significant value in helping rebuild community trust and cohesion in Cambodian culture, and policy makers are urged to reach out to the leaders of reputable Buddhist temples in Cambodian communities to act as brokers for addressing urgent concerns affecting them.

Specific Policy Suggestions for Addressing Key Areas

HELPING PEOPLE REDUCE THEIR DAILY HASSLES AND INCREASE THEIR FUNCTIONING. Policy makers are encouraged to work with existing Western and Cambodian social and healthcare providers and agencies to provide Cambodian clients with essential resources to help them function in mainstream activities. These resources would include English language instruction, training on the use of public transportation, offering day care services, creating a support group for families struggling with intergenerational conflicts, and providing access to affordable or subsidized housing. Single female heads of households who are isolated, in particular, might benefit from job referral services and being reconnected to community social supports.

One effective means of facilitating these changes would be to establish a Cambodian community center to serve as an informational resource center linking individuals to various programs offered in the community. Young people could get involved by offering basic computer classes for the elderly, assisting them with the banking system, and helping them search for employment or social services in order to become economically self-sufficient. On the other hand, the younger Cambodians could learn the Khmer language and culture from the elderly. The purpose of the center would be to provide a safe place for people of all ages to come together to share stories of triumph and exchange valuable knowledge on everything from basic survival/coping skills and community resources to the rich cultural legacy of the Cambodian people.

HELPING PEOPLE ALLEVIATE PTSD AND MENTAL HEALTH SYMPTOMS. The findings from this study have direct implications for policy makers to consider when designing or evaluating counseling and psychotherapy programs, whether such programs are aimed at helping people understand and identify symptoms of mental illness in general, or are specifically aimed at distinct groups in need of immediate psychological and medical intervention. These programs could take the form of specialized treatments or collaborative techniques incorporating indigenous and Western biomedical healthcare models.

These counseling and research programs need to take into account psychosocial adaptation factors, mental health needs, and the traditional healthcare belief systems of Cambodian refugee populations. A top priority of these programs should be to destigmatize seeking and obtaining mental health services. Enhancing relationships with existing health/mental health providers who have established relationships with Cambodian clients is one effective way of ensuring success. Treating mental health concerns among Cambodian refugees requires an applied, cross-cultural perspective; in order to fully understand the group's cultural background, all mental healthcare providers are encouraged to spend time in the Cambodian community and attend community festivities and celebrations.

HELPING EDUCATE PEOPLE ABOUT PREVENTIVE PHYSICAL HEALTHCARE. Frequently, Cambodians do not have adequate health insurance coverage, and those who do seek out medical care do not receive culturally appropriate, comprehensive services. One cost-efficient recommendation is to establish links with local medical schools in areas with large populations of Cambodians, requesting a partnership with existing community health agencies. Community-based medical internship programs could be established to encourage medical students to use their medical knowledge to help educate the Cambodian population through basic health screenings.

HELPING PEOPLE DEVELOP SOCIAL-SUPPORT NETWORKS. Policy makers could maximize the beneficial effects of existing institutional resources in the community simply by helping families become informed about different services and programs. The suggestion provided earlier regarding the establishment of a community center is one effective way to help people develop such networks of social support. As an informational resource center, a community center can unite individuals and families as they learn from each other, face similar life conditions, and access a variety of critical resources and services. The leaders of the Buddhist temples are encouraged to participate in these institutional activities and programs, providing an indigenous source of solace for meditation and spiritual healing.

Conclusion

This research has shown that Cambodians in Massachusetts continue to encounter life challenges as they try to define and establish their identity as refugees. Their difficulties are multifaceted. Most are linked to Cambodia's history and the political events that forced them to emigrate as refugees, often ill-equipped to deal with the harsh realities of modernity in the host society, unable to fully grasp local and national policies that control their access to educational and healthcare resources.

It is evident that the respondents understand that the negative impact of social stressors on their community is made worse by the inadequate response by the host society. These problems are often linked to language and cultural barriers and lack of direct healthcare services or advocacy on behalf of the Khmer population. In the view of many respondents, the misguided if well-intentioned responses of Western healthcare practitioners have created services that are not useful to a vulnerable population traumatized by genocide. There is a desperate need to remove cultural barriers and improve community services as many Cambodians continue to battle psychological and emotional scars while facing resettlement challenges. This assessment echoes the conclusion drawn by Marshall et al. (2005), who noted that:

> The pervasiveness of psychiatric disorders raises questions about the adequacy of existing mental health resources in this community. Addressing this high level of need may require additional research to identify barriers to seeking services as well as efforts at improving treatment for this population. (p. 578)

This conclusion came from a recent study conducted by Marshall and his colleagues (2005) on the mental health of Cambodian refugees two decades after resettlement in the United States (specifically in Long Beach, California). They reported the significant findings that Cambodian refugees have prevalence rates of 62 percent for PTSD and 51 percent for major depression. These rates are much higher than those for the general population (PTSD = 3.5 percent, major depression = 6.7 percent). These disturbing findings complicated the understanding of Cambodians' mental health when community sample data on the rates and correlates of seeking mental health services among Cambodian refugees actually showed high rates of contact with both medical care providers (70 percent) and mental health providers (46 percent). Seeking services from both types of providers was often associated with respondents having limited command of the English language, being unemployed, having three or fewer years of pre-immigration education, and being retired or disabled. Women, particularly those who had health coverage, and persons receiving government aid were especially likely to utilize healthcare services (Marshall et al., 2006). In the current study, higher social support levels were positively associated with increased BSI symptoms; although causality has yet to be proven, this association raises the question of whether access to resources or social support actually results in better health or mental health. This concurs with the findings of Marshall et al. (2006).

The results of the current study suggest that the Khmer Psychosocial Adaptation Model, with some modifications, is effective in leading to increased understanding of the psychosocial well-being of Cambodians in Massachusetts. The modifications include deemphasizing the role of social support as a moderating variable and treating negative life events as having an indirect effect on PTSD. The possibility that the model might be modified to treat daily hassles as the variable that finally influences overall adaptation needs further exploration. It is hoped that the model can be useful for increasing our understanding of the circumstances of other Cambodian communities in the diaspora, and also for calling attention to the importance of adequate health/mental health resources in Cambodian communities.

Acknowledgments

This research was entirely supported by financial and logistical support from the Institute for Asian American Studies, University of Massachusetts, Boston. The author especially wishes to thank Dr. Paul Watanabe, Bou Lim, Kirirath Saing, Stephen Thong, Dorcas C. Grigg-Saito, Sonith Peou, Chan Touch, Samkhann Khoeun, Dr. Anthony Marsella, Dr. Michael Mend, Dr. Patrick Clarkin, Dr. Jeff Davis, and the research participants themselves.

Qualitative research results are available from the Journal of Southeast Asian American Education and Advancement (jsaaea.coehd.utsa.edu/index.php/JSAAEA) or the Institute for Asian American Studies, University of Massachusetts, Boston (www.iaas.umb.edu/).

References

Bjork, S., & Tambs, K. (1995). Social support, negative life events, and mental health. *British Journal of Psychiatry, 166*, 29–34.

Blair, R. G. (2000). Risk factors associated with PTSD and major depression among Cambodian refugees in Utah. *Health and Social Work, 25*(1), 23–30.

Carlson, E., & Rosser-Hogan, E. (1993). Mental health status of Cambodian refugees ten years after leaving their homes. *American Journal of Orthopsychiatry, 63*, 223–231.

Chung, R. C. Y. (2001). Psychosocial adjustment of Cambodian refugee women: Implications for mental health counseling. *Journal of Mental Health Counseling, 23*(2), 115–126.

Derogatis, L. R. (1977). *The SCL-90 manual 1: Scoring, administration and procedures for the SCL-90.* Baltimore: Clinical Psychometric Research.

Derogatis, L. R., & Melisaratos, N. (1983). The Brief Symptoms Inventory: An introductory report. *Psychological Medicine, 13*, 595–605.

Ensel, W. M., & Woelfel, M. (1986). Measuring the instrumental and expressive functions of social support. In N. Lin, A. Dean & W. Ensel (Eds.), *Social support, life events, and depression* (pp. 129–152). London: Academic Press, Inc.

Gruen, R. J., Folkman, S., & Lazarus, R. S. (1988). Centrality and individual differences in the meaning of daily hassles. *Journal of Personality, 56*(4), 743–762.

Holmes, T. H., & Rahe, R. H. (1967). The social readjustment rating scale. *Journal of Psychosomatic Research, 11*, 213–218.

Institute for Asian American Studies (IAAS). (June 2004). *Asian Americans in Massachusetts.* Boston: University of Massachusetts.

Kanner, A., Coyne, J. C., Schaefer, C., & Lazarus, R. S. (1981). Comparisons of two modes of stress measurement: Daily hassles and uplifts versus major life events. *Journal of Behavioral Medicine, 4*, 1–39.

Lazarus, R. S. (1981). The stress and coping paradigm. In C. Bisdorfer, C. Cohen, A. Kleinman & P. Maxim (Eds.), *Conceptual models for psychopathology* (pp. 173–209). New York: Spectrum.

Lie, B., Sveaass, N., & Eilertsen, D. E. (2004). Family, activity, and stress reactions in exile. *Community, Work & Family, 7*(3), 327–350.

Lin, N., Dean, A., & Ensel, W. (1981). Life stress and health: Stressors and resources. *American Sociological Review, 54*, 382–399.

Marshall, G. N., Berthold, S. M., Schell, T .L., Elliott, M. N., Chun, C. A., & Hambarsoomians, K. (2006). Rates and correlates of seeking mental health services among Cambodian refugees. *American Journal of Public Health, 96*(10), 1829–1835.

Marshall, G. N., Schell, T. L., Berthold, S. M., & Chun, C. A. (2005). Mental health of Cambodian refugees two decades after resettlement in the United States. *Journal of the American Medical Association, 294*(5), 571–579.

Menaghan, E. G. (1990). Social stress and individual stress. *Research in Community Mental Health, 6*, 107–141.

Milkie, M. A., & Thoits, P. A. (1993). Gender differences in cognitive coping with positive and negative experiences. Unpublished manuscript, Indiana University, Bloomington.

Mirowsky, J., & Ross, C. E. (1989). *Social causes of psychological distress.* New York: Aldine de Gruyter.

Nicholl, C., & Thompson, A. (2004). The psychological treatment of post-traumatic stress disorder (PTSD) in adult refugees: A review of the current state of psychological therapies. *Journal of Mental Health, 13*(4), 351–362.

Nicholson, B. L. (1999). Group treatment of traumatized Cambodian women: A culture-specific approach. *Social Work*, *44*(5), 470–479.

Nou, L. (2002). Social support, coping, and psychosocial adjustment of Khmer university, college, and technical students in modern Cambodia: A sociological study. Unpublished doctoral dissertation, University of Hawaii at Manoa.

Nou, L. (2006). *A qualitative examination of the psychosocial adjustment of Khmer refugees in three Massachusetts communities.* Occasional papers, Institute for Asian American Studies. Boston: University of Massachusetts.

Pearlin, L. I. (1989). The sociological study of stress. *Journal of Health and Social Behavior*, *30*, 241–256.

Pearlin, L. I., Lieberman, M. A., Menaghan, E. G., & Mullan, J. T. (1981). The stress process. *Journal of Health and Social Behavior*, *22*, 337–356.

Refugee reports (*Indochinese refugee reports* from May 1979 to December 1980). May 1979–Dec. 1995, vols. 1–16.

Thoits, P. A. (1995). Stress, coping, and social support processes: Where are we? What next? *Journal of Health and Social Behavior*, extra issue, 53–79.

Turner, R. J., & Lloyd, D.A. (1999). The stress process and the social distribution of depression. *Journal of Health and Social Behavior*, *40*(4), 374–404.

Uba, L., & Chung, R. C. (1991). The relationship between trauma and financial and physical well-being among Cambodians in the United States. *The Journal of General Psychology*, *118*(3), 215–225.

Weiss, C., & Marmar, D. (1997). Impact of Event Scale—Revised (IES-R). In J. Wilson & T. Keane (Eds.), *Assessing psychological trauma and PTSD*. New York: Guilford Press.

Zucker, N. L., & Zucker, N. F. (1992). From immigrants to refugees redefinition: A history of refugee and asylum policy in the United States. In E. G. Loescher (Ed.), *Refugees and the asylum dilemma in the West* (pp. 54–70). University Park: Pennsylvania State University Press.

About the Author

Leakhena Nou, Ph.D., is an assistant professor of sociology in the Sociology Department at California State University, Long Beach, 1250 Bellflower Boulevard, Long Beach, CA 90840-0906. Phone: 1-562-985-7439. Fax: 1-562-985-2090. E-mail: lnou@csulb.edu.

Understanding the Immigration Experience through a Lifecourse Lens
Four Personal Stories

3

BAHIRA SHERIF TRASK, LAURA THOMPSON BRADY, WEI QIU,
AND DORIT RADNAI-GRIFFIN

Abstract

This chapter highlights the range of diversity (both within and between) immigrant groups. Special attention is afforded focus on the implications of diversity for policy and service. Four personal accounts exemplify the experiences of immigration. Each story highlights lifecourse and immigration experiences and the complexity of issues that make immigration unique to each family and individual. These touching stories demonstrate that age of arrival, country of origin, timing, regionality, family, and marital status coincide to differentiate the immigrant experience. Accounts of immigration to the U.S. from Egypt, Israel, China, and Ireland are portrayed.

Keywords: Policy, Service, Within-Group Diversity, Case History

Address all correspondence to Dr. Bahira Sherif Trask, Department of Individual and Family Studies at the University of Delaware, 111 Alison West, Newark, DE 19716. Phone: 302-831-8187. Fax: 302-831-8776. E-mail: bstrask@udel.edu.

IMMIGRANT POPULATIONS PRESENT a unique challenge to family studies and human service professionals. Most family studies and human service professionals, while increasingly sensitized to issues of diversity, are unaware of the many unique facets of the immigration experience. For example, it is not enough to know the country of origin of an immigrant, their ethnicity, or their socioeconomic status. Factors such as race, ethnicity, gender, age, and shifting immigration policies contribute to significant fundamental differences among immigrants and their experiences (e.g., Cauce, 2005; Hagan, 2004). There are many individuals who have multiple religious, ethnic, or class affiliations that are not captured under our current systems of categorization. Furthermore, the immigrant experience is deeply impacted by historical time of arrival in the receiving society. This raises questions about the knowledge we have about families, how we best train students to understand issues facing families, and how to provide the kind of services that are needed for culturally diverse families.

This chapter unravels some of the complexities of the immigration experience, and focuses on how immigration impacts not only individuals but families across the lifecourse. It examines the topic of immigration both from an academic as well as a personal perspective by drawing on scholarship and case studies that illustrate the experiences of the four authors who represent various parts of the world, including Asia, Europe, the Islamic Middle East, and Israel. Each of their lives has been permanently impacted by the immigration experience. Their stories point to the importance of including a lifecourse perspective in the research and analyses, the provision of services, and the development of policies that influence the lives of immigrants. Further, the authors highlight the impact of immigration not just on the individual but also on the nuclear and the extended families involved. As the United States becomes increasingly diverse, it is more crucial to incorporate an awareness of cross-cultural experiences into social science education (Umana-Taylor & Wiley, 2004). In particular, it is critical to help our students realize the importance of understanding other points of view, beliefs, and values since they will be working with diverse populations in every facet of their lives (Dilworth-Anderson, Burton & Turner 1993).

Who Are Recent Immigrants?

According to the most recent report by the U.S. Census Bureau (Larsen, 2004), the foreign-born population of the United States constituted 11.7

percent of the total population. Furthermore, more than one-fourth of the population is either African American, Latino, Asian, or Native American, and approximately one-third of all American children are nonwhite. According to predictions by the U.S. Census, by 2050 nonwhites will replace whites as the majority in the United States. While some of this growth is propelled by differential fertility rates among racial and ethnic groups (He & Hobbs, 1999), much of this increase is due to changes in the Immigration Act of 1965, which opened America's doors to individuals from all over the globe (Hagan, 2004). This growth in the immigrant population has profound effects on a range of issues including culturally appropriate educational environments and approaches, multilingual healthcare delivery, social welfare policies, and culturally competent family support interventions/models that address the risks and resilience of immigrant families (Fong, 2001; Pratto & Lemieux, 2001).

Traditionally, immigrants settled in New York, California, Texas, Florida, Illinois, and New Jersey: today, other states are seeing an unprecedented rise in their number of immigrants. For example, Nevada has witnessed a 123 percent increase in its Hispanic population between 1990 and 2000, while Nebraska has experienced a 96 percent growth during the same period (Schmidley, 2001). While the statistics are staggering, they tell us little about the actual effect of immigration on the individuals and families who migrate, nor about their experiences in the host society or communities. For example, the experience of an Asian family in California is quite different from one in Arkansas (Cauce, 2005), and the intricacies of these differences are crucial to understanding variations in immigrant experiences.

Oropesa and Landale (2004) point out that, in research with culturally diverse families, ethnicity is often used as a "crude identifier of groups that are assumed to form a communicative system" (p. 908). Even though this is common practice in work on cultural diversity, it is problematic because much intragroup diversity is masked under an implied overarching cultural hegemony. The same argument can be made for understanding immigration and immigrants. Often lumped together under statistical umbrellas, these representations do not reveal the enormous differences in experiences between subgroups, races, classes, educational levels, genders, and arrival times. These issues reveal just how complicated labeling may be and how important it is to represent the multiple views of the members of a particular group.

An equally complex issue is the reality that most immigration to the United States today is from Mexico, Central and South America, Asia, and

Africa. The non-European phenotypes of many of these new immigrants tend to trigger stereotypes and prejudices about the "foreign" backgrounds of these groups. This creates social barriers to their full integration into American society (Buriel & DeMent, 1997). Maher (2002) examines contemporary issues of immigrants and migrant workers from a human rights perspective, and highlights the cultural, economic, and legal dichotomy in the United States (and other industrialized nations) between citizens and aliens. Maher argues that a "neocolonial logic" is used to legitimize claims to rights for individuals according to a "racialized international division of labor" that affords privileges to citizens of the First World over transnational individuals and families from the developing world (p. 21). Although immigrants and migrant workers are embedded in the economic structure of American labor markets (Hagan, 2004), they are not afforded basic human rights (e.g., social, economic rights) that are only available to individuals with citizenship status (Maher, 2002).

The intersection of recent federal and state legislation (e.g., the Anti-Terrorism Act of 1996, the Illegal Immigration Responsibility Act of 1996, the Patriot Act of 2001, California's Proposition 187) (see discussions in Cordero-Guzman & Navarro, 2000; Guest, 2005; Lee, Ottati & Hussain, 2001) and the experiences of immigrant families requires special attention in the twenty-first century. These shifts in policy reflect not only current political and economic events in the United States, but also pervasive attitudes about the demographics of the latest wave of immigrants. Such societal and political issues have important implications for immigrant families' access to resources and opportunities.

The Impact of Immigration on Families

Interestingly, there is relatively little research on immigrant children and families in the field of family studies yet family is the strategic unit in which immigration decisions are made and experienced. Migration decisions are arrived at for a variety of reasons, and are often made in order to maximize family well-being. Yet, we know little about immigrant adaptation processes, the stressors of migration on those parts of the family that have emigrated versus the ones left behind, or about the changes in a family's values or behaviors. Instead, most research on immigration has focused on how immigrants socialize their children and the impact on gender roles (e.g., Dion & Dion, 2001; Raffaeli & Ontai, 2004). There is also a tendency in the immigration literature to focus on the patriarchal role of men in the family. This holds true despite scholarly evidence that immigrant families demonstrate many features and may include patriarchal, role-segregated couples, as well as egalitarian dual-earner families, and variations in between (e.g., Torres, Solberg & Carlstrom, 2002). In addition, this literature often ignores the fact that individuals' lives are bound up with broader systems of inequality, such as race, ethnicity, and social class, and that immigrants' lives are not necessarily solely determined by the culture of their country of origin (Dion & Dion, 2001).

An important area of exploration is that immigrants and their offspring are often embedded in intricate webs of family ties, both in the United States and abroad (Rumbaut, 1997). This relatively unexplored facet of the immigration experience is frequently referred to as "the new transnational family"—a family that is dispersed geographically and that seems to mutate at different parts of the lifespan. At times these families are smaller or larger depending on where members are geographically located at any given point. Transnational families are able to reconstitute and redefine themselves over time, depending on geographical practicality, material needs, and at times, even emotional necessity. Most often, transnational families live apart from one another and, yet, hold together through a collective feeling of welfare and unity (Bryceson & Vuorela, 2002).

All too frequently, contemporary research and policy on immigration does not account for these strong global ties. Instead, much of our understanding about immigrants is predicated on the model of assimilation and racial classification. Traditionally, homogenized cultural explanations were the primary venue for understanding racial minorities and immigrant populations (Phinney, Ong & Madden, 2000). Therefore, it was assumed that the young immigrant African student from Nigeria shared characteristics and experiences with the young African American student raised in the Bronx. Only more recently have scholars such as Glenn (1983), Rumbaut (1997), and Pratto and Lemieux (2001) put forth the argument that the structures and experiences of immigrant families are largely determined by constantly shifting economic, legal, and political factors.

Immigrant Families through the Lifecourse Lens

In order to better understand how the immigration experience impacts individuals and families, variations in ontogenetic, generational, and historical development must be examined (Bengtson & Allen, 1993). Situating the microsocial unit of the immigrant family in the macrosocial context of changing sociopolitical, economic, and ideological paradigms of the United States provides a holistic lens through which to interpret variations in immigration experience. The lifecourse perspective can illumine how immigrant families experience transitions and family change (Hareven, 2000) by taking into account the various ages and backgrounds, cohorts, and arrival times of diverse groups.

Elder (1998) points out that "the lifecourse of individuals is embedded in and shaped by the historical times and places they experience over their lifetime" (p. 3). In addition, the developmental effects of transitions differentiate according to when events occur in an individual's life (Elder, 1998). Variables such as immigration history, timing, generational status, and geographic location of settlement must be considered when interpreting the experiences of immigrant individuals and families. For example, the Latino population in southern Florida is mostly of Caribbean origin, while the majority of Latinos in Texas are of Mexican descent (Cauce, 2005). Clearly, there are sociohistorical, cultural, geographic, economic, and individual variations in these two populations that cannot simply be explained by the broad categorization of *Latino*. Under the umbrella of the Latino category lies great cultural diversity and experience that can be analyzed on microsocial and macrosocial levels (Bengston & Allen, 1993).

Moreover, there is diversity among immigrants who come from the same country of origin, which has implications for microsocial and macrosocial trends. For example, a popular but dated perception of Mexican American marriage patterns is that they are consistently tied to values of the *traditional* family and female chastity. Although cultural factors do play a role in the timing of marriage in the lifecourse for Mexican American immigrants, variables such as economic and demographic constraints also influence the timing of these choices for individuals and families (Raley, Durden & Wildsmith, 2004). Mexican Americans and immigrants from other backgrounds make decisions about the timing of marriage and other family-related choices as they are influenced by cultural values, as well as constraints, demands, and opportunities in their host country. In order to better understand the diverse ancestry and transitional experiences of immigrant families, country of origin, timing of arrival, age at arrival, family constellation, economic and educational resources, and geographic settlement location in the United States must be taken into account.

The developmental processes and living environments of immigrants prior to immigration is another unexplored area of research. Of the 950,000 people who immigrated to the United States in 2004, about 75 percent were above twenty-one years of age (U.S. Department of Homeland Security, 2005). In other words, for the majority of new immigrants, important early developmental stages have already taken place in cultural and historical contexts that are characteristic of their home countries. It is unfair to judge those contextual influences based on what we know about growing up in the United States. Furthermore, it is crucial to understand the impact immigration has on individual and family social networks as adult immigrants adjust to economic and familial demands in their host country. Salaff and Greve (2004) examined the impact immigration has on Chinese immigrant women who are simultaneously working to rebuild their professional careers and organize care for their children in Canada. Using lifecourse and social capital theories, they found that women who no longer had access to the expansive formal and informal childcare support networks in their home countries experienced greater losses in their career trajectories than did their husbands. Ultimately, loss of social capital, building new careers, and arranging childcare were challenging adjustments for the Chinese immigrant women in this sample. In order to more systematically explore the relationship between immigrant experiences and adjustment to U.S. society, we need to take the life experiences and developmental pathways of individuals and their families before and after immigration into account.

To illustrate the complexity of the relationship between lifecourse and immigration, the authors of this chapter have highlighted aspects of their own personal stories. The four following case studies demonstrate that age at arrival, country of origin, timing, regionality, and family/marital status coincide to differentiate the immigration experience.

Case Study 1: Immigration as a Childhood Experience

This story describes the immigration experience of two young children, Amr and Leila, who came to the United States at the ages of six and eight from Cairo, Egypt. Their story is a bit different from those of many children brought to the United States in childhood, due to the fact that their parents originate from different parts of the world—their mother is German and their father is Egyptian. Their parents decided to immigrate to this country in order to give their children opportunities that they felt would be lacking had they decided to stay in Egypt. The immigration decision was impacted by two historical events—the 1967 war between Egypt and Israel, and the 1965 Immigration Act that opened America's doors to immigrants from non-Western parts of the world. The children's father was a professor, and in 1968 (the year they immigrated) the United States had a shortage of academics. Thus, their father was able to apply for a green card and bring his family over. His decision was impacted by this opportunity as well as the unstable political situation in the Middle East, which he felt would not be conducive to raising young children.

While the parents spoke English, the children did not—Amr and Leila were raised speaking German at home (they had attended a German school in Cairo). Thus, the transition to the United States involved a cultural adjustment for the parents and, in particular, a linguistic one for the children. It is important to point out that this migration took place in a time before *diversity*, *bilingual education*, and *multiculturalism* had become popular concepts. Amr and Leila were sent to school and expected to *adjust*—there were no special facilities to assist them with the transition.

The family settled in a white suburb of a small town on the northeast coast of the United States. They had little if any contact with either Egyptians or Germans and all of the children's friends were American. A major consequence of the migration was that for Amr and Leila, all contact with the father's family was lost. The family never went to Egypt to visit, and only twice did a sole uncle come for short business trips. Amr and Leila, thus, grew up without a real sense of either their Egyptian or German backgrounds. Their ties to their cultural backgrounds only persisted through food, since the parents continued to maintain that part of their traditions, and through family stories. Their father, who is one of ten children, liked to tell stories about his life, which sounded as exotic to the children as if they were reading the *Tales of a Thousand and One Nights*. However, Amr and Leila did not associate any of the stories or experiences with themselves. Instead, they insisted that they were *American* all through their childhoods, and resented the fact that they *had to* speak German at home.

As children from mixed parentage, Amr and Leila grew up feeling that they were children of *immigrants*—but not of a specific cultural background. At times, both children served as cultural brokers, explaining aspects of the society to their parents that they did not understand. For example, their parents were not familiar with, nor did they approve of, the school system in the United States, with its emphasis on sports and after-school activities, or social activities such as sleepovers that the children enjoyed. The immigration experience impacted Amr and Leila primarily through the cultural gaps that they experienced with their parents as they were growing up—on issues such as dating, extracurricular after-school activities, and going off to live at college, all of which were discouraged.

It was only in adulthood, through international travel and educational opportunities, that both Amr and Leila started to understand the value of the opportunities that were provided to them through the immigration experience. By coming as young children and going through the

American educational system, they both were able to realize success on multiple levels that may be difficult to achieve for those who come later in life. Their parents were able to provide a stable family environment from which they, as children and young adults, explored and took advantage of various opportunities.

Case Study 2: Immigration and the Single Woman

Dafna was just released from the Israeli army when she decided to fly to the United States. She was almost twenty at the time, and helping an Israeli family with the option to tour the United States seemed to be an ideal opportunity for her. However, after only a couple of months, Dafna realized that being away from her family was very difficult. She tried to adjust. She took two classes at a community college to improve her English, and joined a gym to fill her leisure time. At the gym, Dafna met Rick, who befriended her after seeing her a few times. The relationship soon developed into a romantic one, but Dafna's time in the United States was almost over and saying goodbye was not easy.

Dafna was excited to return to her home in Israel. She had a very close family, and without her they felt that a big piece of their lives was missing. Her brother, who is eight years younger than her, asked her to never leave because the house was not the same without her, and her sister, who is three years younger than her, felt that her best friend finally came back. Dafna tried to get her life back on track, registering at different universities and applying for several jobs. However, she quickly realized that the connection made with Rick was deeper than she thought. It was not easy to get back to ordinary life even though she was home. After much heartache and personal exploration, Dafna and Rick decided they were meant to be together, and doing so would mean for Dafna to leave her family once again.

In order to legally live with Rick in the United States, Dafna had to obtain a student visa that would allow her to have the status of an international student. No other sensible options were possible. She would have had to get married right away or enter the United States legally with a tourist visa and remain in the country illegally after the visa expired. Dafna, who considered herself to be a person of high morals and who aspired to obtain higher educational degrees, believed the student visa to be her only option. With Rick's help, Dafna applied to an American university, sending all the registration materials from Israel. Her acceptance at the university was their only hope. However, Dafna's and Rick's wishes to be together not only influenced their lives, but also impacted her family's life greatly. Her parents helped her financially as much as they could and planned to acquire special loans to pay for their daughter's expensive education.

At almost twenty-two, an emotional Dafna returned to the United States to reunite with Rick after a heartbreaking separation from her family. They moved in together and she began her studies to gain her bachelor's degree. Dafna enjoyed living with Rick, but the distance from her parents and siblings became unbearable at times. She talked to her family every day and most days more than once. Holidays and birthdays were especially depressing, and Dafna felt very lonely. Luckily, she was able to visit her family once or twice a year, which was another financial burden on her parents, but leaving every time was extremely difficult. After dating Rick for almost three years, they were married in a modest ceremony at city hall. At that time, Dafna applied to change her status from a student visa to a permanent residence visa. The journey of becoming a permanent resident was complex, and at times Dafna felt that her privacy was compromised. However, becoming a permanent resident was very exciting. She believed that having a permanent residence visa would open doors that were exclusive to citizens.

After almost a decade, Dafna became a graduate student in a major university. She gave birth to a son more than three years ago and in some ways her life became easier. Dafna's improved English, her local friends, her son, and her strong relationship with her husband made her life brighter and happier. She learned to embrace the reality of being so far away from her family, but also realized that the longing to be close to them would never subside.

Case Study 3: Immigrating as a Married Graduate Student

Xiaomei was an international college student from China. Strictly speaking, she is not an immigrant but a *non-immigrant alien*, based on the categorization by the U.S. Immigration Office. She shared the experience of leaving her home country behind and settling down in a new cultural context as thousands of immigrants do. Starting a graduate program was a stressful time for her, as she had the extra strain of adjusting to different cultural values and foreign language proficiencies that she felt were beyond her academic preparation in China.

Xiaomei was twenty-eight, married, and had a stable job in a Chinese metropolitan city when she moved to the United States. The idea of seeking better educational opportunities in a Western country was very popular among her friends in China. When her husband, also Chinese, received an offer from a doctoral program at a major U.S. university, she was excited about what this opportunity would bring to them. They decided that they would go to America together to study for postgraduate degrees. Both of their families were extremely supportive of their decision. In China, education is given the topmost priority. Most parents, if possible, would give anything in exchange for a better education for their children. The side effect is that the children often have to endure the pressures of trying to excel academically to meet their parents' high expectations.

Xiaomei and her husband left for the United States with dreams of academic achievements and winning honor for the family. Xiaomei studied in a graduate program for about five years. During this period of time, the constant stressor that bothered her most was the physical separation from her parents, relatives, and friends in her remote homeland. She only visited her family once because of the time-consuming procedures of visa application. Telephone calls and e-mails were the only ways to be connected with family and friends. There were moments that Xiaomei felt homesick and lonely, but not too often, especially when she was busy with schoolwork.

The language barrier was another constant stressor in Xiaomei's school life. Although Xiaomei studied English for sixteen years before moving to the United States, she still struggled with completing essays, finishing reading assignments, taking notes during lectures, and communicating with professors due to her limited language proficiency. In addition, the social science program that she majored in taxed her English skills tremendously.

As the time of graduation approached, Xiaomei was faced with a new dilemma in her life. She needed to make a choice between residing in the United States or returning to China. There were benefits and drawbacks to both options. It would be a relatively smoother transition if she chose to stay in the country that she had become used to over the past five years; however, she would be even further away from her beloved family and home culture. On the other hand, if she decided against becoming an immigrant in the United States and returned to China, there would be no worry about family separation. She would, however, have to make another round of adjustments to the culture with which she was once very familiar. A moderating factor in this decision-making process was employment opportunities. In the end, Xiaomei decided to base her decision on career opportunities.

Case Study 4: An American Woman's Marriage into a Transnational Family

Sara was a senior at a liberal arts college in the fall of 2000 when she met Ronan, her roommate's childhood friend. They made an immediate connection and she knew that if she had the opportunity, she would grow to love him. What she did not know was that she would eventually marry him and become part of the second generation of an Irish immigrant family.

Ronan's father, Coman, first came to the United States in 1969 in search of work that was not available to him in Ireland. He dated Marie, Ronan's mother, before he left for America and returned to marry her in 1977. Soon after their marriage, they left their rural hometown in Ireland and made the journey across the Atlantic to raise their family where they believed their children would experience greater educational and economic opportunities. Ronan was born in Brooklyn in the spring of 1978. In the following seven years, Coman and Marie had two more boys and two girls.

When Ronan told Sara about his parents' immigration story, she was amazed by their courage to leave their family, support networks, and culture at the same time they were beginning a family of their own. Sara had trouble imagining how Marie gave birth to five children and took the role of primary caregiver without the help of her mother, siblings, or extended family, while Coman worked long hours as a carpenter to make ends meet. How was it for both Marie and Coman to move from a tiny town in Ireland to the culturally diverse metropolis of New York City? How did they build new social support networks? How did they economically manage in the early years? Did they experience great loneliness and isolation when they first moved to their new home? As a native-born American, Sara had never contemplated what it would be like to start a new life in a foreign country and had great respect for Coman and Marie's resilience and courage.

When Sara first met Coman and Marie she was nervous that they might not accept her. She was scared that they would want their first-born son to marry an Irish Roman Catholic girl who shared their heritage and beliefs. Sara grew up in a small nonreligious family and wondered how she would fit in with Ronan's family members. However, with time Sara grew to be very close with family members and learned that her assumptions about Ronan's parents were inaccurate. Marie and Coman embraced her and Sara found them to be extraordinarily open-minded about individuals from various cultural and ethnic backgrounds.

Ronan and Sara wed in the fall of 2003 in her small New England hometown in a Roman Catholic ceremony that was officiated by his uncle and cousin, both priests. Ronan has about fifty first cousins, most of whom still live in Ireland, and about twenty of those relatives came for their wedding. During this period Sara truly began to understand the complex interconnections between Ronan's nuclear family and extended family in Ireland.

Although Coman and Marie miss the *old country* as they call it, and their brothers, sisters, cousins, nieces and nephews; they have made continuous efforts to stay connected to their family. Marie speaks with her mother, sister, and many of Coman's relatives on the phone regularly. They also keep in touch through letters and e-mail. Most significantly, Ronan and his siblings spent their childhood summers in Ireland, so they have grown up with a clear understanding of where they came from and what it means to be a part of their family abroad.

Marie and Coman sometimes marvel at the fact that their children are *American* and wonder how different life would have been in Ireland. As for Sara, she recently had the opportunity to visit Ireland for the first time and learn more about her new family. When Sara and Ronan arrived at a family party, they were welcomed with great excitement. A cousin immediately approached Sara and exclaimed, "Welcome home!" Throughout her visit to Ireland, Sara quickly realized that even though there is great physical distance between them and a lack of constant interaction, her new nuclear and extended families are deeply connected. Ultimately, she hopes that these ties survive future transnational generations.

Summary

Each of the case studies presented above provides a glimpse into the complexity of immigration processes and pathways for individual members of families. The cases, in particular, illustrate that the lifecourse is a critical factor in understanding at least some of the aspects of the immigration experience. Each of the individuals described here arrived in the United States at a different point in their lives. They also arrived at various junctures in American history. Their stories reflect the fact that no single factor or classification predicts the immigration experience for individuals and their families. Instead, the four case studies highlight the fact that sociohistorical timing, country of origin, ethnicity, educational level, age, marital status, and gender all play critical roles in the immigration experience, sometimes in unexpected ways. This myriad of elements shapes diverse immigration experiences for individuals and their families.

Conclusion

This chapter has illustrated that the lifecourse plays a critical role in shaping the immigration experience. While immigrants are primarily described and studied as a collective body, the case studies demonstrate that there is immense variation in the immigration experience depending on the age of the migrants and the timing of arrival in the host society. Further, the cases point out that family ties provide both negative and positive social capital for immigrant families. The move from one sociocultural environment to another can lead to a variety of family changes, including gender and generational roles, as well as dissonance in marital and parent-child relations. The migration experience can also result in positive transformations, such as stronger unity and cohesion between family members, leading to achievements that benefit both the immigrant family and their extended relations in their home country.

As the number of immigrants increases and their places of residence expand around the country, it is imperative to heighten scholarly awareness about their lives and experiences. In order to prepare future scholars to further research this topic, as well as prepare practitioners who will interact closely with immigrant families, immigration will need to be studied and taught as a multidimensional experience. There is a dire need in the field for professionals who are sensitive, compassionate, and educated about the complexity and the significance of this topic.

Researchers who study families are recognizing the complex and multidimensional nature of issues confronting immigrants. They have become acutely aware of the interaction effects of ethnicity, gender, and class on families. As understanding of the importance of this interface has grown, so too has the realization that family researchers and family-service practitioners must become increasingly culturally competent (Fong, 2001). Cultural competency can be achieved, in part, by understanding how families and service delivery to families are impacted by immigration issues. Social scientists concerned with preparing young scholars and practitioners need to become more sensitive to the complex aspects of the immigration experience for individuals and families in order to better prepare their students for their future careers (Smeiser, Wilson & Mitchell, 2000). In particular, the fields of family studies, human services, and family life education are faced with the challenge of training professionals who will have to meet the needs of an increasingly diverse clientele. It is critical that professionals do not stereotype their students and clients. Unfortunately, it is quite common for educators and service providers to assume that they are culturally competent because they know a smattering about various cultures, religions, or ethnicities. The cases in this chapter illustrate that individual experiences are often quite different from group characterizations. Cultural competency needs to be based on sensitivity to individual lives and sociohistorical context. This can be achieved through teaching listening skills and sensitivity to personal biases. By emphasizing the complexity of individual and family experiences, educators and family professionals can assist in creating and delivering services that will better assist immigrants and their families.

References

Bengtson, V. L., & Allen, K. R. (1993). The lifecourse perspective applied to families over time. In P. G. Boss, W. J. Doherty, R. LaRossa, W. R. Schumm & S. K. Steinmetz (Eds.), *Sourcebook of family theories and methods: A contextual approach* (pp. 469–499). New York: Kluwer Academic/Plenum.

Bryceson, D., & Vuorela, U. (2002). Transnational Families in the twenty-first century. In D. Bryceson & U. Vuorela (Eds.), *The transnational family: New European frontiers and global networks.* New York: Oxford University Press.

Buriel, R., & DeMent, T. (1997). Immigration and sociocultural change in Mexican, Chinese, and Vietnamese American families. In A. Booth, A. Crouter & N. Landale (Eds.), *Immigration and the family: Research and policy on U.S. immigrants* (pp. 165–200). Mahwah, NJ: Lawrence Erlbaum.

Cauce, A. M. (2005). The demographics of the 21st-century family: Examining race, ethnicity, and culture within geographic and generational context. In V. L. Bengtson, A. C. Acock, K. R. Allen & D. M. Klein (Eds.), *Sourcebook of family theory and research* (pp. 206–208). Thousand Oaks, CA: Sage.

Cordero-Guzman, H. R., & Navarro, J. G. (2000). What do immigrant service providers say about the impact of recent changes in immigration and welfare laws? *Migration World Magazine, 28*(4), 20–26.

Dilworth-Anderson, P., Burton, P. L., & Turner, W. L. (1993). The importance of values in the study of culturally diverse families. *Family Relations, 43*, 243–248.

Dion, K. K., & Dion, K. L. (2001). Gender and cultural adaptation in immigrant families. *Journal of Social Issues, 57*(3), 511–521.

Elder, G. H. (1998). The lifecourse as developmental theory. *Child Development, 69*(1), 1–12.

Fong, R. (2001). Cultural competency in providing family-centered services. In E. Walton, P. Sandau-Beckler & M. Mannes (Eds.), *Balancing family-centered services and child well-being: Exploring issues in policy, practice, theory, and research* (pp. 55–68). New York: Columbia University Press.

Glenn, E. N. (1983). Split households, small producers and dual wage earners: An analysis of Chinese-American family strategies. *Journal of Marriage and the Family, 45,* 46–55.

Guest, K. R. (2005). The ideology of terror: Why we will never win the "war." *The Journal of American Culture, 28*(4), 368–376.

Hagan, J. M. (2004). Contextualizing immigrant labor market incorporation: Legal, demographic, and economic dimensions. *Work and Occupations, 31*(4), 407–423.

Hareven, T. K. (2000). Synchronizing individual time, family time, and historical time. *Families, history, and social change: Lifecourse and cross-cultural perspectives* (pp. 151–165). Boulder, CO: Westview Press.

He, W., & Hobbs, F. (1999). *Minority population growth: 1995 to 2050.* Washington, DC: U.S. Department of Commerce.

Larsen, L. J. (2004). *The foreign born population in the U.S.: 2003.* Washington, DC: U.S. Census Bureau.

Lee, Y. T., Ottati, V., & Hussain, I. (2001). Attitudes toward "illegal" immigration into the U.S.: California proposition 187. *Hispanic Journal of Behavioral Sciences, 23*(4), 430–443.

Maher, K. H. (2002). Who has a right to rights? Citizenship's exclusions in an age of migration. In L. Brysk (Ed.), *Globalization and human rights* (pp. 201–225). Berkeley: University of California Press.

Oropesa, R., & Landale, N. (2004). The future of marriage and Hispanics. *Journal of Marriage and Family, 66,* 901–920.

Phinney, J. S., Ong, A., & Madden, T. (2000). Cultural values and intergenerational value discrepancies in immigrant and non-immigrant families. *Child Development, 71*(2), 528–539.

Pratto, F., & Lemieux, A. F. (2001). The psychological ambiguity of immigration and its implications for promoting immigration policy. *Journal of Social Issues, 57*(3), 413–430.

Raffaeli, M., & Ontai, L. L. (2004). Gender socialization in Latino/a families: Results from two retrospective studies. *Sex Roles, 50*(5/6), 287–299.

Raley, R. K., Durden, T. E., & Wildsmith, E. (2004). Understanding Mexican-American marriage patterns using a life-course approach. *Social Science Quarterly, 85*(4), 872–890.

Rumbaut, R. (1997). Ties that bind: Immigration and immigrant families in the U.S. In A. Booth, A. Crouter & N. Landale (Eds.), *Immigration and the family: Research and policy on U.S. immigrants* (pp. 3–45). Mahwah, NJ: Lawrence Erlbaum.

Salaff, J. W., & Greve, A. (2004). Can women's social networks migrate? *Women's Studies International Forum, 27,* 149–162.

Schmidley, D. (2001). *Profile of the foreign-born population in the U. S.: 2000 (Series P23-206)*. Washington, DC: U.S. Census Bureau.

Smeiser, N. J., Wilson, W. J., & Mitchell, F. (Eds.) (2000). *America becoming: Racial trends and their consequences* (Vol. 1). Washington, DC: National Academy Press.

Torres, J. B., Solberg, V. S., & Carlstrom, A. H. (2002). The myth of sameness among Latino men and their machismo. *American Journal of Orthopsychiatry*, 72(2), 163–181.

Umana-Taylor, A. J., & Wiley, A. R. (2004). Family diversity in the classroom: A review of existing strategies. *Journal of Teaching in Marriage and Family*, 4(1), 127–143.

U.S. Department of Homeland Security. (2005). *2004 Yearbook of Immigration Statistics*. Retrieved February 4, 2006, from uscis.gov/graphics/shared/statistics/yearbook/.

About the Authors

Laura Thompson Brady is a doctoral student in the Department of Individual and Family Studies at the University of Delaware, Newark, DE 19716. E-mail: llt@udel.edu

Wei Qiu is a doctoral student in the Department of Individual and Family Studies at the University of Delaware, Newark, DE 19716. E-mail: weiqiu@udel.edu

Dorit Radnai-Griffin is a doctoral student in the Department of Individual and Family Studies at the University of Delaware, Newark, DE 19716. E-mail: doritrg@udel.edu.

Bahira Sherif Trask is a professor in the Department of Individual and Family Studies at the University of Delaware, 111 Alison West, Newark, DE 19716. E-mail: bstrask@udel.edu.

Transnational Families and the Social Construction of Identity
Whiteness Matters

4

LIBBY BALTER BLUME AND LEE ANN DE REUS

Abstract

In this chapter, we offer an alternative theoretical approach that recognizes the multiplicity, fluidity, and intersectionality of immigrant family life. Family science scholars, educators, and practitioners are increasingly sensitized to issues of diversity, yet most remain relatively uneducated about transnational families. In order to develop cross-cultural competencies, family scholars must increase their awareness on multiple levels, including: (1) understanding the identity negotiations of new immigrant families; (2) sensitivity to the meaning of white ethnic identity for immigrant families; and (3) developing reflexive knowledge about one's own racial/ethnic identity and privilege.

Keywords: Racism, White Privilege, Identity, Transnational Feminism, Critical Race Theory

THE MEANING OF ETHNICITY is complicated for new immigrant families who often maintain family links across borders, bridging *homeplaces* in two very different cultural worlds (Dilworth-Anderson,

Address all correspondence to Dr. Libby B. Blume, Department of Psychology and Women's Studies at University of Detroit Mercy, 4001 W. McNichols, Detroit, MI 48221-3038. Phone: 313-578-0446. E-mail: blumelb@udmercy.edu.

Burton & Klein, 2005; Phinney, 2003). Living in one or more cultures and maintaining connections to both is defined as *transnationalism* (Stone, Gomez, Hotzoglou & Lipnitsky, 2005; Waldinger & Fitzgerald, 2003). Transnational families, therefore, are immigrants who sustain social relations across places of origin and settlement (Basch, Schiller & Blanc, 1994; Bryceson & Vuorela, 2002). Because we live in a postmodern world in which air travel, Internet communication, and economic globalization are increasingly common, the traditional distinction between *immigrants* and *those left behind* is no longer clear (Stone et al., 2005). As a result, migration involves a very large, interconnected relationship system, sometimes referred to as *emotional transnationalism* (Falicov, 2005).

As people move physically and virtually between places, the notion of a stable identity becomes problematic. For example, ethnic immigrant families from Middle Eastern countries may be considered people of color when they come to the United States—even though they would be regarded as white in their home countries *and* in terms of the U.S. Census Bureau classification. For example, an older Iranian woman who is a naturalized American citizen may regard herself to be Persian, Muslim, and white (e.g., McConatha, Stoller & Oboudiat, 2001). However, she may be viewed by her neighbors as a person of color due to her country of origin, accent, religion, and appearance. When she visits her family in Iran, who is she? Does her level of social status or privilege change from one location to the next, depending on her perceived identity?

The purpose of this chapter is to raise awareness among educators, researchers, and practitioners about the complexities of the white ethnic identities of new immigrants from homeplaces such as Eastern Europe or the Middle East and to consider what happens when ethnic, religious, cultural, national, social, family, and/or personal identities intersect. Intersectionality is a well-established perspective in feminist theory that describes the multiple identities that people hold simultaneously. For example, *Muslim American woman* describes an individual's *religion* × *nationality* × *gender*. In this chapter, we will use the concept of intersectionality to describe how transnational individuals and families negotiate multiple, fluid identifications with cultural norms and practices when connected to two or more homeplaces, for example, when moving between two cultures. An essential premise of this chapter is our recognition that aspects of collective identity such as race, ethnicity, and nationality are not fixed but are dynamic. In other words, we question the existence of restrictive social categories by recognizing the fluidity and contextual embeddedness of identities (De Reus, Few & Blume, 2005). Lastly, we will suggest how educators, researchers, and practitioners can increase their cross-cultural competence for understanding the complexities of ethnic identities.

In writing this chapter, we relied on critical race theory to examine the dominant cultural discourse of racism. Critical race theorists emphasize the ways that majority groups racialize different immigrant groups at different times in response to shifting needs (e.g., the global labor market, economic fluxes, and/or social and legal movements) to maintain power within a hierarchal social matrix (Delgado & Stefancic, 2001). The writings of critical race feminists offer family scholars, educators, and practitioners an alterative interpretation of the legal history of immigration history from the perspective of transnational family experiences (Wing, 1997). For example, critical race scholars legitimate the narratives of immigrants as part of historical and legal fact-finding that may present a different story of how the law has justified an ideology of racism against a person of color (Parker & Lynn, 2002).

We also utilized transnational feminism to apply our understanding of racism to new immigrant families. Transnational feminists investigate the social, political, and economic conditions comprising imperialism and racism. Transnational feminism brings a global focus and perspective to studying nationhood, race, gender, sexuality, and economic exploitation (Mohanty, 2003). From this perspective, the social construction of race confounds families' navigation of transnational lives (Kim, 2004). In addition, the fluidity of identity is particularly salient as we consider the lives of new immigrant families.

New Immigrant Families and the Social Construction of Difference

Given the globalization of families, the challenge before family scholars, practitioners, and educators is to think differently about *difference*. In 2004, approximately 35 million people, or 12 percent of the U.S. population, were identified as foreign-born, with one out of five children currently living in an immigrant family (Haskins, Greenberg & Fremstad, 2004). While most studies of immigrant families have focused on the two largest groups, those from Latin America and Asia, very little attention has been directed at new immigrants from Eastern Europe. The number of legal immigrants arriving from Bosnia, Romania, and Russia, for example, increased from 18,260 in 1987 to a high of 121,083 in 2001 (Migration Information Source, 2007). This growth is due primarily to the fall of Communism in the late 1980s. Included in this group are new immigrants from countries such as the Czech/Slovak Republics, Hungary, Latvia, Lithuania, Poland, Romania, Russia, Ukraine, and the former Yugoslavia.

Similarly, little research has considered the diverse ethnic identities and experiences of new immigrants from countries in a geographical area labeled (by Westerners) as the "Middle East" (Achar-Naccache, 2006). Middle Eastern individuals have ancestral ties to the Islamic region of the world in Southwest Asia and North Africa (Marvasti & McKinney, 2004). Although the newest Middle Eastern immigrants are often Muslim, most Middle Eastern Americans in the United States are Christian (Marger, 2006). The largest population of Middle Eastern immigrants in the United States is Iranian, a group that is not ethnically or linguistically Arabic. Most Arab Americans (individuals from Lebanon, Syria, Egypt, Palestine, Iraq, Jordan, etc.) are part of the newest immigration that started in the 1970s. Some estimates of the number of Americans of Arab origin are as high as 3 million, with 25,000 Arabs immigrating to the U.S. annually; however, the official U.S. Census described the Arab American population as 1.2 million with the largest number of immigrants from Lebanon, Syria, Egypt, and Palestine (Marger, 2006). This discrepancy in the population statistic is due to the fact that the U.S. Census classifies Middle Eastern Americans as *white*. Despite the addition of a question on national origin in the 2000 census, there is no category available for Arab or Middle Eastern Americans (Marvasti & McKinney, 2004).

The Myth of Race

We can no longer think simplistically and categorically about people. For example, the U.S. Census Bureau defines a white person as someone "having origins in any of the original peoples of Europe, the Middle East, or North Africa, including people who indicate their race as 'white' or report ethnicities such as Irish, German, Italian, Lebanese, Near Easterner, Arab, or Polish" (U.S. Census Bureau, 2001). Whether an individual perceives her- or himself to be white, however, is subjective in the same way that society's determination of "race" is widely regarded by experts as a biological myth.

Biologists, anthropologists, and geneticists have agreed for some time that race has no genetic basis (Marks 2003; Goodman, 1998; Ossorio, 2003). In fact, 85 percent of human genetic diversity occurs within, not between, "races." Whether local populations are Italians, Kurds, Koreans, or Cherokees, about 94 percent of genetic variation can be found within any continent. Consequently, any two Koreans may be as genetically different as a Korean and an Italian (Rose & Rose, 2005; see also Lewontin, 1982).

The "race" of immigrant individuals and families is imposed by a societal perception of what it *means* to be African, Asian, European, Middle Eastern, Latino, or Afro-Caribbean, and so on. Typically based on biological markers such as skin tone and "foreignness," determined by nationality and/or accent, many immigrant families are regarded as people of color. In addition, whites in the United States most often judge newcomers along a binary white-to-black status continuum (Feagin, 2000; Rose & Rose, 2005). Consider the following example offered by Pilar Ossorio, a legal scholar, microbiologist, and bioethicist who teaches at the University of Wisconsin, Madison, "Well, I have a friend who's from the Bahamas; he grew up there. And he was White in the Bahamas. So he lived his life socially positioned as a White person. He came to the United States and instantly he became a Black person. Because our understanding here of what it means to be White and Black is different than the understanding of people in the Bahamas. So what we see and label as Black is different than what other people see and label as Black" (Ossorio, 2003).

It is important to acknowledge that race—like other social constructions such as gender—is performative. In this view, identities are sustained through repeated interactions with the cultural discourse. Furthermore, as we *perform* our whiteness, we are socially constructed by those with whom we interact (Butler, 1990; Hill & Thomas, 2000; Warren & Fassett, 2002). Put another way—with apologies to West and Zimmerman (1987)— "being white" is not "doing white" (see Alexander, 2004). Thus, we regard whiteness as a performative accomplishment, not a biological fact. It is a product of social norms that have designated a particular skin pigment a political signifier of privilege (Warren & Fassett, 2002).

White Privilege

While race may not be genetically definable, it is undoubtedly a powerful social construct that affords varying levels of opportunities and resources to certain individuals. People regarded as white, for example, are afforded social, legal, and economic privileges compared to nonwhites (Delgado & Stefancic, 1997, 2001). "Throughout American history, starting with the 1790 census, a classification of racial groups has been used to regulate relations among the races and to support discriminatory policies designed to protect the numerical and political supremacy of white Americans of

European Ancestry" (Roberts, 2004, p. 143). This arbitrary hierarchy of races was necessary in the eighteenth and nineteenth centuries for the rationalization and justification of slavery. Still in effect today, white culture is dominant in the United States with the power to control resources, set rules, and influence events. For example, only 16 percent of the current U.S. House of Representatives and 5 percent of the U.S. Senate belong to a racial-minority group compared to about 25 percent of the total population (Pearson Education, 2006). Indeed, a preference for white skin has operated structurally, systematically, and at times unconsciously, as a dominant force around the world (Giordano & McGoldrick, 2005).

In the twentieth century, however, whiteness has been examined by scholars in an intentional political strategy to make whiteness visible (e.g., Delgado & Stefancic, 1997; Du Bois, 1935; Roediger, 2003). As Frankenberg (1993) asserted, "most often, whites are the nondefined definers of other people . . . whiteness comes to be an unmarked or neutral category" (p. 197) ascribed with power and privilege. In a now-classic paper entitled, *White Privilege: Unpacking the Invisible Knapsack*, McIntosh (1990) began to unravel and illuminate the numerous, unearned, invisible privileges afforded her in daily life due to the color of her skin. Much as men's lives are viewed as normative and neutral—with most men unaware of their entrenched male privilege—so, too, does McIntosh liken her obliviousness to white privilege and her unconscious role as oppressor. The following is a sample of her daily privileges: (a) I can, if I wish, arrange to be in the company of people of my race most of the time; (b) I can go shopping alone most of the time, fairly well assured that I will not be followed or harassed by store detectives; (c) I can turn on the television or open to the front page of the paper and see people of my race widely and positively represented; (d) I did not have to educate our children to be aware of systemic racism for their own daily physical protection; and (e) I am never asked to speak for all the people of my racial group. McIntosh concluded her essay by challenging whites to end the silence and denial surrounding the unseen dimensions of privilege in order to redesign our current systems of inequality.

In previous waves of immigration, when many European ethnic groups immigrated to the United States from Germany, Italy, and Ireland, most Americans assumed that they were accorded the benefits of being white: access to housing, work, and education. W. E. B. Du Bois referred to such privileges as "the wages of whiteness" (Du Bois, 1935; see also Hartman, 2004). White ethnic groups—although lacking in protection by labor unions from the abuse of wealthy factory owners—nevertheless were accorded more privilege than African Americans, American Indians, or immigrants of color (Roediger, 1991; Thandeka, 2006). Some scholars have claimed, however, that Jews (Brodkin, 1999; Goldstein, 2006), Irish (Ignatiev, 1995)—and more recently Asians (Zhou, 2004)—have *become* white through the interrelated processes of assimilation and accultura-tion. Although initially perceived by the public as separate "races," these immigrant groups established their whiteness by relinquishing their more obvious ethnic traits and by identifying with elite whites in terms of social class (Marvasti & McKinney, 2004). Given their location on an antiquated white-black continuum as ascribed by skin tone, European immigrant groups had an easier assimilation experience than immigrants of color.

Despite studies of early twentieth-century immigrant groups, such as the Irish and Jews who arrived in the United States as nonwhites but later achieved white status, only a small number of researchers have examined the lived experiences of recent immigrants from Eastern Europe and the Middle East. No studies were identified that examined the role of white racial identity and its inherent privilege in the lives of recent immigrants. Thus the question remains, what does a system of white privilege mean for the experiences of contemporary transnational immigrant families?

For the majority of recent Middle Eastern immigrants, their social loca-tion has been severely compromised by the tragic events of September 11. As the authors of a study of Arabs in the Detroit area point out, "You will not fit in here unless you behave appropriately, and this will be possible only if the differences that set you apart from us—your language, your culture, your religion, your attitude—are somehow naturalized, normal-ized, muted, consigned to another time, or linked to a place and a way of life you have left behind" (Shryock & Abraham, 2000, p. 17). The message from the white dominant culture is clear. If Arabs cannot *be* white, they must "do whiteness" and conform to the standards of Americanization if they hope to achieve success in the United States. In this case, ethnicity as defined by brown skin and "foreignness" has transcended identity as an American and relegated Arab immigrants to second-class citizens. In the post–September 11 era of racial profiling and suspicion of anyone "Middle Eastern–looking," many Arab Americans have adopted a variety of coping strategies to address situations in which they are asked to explain them-selves. To avoid this accounting, some Middle Eastern Americans try to "pass" by trading their ethnic identity for one less controversial, such as Hispanic (Marvasti & McKinney, 2004). The extreme irony, of course, is that Arab Americans are classified as white according to the U.S. Census.

A paucity of research regarding Eastern European immigrants prohib-its us from examining their lived experiences regarding ethnic identity and whiteness. That said, there is evidence to suggest that these transnational groups may live at the intersection of assimilation and transnationalism in the form of *hybridization* where "immigrants, especially children, blend rather than alternate cultural meanings" or engage in indigenous/ethnic reaffirmation (Falicov, 1998, p. 74). For example, a new bilingual magazine called *Russian Bride of New York* touts "Martha Stewart Weddings" for young Russian women. Created by an Uzbekistan immigrant, the publication caters to the more than 200,000 single Russian women in the United States, of which a quarter live in New York. The purpose of the magazine is to explain American wedding rituals, while at the same time encouraging the preservation of Russian traditions (Bellafante, 2004). The location of Eastern Europeans on the white-black continuum affords them access to white privilege, particularly if they are of the upper- or middle-class. Honeymoons in Seychelles or Fiji are promoted in the fall issue of *Russian Bride of New York,* as destinations that would allow newlyweds to emulate the likes of Michelle Pfeiffer and Bill Gates. In this case, higher social class enables some Eastern Europeans to move beyond "being white" to "doing whiteness."

Developing Transnational Competencies

Family science scholars, educators, and human service professionals have become increasingly sensitized to issues of diversity, yet most remain relatively uneducated about immigrant families and the implications of racial/ethnic identities beyond a simplistic understanding of difference. For example, the social construction of whiteness often goes unaddressed when researchers mistakenly assume that European American adolescents do not develop an ethnic identity (Perry, 2001). Extensive research with Portuguese American adolescents, however, has revealed that teens navigate diverse cultures, such as family, peer, and school contexts (García Coll, Szalacha & Palacios, 2005).

Understanding adolescents' identities across transnational social contexts has been described as experiencing "multiple selves, multiple worlds" by researchers who use an ecocultural model to "unpack" ethnicity, culture, and family (Cooper, Jackson, Azmitia & Lopez, 1998). Ecoculturalists assume that all families seek to make meaningful accommodation to their ecological contexts through the sustainable practices of daily living. They examine activity settings in terms of (a) who participates; (b) the salient goals, values, and beliefs of the participants; and (c) the recurring patterns of communication as a technique "for moving beyond static labels and categories for ethnicity, culture, and relationships" (Cooper et al., 1998,

p. 113). For example, in focus groups, adolescents talked about their movement within a wide array of worlds, including their families, countries of origin, friends' homes, churches, mosques, academic outreach programs, shopping malls, video arcades, school clubs, and sports. They also discussed how they communicate across these worlds, especially how they respond to their families, friends, siblings, and teachers. A central concern of ecocultural researchers is how to understand the multiple worlds of diverse adolescents without fostering stereotypes based on race, ethnicity, gender, social class, and country of origin (Cooper, 1999).

In an academic symposium on ethnicity, scholars recommended several ways to reconceptualize the relationship between ethnicity and national origin. First, we need to view ethnicity as dynamic and processual, not static and structural (Oommen, 2001). Second, we should specify how ethnic, racial, or national groups are socially constructed through the dominant discourse in a specific place and when people identify themselves—or others—in racial, ethnic, or national terms (Brubaker, 2001). Third, we should recognize that boundaries between categories are not clear-cut (Eriksen, 2001). Fourth, we need to reframe global questions of ethnicity, recognizing that where we are situated spatially, economically, and politically affects our standpoint (Yuval-Davis, 2001). Finally, we need to recognize that *ethnic* is not synonymous with *traditional* but rather is a living construction influenced by new communications media, such as the Internet, that allow new immigrants to maintain a high level of simultaneous participation in the life of their home country (Calhoun, 2001).

To develop cross-cultural competencies, researchers, educators, and practitioners can increase their level of awareness on multiple levels and from several vantage points or locations including: (a) research on the identity negotiations of new immigrant families; (b) knowledge about the meaning of white ethnic identity for immigrant families; and (c) a reflexive knowledge about one's own racial/ethnic identity and privilege. The following are possible conceptual tools for thinking differently about difference.

Intersection of Ethnicity and Identity

Identity development involves defining yourself both as an individual and as a social group member. The socially constructed categories of *race* and *ethnicity* have both been used to define the group membership of new immigrants. While *racial* identity refers to one's sense of self compared to other perceived racial groups, a closely related construct, *ethnic* identity, refers to one's sense of belonging to a cultural group (Dion & Dion, 2004). However, ethnic identity researchers have found that feelings of being "ethnic" or of belonging to a particular "race" may depend on the situation and the people one is with (Rosenthal & Hrynevich, 1985; Hill & Thomas, 2000). For example, in a qualitative study that explored the acculturation experiences and identity development process of American-born adult children of sixteen different immigrant groups, participants who were recognizably different in appearance from the majority reported more powerful and traumatic experiences of the instant when they first became aware of their difference than participants who were nonrecognizable as immigrants. They also described more volatile and conflicted identity processes, including making more efforts to blend into the dominant culture than participants who were nonrecognizable as immigrants. Researchers have concluded that being recognizably different may make the identity development process and acculturation more stressful (Murthy, 2003). When working with new immigrant groups, family professionals need to address individuals' experiences in varied contexts as their "race" or "ethnicity" is socially constructed by others with whom they interact.

As immigrant populations relocate—also referred to as *dislocating ethnicity*—individuals may also construct their own "narratives of location" (Anthias, 2002). These narratives are stories that tell us how families see themselves at particular points in time in specific locations, such as a new country. As a result, some theorists are abandoning the concept of collective identity in favor of the ideas of location and (translocational) positionality (Anthias, 2002). Such ideas are consistent with a feminist framework that describes the intersectionality of multiple identities within changing contexts (see De Reus et al., 2005). Thus it is important that family professionals understand that immigrants' national identities—both as new Americans and as expatriates of their countries of origin—may blend into a newly emergent cultural identity, such as Arab American, that is coconstructed through negotiations with others in one's family and community. For example, residents in Detroit from many different Middle Eastern cultures created a unified pan-Arab movement some thirty-five years ago and formed the Arab Community Center for Economic and Social Services (ACCESS) which today operates health clinics, social service agencies, and cultural programs, such as the Arab American National Museum and Detroit's renowned World Music Festival (ACCESS, 2006).

Dialectics of Whiteness in New Immigrant Families

From a social construction perspective, whiteness can be seen as an ongoing symbolic interactional process. In this view, whiteness is inextricably linked to a discursive process of being American; that is, any cultural practice not identical to the dominant culture is described as "not *really* white" or even as "not *American*" (Frankenberg, 1993; Murthy, 2003). Although most discussions of whiteness in the United States inevitably reproduce an outdated binary of black/white due to America's history of slavery, it is important for researchers, practitioners, and educators to resist such an oversimplification of multiculturalism in the twenty-first century. Often, multiethnicity is conflated with "race" such that culture and nationality are lost (Hartman, 2004). Such oversimplifications can be avoided by examining dialectical processes in new immigrant families (see Montgomery & Baxter, 1998).

In a dialectical model, family-level coconstructions of identities result from the multiple intersections of ethnicity and whiteness. White transnational families thus challenge family practitioners "to understand the location of 'whiteness' in the terrain of culture" (Frankenberg, 1993, p. 202) as they struggle against the pressures of assimilation to maintain their ethnic values, practices, and worldviews. In this dialectical struggle between assimilation to a new country and maintenance of their ethnic traditions, transnational immigrant families may experience mixed feelings of both gains and losses (Falicov, 2005; McConatha, Stoller & Oboudiat, 2001). For example, members of a diasporic community used Iranian television as a source for resisting cultural messages both of the homeland and receiving country by being physically located in one culture while dreaming of an unrealizable return to another. In this situation, a dialectical solution considers "cultural contact zones," where cultures bleed and permeate into one another (Bhatia & Ram, 2001; see also Hermans, 2001).

One ethnicity theorist recommends—albeit symbolically—replacing hyphens (-) with ampersands (&) in our writing of transnational identities (Ifekwunigwe, 1998; see also Fine, 1994). In actual practice then, people with multiethnic or transnational identities could be "both/and" rather than "either/or." This reconceptualization of ethnic identity as fluid enables the transcendence of limiting categories (e.g., race, culture, nationality, or religion), thereby creating a unique space for understanding—in this case—the ethnic diversity within whiteness. As practitioners who work with new immigrant families, we need to help family members identify points of dialectical tension through, for example, the reexamination of family photographs taken in both former and new countries of residence, or the retelling of family narratives from before and after immigration (e.g., Anthias, 2002; Stone et al., 2005). From this dialectical perspective, family stories involve making sense of migration experiences, are produced through social interaction, and contain elements of contradiction (Anthias, 2002). Using discourse approaches that make apparent the socially constructed nature of descriptions and accounts, intergenerational, transnational, and multicultural experiences may be better understood (Bhatia & Ram, 2001; Verkuyten & de Wolf, 2002). For example, as an alternative to conceptualizing identity as *being* from one culture or another, "negotiating one's identity based on 'feeling' [American] or 'doing' [American] does not force an either/or choice, but rather allows one to resist the pressure from each side by incorporating elements of both cultures" (Abbey, 2002, p. 414).

In addition, a dominant discourse of white privilege will more likely be identified and resisted if families make their immigration narratives known. In this regard, family life educators and family therapists can help family members uncover the discursive practices that are hidden in daily conversation about race and ethnicity to maintain privilege of one group over another (e.g., Falicov, 2005). To effectively eliminate racial/ethnic categories in family studies also requires researchers to engage in scholarship that transcends racial binaries and reduces cross-cultural comparisons in favor of within-group designs. Most importantly, it would require that social activists abandon racial lines and identity politics to engage in coalitions for the sake of all immigrant families. In other words, in a postmodern, globalized world, we need to maintain our focus on the agency of individuals to resist the political and social constructions of "race" (Kim, 2004).

Reflexivity, Race/Ethnicity, and White Privilege

The focus of this chapter thus far has centered on transnational immigrant families. However, it is also imperative that practitioners, educators, and researchers reflect on their *own* racism and positions of privilege as Americans (Wing, 2005). To achieve a more inclusive family studies, engaging in a reflexive process is essential to creating family studies scholarship and practice that is accountable to readers, clients, students, ourselves, and the people we study (Allen, 2000). The process of reflexivity is an established tradition in qualitative methods (Lynch, 2000) that involves a critical examination of self as a means for increasing individual awareness and sensitivity to the experience of others (Allen & Farnsworth, 1993). "When we invoke an awareness of the ways our own personalities and experience pass into the constructed products of our research, we are engaged in a process of reflexivity" (Daly, 2007, p. 88). In its simplest form, reflexivity compels practitioners, teachers, and researchers to identify, address, and control their personal bias in their work with or about families (Daly, 2007).

A variety of reflexive exercises and methods have been created for the purpose of examining whiteness. For example, autobiography assignments often require students to write about their experiences of being white (see McKinney, 2005; Vavrus, 2002). Examples of questions to be addressed include: What does it mean to be white? Could you tell your life story without mentioning that you're white? What experiences have made your whiteness most visible to you? Have you been discriminated against because you are white? Predictably, many of the students had difficulty articulating what it meant to be white. Their whiteness was not something they considered. One student wrote, "Whiteness to me is not having to think about being white." Further, the majority of students believed that they are now the victims of reverse discrimination, rather than understanding their whiteness as affording them power and privilege (McKinney, 2005).

Similarly, college educators of preservice teachers have used a pedagogical method called *cultural memoir* to stimulate privileged white students' thinking about their own performance of culture and ethnicity (Allen & Hermann-Wilmarth, 2004). In this journaling process, students created elaborate scrapbooks of their family stories and photos, but they did not spontaneously examine issues of race, class, gender, privilege, and equity until prompted by the self-reflexive memoirs of the instructors themselves, as well as by examples of reflections in bell hooks' *Wounds of Passion: A Writing Life* (1997) and Bell-Scott's *Life Notes: Personal Writings by Contemporary Black Women* (1994). In other words, whiteness went unvoiced.

When considering ethnicity, however, it is equally important to listen to the voices of silence: times when thoughts are not spoken. For example, in a discussion of whiteness among white teachers in a Midwestern urban school district, a qualitative researcher reported five types of (metaphoric) silence: *polite* silences were based on political correctness ("I was afraid I might use the wrong word"); *privileged* silences were words spoken from a position of privilege that afforded the luxury of not even considering the question ("I don't get it"); *veiled* silences were used when their whiteness was conveyed only through an encounter with the Other ("Whites have always been sort of the non-race"); *intentional* silences anticipated how the group might perceive the speaker without her actually expressing an opinion ("I'm in a relationship with a black man"); and *unintelligible* silences were peaceful, nonconfrontive, accepting, and affirming (Mazzei, 2003).

Another reflexive technique—autoethnography—has been recommended by feminist family researchers as a means for revealing whiteness. "Autoethnography can be defined as a self-narrative that critiques the situatedness of self with others in social contexts" (Spry, 2001, p. 710). It is an autobiographical method in the qualitative tradition where an individual is both researcher and subject. In practice, writing an autoethnography facilitates explicit reflection on one's personal experience in order to expose the biases and subjectivities we bring to our work as scholars, educators, and practitioners (Allen & Piercy, 2005).

In the analysis of whiteness, autoethnography can be used to make critical, political, and personal sense of experiences of white privilege (Magnet, 2006; Spry, 2001) by addressing questions such as: (a) How is white privilege a factor in my everyday personal life? (b) What are the ways in which my whiteness and privilege intersect with my work (i.e., interactions with clients, teaching practices and course content, research aims and findings)? (c) How are we as practitioners, scholars, and instructors constrained by our whiteness and privilege? and (d) How does a white person understand and join in the struggles different groups share? (adapted from Allen, 2000). For example, the use of autoethnography as a critique of whiteness was modeled by Allen (2000) in her critical reflection and personal narrative regarding experiences in a discussion group of black and white women academics. Following a heated exchange that occurred over black/white intimate relations, Allen was able to use critical self-reflection as a means for discerning the source of her anger. To her surprise, she uncovered previously unknown stereotypes and assumptions about black women that fueled her defensiveness. Making conscious her prejudice and unexamined beliefs ultimately informed her personal interactions and academic work. Through autoethnography, Allen was able to utilize personal experience as a bridge to other women and, consequently, to open new theoretical and methodological possibilities (Allen, 2000).

Conclusion: Whiteness Matters

The purpose of this chapter was to examine whiteness, not only as a social construction that confounds our understanding of ethnicity but also as a privileging mechanism in American society. Furthermore, we issue a challenge to family scholars, practitioners, and educators to think critically about the role of privilege in the lives of transnational immigrant families as well as its role in our own lived experiences. Critical race theory and transnational feminism can provide tools for such examinations. Through critical race theory we are able to examine the dominant cultural discourse of racism, while recognizing the narratives of immigrants as valid sources of information. The lens of transnational feminisms brings a focus to the multiple intersections among nationality, ethnicity, and social constructions of race in the lives of new immigrants (Grewal & Kaplan, 2000; Ifekwunigwe, 1998). In keeping with the feminist practice of raising self-awareness, reflexive methodologies such as authoethnography will hold us accountable as we position ourselves in relation to our own experiences and work. Whiteness matters—both in the lives of new immigrant families and in the lives of the practitioners, educators, and researchers who interact with them.

Acknowledgments

The authors wish to thank Katherine R. Allen and April L. Few for their insightful comments on an earlier version of this paper presented at the 2006 Theory Construction and Research Methodology Workshop of the National Council on Family Relations.

References

Abbey, E. (2002). Ventriloquism: The central role of an immigrant's own group members in negotiating ambiguity in identity. *Culture & Psychology*, *8*(4), 409–415.

ACCESS (2006). Arab Community Center for Economic and Social Services, 2651 Saulino Ct., Dearborn, MI 48120. Retrieved November 14, 2006, from www.accesscommunity.org/.

Achar-Naccache, T. (2006). *A Lebanese-Arab perspective on Middle Eastern studies.* Retrieved February 2, 2006, from womencrossing.org/naccache.html.

Alexander, B. K. (2004). Black skin/white masks: The performative sustainability of whiteness (with apologies to Frantz Fanon). *Qualitative Inquiry*, *10*(5), 647–672.

Allen, J., & Hermann-Wilmarth, J. (2004). Cultural construction zones. *Journal of Teacher Education*, *55*(3), 214–226.

Allen, K. A. (2000). A conscious and inclusive family studies. *Journal of Marriage & the Family*, *62*, 4–17.

Allen, K. A., & Piercy, F. (2005). Feminist autoethnography. In D. Sprenkle & F. P. Piercy (Eds.), *Research methods in family therapy* (3rd ed.). New York: Guilford Press.

Allen, K. R., & Farnsworth, E. B. (1993). Reflexivity in teaching about families. *Family Relations*, *42*(3), 351–356.

Anthias, F. (2002). Where do I belong? Narrative collective identity and translocational positionality. *Ethnicities*, *2*(4), 491–514.

Basch, L., Schiller, N. G., & Blanc, C. S. (1994). *Nations unbound: Transnational projects, postcolonial predicaments, and deterritorialized nation-states.* Langhorne, PA: Gordon and Breach.

Bellafante, G. (2004, December 13). An immigrant group in a rush to marry young. *New York Times*, A1, A26.

Bell-Scott, P. (Ed.) (1994). *Life notes: Personal writings by contemporary black women.* New York: Norton.

Bhatia, S., & Ram, A. (2001). Locating the dialogical self in the age of transnational migrations, border crossings, and diasporas. *Culture & Psychology*, 7(3), 297–309.

Brodkin, K. (1999). *How Jews became white folks and what that says about race in America.* New Brunswick, NJ: Rutgers University Press.

Brubaker, R. (2001). Symposium on ethnicity: Cognitive perspectives. *Ethnicities*, 1, 15–17.

Bryceson, D., & Vuorela, U. (2002). *The transnational family: New European frontiers and global networks.* New York: Oxford University Press.

Butler, J. (1990). *Gender trouble: Feminism and the subversion of identity.* New York: Routledge.

Calhoun, C. (2001). Symposium on ethnicity: Tradition, but not mere inheritance. *Ethnicities*, 1, 9–10.

Cooper, C. R. (1999). Multiple selves, multiple worlds: Cultural perspectives on individuality and connectedness in adolescent development. In A. S. Masten (Ed.), *Cultural processes in child development* (pp. 25–57). Mahwah, NJ: Erlbaum.

Cooper, C. R., Jackson, J. F., Azmitia, M., & Lopez, E. M. (1998). Multiple selves, multiple worlds: Three useful strategies for research with ethnic minority youth on identity, relationships, and opportunity structures. In V. C. McLoyd & L. Steinberg (Eds.), *Studying minority adolescents: Conceptual, methodological, and theoretical issues* (pp. 111–125). Mahwah, NJ: Erlbaum.

Daly, K. (2007). *Qualitative methods for family studies and human development.* Thousand Oaks, CA: Sage.

Delgado, R., & Stefancic, J. (1997). *Critical white studies: Looking into the mirror.* Philadelphia: Temple University Press.

Delgado, R., & Stefancic, J. (2001). *Critical race theory: An introduction.* New York: New York University Press.

De Reus, L. A., Few, A. L., & Blume, L. B. (2005). Multicultural and critical race feminisms: Theorizing families in the third wave. In V. Bengtson, A. Acock, K. Allen, P. Dilworth-Anderson & D. Klein (Eds.), *Sourcebook of family theory and research* (pp. 447–468). Thousand Oaks, CA: Sage.

Dilworth-Anderson, P., Burton, L. M., & Klein, D. M. (2005). Contemporary and emerging theories in studying families. In V. Bengtson, A. Acock, K. Allen, P. Dilworth-Anderson & D. Klein (Eds.), *Sourcebook of family theory and research* (pp. 35–58). Thousand Oaks, CA: Sage.

Dion, K. K., & Dion, K. L. (2004). Gender, immigrant generation, and ethnocultural identity. *Sex Roles*, 50(5/6), 347–355.

Du Bois, W. E. B. (1935). *Black reconstruction in America.* New York: Russell & Russell.

Eriksen, T. H. (2001). Symposium on ethnicity: Some current priorities for ethnicity studies. *Ethnicities*, *1*, 17–19.

Falicov, C. J. (1998). *Latino families in therapy: A guide to multicultural practice*. New York: Guilford Press.

Falicov, C. J. (2005). Emotional transnationalism and family identities. *Family Process*, *44*(4), 399–406.

Feagin, J. (2000). *Racist America: Roots, current realities, and future reparations*. New York: Routledge.

Fine, M. (1994). Working the hyphens: Reinventing self and other in qualitative research. In D. K. Denzin & Y. S. Lincoln (Eds.), *Handbook of qualitative research* (pp. 70–82). Thousand Oaks, CA: Sage.

Frankenberg, R. (1993). *White women, race matters: The social construction of whiteness*. Minneapolis: University of Minnesota Press.

García Coll, C., Szalacha, L. A., & Palacios, N. (2005). Children of Dominican, Portuguese, and Cambodian immigrant families: Academic attitudes and pathways during middle childhood. In C. R. Cooper, C. T. García Coll, W. T. Bartko, H. Davis & C. Chatman (Eds.), *Developmental pathways through middle childhood: Rethinking context and diversity as resources* (pp. 207–234). Mahwah, NJ: Erlbaum.

Giordano, J., & McGoldrick, M. (2005). Families of European origin: An overview. In M. McGoldrick, J. Giordano & N. Garcia-Preto (Eds.), *Ethnicity and family therapy* (3rd ed.). New York: Guilford Press.

Goldstein, E. H. (2006). *The price of whiteness: Jews, race, and American history*. Princeton, NJ: Princeton University Press.

Goodman, A. H. (1998). The race pit. *Anthropology Newsletter*. Retrieved February 28, 2006, from www.pbs.org/race/000_About/002_04-background-01-10.htm.

Grewal, I., & Kaplan, C. (2000). Postcolonial studies and transnational feminist practices. *Jouvert: A Journal of Postcolonial Studies*. Retrieved February 28, 2006, from social.chass.ncsu.edu/jouvert/v5i1/grewal.htm.

Hartman, A. (2004). The rise and fall of whiteness studies. *Race and Class*, *46*(2), 22–38.

Haskins, R., Greenberg, M., & Fremstad, S. (2004). Federal policy for immigrant children: Room for common ground? *The Future of Children*, *14*, 1–5.

Hermans, H. J. M. (2001). The dialogical self: Toward a theory of personal and cultural positioning. *Culture & Psychology*, *7*(3), 243–281.

Hill, M. R., & Thomas, V. (2000). Strategies for racial identity development: Narratives of black and white women in interracial partner relationships. *Family Relations*, *49*, 193–200.

hooks, b. (1997). *Wounds of passion: A writing life*. New York: Holt.

Ifekwunigwe, J. O. (1998). Borderland feminisms: Toward the transgression of unitary transnational feminisms. *Gender & History*, *10*(3), 553–557.

Ignatiev, N. (1995). *How the Irish became white*. New York: Routledge.

Kim, C. J. (2004). Unyielding positions: A critique of the "race" debate. *Ethnicities*, *4*(3), 337–355.

Lewontin, R. C. (1982). *Human diversity*. New York: W. H. Freeman.

Lynch, M. (2000). Against reflexivity as an academic source of privileged knowledge. *Theory, Culture & Society*, *17*, 26–54.

Magnet, S. (2006). Protesting privilege: An autoethnographic look at whiteness. *Qualitative Inquiry*, *12*(4), 736–749.

Marger, M. N. (2006). *Race and ethnic relations: American and global perspectives*. Belmont, CA: Thomson.

Marks, J. (2003). *Scientific and folk ideas about heredity*. Retrieved February 28, 2006, from www.pbs.org/race/000_About/002_04-background-01.htm.

Marvasti, A., & McKinney, K. (2004). *Middle Eastern lives in America*. Lanham, MD: Rowman & Littlefield.

Mazzei, L. A. (2003). Inhabited silences: In pursuit of a muffled subtext. *Qualitative Inquiry*, *9*(3), 355–368.

McConatha, J. T., Stoller, P., & Oboudiat, F. (2001). Reflections of older Iranian women adapting to life in the United States. *Journal of Aging Studies*, *16*, 369–381.

McIntosh, P. (1990). White privilege: Unpacking the invisible knapsack. *Independent School*, *49*, 31–36.

McKinney, K. (2005). *Being white: Stories of race and racism*. New York: Routledge.

Migration Information Source. (2007). Migration Policy Institute, Washington, DC. Retrieved April 30, 2007, from www.migrationinformation.org/datahub/countrydata/data.cfm.

Mohanty, C. T. (2003). *Feminism without borders: Decolonizing theory, practicing solidarity*. Durham, NC: Duke University Press.

Montgomery, B. M., & Baxter, L. A. (1998). *Dialectical approaches to studying personal relationships*. Mahwah, NJ: Erlbaum.

Murthy, H. D. (2003). The acculturation experiences of recognizable and nonrecognizable ethnic minorities. *Dissertation Abstracts International: Section B: The Sciences & Engineering*, *63*(11-B), 5530.

Oommen, T. K. (2001). Symposium on ethnicity: Situating ethnicity conceptually. *Ethnicities*, *1*, 13–15.

Ossorio, P. (2003). *Race: The power of an illusion*. Retrieved February 28, 2006, from discuss.washingtonpost.com/zforum/03/sp_tv_race050103.htm.

Parker, L., & Lynn, M. (2002). What's race got to do with it? Critical race theory's conflict with and connections to qualitative research methodology and epistemology. *Qualitative Inquiry*, *8*(1), 7–22.

Pearson Education (2006). *Minorities and Women in the 109th Congress*. Retrieved November 14, 2006, from www.infoplease.com/ipa/A0878575.html.

Perry, P. (2001). White means never having to say you're ethnic: White youth and the construction of "cultureless" identities. *Journal of Contemporary Ethnography*, *30*, 56–91.

Phinney, J. S. (2003). Ethnic identity and acculturation. In K. M. Chun, P. Balls Organista & G. Marin (Eds.), *Acculturation: Advances in theory, measurement, and applied research* (pp. 63–81). Washington, DC: American Psychological Association.

Roberts, S. (2004). *Who are we now: The changing face of America in the 21st century.* New York: Times Books.

Roediger, D. R. (1991). *Wages of whiteness: Race and the making of the American working class.* London: Verso.

Roediger, D. R. (2003). *Colored white: Transcending the racial past.* Berkeley: University of California Press.

Rose, S., & Rose, H. (2005). Why we should give up on race. *The Guardian,* April 9. Retrieved November 12, 2006, from www.guardian.co.uk/life/science/story/0,12996,1455716,00.html.

Rosenthal, D., & Hrynevich, C. (1985). Ethnicity and ethnic identity: A comparative study of Greek-, Italian-, and Anglo-Australian adolescents. *International Journal of Psychology, 20,* 723–724.

Shryock, A., & Abraham, N. (2000). On margins and mainstreams. In N. Abraham & A. Shryock (Eds.), *Arab Detroit: From margin to mainstream.* Detroit, MI: Wayne State University Press.

Spry, T. (2001). Performing autoethnography: An embodied methodological praxis. *Qualitative Inquiry, 7,* 706–732.

Stone, E., Gomez, E., Hotzoglou, D., & Lipnitsky, J. Y. (2005). Transnationalism as a motif in family stories. *Family Process, 44*(4), 381–398.

Thandeka (2006). The cost of whiteness. In K. E. Rosenblum & T. C. Travis (Eds.), *The meaning of difference: American constructions of race, sex, and gender, social class, and sexual orientation* (pp. 207–213). New York: McGraw-Hill.

U.S. Census Bureau. (2001). *The White population: 2000.* Retrieved February 25, 2006, from www.census.gov/prod/2001pubs/c2kbr01-4.pdf.

Vavrus, M. (2002). *Transforming the multicultural education of teachers: Theory, research, and practice.* New York: Teachers College Press.

Verkuyten, M., & de Wolf, A. (2002). Being, feeling, and doing: Discourses and ethnic self-definitions among minority group members. *Culture & Psychology, 8*(4), 371–399.

Waldinger, R. D., & Fitzgerald, D. (2003). Immigrant "transnationalism" reconsidered. Los Angeles: University of California Los Angeles eScholarship Repository. Retrieved December 10, 2005, from repositories.cdlib.org/cgi/viewcontent.cgi?article=1006&context=uclasoc.

Warren, J. T., & Fassett, D. L. (2002). (Re)constituting ethnographic identities. *Qualitative Inquiry, 8,* 575–590.

West, C., & Zimmerman, D. (1987). Doing gender. *Gender and Society, 1,* 125–151.

Wing, A. K. (Ed.). (1997). *Critical race feminism: A reader.* New York: New York University Press.

Wing, A. K. (2005, April). *Critical race feminism: Race, gender and the law.* Keynote address at the White Privilege Conference, April 27–30, Pella, IA.

Yuval-Davis, N. (2001). Symposium on ethnicity: Contemporary agenda for the study of ethnicity. *Ethnicities, 1,* 11–13.

Zhou, M. (2004). Are Asian Americans becoming "white"? *Contexts, 3*(1), 29–37.

About the Authors

Libby Balter Blume, Ph.D., CFLE, is a professor in the Department of Psychology and Women's Studies at University of Detroit Mercy, 4001 W. McNichols, Detroit, MI 48221-3038. Phone: 313-578-0446. E-mail: blumelb@udmercy.edu.

Lee Ann De Reus, Ph.D., is an associate professor in the Department of Human Development and Family Studies and Women's Studies at Pennsylvania State University, Altoona, 3000 Ivyside Park, Altoona, PA 16601. Phone: 814-949-5751. E-mail: lad12@psu.edu.

MARRIAGES AND FAMILIES II

Influence of American Culture on East Indian Immigrants' Perceptions of Marriage and Family Life

5

DOUGLAS A. ABBOTT AND PALLABI MOULIK GUPTA

Abstract

The purpose of this research was to identify how the marriages and family life of recent Indian immigrants had changed since coming to America. Personal interviews were conducted with nine Hindu couples who were married in India but had lived in the United States for at least two years. Changes were found in several aspects of marital interaction, in some parenting behaviors, and in the personal identity of husbands and wives. Greater egalitarianism in marriage and more personal parent-child interaction were seen as beneficial changes. It appears that American culture has a powerful influence on changing traditional values and behaviors for some new immigrants from India.

Keywords: East Indian, Egalitarianism, Marriage, Family Life, Assimilation

AMERICAN CULTURE CAN HAVE a powerful effect upon the marriage and family life of new immigrants (Kalita, 2003; Trask & Hamon, 2007). The U.S. media (TV, movies, music), the secular social norms (e.g., egalitarianism, individualism, humanism), and American political values (democracy, freedom of speech, and multiculturalism) may influence various aspects of marital interaction (e.g., increasing sexual interaction), parenting behaviors (challenges to authoritarian discipline), and family interaction (less family time and different leisure time activities) (Ingoldsby & Smith, 2005). Thus, new immigrants face a challenge when they are saturated by American culture: how much assimilation will they embrace or permit and how much will they retain the values and behaviors of their homeland culture (Min, 2005; Parrillo, 2005; Petievich, 1999).

East Indians are an important ethnic group in America for several reasons. The numbers of East Indians emigrating to the United States has increased substantially during the last half century from less than 10,000 in 1947 to 1.7 million in 2002, representing 0.6 percent of the total American population (Passage from India, 2002; Mogelonsky, 1995). East Indians are the third largest Asian American community after Chinese Americans and Filipino Americans. The overall growth rate for East Indian Americans from 1990 to 2000 was almost 106 percent, the largest in the Asian American community (Passage from India, 2002; Sharma, 1995).

Due to their emphasis on education, East Indians are overrepresented in professional fields such as engineering, medicine, and small businesses such as hotel management and start up high technology companies (Iwata, 2006). They have the highest median income (nearly $71,000) of any immigrant group and far above the national average of approximately $46,000 (Kanjilal, 1996; Singh & Koposowa, 1996; Wadha, 2006). East Indians have been widely recognized as one of the most successful immigrant groups in the United States (Clark, 2003; Kanjilal, 1996). In spite of a number of sociocultural and religious differences between East Indians and Euro-Americans these immigrants tend to assimilate well into mainstream society (Khandelwal, 2002; Ramisetty-Mikler, 1993).

East Indian immigration continues yet there is little research on this ethnic group, and few studies have focused on how acculturation issues have influenced marriage, parenting, and family life (Berger, 2004; Helweg, 1987; Pettys & Balgopal, 1998; Sharma, 1995). The purpose of this study is to investigate the impact of American culture on recent East Indian immigrants' marriage, parenting, and personal development (Patel, 2005). The specific issues studied included couples' attitudes toward martial interaction, women's work issues, and changes in child rearing (Rudrappa, 2004; Mogelonsky, 1995).

Review of Literature

There is little extant research on the impact of U.S. culture on marriage and family life of East Indian immigrants. There are a few researchers that have reported on the experience of first generation immigrant couples, and a few studies on changes reported by East Indian adolescents or young adults on issues related to dating, premarital sex, and marriage (Alba & Golden, 1986; Balagopal, 1999; R. Berger, 2004; Davis & Singh, 1989). This review focuses only on studies that assess how new Indian immigrants' marriage, parenting, and family life have changed since coming to the United States.

One conclusion can be drawn from the existing research: immigrants' values, social roles, and lifestyle choices (related to marriage and family life) are affected by the political, economic, and social forces of Western culture, and especially by American media, including TV, music, videos, and magazines (Castro, 2003; Christensen, 1989). For example, thirty years ago, Kornacker (1971) studied the impact of American culture on Indian immigrants' marriage and found that each spouse's marital roles became more flexible and egalitarian when exposed to American culture.

Mangalam (1985) studied post-immigration adjustment of Indian immigrants in Canada. He found the husband's expectations of a patriarchal, patrilineal, extended family and the wife's demands for a more democratic and bilineal family structure led to marital conflict.

Suppal, Roopnarine, Buesig, and Bennett (1996) studied the beliefs of Indian couples about the division of household chores, financial responsibilities, childcare, and filial obligations. They found a residual conservative outlook by East Indian couples regarding the value of arranged marriage, a preference for a patriarchal family structure, and a wife's traditional role as mother and homemaker (also see Niraula & Morgan, 1995; and Srinivasan, 2001). On the other hand, Gupta (1999) studied the struggle of some East Indian American women to conform to traditional Indian gender roles. Some of the women actively rejected traditional patriarchal gender roles and even opted for divorce, which is a serious taboo in Indian culture. Balagopal (1999) observed Indian American women who were attempting to maintain traditional roles at home yet were opting for work outside the home (see also Sinha & Mukherjee, 2001). Balagopal found that many couples in his sample reported more equitable distribution of household chores and childcare after immigrating to America.

Another way to examine changes in family life is to assess the second generation, the children of the immigrants. For example, Davis and Singh (1989) queried Indian students at the University of Texas. The students adopted more permissive attitudes toward premarital sex, cohabitation, women's roles, and divorce than their parents. Interestingly however, they doubted their ability to imitate their parents' skills at making long-term successful marriages. Talbaani and Hasnaali (2000) found that the second-generation

East Indian adolescents in Canada experienced huge acculturation stress. They found traditional gender roles were maintained by their parents in the homes through sex-segregated social activities, dress restrictions, and pressure for arranged marriages. Yet, the adolescent girls believed prevalent conditions on dating, mixed-sex social engagements, and marriage expectations would gradually change (see also Wadhwani, 2000).

In addition to changes in marriage, a few researchers examined changes in parenting of first generation East Indian American immigrants. For example, Jambunathan and Counselman (2002) showed that the Indian immigrant mothers tended to reject corporal punishment and harsh disciplines (common in India), and utilized a more authoritative parenting style than the authoritarian style common in India. Mohammed (1997) described how a small sample of East Indian immigrants favored a blending of both Western and Eastern dating and marriage values and practices and were more flexible in negotiating differences in these areas with their children. Other studies have shown there is conflict between the Indian parents and their teens or young adult children on a variety of issues related to dating and marriage (Dugger, 1998; Jain, 2000; Segal, 1991). For example, Srinivasan (2001) showed that even after living in the United States for ten years East Indian parents reported conservative attitudes toward their children's dating and mate selection.

In summary, these few studies indicate that American culture has a profound impact on many Indian immigrants' marriages, parenting, and family life. The majority of families adopt American values of equality, openness, individuality, and freedom of choice (Singh, Nath & Nichols, 2005). This value shift changes interaction between husband and wife and between parents and children (Myers, Madathil & Tingle, 2005). Thus, the authors of this paper expect couples to report a variety of changes in their marriages, parenting behaviors, and individual life course options.

Theoretical Background

An acculturation framework was used as a background to investigate whether immigration to the United States changes perspectives of East Indian spouses toward marriage, parenting, and family life. The term acculturation was introduced by anthropologists to refer to cultural changes that emerged from intercultural contact. Redfield, Linton, and Herskovits in 1936 defined acculturation as those phenomena that result when groups of individuals having different cultures come into continuous first hand contact that produces subsequent changes in the culture patterns of either or both groups (in Castro, 2003). Acculturation can be viewed as the selective adaptation to the value system of the host culture. Individuals may try to inculcate the values and beliefs of the host culture and at the same time may try to maintain some of their own values and beliefs. Psychological acculturation refers to the changes in individuals' behaviors, attitudes, identities, and values resulting from intercultural encounters at the individual level (Castro, 2003).

Much of the research on acculturation has been guided by two distinct models: linear bipolar models and two dimensional or multicultural models. Linear models assume that acculturation is a process of absorption into the dominant culture. It implies eventual loss of identification with the culture of origin. By contrast, the basic premise of multicultural models is that individuals can maintain positive ties with the original culture and take in selected aspects of the new or mainstream culture.

Two important multicultural models are (1) acculturation-biculturalism model and (2) quadri-modal acculturation model. The proponents of the acculturation-biculturalism model argue that when immigrants interact with other cultural communities (e.g., host society) they need to develop skills that are necessary to participate in both the host and their original culture. This results in two distinct processes: adaptation to the host culture and retention of original cultural characteristics. The major contribution of this model is that it implies that adaptation to a new cultural context does not necessarily result in loss of ties with the original cultural community.

Berry (1980) developed the quadric-modal acculturation model. He argued that during the process of acculturation, individuals and groups are confronted with two basic issues: (a) cultural maintenance with the old culture and (b) contact and participation in the new culture. The former involves a decision to maintain one's cultural identity and patterns and the latter to engage in positive group contact. His model proposes four outcomes of adaptation: *integration, assimilation, separation,* and *marginalization.* Integration refers to maintaining positive relations with the larger society and simultaneously maintaining one's own ethnic identity and traditions. Assimilation occurs when individuals do not wish to maintain their original cultural identity; fully change their values, attitudes, and behaviors; and completely identify with the larger society. Separation results when individuals have a strong identification with their native culture and attempt to minimize contact with the host culture. Marginalization occurs when individuals lose cultural and psychological contact with both their own ethnic group and the larger society. These outcomes indicate the extent to which the immigrants are acculturated in the host culture.

For East Indian immigrants the most likely outcome is *integration*. They may retain many of their Indian cultural values and traditions, yet contact with American society may induce changes in certain aspects of marriage, parenting, and personal development. Thus, the Quadric-model provides an appropriate theoretical framework for the current research. When Indian couples emigrate to the United States, it is likely that they undergo integration because of the continuous exposure to the U.S. society, their participation in high status occupations, and their native fluency with the English language. The integration process may induce changes in many aspects of the marriage including sharing of power, attitudes toward women's employment, and division of household labor.

Because of a large number of immigrants from India, Indian couples also have the opportunity to come in contact with other Indians while living in the United States. Multicultural models suggest that the degree to which couples adopt American marital values and beliefs may be affected by how embedded the couple is with Indian culture in the United States. The more the couple is involved with Indian friends, religious and cultural activities, the less impact U.S. culture may have on their family life (Chekki, 1988).

Methods

Design
This was a qualitative study. "Qualitative research is an umbrella concept covering several forms of inquiry that helps us understand and explain the meaning of social phenomenon with as little disruption of the natural setting as possible" (Merriam, 2001, p. 5). A phenomenological approach was used which attempts to understand the participants' first-hand experience and the meaning they give to the phenomenon under study. Creswell notes (2007) "a phenomenological study describes the meaning for several individuals of their lived experiences of a [specific] phenomenon [e.g., marital changes due to immigration]" (p. 57). The goal of this type of inquiry is to describe what a small group of participants have in common as they experience the same phenomena (Creswell, p. 58). Because little is known about immigration's effects on marriage and family life, and few conceptual constructs or theories has been developed on this issue, the authors chose a flexible, personal interview by a member of the same ethnic group.

Participants and Procedures

PARTICIPANTS. A convenience sample of nine Hindu Indian couples was recruited from two large midwestern cities. The second author knew two couples and found the others by referral. In the first city, six couples were contacted by phone and received an explanation of the study. Three of the couples agreed to participate. Two other couples declined because of unwillingness to share personal information. The sixth couple indicated that their work schedule did not permit time for an interview. In the second city, ten couples were contacted by phone, some of whom were known to the second author. Six couples agreed to participate. The remaining four couples were unwilling to participate because of lack of time or other personal reasons.

Informed consent letters explaining the study were sent to the nine volunteer couples. The participants returned the forms by mail and were then contacted by phone to set up interview times. To be eligible to participate, couples had to be twenty years or older, married for more than three years, married while in India, and lived there for at least one year before coming to the United States. Couples also had to be currently living in the United States for more than two years.

Among the nine couples interviewed, six couples were married for five years, one couple was married for four years and two couples were married for three and a half years. The women's age range was twenty-five to thirty-two ($M = 28.5$) and men's age range was twenty-eight to thirty-eight ($M = 33$). Six out of nine couples had children, aged between two and five years. All the children were born in the United States. Four men and two women were working on graduate degrees. Four men and three women were employed full-time in large corporations. Four women were homemakers and one man was unemployed. Five couples had been living in the United States for six years, three couples for four years, and one couple for three and a half years.

PROCEDURES. The second author (a married Indian immigrant herself) conducted all interviews. She tried to avoid bias by maintaining optimal objectivity in data collection and analysis. During the interviews, she did not interfere or comment on respondent's responses. She did not lead or encourage respondents to give any specific answers. She avoided being involved in any conversation with respondents wherein she would share her opinions or personal experiences about her marriage in America.

Interviews were conducted with individual spouses in participant's homes or in a university campus building. Spouses were interviewed separately so that each individual could freely discuss his or her perceptions of marriage and family life. When both spouses were home, the respondent was alone in one room with the interviewer and the spouse was in another part of the house far enough away so he or she was unable to hear the conversation. Each interview lasted about one hour and was audiotaped.

Instruments

INTERVIEW GUIDE. The interview guide consisted of eight items. Questions aimed at understanding the impact of American culture on married couples' perspectives about marriage, parenting, and personal growth. Several items asked whether couples had faced any marital problems after coming to the United States and whether they attributed these problems to the influence of American culture. Examples of questions included: "Has your relationship with your spouse changed since immigrating to America?" "How do you communicate and discipline your children, and is this different than it would have been if you stayed in India?" and "What values and behaviors regarding family life have you retained from your Indian heritage, and which ones have changed since coming to the United States?"

INTERNAL VALIDITY AND RELIABILITY. Internal validity is concerned with whether findings are congruent with what really happened (Merriam, 2001). Several strategies were used to enhance internal validity: triangulation, member checks, and peer examination of findings. Member checking was conducted by randomly selecting six couples and asking them to discuss our findings. Four agreed to participate. All four couples generally agreed with our interpretations. For peer examination, the authors had a graduate student in family science read the uncoded interview transcripts, and then examine the codes and themes that were created by the authors. The reviewer had few comments and agreed with the majority of the coding themes.

Reliability, in qualitative research, generally refers to the author's ability to faithfully record the points of view of the participants in a natural setting (Creswell, 2003; Merriam, 2001). One method of doing this is to tape-record the interviews, thus the exact words, phrases, and sentences can be analyzed (Newman, 2004). This was done by a similar-aged Indian immigrant, mostly in the homes of the participants.

Qualitative Data Analysis

The audiotapes were transcribed. Names of the respondents were changed to maintain confidentiality. Pseudonyms were given for each spouse. After reading the transcripts several times both authors independently coded answers related to each interview question into initial categories. These categories were discussed until common ground was reached on the majority of categories. The names of the categories resembled, as closely as possible, terms used by participants. Next the authors identified verbatim quotations to support each category. For example, under the category "Marital Changes" (based upon the interview question: "Has your marriage changed in any way since coming to America?") five subcategories immerged: (1) openness in communication, (2) respect of spouse's space, (3) power and control, (4) the meaning of marriage, and (5) marriage as sharing. Direct quotations for each subcategory were then inserted. For each interview question, several categories and subcategories were created.

Results

This study explored the impact of American culture on East Indian couples' marriage, parenting, and personal growth.

Marital Changes

OPENNESS IN COMMUNICATION. One of the important changes noted by men was increased openness in communication with their wives. Many of them said they felt freer to communicate with their spouses especially about things they did not like. Sanjay (male) cites a very trivial matter but it indicates how he is more forthcoming in his communication with his wife after coming to the United States.

> I simply did not like drinking tea in the morning, but my wife would insist that I had tea. I never told her while in India and kept drinking tea (even if I did not like it) because not doing so would be a big thing you know. She might get offended, it may cause a fight. I do not do that here. I mean it is so silly. Why should I? I just told her that I do not want it [to drink tea].

Ed (male) explained that in India his wife would always overrule him in front of their children, and he never liked it. In India, whenever such instances would occur, he would just go into his shell and stop communicating with his wife. He did not do that here. He stated:

> I just tell her what I do not like, especially our interaction in front of our son. I just do not like how she just disregards what I say. I just tell her straight how I feel. I think it is much better calling spade a spade rather than keeping mum, sulking and not communicating.

RESPECT FOR OTHER'S SPACE. Respondents also indicated they had started respecting each other's psychological and physical space (Sinha & Mukherjee, 2001). For instance Ravi (male) stated he valued time for himself and his wife:

> I like being with myself, so Saturday mornings are reserved for myself, that's pretty sacred. I mean I do not let anything else come in my way. I do my reading. I think about myself and my career. I work on my car. I do not really like to be disturbed Saturday morning, not even by my wife. My wife initially felt pretty strange about it, but I think she appreciates it these days. And I make it a point that she gets time for herself too so I do the cooking and household chores Sunday morning and let her take time off for herself.

POWER AND CONTROL IN MARRIAGE. The wives in general reported they felt more power and control in marriage than they had in India. Sita (female) replied:

> Over here it is only I and him. Who else do we have? I can play a greater role in our lives here. We do not have to visit (relatives) every week. I never liked visiting (my in-laws) but that was what we did. Here I don't have to do that. I can decide how we spend time.

Anu (female) commented: "Here all he has is me, so most of his interaction is with me, and that makes a huge difference. We make a lot of decisions together; we do what we want."

One of the major reasons for this perceived control was the absence of in-laws and other family members. Distance from extended family members made a lot of difference to these women. They noted their husbands were more open to listening to them and were more open to implementing their suggestions. This gave them a feeling they were more in control. Wive's jobs also seemed to enhance their perceived power in the marriage. Some wives felt more confident about handling marital problems because of job success and satisfaction. Seema (female) commented:

I just feel very confident these days. I deal with so many issues and crises at my job, that handling day-to-day household frictions does not overwhelm me. I am better able to handle it. I would be very anxious about such things earlier, but not now.

MEANING OF MARRIAGE. When asked about the meaning of marriage, two themes emerged: Marriage as a friendship and marriage as a mutual support system. These notions of marriage were different than they had been in India. For example, Rajan (male) has been living here for four years and has many American friends. As he says, observing his friends' interactions with their spouses changed his thinking and his behavior too.

> I have a ton of friends here, and we interact pretty frequently. I observe how friendly they are with one another [as spouses]. I mean they are friends first and then a couple, and that makes a lot of difference. I think it brings in a different perspective, and that makes a lot of sense to me.

Rajan's wife Radhika had a similar opinion.

> Our parents got married and then they were together for forty-five years. They were pretty close, but I don't think they ever tried to develop friendship. I may be wrong; they were companions but were they friends? I do not know. Well, we try to inculcate this sense of friendship between us. We try to be buddies.

Seema (female) reflected the same opinion.

> If you think of your husband as a friend, it makes such a huge difference. I don't know what changes, but you know my whole perspective has changed. I feel more open and I communicate much better with him.

Sandeep (male) explained how they had evolved as friends:

> Of course there is a huge change in marriage. I think we have evolved as friends, partners, as individuals. We share everything. If I have something, my partner has to have it. If I am having a good time, so should she.

A second important theme that emerged from both men's and women's responses was that they also looked at marriage as a mutual support system. Sita's (female) response was:

> There are no people [relatives] here, so I have to keep talking to him. Back home you have your parents, siblings, and neighbors. But you can't make an international call to talk all those silly things with your relatives. So I

would tell him all sorts of things. So that way you can say our interaction has increased a lot.

Reema (female) mentioned:

Marriage in India is a feeling of security. You have a man who would take care of you for the rest of your life. But after I came here, I have a different view about marriage. Marriage is not only dependency, it's mutual.

Raj (male) stated:

My wife is much more a source of support here than she would have been in India. [Because we are] away from the rest of the family each of us is probably the only support the other has. So marriage is much different here.

Anu (female) also commented that being geographically distant from other family members increased dependence of spouses on one another.

The biggest reason for us evolving in marriage here is we are away from the rest of the family. Back there whatever you do there is always "what will the family members think?" But here it is only I and him; it is so very different.

MARRIAGE AS SHARING. The majority of the husbands reported they looked at their marriage more as sharing of resources and responsibilities than in India where rigid sex roles are the norm. While in India, they would not share day-to-day household chores with their wives. However, many of them reported their views changed significantly over the last few years of living in America. They no longer assigned a specific job to one person, for instance, cooking became a joint responsibility and it no longer remained the wife's job. Ravi (male) commented:

We no longer believe that a particular work is mine or hers. Both of us have learned to do it. I think it makes sense, you never know when I will be swamped with work and then she just takes over and manages the entire thing.

Prashant's (male) comment also suggests more sharing: "For me, marriage is about sharing. You just cannot think of your own self. We share a lot of things together."

WORK AND RELATED ISSUES. Did the challenges faced at the workplace influence the couples' marital lives in the United States? Respondents felt that work had both positive and negative impacts on the marriage. Most of the respondents (who were employed) came to the United States for rewarding careers. The challenge of work and the overall job satisfaction appeared to have a positive influence on marriage. For example, Sandeep (male) said:

> I love my job. It's very challenging, but I love the challenge. It gives me a sense of achievement that kind of reinforces my own confidence and makes me feel positive about life. Yes, it does change married life. Imagine if I were struggling and then would come home and take out all the frustration on my wife and children.

Two other couples reported that job stress was causing trouble in their marriages. In both cases, the wife was employed full-time and the husbands were either taking care of the household or attending school. Husbands reported a sense of frustration owing to the lack of monetary power, and a feeling of inferiority. Prashant (male) commented:

> These days, many a time, we are just not talking. If we talk, many times, we end up just fighting. I sometimes wonder whether it was a wise decision to leave everything and come to the U.S. I hope I have a career soon and things change in the near future.

Rani, Prashant's wife, added:

> I think the biggest problem is that he does not have a job. So I am the breadwinner. I have no problem with that, but I think it hurts him. I mean his ego. He is really upset most of the times, and then we end up fighting and not talking.

SEXUAL INTERACTION. We wanted to explore how sexual activities had changed after coming to America. Respondents were not forthcoming discussing marital sex. Only four couples responded to this question. Two of the couples said that there was no change in marital sex after coming to the United States. Ed (male) said: "I don't think there is any change [in sexual interaction]. In India we talked sex and we did sex. We do the same here, so where is the change." Two of the couples stated that their sex life was worse. They attributed this to the workload, work-related anxieties, and increasing friction between spouses that was the result of coming to the United States.

DIVORCE. Couples were asked if they felt differently about divorce since coming to America. In India, even though the rate of couples divorcing is increasing, divorce is associated with severe social stigma. In many cases, people look down upon divorced couples as incompetent in handling interpersonal issues. Many couples continue to live together to avoid the social stigma of divorce. This sense of shame associated with divorce was not prevalent in this sample of immigrant couples. Radhika (female) commented:

> Divorce happens. I remember when my friend got divorced [in India]. She would face many curious and penetrating looks, and people would talk behind her back almost as if she was a failure. Immediately after her divorce she was so hesitant to interact; almost as if she had committed a crime. I do not know what I thought of that then, but now if I think it is so wrong [to think badly of a divorced person].

However, some participants retained a negative view of divorce after coming to America. Ed stated:

> If you can't get along, well, divorce is an option. But I have always thought of it that way. I don't think I have changed or have become more liberal after coming here. I think my views are just the same.

Sita (female) replied:

> I was never in favor of it [divorce]. Back home I didn't like the idea of divorce, and after coming here I confirmed my idea. Kids suffer a lot because of that [divorce]. If the relationship is not that sour, they should think about the kid. There are lots of ways you can handle a bad relationship, but whatever it is, my personal opinion is that adults can sacrifice for the sake of the little one.

Child Rearing Changes

We asked if their ideas or behaviors regarding raising children had changed since coming to America. Six of the nine couples had children. The children were ages two to five years old. All were born in the United States. These couples reported substantial changes in many aspects of parenting. Husbands were more concerned about child safety (from drugs and violence), and they were more focused on the overall *development* of their children, not just academic success as they would be in India. Wives, on the other hand, said that their communication with their children had become more open and more frequent. They also said that they treated children as more grown up, more so than they would have done in India. For example, Raj (male) explained:

I probably would not have thought of involving myself in my child's life as much here as I would if I were in India. In India the children would have their friends and relatives and everyone would watch over them. But over here it is only me and my wife, so the responsibility is much more.

Ravi (male) had a similar opinion:

I think they [children] need closer attention and deeper involvement. I would not have involved myself as much if I were back home. First, there would be my parents and her parents so he would have had many people looking after him. So yeah, there is a huge difference in how I will raise him [here in the United States].

Prashant (male) responded:

We are much more involved in his [the son's] life and in a variety of ways, much beyond whether he is hungry or not. I think we are pretty different as parents. We are more like his [the child's] friends. We ask him what he did in school, how was the day, has anybody said anything to hurt him. It's like total interaction. My parents never had this kind of conversation with me.

One of the reasons for parents' increased involvement in children's lives in America was parental concern about "outside temptations." In order to keep children from "falling into the wrong traps," they paid close attention to children's daily activities. Rajan's (male) opinion reflected this:

I feel it is necessary to give complete attention to their overall growth. Look at the temptations that exist outside. If you are not involved fully in their lives, then there is always a danger of kids slipping out of your hand. I am more involved here. You have to be that way to save your kid from the crime, drugs, sex.

Four respondents that were interviewed said that raising children in this country was a tough challenge. Both couples have been living here for four years. Because temptation for drugs, sex, and alcohol are so high, they thought that going back to India once the child grows older would be a better alternative. Ed (male) comments on this: "We don't want to stay here for a long [time] . . . We want to move back to India. . . . The way kids are raised here they don't learn the values as we learn [them] in India."

CONCERN BEYOND ACADEMICS. Husbands were interested in the development of their children beyond academics. Some insight into India may be helpful to understand this concern. First, most schools in India do not have extracurricular activities. Second, parents from all strata of Indian society place a high emphasis on the child's academic performance. As a result of this intense focus on grades, children are seldom encouraged to be involved in activities that might interfere with their studies. The situation in the United States is different, nonacademic activities were readily available. Sanjay (male) commented on his son's sports activities:

> I would like him to grow as a person and not only be involved in his studies. Studies are important and he should do well, but I think both of us emphasize that he develop an overall personality. I am a big supporter of his sports activity. I never had a basketball team or a football team in my school.

A similar point of view was expressed by Prashant (male): "We take special care that we are involved in his day-to-day happenings, what he does in school, and his sports team. We take a much greater interest in his [non-academic] activities."

INCREASED FREQUENCY OF COMMUNICATION. Parents felt the need for frequent communication with their children because children did not have an opportunity to talk with their cousins, grandparents, and neighbors. Anu (female) reflected on this:

> I think I am a completely different mom than what I would have been if I were in India. I see my sister and my brother's kids [in India], they are being raised with good values and everything, but I mean there is a huge difference [in communication]. I talk with my daughter so much about everything, her school, her friends, what she likes and dislikes, everything. We never seem to have enough time for our chatting. Back in India, I don't think I would have done that.

Parents said that in addition to the frequency of communication, the quality of their communication had also undergone a significant change. Parents said that they liked how American parents treated their kids with a sense of maturity and tried not to dismiss their opinions as childish. They contrasted this approach with the traditional Indian way of not taking children's opinions seriously. Rani (female) stated:

> After coming here, I saw people interacting with their kids [differently]. The way they were raising their kids just opened my eyes. You talk with

them [children] intellectually, you communicate with them and give their views due importance.

Personality and Sense of Self

We discovered that respondents felt their personalities had changed since immigrating, especially in areas of independence and autonomy. Both women and men reported they had a different perception of themselves after coming to the United States. Men noted they were more assertive whereas women felt they developed individuality and a personal sense of identity.

ASSERTING CHOICES. Raj (male) said this:

> We think differently here, and we talk pretty straight, no beating around the bush. Like I enjoy drinking beer every night. I have been drinking for years, but in India, my wife would not tell me directly [how she felt]. She would give me hints that she did not like it, but she never told me [to] my face. Not that she was afraid of me, but she just did not want to be very forthright. But here it is not the same. If she doesn't like it, she tells me [to] my face. That's pretty assertive.

This openness was observed in many other small day-to-day matters as well. Sandeep (male) explained: "I think we are pretty open about issues here. For example, if my wife wanted me to go for a workout with her, and I didn't want to go, I could say so."

IDENTITY DEVELOPMENT. The changed perception of self was reflected somewhat differently for women. Most of the women indicated they were forthright with their husbands and did not sacrifice their choices in favor of either husband or family. More importantly, they were able to develop an identity for themselves. They started insisting on their personal space and felt they needed to attend to their inner selves as much as they needed to attend to the duties of mother or wife. Priya's (female) comment was pertinent:

> I have started thinking of myself without any identity tags. I am someone's mother and someone's wife and daughter-in-law, but at the same time I am myself too. I have begun to realize that much more than what I would if I were not to come here. It's not self-centeredness, but I do think about what "I" really want to do, too. [For example] sometimes I cook what I really like and not always what my husband or my son like.

Discussion

The purpose of this research project was to examine changes in marriage, parenting, and personal growth of recent East Indian immigrants due to exposure to American culture. Results of this qualitative study indicated that interaction in U.S. society may engender several types of changes in the marriages and family life of some Indian immigrants. Old ways of thinking and behaving within marriage (i.e., that were learned in India) may be modified by the values and norms of American society. For example, couples saw their spouses as friends and companions, where in India the marital relationship is more formal and businesslike. The husbands' notion of "marriage as sharing" and the wives' notion of "marriage as a mutual support system" indicates further that for these couples marriage meant more than just an "auspicious" bond between two individuals.

Greater assertiveness in marriage and an increased sense of self for both spouses may reflect American values of individualism and autonomy (Ramisetty-Mikler, 1993). This is in contrast to the values of a collectivistic society like India, where marriage is seen as a personal sacrifice for spouse and children (Srinivasan, 2001). Couples indicated living in America and observing friends' families had changed their interaction with their spouses and children. There was greater openness in communication and greater respect for each other's physical and psychological space compared to what it may have been in India (Sinha & Mukherjee, 2001).

Absence of immediate and extended family members appeared to be associated with some marital changes. The absence of in-laws may bring spouses closer together. Couples could decide how to spend their free time and whom to spend it with. In India couples are expected to visit extended kin most of the time. Lack of kin also may foster greater engagement by parents in the lives of children. In India, child rearing is more of a shared responsibility. Children are looked after by their grandparents, aunts and uncles, and cousins. Children are rarely left unsupervised. In addition, schools in India are different than U.S. schools. Problems such as sex, violence, gangs, and drug use are not a major concern for most parents in India. But here in the United States, parents are worried about those things. Thus the couples reported being more involved in their children's lives because of lack of extended family and the numerous problems in schools.

Men in India generally do not assist their spouses with childcare (Rout et al., 1999). However, for this sample, child rearing was an important father responsibility. The data suggested that fathers had higher overall involvement in children's lives (beyond academics) than would be expected in India. The nature and frequency of parents' communication with children was also more than would be expected in India. Parents also said they treated their children as more mature and adult-like, whereas in India, children's opinions are considered to be childish and not taken seriously.

It was expected that exposure to American culture would have some effect on marital sex. But these immigrant couples were not comfortable discussing marital sex. This was not surprising since Indian society treats sex as a secret and shameful activity (Singh, 1999). Possibly, using anonymous surveys may have elicited more open and honest answers to any changes in sexual interaction that may have occurred since immigrating to America.

In many families in India, wives occupy a subordinate and subservient role and their status in their husband's family is marginal. In India, husbands' parents' opinions on matters such as children's schooling are given more significance than wives' opinions (Suppal et al., 1996). But for this sample of immigrants, exposure to American society has inculcated a sense of equality among the spouses. This egalitarianism was reflected in areas such as treating each other as friends, sharing household chores, respecting one another's space, and increased marital communication. None of the husbands indicated they insisted on a patriarchal model of family life. On the contrary, they were open to sharing responsibilities including housework and parenting. The wives reported a greater sense of self, and they also acted more assertively in marriage. Women in this sample also mentioned that job success made them feel in charge of their lives, more confident and powerful. This confidence and perception of power positively impacted their marriage and the way they were raising their children.

Limitations

Overall, the results of this preliminary qualitative study indicated changes in East Indian couples' marriages, parenting, and personal development due to immigration to America. The results are not meant to prove or test a theory but simply to identify concepts and theoretical propositions that could be tested in quantitative studies using larger, random samples of Indian immigrants. Thus, our conclusions are only tentative conjectures that may be informative for developing theory about how the assimilation and acculturation processes influence family life of recent immigrants.

A sample with different demographic factors may result in different influences of immigration on marriage and family life. Results may be mediated by many factors such as age of respondents, years spent in America, spouses' education level and occupational status, and contact with Indian culture in the United States (i.e., involvement with East Indian friends, practice of the Hindu religion, and contact with Indian relatives also living in America). Another explanation of our data could be that India has witnessed a substantial sociocultural change in the last ten to fifteen years, and many of the traditional concepts about marriage (such as patriarchal structure or women sacrificing for the sake of husband and children) are less prevalent in contemporary India. These changes may have facilitated the ease with which recent Indian immigrant couples assimilate into American culture and make changes in their marriage and parenting.

Implications for Professionals

Knowledge obtained from studies like this can help increase awareness about one of the most successful immigrant minorities in America. This research can help family counselors to understand the impact American culture can have on marriage and family life. Changes in marriage and parenting may be more or less accepted by Indian immigrant spouses. Thus, a well-informed counselor may help immigrant family members cope with acculturation effects on family processes. Paniagua (1996) provided specific therapeutic guidelines for dealing with Indian American families especially with issues such as open communication, rigid gender roles, and patriarchal power structure. Information about East Indian family acculturation may be useful to teachers and educators. East Indian American parents may have different opinions about American parenting styles and American school systems but feel under pressure to accept the changes since they live in this country. If educators are knowledgable about the differences in parenting styles and the worries these parents have they will be better able to serve Indian American children and families.

Conclusion

The East Indian population is increasing in America. In 1960, there were only 12,000 East Indians in the United States and now there are nearly 2 million (Bames & Bennette, 2002). Continued research with this minority population seems warranted because they are becoming a considerable force in America's economy, politics, and culture (Trask & Hamon, 2007). This research is unique for two reasons. First, few researchers have examined issues related to the impact of American culture on Indian marriages in recent Indian immigrants; and second, this study adds to the theoretical concepts that may help us understand how American culture influences the marriage and family life of recent immigrants.

References

Alba, R. D., & Golden, R. M. (1986). Patterns of ethnic marriage in the United States. *Social Forces, 65*(1), 202–224.

Balagopal, S. S. (1999). The case of the brown memsahib: Issues that confront South Asian wives and mothers. In S. R. Gupta (Ed.), *Emerging voices: South Asian American women redefine self, family, and community* (pp. 146–168). Walnut Creek, CA: AltaMira Press.

Barnes, J. S., & Bennette, C. E. (2002, February). *The Asian population: 2000.* Retrieved April 22, 2004, from www.census.gov/prod/2002pubs/c2kbr01-16.pdf.

Berger, R. (2004). *Immigrant women tell their stories.* Binghamton, NY: Haworth Press.

Berry, J. W. (1980). Acculturation as varieties of adaptation. In A. Padilla (Ed.), *Acculturation: Theory, models, and some new findings* (pp. 9–25). Boulder, CO: Westview Press.

Castro, V. S. (2003). *Acculturation and psychological adaptation.* Westport, CT: Greenwood.

Chekki, D. A. (1988). Family in India and North America. *Journal of Comparative Family Studies, 19*(2), 171–327.

Christensen, C. P. (1989). Cross-cultural awareness development: A conceptual model. *Counselor Education and Supervision, 28*, 270–289.

Clark, W. (2003). *Immigrants and the American dream: Remaking the middle class.* New York: Guilford Press.

Creswell, J. W. (2003). *Research design qualitative, quantitative, and mixed methods approaches.* Thousand Oaks, CA: Sage.

Creswell, J. W. (2007). *Qualitative inquiry and research design: Choosing among five approaches.* Thousand Oaks, CA: Sage.

Das, A. K., & Kemp, S. F. (1997). Between two worlds: Counseling south Asian Americans. *Journal of Multicultural Counseling & Development, 25*(1), 23–34.

Dasgupta, S. (1986). Asian Indian Community in the U.S.: A Case of Cultural Reaffirmation within an Ethnic Enclave. *International Sociological Association.*

Davis, V. T., & Singh, R. N. (1989). Attitudes of university students from India toward marriage and family life. *International Journal of Sociology of the Family, 19*(2), 43–57.

Dugger, C. W. (1998, July 20). In India, an arranged marriage of 2 worlds. *New York Times* (p. A1).

Gravetter, F. J., & Walnau, L. B. (Eds). (2000). *Statistics for the behavioral sciences* (5th ed.). Belmont, CA: Wadsworth / Thomson Learning.

Gupta, S. R. (1999). Walking on the edge: Indian-American women speak out on dating and marriage. In S. R. Gupta (Ed.), *Emerging voices: South Asian American women redefine self, family, and community* (pp. 120–145). Walnut Creek, CA: AltaMira Press.

Helweg, A. W. (1987). Why leave India for America? A case study approach to understanding migrant behavior. *International Migration, 25*(2), 165–178.

Ingoldsby, B., & Smith, S. (2005). *Families in global and multicultural perspective.* Thousand Oaks, CA: Sage.

Iwata, E. (2006, 6 June). Immigrants from India spread business success to homeland. *USA Today* (p. B3).

Jain, J. M. (2000). Co-existing in two cultures: Parental belief and children's activities in an Indian immigrant community (Doctoral dissertation, University of Illinois, 2000). *Dissertation Abstracts International, 60,* 12.

Jambunathan, S., & Counselman, K. P. (2002). Parenting attitudes of Asian Indian mothers living in the United States and in India. *Early Childhood Development and Care, 172,* 657–662.

Kalita, S. M. (2003). *Suburban sahibs: Three immigrant families and their passage from India to America.* Piscataway, NJ: Rutgers University Press.

Kanjilal, T. (1996). The Indian-Americans in the United States: Participation in the U.S. political process. *India Quarterly, 52*(4), 85–118.

Khandelwal, M. S. (2002). *Becoming American, being Indian: An immigrant community in New York City.* Ithaca, NY: Cornell University Press.

Kornacker, M. (1971). Cultural significance of intermarriage: A comparative approach. *International Journal of Sociology of the Family, 1,* 147–156.

Mangalam, J. J. (1985). Post-immigrant adjustment of India's immigrants in Canada: A case study. *Population Review, 29*(1/2), 95–112.

Merriam, S. B. (2001). *Qualitative research and case study applications in the education.* San Francisco: Jossey-Bass.

Minn, P. G. (2005). *Asian Americans: Contemporary trends and issues.* Thousand Oaks, CA: Sage.

Mogelonsky, M. (1995). Asian-Indian Americans. *American Demographics, 17*(8), 32–38.

Mohammed, P. (1997). The idea of childhood and age of sexual maturity among Indians in Trinidad: A sociohistorical scrutiny. In J. L. Roopnarine & J. Brown (Eds.), *Caribbean families: Diversity among ethnic groups* (pp. 115–146). Greenwich, CT: Ablex.

Myers, J., Madathil, J., & Tingle, L., (2005). Marriage satisfaction and wellness in India and the United States: A preliminary comparison of arranged marriages and marriages of choice. *Journal of Counseling & Development, 83,* 183–190.

Newman, W. L. (2004). *Basics of social research: Qualitative and quantitative approaches.* Boston: Pearson Education.

Niraula, B. B., & Morgan, S. P. (1995). Son and daughter preferences in Benighat: Implications for fertility transition. *Social Biology, 42*(3–4), 256–273.

Paniagua, F. A. (1996). Cross-cultural guidelines in family therapy practice. *The Family Journal: Counseling and Therapy for Couples and Families, 4*(2), 127–138.

Parrillo, V. N. (2005). *Diversity in America*. Thousand Oaks, CA: Sage.

Passage from India: A brief history if Indian immigration to the U.S. (2002). Washington, DC: The American Immigration Law Foundation Report.

Patel, T. (2005). *The family in India: Structure and practice*. Thousand Oaks, CA: Sage.

Petievich, C. (Ed.). (1999). *The expanding landscape: South Asians and the Diaspora*. New Delhi: Manohar Publishing.

Pettys, G. L., & Balgopal, P. R. (1998). Multigenerational conflicts and new immigrants: An Indo-American experience. *Families in Society, 79*(4), 410–423.

Ramisetty-Mikler, S. (1993). Asian Indian immigrants in America and sociocultural issues in counseling. *Journal of Multicultural Counseling & Development, 21*(1), 36–49.

Rout, U. R., Lewis, S., & Kagan, C. (1999). Work and family roles: Indian career women in India and the west. *Indian Journal of Gender Studies, 6*(1), 91–105.

Rudrappa, S. (2004). *Ethnic routes to becoming American: Indian immigrants and the cultures of citizenship*. Piscataway, NJ: Rutgers University Press.

Segal, A. U. (1991). Cultural variables in Asian-Indian families. *Families in Society, 72*(4), 233–241.

Sharma, P. (1995). Asian Indian attitudes toward seeking professional psychological help (Doctoral dissertation, University of Texas, Austin, 1995). *Dissertation Abstracts International, 55*, 10-B.

Singh, G. K., & Koposowa, A. J. (1996). Occupation-specific earnings attainment of Asian Indians and whites in the United States: Gender and nativity differentials across class strata. *Applied Behavioral Science Review, 4*(2), 137–175.

Singh, M. D. (1999). The paradox of Kama Sutra and the veil: Women reflect on their marriages, divorces, and on rebuilding lives. In S. R. Gupta (Ed.), *Emerging Voices: South Asian American women redefine self, family, and community* (pp. 169–192). Walnut Creek, CA: AltaMira Press.

Singh, R., Nath, R., & Nichols, W. (2005). Introduction to treating Indian families. *Contemporary Family Therapy: An International Journal, 27*, 281–283.

Sinha, S. P., & Mukherjee, N. (2001). Marital adjustment and personal space orientation. *The Journal of Social Psychology, 130*(5), 633–639.

Srinivasan, S. (2001). "Being Indian," "being American": A balancing act or a creative blend? *Journal of Human Behavior in the Social Environment, 3*(3/4), 135–158.

Suppal, P. G., Roopnarine, J. L, Buesig, T., & Bennett, A. (1996). Ideological beliefs about family practices: Contemporary perspectives among North Indian families. *International Journal of Psychology, 31*(1), 29–37.

Talbaani, A., & Hasnaali, P. (2000). Adolescent females between tradition and modernity: Gender role socialization in South Asian immigrant culture. *Journal of Adolescence, 23*(5), 615–627.

Trask, B. S., & Hamon, R. R. (2007). *Cultural diversity and families: Expanding perspectives*. Thousand Oaks, CA: Sage.

Wadha, V. (2006, September 14). Are Indian immigrants the model immigrants? *Business Week* (pp. 7–8).

Wadhwani, S. M. (2000). An assessment of the concerns and service needs of Asian Indian college students (Doctoral dissertation, The State University of New Jersey–New Brunswick, 2000). *Dissertation Abstract International, 62*, 01B.

About the Authors

Douglas A. Abbott, professor, Child, Youth, and Family Studies, University of Nebraska–Lincoln, Lincoln, NE 68583. Phone: 402-472-1665. E-mail: dabbott1@unl.edu.

Pallabi Moulik Gupta, M.S., University of Nebraska.

Strong Marriages in Latino Culture   6

LINDA SKOGRAND, DANIEL HATCH, AND ARCHANA SINGH

Abstract

This study used a qualitative research methodology to understand the cultural values, practices, and strengths of twenty-five Latino couples who had strong marriages. The study was conducted in the context of Latino culture. According to the participants in the study, the components of strong marriages in Latino culture were children, communication, and religion. Implications for culturally appropriate marriage education for Latino couples are provided.

Keywords: Latino, Marriage, Family Strengths, Familism, Qualitative, Marriage Education

THE UNITED STATES is becoming culturally more diverse and the Hispanic/Latino population is now the largest minority group in the United States (El Nasser, 2003). As this growth in the Latino immigrant population in the United States continues, there will be an increasing need to better understand Latino marriage and family life in

Address all correspondence to Dr. Linda Skogrand, Department of Family, Consumer, and Human Development at Utah State University, 2705 Old Main, Logan, UT 84322-2705. Phone: 435-797-8183. Fax: 435-797-7220. E-mail: lindas@ext.usu.edu.

order to provide culturally appropriate marriage and family education. There is a dearth of research in the United States about this growing population to inform such education (DeBord & Reguero de Atiles, 1999; Ooms & Wilson, 2004; Powell, 1988; Vega, 1990). Instead, most research that informs family life education is based upon European American, middle-class families (Santiago-Rivera, Arrendondo & Gallardo-Cooper, 2002). Most programming based upon marriages and family life from the dominant culture is not a good fit for Latino families, because the information and programming are not culturally relevant (Ooms & Wilson, 2004). There is, therefore, a need for research to be conducted within a cultural context to inform programming for the Latino immigrant population (De-Maria, 2005; Doherty & Anderson, 2004; Wiley & Ebata, 2004).

We might ask, "Why is it important to address the issue of family life from the perspective of the immigrant population's culture?" There are two responses to this question. First, if there is a cultural clash between educational information provided and the values of a population, they will usually not attend educational programs (Ernst, 1990). If they do attend, they will not benefit from the information provided (Ernst, 1990) and harm may result if individuals embrace programming ideas that destroy components of their cultural heritage. Secondly, there is evidence that relying upon one's cultural heritage, the way one's people deal with struggles, is the most effective way for people to be resilient and capable of handling difficulties (Delgado, 1998). McGoldrick and Giordano (1996) also assert that those who try to completely assimilate into the dominant culture, rather than maintaining a connection to their cultural values, are likely to have difficulties in dealing with life's problems. In addition, there is evidence that not completely assimilating, by being bicultural and continuing to maintain one's original cultural values, contributes to positive mental health (Falicov, 1998; LaFramboise, Coleman & Gerton, 1993). Consequently, it is important to draw on and reinforce the existing family values that are evident in the Latino culture (DeBord & Reguero de Atiles, 1999; Ooms & Wilson, 2004; Powell, 1988; Vega, 1990).

The research about strong Latino marriages drew upon the family strengths framework, which focuses on the strengths evident in families, rather than focusing on why families do not do well (Stinnett, Sanders & DeFrain, 1981). Using the family strengths framework, we sought to understand the cultural values, practices, and strengths evident in these strong marriages. The purpose of this study was to describe what strong marriages look like from the perspective of Latino couples who identified themselves as having strong marriages and who were willing to tell us about their marriages. The current study identified components of strong Latino marriages, with the ultimate goal of using these findings to provide culturally appropriate marriage education to members of the Latino community.

What We Know about Latino Marriages and Families

Social science literature informs us about features and cultural themes of the Latino culture that are part of marriage and family life, but there is very little research data available about what makes Latino marriages or families work (McGoldrick, Preto, Hines & Lee, 1991; Myers-Walls, 2000; Wiley & Ebata, 2004). We, therefore, relied primarily on descriptions of cultural themes in the literature to guide our research and interpret findings.

The concept of *familism* is a dominant theme in Latino culture (Falicov, 1998; Santiago-Rivera et al., 2002). *Familism* refers to the close relationships that are promoted and exist among Latino family members, which includes interdependence and cooperation among family members with a willingness to sacrifice individual needs for the welfare of the group or family (Falicov, 1998; Santiago-Rivera et al., 2002). There is also an emphasis on the creation of families, such as marriage and fertility, as well as maintaining a close relationship with both nuclear and extended family members (Hurtado, 1995; Oropesa & Landale, 2004; Santiago-Rivera et al., 2002). Family members are instrumental as a source of social and emotional support when problems occur (Hurtado, 1995; Santiago-Rivera et al., 2002; Vega, 1990).

Family affiliation is so important that "parenthood" is considered to be more important than "partnerhood" (Falicov, 1998). The primary goal of marriage is to have children and be part of the family that ensues. Marital happiness may not be the primary goal of marriage and may not be viewed as necessary in achieving a satisfying family life (Falicov, 1998). Intergenerational connections, such as the relationship of a parent to a child, often take precedence over the marital relationship, with the children having a higher priority than the marriage (Falicov, 1998; Penn, Hernández & Bermúdez, 1997). Researchers have found that *familism* is an enduring trait even when families become highly acculturated (Santiago-Rivera et al., 2002).

Personalismo, which is valuing warm, friendly, and somewhat informal interpersonal relationships, is also an important value in Latino culture (Santiago-Rivera et al., 2002). This focus on warm and positive interpersonal relationships is especially important among family members (Santiago-Rivera et al., 2002). Having a positive relationship with a person may be more important than the task at hand, and this is true in family relationships as well (Santiago-Rivera et al., 2002)

Finally, religion is highly valued in Latino culture (Falicov, 1998; Santiago-Rivera et al., 2002). One random sample of Latino immigrants in the United States found that 94 percent of Latinos self-identified as having a religious affiliation, with the majority self-identifying as being Catholic (Espinosa, Elizondo & Miranda, 2003). This is compared with the national population where 81 percent cited a religious preference (Lampman, 2002).

It has been suggested that Catholicism has been so pervasive in Latino culture that it has affected Latino family characteristics such as large family size and marriage (Falicov, 1998). Researchers conclude that Catholicism has become an integral part of the Latino culture even when people practice other faiths (Becerra, 1998; Santiago-Rivera et al., 2002). Religious practices and doctrine provide the Latino culture with prescriptions for behavior and a connection to God as a source of support (Santiago-Rivera et al., 2002).

Method

The study was conducted using the model provided by Grills and Rowe (1999), which encourages researchers to become familiar with and develop a value orientation that is respectful and knowledgeable about the community being investigated. The study was done by gathering and analyzing data using a qualitative methodology, which allowed the strengths of Latino marriages to be described within the context of culture.

The major instrument used for gathering data was a semi-structured interview schedule, which was based on features and cultural themes in Latino family life as described in the literature. The instrument was piloted, revised, and ultimately included twenty-eight open-ended questions about marriage around the following issues: how the couple met; their descriptions of strong marriages; qualities of strong marriages in other couples they knew; what made their marriages strong; the effect of children on their marriages; and, if they were involved in church or religion, the role the church or religion played in the marriages.

Marital partners were interviewed separately. The interviews were conducted in a location convenient for the couple, and all the couples except one chose to do the interviews in their own homes. The average interview lasted approximately forty-five minutes per person. The interviews were audio recorded and conducted with a bilingual researcher. The interviews were translated and transcribed by a bilingual transcriber. Demographic data that affects marriage relationships, such as length of marriage, age at marriage, educational level, and number of children, were also collected from each couple.

The participants interviewed for this study included twenty-five couples (fifty individuals). Purposive and snowball sampling techniques were used to identify participants. We asked two leaders of Latino social service organizations that had no religious affiliation and two Catholic priests who had large Latino membership in their congregations to help us identify couples who had strong marriages. Nine of the couples were recruited by way of the leaders of social service organizations and nine were recruited through Catholic churches. In addition to these eighteen couples, seven couples were referred by the first eighteen couples who were interviewed. Even though referrals were made by others, each of the individuals had to agree that their marriage was strong to be included in the study. One couple who was referred was excluded from the study because they did not feel they had a strong marriage. Each couple determined for themselves what the definition of a strong marriage might be.

The majority of participants (n = 38) in this study were of Mexican decent and the remaining participants (n = 12) were from the Central and South American countries of Chile, El Salvador, Guatemala, Nicaragua, and Uruguay. The couples' countries of origin were consistent with the composition of Latinos in the United States, with about two-thirds of the Latino immigrants coming from Mexico and the remainder coming from Central and South America, Puerto Rico, and Cuba (U.S. Census Bureau, n.d.). The couples resided within a fifty-mile radius, in metropolitan communities and small towns. Of the fifty participants, forty-three were first generation immigrants and seven were second-generation immigrants. The primary language spoken in all the homes was Spanish and twenty-three of the twenty-five couples chose to be interviewed in Spanish.

The couples had an average household income of $30,000, with the range being from $10,000 to $80,000, and most participants were employed in working-class occupations. The individuals had education levels ranging from no formal education to completing graduate school with the average education being completion of high school. All of the couples self-identified as having a religious affiliation, even though approximately half of the couples were recruited by way of nonreligious organizations. Fifteen couples self-identified as Catholic and ten self-identified as being affiliated with Protestant denominations. Three couples had no children and the remaining couples had from one to seven children. They had been married from three to fifty years with the average length of marriage being sixteen years.

Data were analyzed using the procedure described by Bogdan and Biklen (2003) in that the researchers (a project director and two research assistants) identified coding categories in answer to the research question: What makes strong Latino marriages? All three of the researchers immersed themselves in these data, as suggested by Bogdan and Biklen, by reading the transcribed data from all fifty participants all the way through a couple of times to get a sense of the totality of the data. The researchers then read through the data and developed coding categories that were reflective of the patterns and regularities described by the respondents, focusing on what was necessary to have a strong marriage. Although answers to the research questions were often found in response to specific questions about what was essential for strong marriages, their thoughts about components of strong Latino marriages were found throughout the transcribed interview.

The coding was done independently by each data analyst and the coding schemes were shared. When the researchers identified differences in the coding categories, we went back to the data and developed a consensus about which categories best reflected the participants' responses. Throughout this process coding categories were collapsed and refined. The coding categories were then used to code all of the data. The findings in this paper reflect the coding categories that were cited by the largest number of respondents, with children, communication, and religion being identified by the majority of the participants as being necessary components of strong marriages.

The questions were open-ended to allow the participants to share their thoughts about strong marriages. When we report that a certain number talked about one of the components, the remaining participants did not volunteer that category as being necessary—they did not talk about it. For example, if forty-seven out of fifty participants said that children were an important component of strong Latino marriages, the remaining three participants did not volunteer that component as being necessary.

Findings

According to the participants in this study, the components of strong marriages in the Latino culture in order of importance were: children, communication, and religion. These components were identified most often by both husbands and wives in this study. Couples also described how these components contributed to making their marriages strong.

Children

Of the individuals interviewed, forty-seven of the fifty participants indicated that children were an essential component of a strong marriage. Two parents had this to say about the importance of children in having a strong marriage:

> If you want to have a good marriage you have to have a good family. That's the point. I think we have a good marriage because we have good kids together.

> I think by far the high points [of our marriage] were when our boys were born. It really brings you close; it really makes you one person.

One individual who was unable to have children said, "The worst thing about us is not having children. The hardest thing for us is that we don't have a family here in the home." Another person indicated that children were so important to a marriage that if the woman could not have children they should adopt.

Children made the marriages strong by being the "glue" of the marriage, being a source of happiness, providing support to the parents, and being a reflection of the couple's love. Couples also viewed their marriages as subsumed within the context of the family.

CHILDREN ARE THE "GLUE" OF THE MARRIAGE. Children were the reason for getting married and the reason for staying married. We asked individuals why they got married and often got an answer like this:

> I decided to get married because I always wanted to form a home. I always wanted to have a family. I always wanted to have a husband and two kids; that was always my desire. . . . It was more than a goal; it was a purpose, to share my life with someone.

Individuals often described having children as a lifelong goal, an expectation they had since they were children. As one woman said, "The main reason to get married was to bring my family into the world, and to raise them the way I was raised, in the way of the Lord."

Individuals in this study also described children as being what held the marriage together over time. The participants talked about children "uniting the family," and bringing the couple closer together. One participant said that, "Before children arrive, a couple fights more and it is the children that make the marriage strong." Several individuals stated that there had been times when the children were the reason they had stayed together during difficult times. One participant said, "If it wasn't for them [the children] we wouldn't be together at all." Another participant described at length how it is easy to walk away from a spouse, but it is not easy to walk away from one's children:

> I think that if it had been she and I without children, we would have divorced. I think that if a marriage doesn't have children the man can easily find another woman. In some moment when he is mad and fighting with his wife, he can easily find another woman. He can leave the house and find someone else, and the woman too. But you can't find other children. So, I think the love for children is what makes the woman put up with the husband. And the same with the husband, he has more tolerance with the woman.

CHILDREN ARE A SOURCE OF HAPPINESS. Only two individuals out of fifty indicated that, at times, children could be a source of friction and stress. Instead, the great majority of the participants described the fun times they had with their children:

> Something very nice has been the many trips that we have had. We have visited some beaches, and the truth is that it has been fun being with the children and enjoying them. I feel like the most fun is enjoying our children. When they were small and even now we enjoy them.

Children strengthened the marriage and even the most menial tasks were turned into meaningful times that strengthened the marriage relationship and the family. One person said, "We try to spend time with the family. It makes our marriage stronger." Many said they wanted to do things as a family; they did not want to be away from their children.

CHILDREN PROVIDE SUPPORT. Children make a marriage strong because they provide a kind of reciprocal support; the couple supports the children and the children support the couple. This support happens in a number of subtle and obvious ways. A couple's children contribute to building the love between a husband and wife which in turn comes back to the family:

> They [children] make you feel good. They have made our marriage better because the love that you have with the woman and the children, now that is coming back. They love you. When they love you they make your marriage stronger, they bring the couple closer together.

Many of these couples saw their children as critical components in the family unit who could provide them with support. The children's love rejuvenated the love the couple felt for each other. There was a reciprocal benefit in that children benefited from the unity of the couple and the couple benefited from the love the children gave back to them.

CHILDREN ARE A REFLECTION OF A COUPLE'S LOVE. Several couples talked about children as a reflection of the love the husband and wife felt for each other. As one person described it, "[as a couple] we are two things with one purpose." Another participant viewed it in this manner: "The home will be good. Our children, even if they are poor and whatever happens to them, they are always going to be a part of us." The knowledge that their children were a reflection of the couple's love and were always going to be a part of them became a unifying factor that strengthened marriage relationships. One person exemplified this idea as she described her pregnancy, "When I was pregnant, we were all happy because it was from both of us."

MARRIAGE IS SUBSUMED WITHIN THE CONTEXT OF FAMILY. We asked Latino couples who were identified as having strong marriages a variety of questions designed to determine what made their marriages strong. To such questions, they typically responded with an answer describing their family life. Of the fifty individuals interviewed, only five participants actually focused on discussions specifically about their marriages. The remaining forty-five individuals consistently would respond with answers about their families. "Family" was the more important umbrella and their spouse and children were under that umbrella. These Latino couples viewed their marriages as subsumed within the context of family.

When we asked individuals to tell us about high points in their marriage, we also often got a response about their family life. Some of the respondents indicated that without children there was no marriage. One person said, "It's the children that make the marriage." Another had this to say:

> Without children, I think there aren't marriages. Almost 90 percent of couples who don't have children separate. They always separate. . . . So if there aren't children, I don't think there is a marriage. The children are the happiness of the house.

Communication
We found that forty-five of the fifty individuals interviewed volunteered that communication was an essential component of a strong marriage.

Individuals said things like, "Without communication . . . nothing is going to work," "[Other couples] have a lot of communication, her to him, him to her, so that marriage is good," or "When the marriage doesn't work, it is because there isn't communication." One participant concluded, "Communication is everything. If there is not communication, everything breaks."

The participants described how communication happened in their marriages. They said they needed to spend time together and talk often. Talking with each other helped them understand each other, which led to greater love for each other. They also stated that couples need to talk in order to solve problems and make decisions.

SPENT TIME TOGETHER AND TALKED OFTEN. Participants would say things like: "We talk continuously," "We talk and talk," or "We talk a lot about everything." One woman said:

> We talk about things all the time. Very rarely do we have a formal sit-down to make a decision. Decisions are made slowly because we talk about it all the time.

Several couples also indicated that they needed to spend time together in order to have the opportunity to talk and communicate effectively. One man said:

> It's really important to talk. If you cannot do it every day, do it at least once a week. For me it's important to have one day a week that you can go with your wife, you and her, and share time. You can go play basketball. You can watch a movie. You can go to a restaurant. Those kinds of things help the communication. I think communication is the key.

Spending time together allowed the participants the opportunity to communicate about issues that affected their marriage and family.

UNDERSTANDING THE OTHER PERSON: BUILDING LOVE. One of the outcomes of talking often was that the husband and wife were able to better understand each other. This communication began as they were boyfriend and girlfriend and continued into marriage.

For many participants, communicating and getting to know each other resulted in love.

One woman said, "You need to understand your partner. Try to understand what he believes, what he thinks." A participant said that a person needed to understand how their spouse was feeling regarding how the children were doing at school and other issues that involved the family. Participants talked about how they needed to understand their spouse's point of view about everything:

> Misunderstanding can result because of lack of communication or lack of attention and lack of understanding. If you don't clear something up, it can be really small but will become very big.

One person summarized this relationship between communication and love by saying, "If there isn't communication there isn't love either because the communication helps us build love."

COUPLES TALKED TO SOLVE PROBLEMS AND MAKE DECISIONS. Communication was an important component in having a strong marriage, because communication was necessary to solve problems and make decisions in their marriages. Almost all of the couples, when trying to solve problems in their marriage, preferred talking to each other before they discussed their problems with someone else. Participants said communication was important so that problems did not develop in the first place. Some participants concluded that, if they did not communicate to solve problems and make decisions, their marriages would probably end. One woman said that talking to solve problems brings the husband and wife closer: "Don't give up; don't give up. One has to help the other so this doesn't end. So instead of ending it, you grow closer."

Religion

Of the fifty participants, thirty-seven volunteered that religion was a necessary component of a strong marriage. One participant responded to an interview question about what is essential for a strong marriage this way:

> I think that the church has been the most important thing in our marriage because of the values we believe in, that the family is the most important thing . . . and the plan that God has for us.

Another participant had this to say about other couples who have strong marriages:

> I think the ones [couples] that I know who have a strong marriage, that you can see they live well, they are the ones who go to church the most. . . . They know how to handle marriage situations.

Couples described how religion affected several aspects of their marriages. Religion affected their marriages by providing them with guidance to stay on the right path in marriage, spiritual strength that helped them cope with crisis, and it helped them stay committed to their spouse.

GUIDANCE: LEADING A CHRISTIAN LIFE. Religion provided guidance that came from religious teachings and church leaders, which helped make the marriage strong. Religious teachings made couples aware of the fact that they needed to take care of each other as family members, which supported their interdependence. Religious teachings also taught virtues like respect, healthy communication styles, empathy, and compassion, all of which helped to build healthy relationships:

> The Commandments direct us by telling how to live our lives. Without them we would be lost. . . . The Commandments teach us the virtues of life that prevent us from being destructive.

Religious teachings not only provided guidance about the right things to do in marriage, but also kept them from engaging in behaviors that would have a negative consequence for their marriage. Several husbands in this study had at one time engaged in activities such as drinking and hanging out with friends, but realized that those activities were causing problems in their marriages. Religion helped them by providing direction about what was expected from them as husbands:

> When the person doesn't have religion it's different. They drink, they smoke, they go out with friends, they do what they want, and the wife is left aside. And I was afraid of living like that. . . . But, thank God that hasn't happened to me. Religion has a lot to do with it. It changes the person's life.

Many turned toward religious leaders when they faced problems in their marriages. The religious leaders were respected as authority figures that could intervene in their lives to help them. In turn, the religious leaders had the responsibility for looking after the well-being of the members of the religious organization. The leaders accepted them unconditionally, and they worked together to find solutions to problems:

> It is always very helpful to know that there is someone there that can listen to you. Or, if you feel like you have sinned and you know you can always go in and talk to him [clergy person] and, hopefully, resolve things. You feel happy that you did not do something and God just helps you through

that. And when you want to go and talk to someone, it's private; you can talk to that one person.

SPIRITUAL STRENGTH: GOING TO GOD. Organized religion guided the couples through their daily activities. In addition, many developed a close personal relationship with a God who was involved with their lives and their problems. God was seen as a powerful figure, and faith in Him was a source of comfort because they felt He could take care of personal problems and problems in their marriage. One person described this by saying, "When I have had problems in my marriage. . . . What I have done is pray. I ask God for help because I can't do it alone. He is the only one that helps me."

COMMITMENT. All of the participants in this study who talked about commitment described it in the context of religion. Marriage was a life-long commitment, which made them feel they needed to stay together through difficult times. They sacrificed personal benefits for the good of the family. Since the religious teachings were also against divorce and living together outside marriage, there was an increased commitment to marriage:

> You commit in front of everyone, including God, so that a marriage will go well, so that the man isn't unfaithful and the woman isn't either . . . it's part of a religion. We are very much involved in the Catholic religion and it unites us and makes sure that everything goes very well.

Conclusions

This study provided in-depth understanding of what makes marriages strong from the perspective of fifty Latino individuals who had strong marriages. The findings are consistent with findings of other research about Latino marriages and families. This study supports the cultural theme that the family, which includes children, is more important than the marriage (Falicov, 1998). For these couples, children were important and, for many, an essential component of a healthy marriage. In fact, children were so important to some of these couples that at times "parenthood" was more important than "partnerhood" (Falicov, 1998). The couples in this study clearly viewed the family as the most important point of reference, and the marriage was part of the family. The couples in this study also indicated that family members were a source of social and emotional support when problems occurred, which is consistent with the findings of Hurtado (1995) and Vega (1990).

Literature about the features of Latino culture does not directly state that communication is an important value in the Latino culture. The concept of *personalismo*, however, may be related to or encompass the communication component that was described by these couples. Communication that is necessary to have a strong marriage is really an aspect of *personalism*, the warm and friendly interpersonal relationships that are important in family life (Santiago-Rivera et al., 2002).

The couples who had strong marriages also described how religion was an integral part of their marriage and family life, which is consistent with the literature (Falicov, 1998; Santiago-Rivera et al., 2002). Religion was not a separate entity and something given attention only on Sundays; it was an everyday matter. The couples described how it was an integral part of many aspects of their family lives, from solving problems to the role of commitment to their marriages.

Implications for Education, Service, and Research

This study, along with features and cultural themes evident in the Latino culture, has important implications for how we think about marriage and family education. There are implications for how one thinks about providing social services to this population. These findings also indicate a need for continued and more focused research into the dynamics of Latino families, within a cultural context. This should be done in order that Latino families may be better served.

The findings of this study, along with features and cultural themes evident in Latino culture, provide direction for marriage and family education that is culturally relevant. Marriage and family life should not be considered as separate entities. Children are an integral component of Latino couples' lives. The couples in this study would not likely attend educational programming if their children were not present.

What might marriage and family education look like if the entire family was included rather than just the couple? This programming could include a series of family events where the parents and children are involved in activities designed to strengthen the family unit. The family time could include activities that show how family members rely on each other and how love and support go from parents to children and from children to parents. It could also include time to have fun together, which was described as an important benefit of having children. Another part of the educational event might include activities for children in a nearby facility, while couples engage in programming focused on the things unique to the couple relationship. Educational programming for Latino families such as those provided through the Cooperative Extension Service and other community education programs could also benefit from these findings, in that the entire family should be included in programming.

Social services provided to Latino families might also be more effective if they, whenever appropriate, provided information to the family rather than the individual. Services that involve the entire family might include counseling and therapy, consultations regarding health care, and social service assistance. We typically think of some of these areas as being inappropriate for children, but they may support the cultural theme of *familism* (Santiago-Rivera et al., 2002) to help strengthen the family. The physical environment of public health facilities, clinics, and other human service organizations might also provide waiting rooms, meeting rooms, and examining rooms for larger groups of people. The first author's experience in designing and building a group home for Latino individuals in the end stages of AIDS resulted in designing larger individual rooms and a much larger dining area to accommodate the family units that would visit the client.

Education designed to develop effective marriage and family communication could also be included in marriage and family education. Latino couples did not talk about sharing feelings in a particular way or having effective listening skills. Instead, they spoke of spending time together so they could talk, understand each other and, therefore, love each other. This was reflective of *personalism*, the warm and friendly interpersonal relationships, which is a highly valued Latino cultural characteristic (Santiago-Rivera et al., 2002). Because of the strong integration between marriage and family life, information about communication could also include communication among all family members.

Because religion was pervasive in the lives of most of these couples, which is supported by existing literature, programming might include content about how some couples benefit from affiliations with religious institutions or how a spiritual connection can be helpful in marriage and family life. Another implication might be that marriage education programming could be planned in partnership with spiritual leaders. Although many of the participants in this study were Catholic, any religious group that serves Latino families might exist where this programming might take place. Religious facilities are likely to be a trusted meeting place for couples and families. Because these couples relied on such leaders for help in many aspects of their marriage and family life, religious leaders might

be appropriate and respected co-facilitators of marriage and family education. Religious organizations might be important resources for providing
social services as well. Because religious institutions are trusted organizations, they may be important avenues for delivering services such as food
pantries or health services. In addition, social services may need to integrate
religion into the services they provide for those who are religious. For example, referring again to the house that was designed and built for Latino
individuals living with AIDS, small altars were built into a wall of each
client's room. Clients were better able to practice their religious beliefs if
they chose to do so.

This study has important implications for further research. The findings of this study and the features and cultural themes identified in the
literature make it very clear that we must provide education and services
in culturally appropriate ways. To do that, we must gain more knowledge
from additional research to learn about this growing population in order
to provide education and services in ways that better serve Latino families. It is not sufficient to say that we have included Latinos in research
that is conducted with a primarily European American sample because
the uniqueness of the Latino population will be lost. In addition, this research should be strength-based, rather than looking at problems, so that
programming can capitalize upon the strengths evident in Latino families.
The resulting programming can allow Latino families to draw upon their
cultural heritage, as suggested by Delgado (1998), to handle difficulties
and solve problems in their lives.

References

Becerra, R. M. (1998). The Mexican-American family. In C. H. Mindel, R. W.
    Habenstein & R. Wright (Eds.), *Ethnic families in America.* Upper Saddle River,
    NJ: Prentice Hall.

Bogdan, R. C., & Biklen, S. K. (2003). *Qualitative research for education: An introduc-
    tion to theory and methods* (4th ed.). Boston: Allyn and Bacon.

DeBord, K. B., & Reguero de Atiles, J. T. (1999). Latino parents: Unique prefer-
    ences for learning about parenting. *The Forum for Family and Consumer Issues,
    4.* Retrieved January 20, 2006, from www.ces.ncsu.edu/depts/fcs/pub/1999/
    latino.html.

Delgado, M. (1998). *Social services in Latino communities: Research and strategies.* New
    York: Haworth Press.

DeMaria, R. M. (2005). Distressed couples and marriage education. *Family Rela-
    tions, 54,* 242–253.

Doherty, W. J., & Anderson, J. R. (2004). Community marriage initiatives. *Fam-
    ily Relations, 53,* 425–432.

El Nasser, H. (2003, June 18). 39 million make Hispanics largest U.S. minority group. *USA Today*. Retrieved August 10, 2004, from www.usatoday.com/news/nation/census/2003-06-18-Census_x.htm.

Ernst, L. (1990). Value differences in families of differing socioeconomic status: Implications for family education. *Family Perspective, 24*, 401–410.

Espinosa, G., Elizondo, V., & Miranda, J. (2003). Hispanic churches in American public life: Summary of findings. *Interim Reports* (Vol. 2003.2). Notre Dame, IN: Institute for Latino Studies, University of Notre Dame.

Falicov, C. J. (1998). *Latino families in therapy: A guide to multicultural practice*. New York: Guilford Press.

Grills, C. N., & Rowe, D. M. (1999). Constructing and managing culturally competent research teams for community-based investigations. *Drugs & Society, 14*, 247–268.

Hurtado, A. (1995). Variations, combinations and evolutions; Latino families in the United States. In R. E. Zambrana (Ed.), *Understanding Latino families; scholarship, policy, and practice* (pp. 40–51). Thousand Oaks, CA: Sage.

LaFramboise, T., Coleman, H. L., & Gerton, J. (1993). Psychological impact of biculturalism: Evidence and theory. *Psychological Bulletin, 114*, 395–412.

Lampman, J. (2002, October 10). Charting American's religious landscape. *The Christian Science Monitor*. Retrieved January 31, 2006, from www.csmonitor.com/2002/1010p12s01.html.

McGoldrick, M., & Giordano, J. (1996). Overview: Ethnicity and family therapy. In M. McGoldrick, J. Giordano & J. K. Pearce (Eds.), *Ethnicity and family therapy* (2nd ed.). New York: Guilford Press.

McGoldrick, M., Preto, N. G., Hines, P. M., & Lee, E. (1991). Ethnicity and family therapy. In A. Gurman & D. Kniskern (Eds.), *Handbook of family therapy* (Vol. 2, pp. 546–582). New York: Brunner/Mazel.

Myers-Walls, J. (2000). Family diversity and family life education. In D. Demo, K. Allen & M. Fine (Eds.), *Handbook for family diversity* (pp. 359–379). New York: Oxford University Press.

Ooms, T., & Wilson, P. (2004). The challenge of offering relationship and marriage education to low-income populations. *Family Relations, 53*, 440–447.

Oropesa, R. S., & Landale, N. S. (2004). The future of marriage and Hispanics. *Journal of Marriage and Family, 66*, 901–920.

Penn, C. D., Hernández, S. L., & Bermúdez, J. M. (1997). Using a cross-cultural perspective to understand infidelity in couples therapy. *The American Journal of Family Therapy, 25*, 169–185.

Powell, D. R. (Ed.). (1988). *Parent education as early childhood intervention: Emerging directions in theory, research, and practice*. Norwood, NJ: Ablex.

Santiago-Rivera, A. L., Arredondo, P., & Gallardo-Cooper, M. (2002). *Counseling Latinos and la familia: A practical guide*. Thousand Oaks, CA: Sage.

Stinnett, N., Sanders, G., & DeFrain, J. (1981). Strong families: A national study. In N. Stinnett, J. DeFrain, K. King, P. Knaub & G. Rowe (Eds.), *Family strengths 3: Roots of well-being* (pp. 33–42). Lincoln: University of Nebraska Press.

U.S. Census. (n.d.). *Profile of general demographic characteristics: 2000*. Retrieved January 24, 2006, from www.census.gov/main/www/cen2000.html.

Vega, W. A. (1990). Hispanic families in the 1980s: A decade of research. *Journal of Marriage and the Family, 52*, 1015–1024.

Wiley, A. R., & Ebata, A. (2004). Reaching American families: Making diversity real in family life education. *Family Relations, 53*, 273–281.

About the Authors

Daniel Hatch is a doctoral student in the psychology department at Utah State University, 2705 Old Main, Logan, UT 84322-2705. E-mail: Harvold _2000@yahoo.com.

Archana Singh is a doctoral student in the Department of Family, Consumer and Human Development at Utah State University, 2705 Old Main, Logan, UT 84322-2705. E-mail: archanasingh@cc.usu.edu.

Linda Skogrand, Ph.D., is a cooperative extension specialist and assistant professor in the Department of Family, Consumer and Human Development at Utah State University, 2705 Old Main, Logan, UT 84322-2705. E-mail: lindas@ext.usu.edu.

Family Strengths of Hmong and Somali Refugees in the United States

7

DANIEL F. DETZNER, AYŞEM R. ŞENYÜREKLI, PA NHIA D. YANG, AND KHADIJA S. SHEIKH

Abstract

Refugees face multiple hardships upon arrival in their countries of destination. We use in-depth qualitative interviews to explore how three-generation Somali and Hmong families stay strong in the face of difficulties. Results indicate: (a) Somali and Hmong families learn family strengths through intergenerational transmission; (b) Somali and Hmong families conceptualize family strengths as overlapping constructs; (c) Somali families have greater agreement on family strengths than Hmong families; and (d) the experiences of Somali and Hmong immigrant families are consistent with the family strengths identified in the literature. Each finding is discussed, followed by implications for research, policy, and practice.

Keywords: Immigrant, Hmong, Families, Somali, Family Strengths

INDIVIDUALS WHO ARE FORCED from their homes experience multiple types of stress and adversity as they flee to refugee camps and resettlement countries. Unlike immigrants who migrate voluntarily at a time of their choosing, refugees are compelled to leave their homeland and family members in the midst of war, political crisis, or ethnic and religious conflict. Many experience traumatic events during the escape or detention, or during the years spent in unsafe camps before resettlement in a third country (Weine et. al., 2004; Halcon et. al., 2004; Rousseau, Abdelwahed & Moreau, 2001). After finding a safe haven, they confront a series of hardships, including the need to find food, shelter, and clothing, acquire language and work skills, establish support networks, adapt to the expectations of the host society, manage long-lasting economic hardships, and cope with the psychological impact of violence and the leaving of some family members behind (Detzner, 2004).

According to the Immigration and Naturalization Service, 12 percent of all the immigrants who arrived in the United States in 2002 were refugees (Ronningen, 2004). In 2005 alone, over 53,738 new refugees arrived in the United States, and 10 percent of all the immigrants who obtained legal permanent resident status in this country were refugees (Office of Immigration Statistics, 2006). In the past three decades, the Laotian Hmong and the East African Somali have been among the largest refugee populations arriving in the United States. However different their cultures and circumstances of arrival, both contemporary groups settled in large numbers in Minnesota, especially in the metropolitan area of the Twin Cities.

Following the Vietnam War, the Hmong were placed in refugee camps, primarily in Thailand, and began arriving in the United States during the late 1970s through sponsorship by families and religious organizations (Detzner, 2004). The U.S. Census estimates that the Hmong population has grown to more than 180,000 in 2000, the fourth largest population of Hmong in the world following China, Vietnam, and Laos (Hmong Cultural and Resource Center in St. Paul, Minnesota). The Hmong who came to the United States represent a diverse ethnic population who lived primarily in the highlands of Laos prior to emigration. After the end of the Southeast Asia war in 1975, the Hmong settled in large numbers in Wisconsin, Minnesota, and California. The Immigration and Naturalization Service estimates that Minnesota currently has the second highest population of Hmong in the United States at approximately 65,000 (Ronningen, 2004). While many have grown up in the United States, others are newcomers. The Hmong have blended religious values including animism, shamanism, Christianity, and Buddhism. St. Paul has the largest urban population of Hmong in America, and is known as the "Hmong capital of the United States."

Somalis are an ethnic group with nomadic roots who occupy Somalia, part of the Djibouti Republic, Eastern Ethiopia, and Northern Kenya (Heitritter, 1999). Upon the beginning of the civil war and the subsequent collapse of the central government of Somalia in 1991, many Somalis who escaped were placed in Kenyan refugee camps while awaiting resettlement. Since the early 1990s, large numbers of Somalia immigrants came to the United States in search of safety and economic and educational opportunities. The 2000 U.S. Census showed more than 36,000 Somalis in the United States, including more than 11,000 living in Minnesota (Ronningen, 2004). More recent data collected in 2004 by the Minnesota Department of Education and Minnesota State Demographic Center estimates that approximately 25,000 Somalis currently live in Minnesota, most of them in Minneapolis (Darboe, 2003). Somali people's religious values are shaped by Muslim beliefs as revealed in the *Qur'an*, with strict obligations to frequent prayer, fasting, and for women, conservative dress and wearing the *hajib*. Many came to Minneapolis through primary or secondary migration, and the large and growing population quickly gave the city the title of "Somali capital of the United States."

Despite significant historical, cultural, and religious differences, the Somali and Hmong share several traits that led to their inclusion in this comparative study. First, both groups have a history of war and forced displacement. Second, despite their roots in tropic and desert climates, large numbers from both groups decided to resettle in Minnesota, a most unlikely cold winter state for peoples from sub-Saharan Africa and Southeast Asia. Third, both groups observe strict hierarchy in familial and community structures. These similarities between the Hmong and Somali suggest that a comparison between them could be quite revealing. For example, if these two highly diverse groups identified similar family strengths as critically important, it would suggest that these strengths should be pursued in future research and program development designed to facilitate adjustment. Further implications for research, policy, and practice are discussed in the final section of this chapter.

Several questions guided this investigation and the larger study from which these data are drawn. What are the similarities and differences between groups in beliefs about the core family strengths needed to be successful in a new environment? How are the strengths they identify similar or different from the characteristics identified in the family strengths research literature? What are the similarities or differences in meaning attributed to core family strengths by the two groups? How can this knowledge be used to assist immigrant families in the future?

A significant body of the social and behavioral research on refugees and their families naturally focuses on the problems forced migrants confront or the problems that societies with large numbers of refugees must address.

This chapter approaches refugee families not from a victim, deficit, or problem-oriented model, but rather from a comparative family strengths perspective in hopes that a preliminary elaboration of the nature and characteristics of these strengths will reorient how we think about new immigrant populations.

Background

Family Strengths

While family scientists have historically been interested in studying the problems of families, the latter part of the twentieth century has revealed their growing interest in what is going *right* with families. Family *strengths* (Stinnett & Sauer, 1977; Royse & Turner, 1980), family *resiliencies* (McCubbin & McCubbin, 1988; Hawley & DeHaan, 1996), family *coping* (Reiboldt & Goldstein, 2000), and *well-functioning families* (Greeff, 2000), are concepts which have been studied to contribute to this growing literature. This study focuses particularly on family strengths, defined by Stinnett (1979b) as:

> [R]elationship patterns, interpersonal skills and competencies, and social and psychological characteristics which create a sense of positive family identity, promote satisfying and fulfilling interaction among family members, encourage the development of the potential of the family group and individual family members, and contribute to the family's ability to deal effectively with stress and crises (p. 2).

The ability of families to be satisfied with and supportive of one another during times of stress or adversity is a particularly useful frame for the study of refugee families. According to McCubbin and McCubbin (1988), how and why certain families adjust to major life changes can be identified by focusing on family strengths. Littlejohn-Blake and Darling (1993) proposed that being strong leads families to have satisfying and fulfilling interactions, which then allows them to deal effectively with stress and crisis. Similarly, both Hawley and DeHaan (1996) and Greeff and LeRoux (1999), suggested that it is the strengths possessed by families that allow them to be resilient when faced with difficult situations. A review of eleven peer-reviewed empirical journal articles on family strengths between 1977 and 2002 revealed that religion, time/activities together, communication, appreciation, and respect were the most frequently identified family strengths in these studies (see appendix 7B).

Research on what families *do right* can have a positive impact on families themselves, by encouraging service providers to focus on strengths as well as pathologies. In order to prevent the assumption that all families thrive on the same strengths, however, this type of research must carefully define which families are being investigated and how these families define their strengths. Cross-cultural comparisons can enrich our understanding of the similarities and differences in context and meaning, and add new insight into the elaboration of this construct. In our review of the family strengths literature, few of the studies included a diverse sample and none compared two groups. Only the two studies which focused on African American families (Royse & Turner, 1980; Hurd, Moore & Rogers, 1995) identified achievement and kinship bonds as family strengths. This might indicate that African American families have different or additional strengths that need to be explored. Additionally, only four studies asked participants to define the family strengths they identified (Royse & Turner, 1980; Hurd, Moore & Rogers, 1995; Medora, Larson & Dave, 2000; Usita & Blieszner, 2002).

Research Objectives

This study is exploratory. We aim to make a contribution to the family strengths literature in three ways. First, we investigate the family strengths of two new populations of immigrants in the United States that are increasing in size. As refugees, these immigrants are more likely to need financial, educational, and mental-health services as they adapt to life in a new country. Knowledge about how these families succeed, and how they develop, maintain, and promote strengths within their extended families will help us to better understand what they are able to do for themselves and what appropriate service providers can do to assist.

Second, we seek to understand family strengths in a generational context by interviewing adolescents, parents, and grandparents from the same family. Because Hmong and Somali families often draw their direction and moral values from elders, it is important to include their voices. Middle generation adults must adjust to the new society while trying to please elders and maintain cultural coherence for children. Adolescents experience a powerful pull toward the new culture, while continually trying to please older adults in the family and community. We believe adding a generational component to the dialogue on family strengths will increase our understanding of the complexity of the construct within multigenerational immigrant families.

Finally, we aim to contribute to the family strengths literature by comparing the most commonly identified family strengths from three separate sources: the family literature, Somali families, and Hmong families. This not only allows us to identify variations by cultural group, but allows us to determine if findings in the literature *fit* the experiences of Somali and Hmong families.

Research Methodology

As with all comparative research on immigrant families, there were several challenges that had to be overcome to conduct this study (Kamya, 1997). The language and cultural barriers were perhaps the most difficult. To develop trust and familiarity with the Hmong and Somali communities, the first author spent several years engaged with the Hmong community and a shorter time period engaged with Somali leaders and organizations. From participating in and observing community meetings, teaching Somali high school and college students, and in-depth interviews with twenty Hmong and twenty Somali leaders, he and the research team were able to gain a certain level of familiarity and acceptance within each community. In order to achieve and maintain respectful cultural protocols throughout the duration of the study, the research team included three Hmong and two Somali research assistants. As cultural insiders, the Hmong and Somali research assistants were responsible for the note-taking during interviews and translating their conversations from their respective languages to English for analysis. A Hmong research assistant coded and analyzed the Hmong interviews. A research assistant from outside these cultural groups coded and analyzed the Somali interviews, and worked closely with a Somali research assistant to ensure cultural sensitivity in her interpretations.

The second challenge was to identify three-generation families that ethnic community leaders would perceive to be matching their perceptions of a *strong* family. Since our interests in family strengths extended into the different ways that young, middle, and elder generations might define strengths, the research protocol called for interviews to be with co-residing three-generation families. Refugee families are often scattered across several camps outside the country of origin, and many are resettled in different countries. Others have lost family members due to the precipitating conflict and the aftermath, or in transit toward a safe haven. For these reasons, and because Somali families are relative newcomers to the United States with many still seeking family reunification, it was difficult to identify three-generation families. One out of the four Somali families we interviewed consists only of mother and daughter interviews, because we were unable to schedule interviews with the elders.

The third challenge in this study that was unique to the Somali community occurred because we were seeking to conduct interviews with the largest Muslim group in Minnesota in the aftermath of September 11, 2001. Although the interviews were conducted in 2003, racial and ethnic tensions surrounding the Somali community in Minnesota were ongoing. There were a series of front-page headlines about the police shooting of a Somali man with mental illness that sparked street demonstrations, and the closing of all Somali money remittance centers because they were allegedly used to fund terrorist organizations. This had an impact on our method of data collection. Given the potentially hostile environment at the time, our Somali interviewees requested that no audio or videotaping be used during the interviews. In addition, we were advised by community leaders not to seek private information such as citizenship status, finances, and other information about those left behind. We agreed and used the same method of data collection with our Hmong participants in order to provide a parallel set of interviews. This is a limitation of the study and the time in which we live.

Sample

This chapter reports on the interviews with Hmong and Somali individuals who are members of three-generation co-residential families identified as *strong* by community leaders. A total of four three-generation Hmong families and three three-generation Somali families agreed to be interviewed. Individuals ($N = 43$) from each generation in the seven families were interviewed using either Hmong and English or Somali and English, depending on the informant's preference. Elders typically preferred their native language and adolescents preferred English. Interviews conducted in the native language were later translated into English by research assistants who were bilingual. The Hmong sample consisted of twenty-four participants (two grandfathers, four grandmothers, three fathers, four mothers, five sons, and six daughters). The Hmong elders ranged in age from fifty-seven to eighty-two, with a mean of twenty-six years living in the United States at the time of the interview. Hmong adults ranged in age from thirty-five to forty-three, with a mean of twenty-six years living in the United States. Finally, the Hmong adolescents ranged in age from fourteen to nineteen, with all being U.S.-born except one.

The Somali sample consisted of nineteen participants (one grandfather, one grandmother, three fathers, four mothers, five sons, and five daughters). Five Somali informants did not provide data on age or years in the United States. The Somali elders ranged in age from seventy to seventy-four, with a mean of almost eight years living in the United States. The Somali adults ranged in age from twenty-six to forty-four, with a mean of ten and a half years in the United States. Lastly, Somali adolescents ranged in age from fourteen to twenty, with a mean of ten and a half years living in the United States. In most cases, the Somali adults and elders were highly educated and all the adolescents were students in high school or college. As reflected by the demographic profile of our sample, Somalis are typically recent newcomers in contrast to the Hmong who have lived in the United States for more than two decades. In contrast to Somali adolescents who were all born in Somalia, the Hmong adolescents in this study were all born in the United States, with one exception. Each individual informant was offered a $20 stipend for their time.

Data Collection

Individuals were interviewed separately but in the same home where other family members were present. They were asked questions related to their own definitions of family strengths, the community leader's conceptualization of family strengths, and the methods they used to cope with stressors in their lives. For the purposes of this chapter, only the questions related to the individuals' own definitions of family strengths are analyzed (see appendix 7A for a list of the interview questions analyzed here).

Interviews were conducted by research assistants who were cultural insiders from the Hmong and Somali communities. During regular meetings with the research team over the span of one year, the assistants reviewed the interview guides, discussed interview strategies, and received feedback on questions that emerged during the interview process. For the Somali families, special attention was given to the cultural inappropriateness of having a young, single female researcher spend time with males during an interview. To be culturally appropriate, a female research assistant interviewed the female family members and a male research assistant interviewed the male family members. Because of the experience, community standing, and maturity of the Hmong female graduate student, she interviewed both female and male informants. Extensive and detailed note-taking on each of the key questions was used to record the interviews.

Data Analysis

Coding was conducted using the qualitative software MAX QDA 2 (see www.maxqda.com). Within this software, it was possible to analyze the responses to each question within and across cultural group and generations. The two research assistants responsible for data analysis met with the principal investigator of this study on a biweekly basis to discuss coding and interpret findings. Given the inability to use audiotaping, the interviewee statements included in the results section are not direct quotations from the informants, but are drawn from the words and ideas recorded in interview notes. The most frequently identified strengths within each cultural group were noted through analysis of question 1a, and further elaborated upon through analysis of questions 1b–f (see appendix 7A). Due to the small sample size in this study, the family strengths are discussed by cultural group with some attention to generation. Generational trends are noted and later discussed with respect to implications for future research and practice. Given the preliminary nature of the study, no attempt to generalize beyond these samples or comparisons is attempted.

Results

For the purposes of this analysis, the informants are grouped according to cultural background and generation. In the family strengths literature, there is widespread disagreement about which strengths are the most important in their ability to help families succeed in the face of adversity. This is supported by the fact that in our review of eleven empirical studies, a total of twenty-nine different family strengths were identified (see appendix 7B). Given this lack of consensus in the family strengths literature, we do not claim, for example, that the nine Somali informants out of nineteen who identified respect or communication as important components of strong families speak definitively for all Somalis. We do assume, however, that knowing which strengths are most frequently mentioned by insiders from strong three-generation families can provide us with useful information about these families and allow for a cross-cultural analysis of the similarities and differences between the strengths of the Hmong and Somalis. We also believe that the information provided by informants about the meaning of such concepts as respect or communication will be particularly relevant in our ability to better understand how strengths are operationalized within refugee families.

Hmong Families

When asked, "What do you think are some characteristics that make your family strong?" Hmong informants most frequently identified *love* (ten out of twenty-four) and *communication* (eight out of twenty-four). Additional strengths emerged when analyzed by generation. Grandparents most frequently identified *love* (four out of six) and *role modeling* (four out of six), parents identified *communication* (three out of seven) and *religion* (three out of seven), and adolescents identified *communication* (five out of eleven) and *love* (four out of eleven). The elaborations of Hmong families on each of these constructions reveal the overlapping characteristics of family strengths.

Hmong informants defined *love* as mutual caring and help. The ability of children to aid parents during times of need was seen as a particularly important way to display love. When asked to provide an example of how love was shown in her family, a grandmother described a situation in which her grandchildren knew their mother was the sole provider for their family. They demonstrated their love by listening to their mother and each other, and assisted in caring for each other in her absence. Similarly, an adolescent girl defined love as doing things for parents without expecting to be paid, and providing money for family members during times of need. Although older family members typically modeled love for younger members of the family, everyone in the home was responsible for showing love. The overlapping nature of family strengths was revealed when families were asked to talk about the effects of love. When it was present, family members experienced general well-being, including patience, respect, happiness, and good communication. In its absence, they felt the family would disintegrate. An adolescent boy stated that without love, parents would give their children up for adoption and family members would hate each other. Similarly, an adolescent girl stated that family members would hate and disown each other, and not be able to live in the same room or house with one another.

Communication was defined as talking to one another and addressing problems together. The mutuality of communication was emphasized. One father stated the importance of parents not only talking to their children but allowing children to talk to them as well. One family encouraged their children to write down their thoughts and share them with parents so that parents could then provide explanations or specific examples. Similarly, an adolescent girl's example of communication was that of siblings talking to one another about stressful issues in their lives and helping one another as needed. She also described the importance of family members keeping current on each other's lives by talking to one another during dinner. Family meetings were frequently used as a way to increase communication, and these meetings often occurred during dinner time when all family members were present. Other everyday events during which communication occurred were when parents were driving the children to school, or at the end of a day prior to going to bed. One mother stated that she talks to her children before bedtime to hear about their day and determine if they have any concerns. If she finds that they are unable to solve whatever problem may have emerged, they then consult someone who can help them identify a solution. As with love, family members learned about communication through elderly family members. When communication was present in the home, family members were happy and provided help to each other as needed. In the absence of communication, it was thought by some that relative chaos would result. When describing such a scenario, a mother stated there would be yelling, misunderstandings, and family members would not know what was happening in each other's lives. An adolescent girl stated that without communication in the home, parents would not be able to tell children right from wrong and children would not try to do well in school.

Somali Families

When asked, "What do you think are some characteristics that make your family strong?" Somali interviewees most frequently identified *respect* (nine out of nineteen), *communication* (nine out of nineteen), *unity* (eight out of nineteen), and *religion* (seven out of nineteen). Their answers varied by generation, where grandparents most frequently identified *religion* (two out of two), parents identified *religion* (four out of seven), and adolescents identified *respect* (six out of ten), *communication* (six out of ten), and *unity* (six out of ten). As with the Hmong families, their elaborations on each of these constructions reveal the overlapping nature of family strengths.

Somalis define *respect* as listening to older family members and taking their advice. When expanding on how her family demonstrates respect, a grandmother described a situation in which her grandson was suspended from school due to a fight with another child, and planned to return to school to fight the boy. When the grandmother talked to him about the consequences of fighting, including how it may bring harm to their family, he demonstrated respect for his grandmother by taking her advice and calling an end to the fight. As illustrated here, older members of Somali families typically modeled respect to younger members. They also placed emphasis on mutuality, as each member of the family was expected to be respectful to others. When asked about the consequences of having respect in the family, family members felt the presence of respect would prevent problems, and its absence would lead to family disintegration. In a typical answer given by Somalis across generations, an adolescent girl stated that without respect, family members could not reside in the same house due to "fighting and rudeness."

Communication was defined by Somali interviewees as both listening to one another and talking out concerns. The concept of sharing was a common thread in this construction. From everyday events to plans for the future, communication was viewed as an opportunity to share thoughts with one another. When recalling her family's initial arrival in the United States, a mother stated that the family was able to become strong because she and her husband communicated with their children. In addition to talking with them about problems at school, the parents listened and discussed their children's fears, hopes, and dreams for the future. Communication meant sharing in the problems of the family as well as the joys. An adolescent girl stated that if one family member had a problem, the entire family rather than the individual would work toward a solution. As with respect, family members learned how to communicate in this way from older family members. An overlap in family strengths was revealed when a mother stated that because she and her husband modeled good communication to their children, the children in turn became mature young adults who respected them. As with respect, an absence of communication in the family was expected to create family disintegration.

Somalis defined the strength of *unity* as a physical connection. This included both living together in the same home and engaging in activities together. An adolescent boy stated he and his family members "stick together" by living together until they are mature enough to manage their own lives. In a more specific example of unity, a mother described how during religious holidays, her family members "come together" to shop and have fun despite scheduling difficulties due to school and work. When asked whose responsibility it was to make sure the family had unity, several Somali informants stated that while parents taught their children about unity, it was the responsibility of the entire family to maintain it. The metaphor of family disintegration reemerged when interviewees were asked to describe what would happen in the absence of unity. As a poignant reminder of her family's history, an adolescent girl stated that her family would not be able to reside in the same home because they would be scattered around the world.

Lastly, *religion* was defined by Somali families as not only believing Islamic principles, but practicing them. Belief in *Allah* was one of the cornerstones of having religion. A grandfather viewed religion as a path to follow in life and felt it helped create family unity. He described how his family gathers at the home of one of his children to break fasting during religious holidays and discuss issues related to the family. "Sticking to religion," he stated, could keep a person "good forever." As exemplified in this statement, Somali families felt religion had a certain protective power. A father described his family's devotion to religious values and *Allah*, and stated that *Allah* accepted their prayers and kept them safe during the civil war. The overlapping nature of family strengths was again revealed through discussions about religion. Interviewees believed that the absence of religion would diminish other strengths, from the family's respect for one another to their ability to maintain unity. The recurring theme of family disintegration emerged when a mother explained that in the absence of religion, her family could not have survived. They would have "broken apart" and experienced "unbearable" events such as children running away from home and being disrespectful and disobedient. As with each of the other strengths identified by Somali informants, religion was taught by the older members of the family. Although the responsibility of teaching religion seemed to weigh more heavily on young adults after they married, the overall responsibility remained with the grandparents.

Discussion

This exploratory study presents the results of a comparative investigation of Hmong and Somali family strengths. The results indicate several interesting comparisons, each with implications for those who seek to understand family strengths and those who make policies for and work directly with immigrant families like the Hmong and the Somali.

Somali and Hmong families learn family strengths through intergenerational transmission. Family members from both groups and all three generations consistently emphasize the role of elders in teaching family strengths. Whether it is through verbal communication or role modeling, older family members are responsible for transmitting family strengths to younger generations. This finding is consistent within the hierarchical structure of both the Hmong and Somali cultures, where hierarchy is observed within the family and externally through clan systems in the community.

Somali and Hmong families conceptualize family strengths as overlapping constructs. For the families in this study, the effects of having one family strength was likely to lead to the presence of others. Somali families, for example, felt the presence of communication in the family would also lead to respect, whereas Hmong families felt it was the presence of love which would lead to respect. This finding is consistent with previous findings on the overlapping nature of family strengths (Schumm, 1985).

Somali families have greater agreement on family strengths than Hmong families. As a group, Somali informants consistently identified respect, communication, unity, and religion more frequently than any other family strength. Hmong informants, on the other hand, had less agreement overall that their most frequently mentioned family strengths such as love, communication, role modeling, and religion were'the most salient. While it is difficult to make any generalizations when fewer than half the informants identify the same strength, the case can be made that the amount of agreement on unprompted key words identifying the same family strengths consistently cited in Western research literature is quite remarkable. The apparent distinction between rates of agreement between Hmong and Somali informants could be a result of different rates of acculturation into U.S. society based on length of time spent living in the United States. Whereas many Hmong families have adolescents who were born and raised in the United States, a majority of Somali adolescents emigrated to the United States with their families within the past decade. Given their more recent arrival and fearful status in the post-9/11 environment, the shared understanding of family strengths for Somalis may be the result of the overtly hostile environment and their understanding that they need to stay strong and unified in the face of it. Most of the Hmong, on the other hand, have been in the United States for a longer time period than the Somalis, and are likely to be more divergent in their thinking about the nature and characteristics of family strengths and achieve a lesser degree of consensus across generations. This suggests that family strengths may be more consistently understood and valued in the early years after migration, and become less important as each generation adapts to life in their new environment.

Family strengths identified in the literature fit *the experiences of Somali and Hmong families.* Communication, religion, and respect were among the most frequently identified family strengths in the literature and by both the Somali and Hmong individuals in this study. This link between the two ethnic groups and the literature on family strengths is helpful as researchers, service providers, program leaders, and educators attempt to discern which of the many characteristics that have been identified by one study or group are most important for immigrant families.

Intergenerational Variation in Family Strengths

Given the very different lives led by elder, middle, and younger generations of immigrants, it is not altogether surprising that some intergenerational differences were identified with respect to family strengths. In Hmong families, grandparents more frequently identified love and role modeling, while there were no apparent patterns for parents or adolescents. For Somalis, the older generations most frequently named religion, whereas adolescents named respect, communication, and unity. While we have little information about these diverse perspectives within Somali families, different rates of acculturation could also be a factor. Despite the small sample size in this study, it was the adolescents who more often stressed the mutuality of strengths like communication, including both listening and speaking. This is noteworthy given that most of these adolescents lived in hierarchical family structures where typically the parents talk and the children listen. This finding reveals the importance of uncovering different meanings of strengths across generations in order to obtain a more holistic picture of what constitutes a strong immigrant family.

Additional findings of interest in this study included the seemingly categorical thinking of Hmong and Somali families. They believed that the absence of any one strength would lead to family disintegration, whereas its presence would lead to a well-functioning family. This dichotomy could be a byproduct of interview question 1d, which asked what would happen if the family did not have a particular family strength. It could also be the result of strongly held beliefs that represent powerful value orientations within families. For example, according to Hmong culture, if the young are disrespectful of elders, the entire structure of filial piety is threatened, and along with it the family beliefs and practices that uphold the hierarchical structure of the family.

Strengths, Limitations, and Implications

The principal strength of this study was its attention to two new groups of refugees in the United States within the context of the family strengths literature. By taking a strengths, rather than deficits approach to studying these groups, this study provided several implications for practice which could be used to empower such families by both recognizing and building on the strengths they bring to a new environment. This is more important today than ever, given that increasing numbers of both Hmong and Somalis in the United States make it more likely that they will be seen by service providers and educators in the context of counseling, education, and social work. Another strength of this study was its inclusion of three-generation Hmong and Somali families. Despite a small sample size, the preliminary data obtained from Somalis in particular, showed that religion may not be as important a family strength for adolescents as it is for their parents and grandparents.

The main limitation of this study was its small sample size. Despite significant amounts of time spent within the respective communities, only four three-generation Hmong families and three three-generation Somali families were successfully recruited into this study. Although the overall sample size of forty-three informants is respectable for a qualitative study, more insights about generational perspectives could be added with a larger number of interviews with each generation. Another limitation in this study was the inability to tape-record participants and capture their own voices. The request by Somali families to forego tape-recording was honored and applied to Hmong interviews as well. Consequently, it was not possible to capture the richness of the informants' language and the fullness of their stories through note-taking.

The findings in this study have several important implications for research, policy, and practice. The emphasis on both divergent and congruent meanings of family strengths across generations within strong families deserves additional attention by researchers. Each generation in immigrant families is likely to view the family and the resettlement problems it faces in diverse ways, depending on its knowledge base and its position within the family structure and community. Elders, adults, and adolescents can be expected to define strengths in somewhat different ways and to judge which strengths are most important in the new context. Attention to this diversity will help to further elaborate the family strengths construct. The convergence of the research literature and both Hmong and Somali informants around the family strengths of communication, religion, and respect seems important as a starting point for future research with immigrant populations and program/service development for migrating families. Future studies that examine how and under what circumstances individuals, generations, and families demonstrate, build, and use these strengths can provide useful information for policy makers and family service providers who seek to facilitate adaptation to the new environment.

These findings also have implications for policy. As refugees, these immigrants are more likely to need financial, educational, and mental-health services as they adapt to life in a new country, although pride and other barriers may inhibit the likelihood that they will use such services. Knowledge about how these families succeed, and how they develop, maintain, and promote strengths within their extended families, can help policy makers and service providers to better understand what the newcomers are able to do for themselves and what types of policies would be both appropriate and helpful. As indicated in the present study, for example, it makes little sense to restrict family reunification to the adult and younger generations, while restricting the older generation since elders assist families to be strong in the face of resettlement adversity.

Finally, if service providers such as social workers and resettlement workers are able to identify one or more strengths within immigrant families, perhaps they will be able to assist them to develop other overlapping strengths that lead to successful adaptation. Knowing what to look for and how to develop strengths may assist service providers to focus on the competence of these families rather than their deficits. As indicated by the present study, family service providers who work in these communities should involve older family members as *consultants* and be aware that the hierarchy of elders may support or counteract their efforts.

Appendix 7A: Questions Asked of Respondents

1. [A community leader] has identified your family as being a strong one. What do you think are some characteristics that make your family strong?
   a. What do you mean by [each characteristic identified by interviewee]?
   b. What does it look like or what happens when your family is being [each characteristic identified by interviewee]?
   c. Please give me an example of a time when your family was [each characteristic identified by interviewee]?
   d. What do you think would happen if your family did not have [each characteristic identified by interviewee]?
   e. How did your family develop or learn to have [each characteristic identified by interviewee]?
   f. Who in the family is responsible for making sure that the family has/ is being [each characteristic identified by interviewee]?

Appendix 7B: Twenty-nine Family Strengths Identified in the Empirical Literature

See the table on the following page.

Table 7B.1.

Article / Strengths	Stinnett & Sauer (1977)	Stinnett (1979)	Royse & Turner (1980)	Stinnett et al. (1982)	Casas et al. (1984)	Knaub et al. (1984)	Brigman et al. (1986)	Hurd et al. (1995)	Greeff & LeRoux (1999)	Medora et al. (2002)	Usita & Blieszner (2002)
Strengths											
Achievement			X								
Adaptability		X	X								
Appreciation	X				X				X	X	
Closeness						X	X			X	
Commitment		X		X		X	X			X	
Communication	X	X		X	X	X				X	X
Concern						X	X				
Consensus											X
Cooperation			X								
Coping			X						X	X	X
Education									X		
Effectiveness of handling conflict							X	X			
Feeling of worth						X	X	X			
Humor				X							
Individuality				X							
Kinship bonds			X						X		
Love/affect expression				X	X			X			
No strict discipline of kids			X								
Optimism about future			X								
Perceptions of happiness						X					
Religion/spirituality	X	X	X	X	X		X	X	X	X	
Rely on others											
Respect			X	X				X	X		X
Seek clarification											
Self-reliance									X		
Time/activities together	X	X	X	X	X	X	X			X	
Trust					X			X			X
Understanding				X				X	X		
Work orientation			X								

References

Brigman, K. M., Schons, J., & Stinnett, N. (1986). Strengths of families in a society under stress: A study of strong families in Iraq. *Family Perspective, 20*(1), 61–73.

Casas, C. C., Stinnett, N., Williams, R. C., DeFrain, J., & Lee, P. A. (1984). Identifying family strengths in Latin American families. *Family Perspective, 18*, 11–17.

Darboe, K. (2003). New immigrants in Minnesota: The Somali immigration and assimilation. *Journal of Developing Societies, 19*(4), 458–472.

Detzner, D. (2004). *Elder voices: Southeast Asian families in the United States.* Walnut Creek, CA: Alta Mira Press.

Greeff, A. P. (2000). Characteristics of families that function well. *Journal of Family Issues, 21*(8), 948–962.

Greeff, A. P., & LeRoux, M. C. (1999). Parents' and adolescents' perceptions of a strong family. *Psychological Reports, 84*, 1219–1224.

Halcon, L. L., Robertson, C. L., Savik, K., Johnson, D., Spring, M. A., Butcher, J. N., et al. (2004). Trauma and coping in Somali and Oromo refugee youth. *Journal of Adolescent Health, 35*, 17–25.

Hawley, D. R., & DeHaan, L. (1996). Toward a definition of family resilience. *Family Process, 35*, 283–298.

Heitritter, D. L. (1999). Somali family strength: Working in the communities. A report prepared for Family & Children's Service, Minneapolis, Minnesota and the University of Minnesota Extension Service for use in Community Outreach.

Hmong Cultural and Resource Center. Retrieved February 22, 2006, from store .yahoo.com/hmongcultural/index.html.

Hurd, E. P., Moore, C., & Rogers, R. (1995). Quiet success: Parenting strengths among African Americans. *Families in Society: The Journal of Contemporary Human Services, 76*, 434–443.

Kamya, A. H. (1997). African immigrants in the United States: The challenge for research and practice. *Social Work, 42*(2), 154–165.

Knaub, P. K., Hanna, S. L., & Stinnett, N. (1984). Strengths of remarried families. *Journal of Divorce, 7*(3), 41–55.

Littlejohn-Blake, S. M., & Darling, C. A. (1993). Understanding the strengths of African American Families. *Journal of Black Studies, 23*(4), 460–471.

McCubbin, H. I., & McCubbin, M. A. (1988). Typologies of resilient families: Emerging roles of social class and ethnicity. *Family Relations, 37*, 247–254.

Medora, N. P., Larson, J. H., & Dave, P. B. (2000). Attitudes of East-Indian college students toward family strengths. *Journal of Comparative Family Studies, 31*(4), 407–425.

Office of Immigration Statistics. (2006). *Yearbook of Immigration Statistics: 2005.* Washington, DC: U.S. Department of Homeland Security.

Reiboldt, W., & Goldstein, A. E. (2000). Positive coping strategies among immigrant Cambodian families: An ethnographic case study. *Family and Consumer Sciences Research Journal, 28*(4), 489–513.

Ronningen, B. J. (2004). Minnesota State Demographic Center. Retrieved February 21, 2006 from www.demography.state.mn.us/PopNotes/EvaluatingEstimates .pdf.

Rousseau, C., Abdelwahed, M.-B., & Moreau, S. (2001). Trauma and extended separation from family among Latin American and African refugees in Montreal. *Psychiatry, 64*(1), 40–59.

Royse, D. D., & Turner, G. T. (1980). Strengths of black families: A black community's perspective. *Social Work, 25*, 407–409.

Schumm, W. R. (1985). Beyond relationship characteristics of strong families: Constructing a model of family strengths. *Family Perspective, 19*(1), 1–9.

Stinnett, N. (1979b). Strengthening families. *Family Perspective, 13*(Winter), 3–9.

Stinnett, N., Sanders, G., DeFrain, J., & Parkhurst, A. (1982). A nationwide study of families who perceive themselves as strong. *Family Perspective, 16*(1), 15–22.

Stinnett N., & Sauer, K. H. (1977). Relationship characteristics of strong families. *Family Perspective, 11*(4), 3–11.

Usita, P. M., & Blieszner, R. (2002). Immigrant family strengths: Meeting communication challenges. *Journal of Family Issues, 23*(2), 266–286.

Weine, S., Muzurovic, N., Kulauzovic, Y., Besic, S., Lezic, A., Mujagic, A., et al. (2004). Family consequences of refugee trauma. *Family Process, 43*(2), 147–160.

About the Authors

Daniel F. Detzner, Ph.D., is a professor in the Department of Post Secondary Teaching and Learning at the University of Minnesota, 246 Appleby Hall, 128 Pleasant Street SE, Minneapolis, MN 55455. Phone: 612-625-5366. E-mail: ddetzner@umn.edu.

Ayşem R. Şenyürekli, Ph.D., is a graduate research assistant in the Department of Post Secondary Teaching and Learning, and instructor in the Department of Family Social Science at the University of Minnesota, 290 McNeal Hall, 1985 Buford Avenue, St. Paul, MN 55108. E-mail: kara0100@umn.edu.

Khadija S. Sheikh, B.S., is a graduate student in the Master of Social Work program at the University of St. Catherine/St. Thomas University, St. Paul, Minnesota. E-mail: shei0028@umn.edu.

Pa Nhia D. Yang, M.A., is a research assistant in the Department of Post Secondary Teaching and Learning and doctoral student in the Department of Family Social Science at the University of Minnesota, 290 McNeal Hall, 1985 Buford Avenue, St. Paul, MN 55108. E-mail: pnyang@umn.edu.

Migrating Latinas and the Grief Process 8

RICHARD B. MILLER AND DAIANA A. GONZÁLEZ

Abstract

The authors applied a theoretical model of the bereavement grief process to examine grief experienced by immigration and loss of home country. Interviews were conducted with twelve Hispanic immigrant married women in Utah. The sample represented individuals from different Latin American countries and the data were collected in four different cities. They had been living in the United States from two to ten years. Results indicated that the grieving process from immigration is similar to that experienced upon the loss of a loved one.

Keywords: Grief, Bereavement, Grief Process, Latinas, Acculturation, Qualitative

THE HISPANIC POPULATION in the United States is growing rapidly. It has increased 50 percent between 1990 and 2000 and, by 2002, more than one in eight people in the United States was of Hispanic origin. A significant percentage of Hispanics residing

Address all correspondence to Dr. Richard B. Miller, School of Family Life at Brigham Young University, office number 2086B JFSB, Provo, UT 84602. Phone: 801-422-2860. Fax: 801-422-0230.

in the United States was born in foreign countries, with two in five (40 percent) of Hispanics being born abroad (U.S. Census Bureau, 2002). As the percentage of Hispanics in the United States increases, the need for research in the mental health fields pertaining to that population also becomes more necessary.

Migrating to a new country requires substantial physical and psychological adjustment. As immigrants adjust to the new country, they undergo an acculturation process. As acculturation takes place, cultural minorities begin to take part in the cultural traditions, values, beliefs, and practices of the host culture (Buddington, 2002; Landrine & Klonoff, 1994). Acculturative stress is a factor affecting Hispanic immigrants. Migrating families often move into an unknown environment, leaving their loved ones behind, while knowing that a return to their native countries will be difficult, if not impossible (Guarnaccia, DeLaCancela & Carrillo, 1989).

When Hispanics come to the United States, they experience multiple losses. Parkes (1996) defined grief as a reaction to loss. Grief is a consequence of losses perceived as significant. Therefore, loss and grief are both components of the psychological experience of Hispanic immigrants. This study qualitatively examines the experience of Hispanic married women as they migrate to the United States. Due to the amount of literature supporting Parkes's model of the grief process with other populations, it was used as the theoretical framework for the present study (Bartrop, Hancock, Braig & Porrit, 1992; Cleiren, 1993; Levy, Derby & Martinkowski, 1993; Parkes, 1970, 1996; Parkes & Weiss, 1983; Prigerson et al., 1996; Zisook & Shuchter, 1993).

Immigration and the grief process have been studied to some extent; however, the amount of research targeted specifically at Hispanic immigrants and the grief process is minimal. As the Hispanic population increases, the demand for research related to this specific population also increases. Using the theoretical frame of loss and grief, the present study looks at the psychological and emotional effects of Hispanics relocating to a new country.

Literature Review

The Grief Process

In his book *Bereavement: Studies of Grief in Adult Life*, Parkes (1996) proposed a theory on grief in which he described grief as being a process, not a state. In addition, Parkes did not describe grief as having a prolonged period of depression, but rather as acute and episodic pangs that are severe episodes of pain and anxiety. At first, following bereavement, these pangs occur frequently, but as time passes they become less frequent and are mainly triggered by events that bring memories of the loss.

Parkes described *numbness* as the first phase of grief. Numbness leads to a lack of overt emotion. Disbelief is also part of this phase and occurs when the person denies that a loss has occurred. The function of disbelief is to enable the bereaved person to avoid pain-provoking thoughts or to take away the pain associated with the thoughts.

Searching (pining), a restless desire of the bereaved person to find the lost person, is the second phase of grief. It can become manifest in more than one way. As the person searches for the dead person, she is involved in selecting places in which to look for her. Parkes described searching as having seven different components, which are: (a) alarm, tension, and a state of arousal; (b) restless movement; (c) preoccupations with thoughts of the lost person; (d) development of a perceptual set for that person; (e) loss of interest in personal appearance and other matters that normally occupy attention; (f) direction of attention toward those parts of the environment in which the lost person is most likely to be; and (g) calling for the lost person. Other aspects of the searching phase are preoccupation with thoughts of the events leading up to the loss of the person, happy memories replacing painful recollections, and repeating habits that were performed with and by the lost person.

Parkes (1996) emphasized feelings of anger and guilt. Guilt is expressed in the form of self-reproach, and anger is often associated with guilt. The target and expression of anger varies among people. At times, the person left behind seeks someone to blame, such as someone else or her own self. Parkes found that anger is apparent in the pining phase of grief and dissipates in the next phase.

As pining diminishes, a period of *disorganization and despair* follows, during which time there is uncertainty, aimlessness, and apathy. The phase of disorganization and despair is not a clear-cut phase, and it can reoccur multiple times. The leading emotion during this phase is depression. In many cases, the roles of the survivor change since she has to fill the gap left by the dead person. As this takes place, one starts to identify more with the dead person by performing the activities and roles that the dead person used to perform. During the disorganization and despair phase, the person left behind concentrates more in the past rather than in the future.

Recovery, the final element of the grief process, constitutes gaining a new identity. In the case of a widow, recovery is achieved as the widow goes from living a *widow* identity into living a *woman* identity. The bereaved person progressively regains interest in the world. Furthermore, she gradually stops looking at the past and starts looking at the future. Recovery involves her starting to gain a new identity independent of the dead person.

Research on Immigrants and Grief

There has been little research studying the grief process as it relates to Latino immigrants. While some research has been conducted on immigration and grief, the amount relating to Latinos and migratory grief is limited. Nevertheless a modest amount of qualitative and quantitative research has been conducted.

Qualitative research to explore the topic of migratory grief in divergent cultures has been performed. Schneller (1981) interviewed thirteen Soviet-Jewish immigrants and identified three different phases and symptoms of mourning. She discovered that the women found a barrier to integrating and adjusting to the new culture. Men, on the other hand, indicated a more complete resolution of mourning than women. This finding concurs with Espin's (1987) assertion that the psychological impact on migrating women is different than that on migrating men.

Additional qualitative research exploring migratory grief has been conducted. Aroian (1990) interviewed twenty-five Polish immigrants and identified common themes in the interviewees' responses. The themes were loss and disruption, occupation, language, subordination, feeling at home, and grief resolution and return visits. Emmenegger-Hindin (1993) found a universal theme of grieving based on a sample of twelve women from three different countries (Ecuador, Russia, and Japan). Her research results indicated that grieving is a normal part of the acculturation process. Ward and Styles (2003) conducted a study in which they surveyed 154 participants and interviewed 40 of them. They found that women who fostered a new identity were able to reinvent themselves. On the other hand, those who did not experienced distress. Significantly, in their study interviewees experienced growth in the self in that they indicated being more confident and having more emotional strength and independence. Nevertheless, not all of them reported a sense of belonging to the new country.

All of the qualitative studies mentioned thus far show that immigrants experience different aspects of migratory grief. A difference was found in gender and the intensity of grief. However, even though these studies supported the notion that immigrants experience grief, none of the studies were specifically targeted to the Hispanic population.

The quantitative research performed in the realm of migratory grief has identified the existence of distress and depression. Prudent (1988) conducted a study which involved one hundred Haitian men and women, in which she found a correlation between Haitians' symptoms of psychological distress and their level of grieving. These symptoms diminished with the passage of time. Brenner (1991) conducted a study with Mexican immigrant subjects and found a relationship between low acculturation, high depression, and high-perceived losses. Lakatos (1992) identified migratory grief as being one of the predictors of psychological symptomatology in Hispanic immigrants. Casado and Leung (2001) researched migratory grief in Chinese elderly immigrants. In their sample of 150 Chinese immigrants, those who had higher degrees of migratory grief, had lower English proficiency, were younger, and visited their home country were more likely to feel depressed. The present qualitative study examined the grief process of Hispanic immigrants through the lens of Parkes's (1996) theory. Thus, it contributes to the existing knowledge on migratory grief, in general, and to the Hispanic experience, in particular.

Methods

Semi-structured, face-to-face interviews were conducted to examine the grief process of Hispanic immigrant married women. Seidman (1998) stated that because the stories of those we interview are of worth, people we interview are hard to code with numbers, and finding pseudonyms for subjects is a sensitive task. Most importantly, through semi-structured interviews, the researchers were able to acquire a deeper and fuller understanding of the experience of Hispanics who migrate into the United States.

Sample

Due to the difficulty in identifying and selecting participants randomly, this study used a convenience sample of subjects located through different contacts. A snowball sample was used. Participants were recruited from four different cities where there is a large concentration of Hispanic immigrants in the state of Utah.

The researchers sampled twelve female Hispanic immigrants who migrated with their spouses from various Latin American countries (Peru, Mexico, Argentina, Chile, Ecuador, Uruguay, and Colombia). The ages of the participants ranged from twenty-eight to forty-three, with almost half of the participants being in their thirties. In order to be eligible to participate, participants had to have resided in the United States for a minimum of two years and a maximum of ten years. It was not expanded past ten years since too long of a time span might cause problems with the accuracy of information.

Interview Procedures

Each participant was interviewed separately by one interviewer and the interviews were audio-taped. Since the interviewer is the main research tool in a qualitative interview (Payne, 1999), careful consideration was given as to who the interviewers should be. Three Hispanic female interviewers were used, based on the assumption that Hispanic immigrants would feel more comfortable talking to someone of their ethnicity about sensitive immigration issues. The interviews were conducted in Spanish.

Instruments

QUESTIONNAIRE. The protocol of the semi-structured interview was designed by the researchers. Questions were based on the grief process identified by Parkes (1996). In order to avoid biases in the questions, three separate researchers participated in adapting the questions for the interview.

The questionnaire consisted of three main sections. The first section was designed to gather general information regarding the participants' experience when coming to the United States. The second was composed of more specific questions related to the participants' experience in the United States as it relates to Parkes's theory of the grief process. The last set of questions aimed at understanding the dynamics of the couple's marital relationship as they migrated into the United States. Interviews lasted approximately ninety minutes. The data presented here will only cover the two first sections.

Analysis of Data

The interviews were audio tape-recorded and then transcribed. Data management was the first step toward data analysis (Brewer, 2000). Data management is a means of organizing data into manageable units. The coders then moved into qualitative description and pattern-searching (Brewer, 2000). As part of the process, coders picked out events that were considered focal for the participants. They further found descriptions of the behaviors that each code represents. Following the qualitative description of the codes, coders searched for patterns within the data. The culminating step in the data analysis was finding deviant cases.

Results

Initially, Parkes's grief framework was used to establish the categories. One additional category was uncovered through the process. The new category was *initial mixed emotions*. The original Parkes's categories were numbness, searching, anger and guilt, disorganization and despair, and recovery. Two categories (searching and disorganization and despair) were further divided into subcategories. The following chart illustrates the findings as they compare to the grief process:

Bereavement Grief	*Migratory Grief*
1. *Numbness*	1. *Initial Mixed Emotions*
2. *Searching*	2. *Searching*
a. Preoccupation with thoughts of the lost person	a. Preoccupation with thoughts of the lost country
b. Direction of attention toward parts of the environment in which the lost person is likely to be	b. Direction of attention toward parts of environment that remind them of their country
c. Calling the lost person	c. Calling those they left behind
3. *Anger and Guilt*	3. *Anger and Guilt*
4. *Disorganization and Despair*	4. *Disorganization and Despair*
a. Depression	a. Sadness
b. Change in Roles	b. Change in Roles
	c. Language
5. *Recovery*	5. *Recovery*

Numbness

None of the women interviewed related experiences similar to those of the numbness phase described by Parkes (1996). Additionally, they did not describe outright disbelief that the loss occurred. As part of disbelief, Parkes illustrates widows as trying to convince themselves that the loss had not happened. He further specified that this type of outright disbelief is rare. Disbelief as described by Parkes was not a theme that emerged in the interviews.

    Instead, the women interviewed described their initial emotional reaction to having left their native country and arriving to a new country as one of having *mixed emotions*. Only two women described their initial reaction as entirely positive, and two women described it as being entirely negative. The remaining women reported having had both positive and negative reactions. They described being amazed by the novelty of the host country. They used words such as "surprise" and "amazement" to describe their reaction to the United States. However, they also reported having experienced negative emotions, such as sadness and frustration. When asked how she first felt when arriving, a thirty-five-year-old woman who had been in the United States for three and a half years stated, "The truth is that when I first arrived, I felt the novelty of having arrived here. The environment, another type of life, the United States seemed so beautiful."

However, she later stated, "I would cry because I missed my customs. I wanted to go back after the first week, but I would tell myself, no, an airplane ticket is too expensive." Thus, most of the women described their initial reaction as one of having mixed feelings. They were surprised by the novelty of being in a new country as well as sad for having left behind components of their native country.

Searching

Three components of searching were evident in the data gathered. These were: preoccupation with thoughts of their native country, direction of attention toward parts of the environment that remind them of their country, and calling those they left behind.

PREOCCUPATION WITH THOUGHTS OF THEIR NATIVE COUNTRY. All the respondents reported that during the early period of time in the United States, they mainly thought about the past. They were preoccupied with thoughts of the family and culture left behind. As time progressed, thoughts started to turn toward the present and future. However, thoughts about the past and their native country were still present to a lesser extent. Only one of the respondents, who had been in the United States for four years, seemed to still be constantly concentrating on what she left behind. Another respondent, originally from Chile, specified that she mainly thought about the past for the first two years of her time in the United States. The factor that made her start thinking about the future in the United States was having a baby. When talking about the future, all but one talked with optimism.

ATTENTION TO PARTS OF THE ENVIRONMENT THAT REMIND THEM OF THEIR COUNTRY. This category has been divided into three subcategories: activities, traditions, and return visits. They all fit under the main category in that they involve a behavior that will guide them to momentarily find elements of their culture that they have to some extent left behind. Commonalities in all three subcategories were found amongst the interviewees' responses.

All but three of the respondents reported going to places and activities that reminded them of their native country. These activities can either be in their homes or outside their homes. One of the respondents had actively been involved in planning cultural activities. Others reported trying to celebrate special dates in the manner that they did in their countries. Other forms of being involved in behaviors that direct them to their cultural roots included listening to music and watching videos of their countries.

Half of the interviewees reported trying to maintain their cultural traditions. Food was an essential part of this. They tried to make the same food they ate in their countries. As one of the interviewees stated, "The days when I cook, we always eat Peruvian food." Most of the women interviewed stated that cooking and eating food from their country reminds them of their country.

Only two of the interviewees had the opportunity to have a return visit to their native country. Nevertheless, there was a big proportion of the interviewees who either planned on returning or at times had the desire to return. One participant said that she missed her family so much that she frequently had thoughts of returning to her native Peru. Other women also described having had, at some point or another, the desire to return. One interviewee stated that her family makes plans every year to go visit their country, but that they have never been able to do so. Both the thought and action of returning to their native countries illustrates a search for what they left behind.

CALLING THOSE THEY LEFT BEHIND. All of the respondents reported frequent telephone calls to family members left behind, regardless of the amount of time they had been in the United States. The number of times they called varied from two to three times a week, to every other week. The frequency of the calls did not diminish over time.

Anger and Guilt

Anger was mainly shown in terms of discontent and blaming. Similar to the anger characteristic of those mourning the loss of a loved one, the expression of anger varied from person to person. It was directed both outwardly toward external factors and inwardly upon themselves. For all of the respondents, most of the anger occurred in the early stages of life in the new country. As time progressed, most of the women demonstrated more affection toward the host country and less bitterness, discontent, and blaming. Nevertheless, there was one interviewee who, after having been in the United States for four years, still showed high levels of anger.

The most frequent form of anger described by more than half of the women interviewed was feeling discontent toward the people in the United States. In many cases, these women perceived racism directed toward them. However, most of the women recognized that only a few U.S. citizens expressed racism; the majority of Americans were kind people. One particular interviewee stated having felt upset toward the foreigners residing in the United States. She further specified that there is racism among the Hispanic population itself. This form of anger was expressed through discontent with others.

Anger was also demonstrated in the form of blaming. Interviewees reported blaming themselves for their problems as a consequence of migrating to a new country. At other times they blamed their husbands. One individual reported solely blaming her husband. She directly stated that at times she blamed her husband and then said, "I say to him: Why did you want to come here if we were fine in our country? I say that many times, but then my anger dissipates. Sometimes one speaks out of anger."

They all reported having found themselves in a state of blaming when they were enduring hardships. A pattern as to when blaming is most prevalent on a time line was not evident. Most of the respondents stated that they still sporadically found themselves engaged in blaming, and the blaming is usually triggered by current stressful situations.

Other forms of anger included resentful feelings toward the host country and toward their native countries. These forms of anger were not as prevalent as those described above. Two women reported feeling upset at the host country. One of them reported that her feelings toward the United States were of anger for it being such a good country. She stated when referring to the United States, "Why did it have to be such a good country? Why did we have to move so far away from our family?" Resentfulness was also expressed toward the native countries. Two women reported having strong negative emotions with regard to their native countries. One of them said the following when asked if she ever found herself blaming herself or others for the problems arising as a result of immigration:

Yes, I blame Mexico's government. If they would have good job opportunities with good salaries, if they would not increase the price of food
because they increase the price of food but not the salaries, if I could make
good money there in my country, of course I would not be here.

This statement shows resentment toward the native country. Furthermore, it
blames the native country for problems that arose as a result of immigration.

Disorganization and Despair

The interview data illustrated three main components of disorganization
and despair, which are: feelings of sadness, role changes, and language.

SADNESS. Parkes (1996) defined depression as the characteristic emotion
of the disorganization and despair phase. Although depression was not directly measured in this study, moments of sadness were described by all of
the interviewees. Hence, we chose to base this category on descriptions of
times when the respondents reported feeling sad. Measuring the severity
of depression (clinical versus situational) was not within the scope of this
study. However, most of the responses pointed toward situational depression, since it mainly occurred during stressful times.

All of the interviewees stated that the first year was the time during
which feelings of sadness were most prevalent. It coincided with being the
most stressful time, with finances being the main stress-provoking factor.
As time passed, feelings of sadness diminished. This indicates that their
experience is not characterized as a prolonged period of depression.

It was evident that following the initial period of sadness, it periodically
reemerged as acute and episodic pangs. The interviewees reported feeling
nostalgic during special events, such as birthdays and Christmas. A few
women reported feeling sad when their babies were born. They wished
that they could share that experience with family members not present in
this country. Other women started feeling sad when difficult events, such
as the death of family members, happened in their native countries. Many
of the participants reported feeling sad as a consequence of their inability
to be with their loved ones during such hard times.

This theme also included the extent to which they missed their native
country as a factor that affected their mood. The participants mainly missed
their families and their customs; they did not necessarily miss the country
itself. As one of the women stated, "Look, if we talk about missing Peru, I
never missed it. Missing my family is a whole different story."

CHANGE IN ROLES. An important component of disorganization and despair is the change in roles and how it affects those experiencing such changes. Only one of the interviewees reported not having had a change in roles. She specified that she worked in her native country, just like she does now. She also took care of her children in her country, which had not changed in the United States. On the other hand, many of the women said that they worked in their native and host countries, but that they still experienced a change in roles when coming to the United States. One woman reported that she does not currently work. She described being able to stay in the home with her children as a positive change. A few interviewees stated that their work status diminished in the United States. One expressed discontent with not being able to find a job similar to the one she had in her native country. She was the main provider in her native country and now her husband is the main provider. Although their role as members of the workforce has not changed drastically, many reported a change in their roles. Some reported working more hours and others reported working less.

Almost all of the women mentioned that there have been changes in their roles as women. One of them explained feeling more equal to her husband now. She noticed that her husband also changed his attitude toward women. Another respondent reported feeling she has more of an opportunity to develop as a woman in this country. She also mentioned she is able to do community work here that she would have never been able to do in her country of origin. In addition, an interviewee who was in the process of acquiring an advanced education degree along with her husband reported becoming more independent in the United States. All who described a change in their role as women in society reported being satisfied with the change.

LANGUAGE. Language was included as a subcategory of disorganization and despair. Not only were the interviewees exposed to a new culture and new roles, but they also found a language barrier. This language barrier led to more disorganization and despair. All of the interviewees reported language as being an essential component of their migratory experience. They stated feeling lost and unable to communicate with others.

Recovery

Although all of the women interviewed demonstrated different elements of recovery described by Parkes, only one of them illustrated full recovery.

They have gradually started looking at the future more than at the past. Furthermore, they all seemed to be gaining a new identity in the sense that they are integrating their old identity with the creation of a new identity. A woman from Ecuador described this process remarkably well:

> You leave your whole life behind. Everything that you were before, everything that you did before, you leave it all behind, because it is not enough here to say, "I was this." That does not count. What counts is what you are doing right now and what you have achieved here. I used to feel like I had left my whole past behind. It is like starting again here, trying to build everything from point zero. I then realized that everything that you were before is the base for everything that you will be in the future, for what you achieve in the future. But during the period of adaptation, during the first few months, one has little identity.

Parkes (1996) described recovery as gaining a new identity independent of the dead person. However, all of the interviewees' countries still seemed to be very present in their lives. Searching was a predominant characteristic of their responses. They still seemed to be making sense of the new culture and how it blends with their old culture.

Discussion

The results of this study suggest that, although there are some differences in the emotional reaction of those reporting the loss of a person by death and those migrating to a new country, the similarities seem to be more prevalent. While the grief of the bereaved can be traced to a specific person, the grief of Latina immigrants points toward the family and customs left behind.

The results of the study concur with Schneller (1981) and Arredondo-Dowd (1981) who described the migratory grief process in terms of phases. Arredondo-Dowd described a connection, mainly based on her clinical experience, between an immigrant's grief and Bowlby's (1961) phases of grief. Schneller identified three phases of mourning based on research done with Soviet-Jewish immigrants. The first phase presented was the protest phase, including the components of anxiety, physical stress, anger, preoccupation with the lost country, and idealization. The second phase was disorganization and depression. Most of the immigrants reported varying degrees of depression related to their immigration experience. The final phase in the process, as described by Schneller, was the detachment phase. Some of the similarities between the components of Schneller's phases and the ones found in the present study include anger, disorganization, and depression. The present study on Latina immigrants and the grief process supports the literature that describes the grief process in terms of phases.

The interviewees demonstrated having experienced anger and guilt similar to that described by Parkes. Anger, which was found both in Schneller's (1981) study and the present study, was a common theme among all of the respondents. It was mainly present in the form of discontent and blaming. Interestingly, anger was mainly prevalent during the first period of their migratory experience. This coincides with Parkes's and Schneller's research in that anger tends to occur during the first stages of grief. This study found that as time progresses, the feelings of anger begin to dissipate.

The second phase described by Schneller concurs with the third phase of this study. Experiences of disorganization and despair were related by those being interviewed. The most salient descriptions of disorganization and despair involved feelings of sadness, role changes, and language, all of which had an impact on the experience of the immigrants interviewed.

We decided to categorize despair in terms of sadness. All of the respondents reported feeling sad at some point or another. They described the first year as the hardest one, during which time sadness predominated. This indicates that sadness is not a prevalent characteristic present in the whole migratory grief process. Nevertheless, they did experience occasional pangs of sadness after the first year. These pangs of sadness were usually precipitated by events that made them think of their native country. These events were either of a dramatic or happy nature. When describing happy events, they described mixed feelings in which they were happy for what had happened, and at the same time sad for not being able to share those experiences with far away family members. Sadness was a part of the experience described by all of the interviewees. Our findings correlate with past research that connected distress and depression to migratory grief (Brenner, 1991; Casado & Leung, 2001; Prudent, 1988).

Much to our surprise, the study's participants did not miss the country itself, but what the country represents. The two main common denominators that they all started missing were their old customs and their families. This supports the literature on Latinos and their social support network. Smart and Smart (1995) described the loss of social support as being one of the most significant aspects of acculturative stress for Latinos. Once they come to the United States, they lose that social support network that is so essential to them. Many reported feeling lonely and missed having a physical interaction with their family. That may explain in part why contact with family in their country of origin did not decrease over time.

Language was mentioned by all the respondents as an important part of their experience. Hence, it cannot be ignored. Furthermore, language has been a prevalent theme in the immigration literature. Padilla and Perez (2003) hypothesized that having to cope with a new language is one of the factors that makes acculturation so difficult. Mirsky (1991) suggested that the loss of a mother tongue is accompanied by an internal loss. She argued that most immigrants struggle with learning the new language because of emotional and psychological factors that are tied to it. The results of the present study are consistent with the literature.

Although the literature on migratory grief and this study present many similarities between the experience of a bereaved person and immigrants, there are also differences. These differences could account for the difference in the initial emotional reaction. All of the immigrants interviewed came to the United States on their own volition; they all reported having voluntarily made the decision to migrate. According to the social exchange approach described by Ben-Sira (1997), the decision to migrate is made after the evaluation of the perceived costs and benefits of migrating. Taking this into account, when change is perceived solely as a gain, acceptance may not be hard. Immigrants migrate with the hope of finding a positive and more beneficent life. On the contrary, in most cases when one loses a loved one through death, it is not through one's own volition.

Differences were also found in the duration of time leading to recovery. The data gathered does not concur with Ward and Styles's (2003) findings that reinvention of the self can happen for some immediately after migration. On the contrary, the creation of a new identity is a process that takes time. The interview data of the present study concurs with Schneller's (1981) study, who found that twelve out of the thirteen participants had not completed the grief process. In the current study, only one out of the twelve participants had reached full recovery. Based on this information, it was found that migratory grief can be a lengthy process. This might be due in part to the length of the acculturation process, which some scholars believe can be present up to the third generation (Phinney & Flores, 2002).

The results of this study indicate that, although there are some differences between grieving for a deceased person and migratory grief, the similarities outnumber the differences. Furthermore, these results confirm that grief is a strong component of the migratory experience. It was also evident that the phases of migratory grief are not linear. The interviewees' accounts described how they at times fluctuated back and forth from one phase to another. Many similarities between the grief process described by Parkes and the experience of married Latina immigrants were found.

Limitations and Directions for Future Research

There are limitations that must be taken into account when examining the findings of this study. First, due to the nature of the qualitative study, the sample size was small and not chosen in a random process. Consequently, participants are not necessarily representative of the general population of Latina immigrants. However, participants were selected in a fashion that could increase the generalizability of the findings. The sample was gathered from four different cities in the Utah area, and it was representative of more than one nationality. These factors help reduce problems with generalizability. Nevertheless, the results should be looked at with caution prior to generalizing them to the entire female immigrant Latina population.

Using Parkes's theory as the main model for creating categories was a constraint of the study as well as one of the strengths. It was a strength in that it gave the researchers a well-grounded model as a comparison point for the experience of immigrants. Using Parkes's model was constraining in that it limited the researchers from finding other categories.

The findings of this study have specific implications for future research, in particular, migratory grief pertaining to Latino male immigrants. No research to date has been done solely targeting that specific population. Doing so would contribute to the general knowledge of migratory grief. It would also give researchers and those interested in the field the opportunity to compare the experience of Latina immigrants to that of Latino immigrants. Doing similar research to that presented here, but with male participants, would add to the existing knowledge on migratory grief.

Due to the scope of this study, we did not look at all of the possible factors that could affect an individual's response when migrating to a foreign country. Doka (1998) identified circumstances surrounding a loss and social factors such as age as having an effect on the impact of the loss. The present study only looked at voluntary migration; thus, the results of political exile might be different. Furthermore, this study did not take into account the participants' ages and how that might be a factor affecting the results. Nevertheless, the ages of the participants were between twenty-eight and forty-three, with almost half of the participants being in their thirties. Further research could be done on the effects of migration at different developmental stages, and on those who have migrated involuntarily. Having such information would help create a more comprehensive model of migratory grief.

Implications

The results of this study have important implications for those working with the Latina immigrant population. It gives service providers a better understanding of the emotional experience undergone by immigrants, and it can help increase the provider's sensitivity to her immigrant clients. It may be useful in some cases for providers to help immigrant clients understand some of their feelings from the perspective of loss and grieving. Helping clients understand that leaving their country has many similarities to losing a loved one may make it easier for them to understand their feelings.

In addition, this study gives providers a theoretical perspective from which to validate their clients' feelings. As clients struggle to understand and justify their feelings, providers can help them realize that their feelings are normal and understandable. It would be useful for clients to realize that many other immigrants have similar feelings. It might bring hope to those who are in the beginning phases of migratory grief to know that, over time, sadness and anger will dissipate.

This understanding of immigrant grief will provide guidance in the assessment of Latino immigrants' needs. Santiago-Rivera and Altarriba (2002) suggested that a thorough assessment of Latinos should include factors such as language proficiency, level of acculturation, and cultural expressions. Santiago-Rivera (1995) suggested that the levels of acculturation, language proficiency and preference, cultural norms, values, and beliefs affect the assessment of psychological factors. They proposed that these factors should be assessed prior to designing a treatment plan. The present study suggests the importance of including migratory grief to the assessment list. Doing a comprehensive assessment that includes migratory grief, will lead to a more thorough treatment plan accounting for factors that would otherwise be neglected.

Issues related to migratory grief might also arise during the service delivery process. For example, Hoffman, Dana, and Bolton (1985) stated that one of the most salient acculturative-related issues presented in psychotherapy is the failure to mourn the loss of the native country. Consequently, recognizing the significant impact of the migratory experience and understanding the experience from the perspective of loss and grief will enable providers to better provide more effective services to immigrants.

References

Aroian, K. J. (1990). A model of psychological adaptation to migration and re-settlement. *Nursing Research*, *39*(1), 5–10.

Arredondo-Dowd, P. M. (1981). Personal loss and grief as a result of immigration. *Personnel and Guidance Journal*, *59*(6), 376–378.

Bartrop, R. W., Hancock, K., Braig, A., & Porritt, D. W. (1992). Psychological toxicity of bereavement: Six months after the event. *Australian Psychologist, 27*, 192–196.

Ben-Sira, Z. (1997). *Immigration, stress, and readjustment.* Westport, CT: Praeger.

Bowlby, J. (1961). Processes of mourning. *International Journal of Psychoanalysis*, *42*, 317–340.

Brenner, E. (1991). Losses, acculturation and depression among Mexican immi-grants. *Dissertation Abstracts International, 51*(12-B), 6148.

Brewer, J. D. (2000). *Ethnography* (2nd ed.). Philadelphia: Open University Press.

Buddington, S. A. (2002). Acculturation, psychological adjustment (stress, depres-sion, self-esteem) and the academic achievement of Jamaican immigrant college students. *International Social Work, 45*(4), 447–464.

Casado, B. L., & Leung, P. (2001). Migratory grief and depression among elderly Chinese American immigrants. *Journal of Gerontological Social Work, 36*(1–2), 5–26.

Cleiren, M. (1993). *Bereavement and adaptation: A comparative study of the aftermath of death.* Washington, DC: Hemisphere.

Doka, K. J. (1998). *Living with grief: Who we are, how we grieve.* Philadelphia: Brunner/ Mazel.

Emmenegger-Hindin, I. (1993). The experience of culture loss, grieving/mourning, and acculturative stress associated with depressive symptomatology among adults in cultural transition. *Dissertation Abstracts International, 54*(4-B), 2195.

Espin, O. M. (1987). Psychological impact of migration on Latinas. *Psychology of Women Quarterly, 11*, 489–503.

Guarnaccia, P. J., DeLaCancela, V., & Carrillo, E. (1989). The multiple mean-ings of ataques de nervios in the Latino community. *Medical Anthropology, 11*, 47–62.

Hoffman, T., Dana, R. G., & Bolton, B. (1985). Measured acculturation and MMPI-168 performance of Native American adults. *Journal of Cross-Cultural Psychology, 16*, 243–256.

Lakatos, P. (1992). The effects of migratory grief on the adjustment of the adult Hispanic immigrant. *Dissertation Abstracts International, 53*(8-B), 4367–4377.

Landrine, H., & Klonoff, E. A. (1994). *African American acculturation: Deconstructing race and reviving culture.* Thousand Oaks, CA: Sage.

Levy, L. H., Derby, J. F., & Martinkowski, K. S. (1993). Effects of membership in bereavement support groups on adaptation to conjugal bereavement. *American Journal of Community Psychology, 21*, 361–381.

Mirsky, J. (1991). Language and migration: Separation individuation conflicts in relation to the mother tongue and the new language. *Psychotherapy, 28,* 618–624.

Padilla, A. M., & Perez, W. P. (2003). Acculturation, social identity, and social cognition: A new perspective. *Hispanic Journal of Behavioral Sciences, 25*(1), 35–55.

Parkes, C. M. (1970). The first year of bereavement: A longitudinal study of the reaction of London widows to the death of their husbands. *Psychiatry, 33,* 444–467.

Parkes, C. M., & Weiss, R. S. (1983). *Recovery from bereavement.* New York: Basic Books.

Parkes, C. M. (1996). *Bereavement: Studies of grief in adult life.* Philadelphia: Taylor & Francis.

Payne, S. (1999). Interviewing in qualitative research. In *Handbook of the psychology of interviewing.* New York: John Wiley.

Phinney, J. S., & Flores, J. (2002). Unpackaging acculturation: Aspects of acculturation as predictors of traditional sex role attitudes. *Journal of Cross-Cultural Psychology, 33*(3), 320–331.

Prigerson, H. G., Bierhal, A. J., Kasl, S. V., Reynolds, C. F., Shear, M. K., Newsom, J. T., et al. (1996). Complicated grief as a disorder distinct from bereavement-related depression and anxiety: A replication study. *American Journal of Psychiatry, 153,* 616–623.

Prudent, S. (1988). The grief associated with immigration: An examination of Haitian immigrant's psychological adjustment in the United States. *Dissertation Abstracts International, 49*(10-B), 4555–4556.

Santiago-Rivera, A. L. (1995). Developing a culturally sensitive treatment modality for bilingual Spanish-speaking clients: Incorporating language and culture in counseling. *Journal of Counseling and Development, 74,* 12–17.

Santiago-Rivera, A. L., & Altarriba, J. (2002). The role of language in therapy with the Spanish-speaking bilingual client. *Professional Psychology: Research and Practice, 33*(1), 30.

Schneller, D. P. (1981). The immigrant's challenge: Mourning the loss of homeland and adapting to the new world. *Smith College Studies in Social Work, 51*(2), 95–125.

Seidman, I. (1998). *Interviewing as qualitative research: A guide for researchers in education and the social sciences.* New York: Teachers College Press.

Smart, J. F., & Smart, D. W. (1995). Acculturative stress of Hispanics: Loss and challenge. *Journal of Counseling and Development, 73*(4), 390–396.

U.S. Census Bureau 2002: The Hispanic population in the United States, March 2002. Retrieved March 14, 2004, from factfinder.census.gov.

Ward, C., & Styles, I. (2003). Lost and found: Reinvention of the self-following migration. *Journal of Applied Psychoanalytic Studies, 5*(3), 349–367.

Zisook, S., & Shuchter, S. R. (1993). Uncomplicated bereavement. *Journal of Clinical Psychiatry, 54,* 365–372.

About the Authors

Daiana A. González, M.S., is a graduate from the Brigham Young University Marriage and Family Therapy program, Brigham Young University, office number 2086B JFSB, Provo, UT 84602. E-mail: dg46@byu.edu

Richard B. Miller, Ph.D., is the director and a professor in the School of Family Life at Brigham Young University, office number 2086B JFSB, Provo, UT 84602. E-mail: rick_miller@byu.edu.

Career and Employment Concerns of Immigrant Women

9

OKSANA YAKUSHKO

Abstract

Information about career development and employment transition issues of immigrant women is limited. This chapter focuses on immigrant women's experiences of work and career development. Stress due to relocation can serve as a barrier to positive work adjustment. Immigrant women are more likely to find jobs than men, however they are most likely to be in low skill, low-level jobs with no opportunity for advancement. Social cultural forces, such as xenophobia, racism, sexism, and poverty, may be interconnected and contribute to oppression and discrimination.

Keywords: Relocation, Immigrant Women, Career Development, Xenophobia

THE U.S. CENSUS BUREAU reports that 10.4 percent or approximately 28 million individuals in the United States are immigrants (Schmidley, 2001). Almost half of this group (43.6 percent) reported on the most recent census that they have moved to the United States since 1990. Although a large number of individuals have undergone a relocation to the United States, their visibility in scholarly literature has only recently begun to grow (Hovey, 2000; Gonsalves, 1992; Pernice, 1994; Yoshihama & Horrocks, 2002).

Even less information exists on the impact of immigration on women, because most research has focused on men (Hondagneu-Sotelo, 1999). Recent census estimates reveal that approximately 15 percent more women than men legally immigrated to the United States between 1990 and 2000 (Perry, Vandervate, Auman & Morris, 2001). In part, this difference is explained by the U.S. immigration law, which favors admission of spouses and children, as well as certain types of skilled workers, such as nurses (Simon, 2001).

Information about the career development and employment transition issues of immigrant women remains even more limited. This chapter focuses on immigrant women and the work/career issues they face in the United States. A majority of immigrant women seek and find employment, even though their occupations will be low prestige and paying occupations (Schmidley, 2001). The significance of attending to women's employment has been highlighted by the United Nations resolution on women refugees, which urges that host nations focus on providing women with educational opportunities about employment after relocation (Office of the United Nations High Commissioner for Refugees, 1991). However, immigrant and refugee women continue to face many barriers in finding meaningful work and rewarding careers after their relocation (Yakushko, 2006).

This chapter is divided into several parts. First, a brief description is provided of the circumstances surrounding migration that bring women to the United States and the impact of these circumstances on their possible employment. Second, the existing literature on immigrant women and work in the United States is reviewed. Third, the chapter discusses the unique issues immigrant women face that may have an impact on their career adjustment and career transition. Fourth, brief implications for working with immigrant women are provided.

The Circumstances of Relocation

Immigration constitutes a wide array of relocation circumstances. These circumstances bear significant repercussions for individuals who enter the United States and their experiences while in this country. Furthermore, women's immigration status is often essential to their subsequent work experiences in the United States.

Legal immigration refers to noncitizens who are granted *legal permanent residence* or a green card by the federal government, or who reside in the United States and may ultimately be granted citizenship status. Legal permanent residence includes the right to remain in the country indefinitely, to be gainfully employed, and to seek the benefits of U.S. citizenship through naturalization (Mulder, Hollmann, Lollock, Cassidy, Costanzo & Baker, 2001). It does not include the right to vote. The majority of women immigrants are likely to enter the United States on family-sponsored immigrant visas (Schmidley, 2001).

One category of such immigrants are so-called *mail-order brides*. Simons (1999) argues that American men have had a propensity to marry foreign women. Chittenden (2000) reports that nearly 600 agencies offering international marriage matching services exist online, and that between 4,000 and 6,000 K-1 fiancé visas yearly are granted to foreign women entering relationships with American men through such services.

Women also can gain immigrant visas through a practice called *brain drain* (Simon, 2001). This brain drain is achieved through immigration policies that allow for legal immigrant status to be given to those who are deemed to be "persons of extraordinary ability" or to have advanced training or skills in occupations important for the U.S. labor market, such as nurses. These individuals receive their immigrant status through companies or agencies who sponsor them (U.S. Census Bureau, 2000).

One of the more recent developments in U.S. immigration policy is focused on creating more equal opportunities for individuals of various countries. Each year, the Diversity Lottery Program makes 55,000 immigrant visas available through a lottery to people who come from countries with low rates of immigration to the United States (U.S. Department of Justice, 2002). Through this program, women can either come by themselves or with their families by obtaining a legal immigrant status for residing and working in the United States.

Another type of immigration status is granted to individuals who are considered refugees. *Refugees* are defined as those people outside their country of nationality who are unable or unwilling to return to that country because of persecution or a well-founded fear of persecution, which coincides with the definition determined by the 1967 United Nations Protocol on Refugees (Mulder et al., 2001). The U.S. Refugee Act of 1980 states that under circumstances outlined by the UN Protocol, the U.S. will allow a number of individuals of any country to enter the United States (U.S. Census Bureau, 2000). This number is determined by the U.S. president and Congress, and has a ceiling.

The last group of immigrants is often referred to as the *illegal* or *undocumented* population. This unauthorized migrant population consists primarily of two groups: (1) those entering the United States (primarily across land borders) without inspection and (2) those entering the United States with legal temporary visas who violate the terms or stay beyond the specified time allotment of their visa (Mulder et al., 2001). The U.S. Census Bureau (2000) estimated that in recent years approximately five million individuals remained in the United States illegally. Undocumented immigrant women remain in the United States because of economic benefits and the possibility of gaining legal resident status.

The attacks on September 11, 2001, have spurred new calls for reform of the immigration laws and the immigration agencies (Dillon, 2001; Hutchinson, 2001; Toy, 2002). These reforms typically sought to restrict immigration and limit services to immigrants. In addition, the current anti-immigrant atmosphere in the United States may contribute to the additional difficulties experienced, especially by the undocumented immigrants who are now residing in the United States (Yakushko, in press).

Issues that Impact Immigrant Women's Employment and Career Experiences in the United States

The ecological model proposed by Bronfenbrenner (1979) and extended to career development and career counseling by Cook, Heppner, and O'Brien (2002), is helpful in conceptualizing the types of issues that may impact employment and career trajectories of immigrant women. Bronfenbrenner suggested that individuals' behavior is influenced by four major subsystems: the microsystem (i.e., interpersonal interactions in individual's life such as school or family), the mesosystem (i.e., interaction between two or more microsystems), the exosystem (i.e., subsystems that influence individuals such as neighborhood or the media), and the the macrosystem (i.e., societal ideology). Cook, Heppner, and O'Brien (2002) propose that this ecological model can help to conceptualize the "dynamic interaction between the individual and the environment" in a way that helps to recognize the complexity of multiple identities and multiple sociocultural influences on individuals (p. 291).

This model appears to provide a good explanation for the realities faced by the immigrant women in the United States. Immigrant women are influenced by a number of intrapersonal, interpersonal, and societal forces, which have a significant bearing on their career well-being and employment. The following section highlights these forces from the intrapersonal to interpersonal to societal issues that may have an impact on work and career functioning of immigrant women.

Intrapersonal Issues

Immigration is a highly stressful experience. Rumbaut (1991) states that "migration can produce profound psychological distress even among the most motivated and well prepared individuals, and even in most receptive circumstances" (p. 56). The stress experienced by women immigrants may result from a number of processes of relocation and adjustment to a new culture. Espin (1999) suggested that among the stressors experienced by immigrant women may be posttraumatic stress, mourning and grieving of multiple losses as the result of moving, and acculturative stress. Transition to a new culture may result in loneliness, loss of self-esteem, strain, and fatigue from cognitive overload, a sense of uprootedness, and the perception that one is unable to function competently in the new culture (Bemak & Chung, 2002; Espin, 1997; Garza-Guerrero, 1974; Prendes-Lintel, 2001).

Refugee women may experience a host of difficult intrapersonal psychological states that may have resulted from their traumatization history. Refugee women may be experiencing intense reactions of stress due to forced relocation and conflicts around having to flee their homes (Bemak & Chung, 2002; Roe, 1992; Saldana, 1992). Posttraumatic stress reactions of refugee women may be related to their experiences of rape and sexual violence (Friedman, 1992), torture (Chester, 1992; Herbst, 1992), or the experiences of war traumas (Bowen, Carscadden, Beighle & Fleming, 1992; Prendes-Lintel, 2001; Shepherd, 1992).

Immigrant women may also have strong internal resources. They may seek to improve their self-esteem through service to their families and community (Prendes-Lintel, 2001; Yee, 1992). Immigrant women may also participate in political and cultural activism, which may help buffer them from the disempowering and stressful events of relocation (Bemak & Chung, 2002; Light, 1992).

The intrapersonal issues encountered by immigrant women bear significant consequences for their career development and work transitions in the new culture. On one hand, women immigrants may have been employed in their homelands and have abilities, attitudes, and skills that can be viewed as facilitative of their positive career transition or adjustment. On the other hand, the barriers may also be significant. Betz (2006) asserts that such individual barriers as low self-esteem impede women's career development. Certainly, the cognitive and emotional overload immigrant women may experience is another such barrier. A unique intrapersonal barrier is women's inability to learn new language adequately.

Interpersonal Issues

Family and ethnic community are considered the primary environmental resources for immigrant and refugee women (Ben-Sira, 1997; Prendes-Lintel, 2001). Family may include not only individuals of blood relations, connections with whom may be severed by relocation, but also persons with whom immigrant women may have had prolonged contact during or following their relocation (Gold, 1989). Furthermore, ethnic communities often become sources of social support as well as networking for women immigrants, which is likely to have enormous impact on their employment seeking strategies (Ben-Sira, 1997).

Women immigrants may report their relationships with their partners and children have remained the same or even improved with the relocation. Kosmarskaya (1999) studied Russian women who immigrated from the Central Asian areas of the former Soviet Union. She found some of the women in her sample felt a new sense of freedom in moving away from sharing a household with in-laws.

Women immigrants may, however, encounter a number of difficulties in their nuclear and extended family due to their relocation. Women, who are viewed in many traditional patriarchal societies as the keepers and transmitters of cultural values, may experience an increasing pressure to focus on their families after the relocation (Espin, 1999; Narayan, 1997; Prendes-Lintel, 2001; Simons, 1999; Toren, 2001). Itzhaky and Ribner (1999) found that in a sample of 200 men and women Jewish refugees, women had a higher sense of individual responsibility than did men. At the same time, women may not have the resources of extended families and the knowledge of local community resources to be able to *care* for their families to the same degree they were expected to in their host cultures (Zlotnik, 2000). Furthermore, Weeks (2000) found that women, whose male partners gained entrance to the United States for employment purposes, experienced the U.S. culture as pressuring them toward greater gender-role traditionality than even their home cultures.

Immigration can be a source of relational stress for many women. Domestic violence against women by their intimate partners is one source of difficulty. The National Council for Research on Women (1995) reports in a survey of immigrant women in the San Francisco Bay Area, 34 percent of the Latina, 30 percent of the Chinese, and 20 percent of the Filipina women reported experiencing domestic violence since their relocation to the United States. Forty-eight percent of the Latinas in this sample reported the intensity and frequency of the abuse had increased since moving to the United States. Russian women refugees in Kosmarskaya's (1999) sample attributed the serious worsening of their marital relationship to the overall instability of the individuals in the immigrant household and specifically, to the male partners who were "drinking and unemployed" (p. 192). Women, whose immigrant status depends on their marriage to a U.S. citizen or legal resident, may be even at higher risk of domestic violence. Narayan (1995) wrote about mail-order brides and cited that women who enter the United States through this arrangement are more economically, psychologically, and linguistically dependent on their partners than other women.

Immigration, however, has been seen as an impetus for challenging traditional gender roles. Women may use their opportunity to emigrate as a chance to leave their partnerships. Various studies have shown that immigrant women report improvement of their gender-role status as the result of migration, because of their perception of increased control over the decision-making in the household, greater personal autonomy, and opportunity to challenge their culture's gender stereotypes (Foner, 1986; Foner, 2001; Hondagneu-Sotelo, 1994; Pedraza, 1991; Simon, 1992).

The interpersonal issues immigrant women encounter in the United States will have an impact on their career development and career transitions. Betz (2006) postulated that interpersonal barriers, such as family-career conflicts may negatively impact women's career development. McWhirter, Torres, and Rasheed (1998) similarly suggest that multiple-role stress can serve as a barrier in women's career adjustment process. On the other hand, women's entrance into the new culture may create space for challenging gender-role stereotypes in new ways. The nontraditional gender-role orientation may function as a facilitator of immigrant women's career transition or adjustment (Betz, 1994).

Sociocultural Issues

Immigrant women in the United States may experience a number of difficulties because of the multiple oppressive forces that are sociocultural in nature. The ecological model would define these forces as belonging to the exosystems and macrosystems of the culture. These forces are likely to include xenophobia, racism, sexism, poverty and employment difficulties, and other systems of oppression.

Yakushko (in press) defined *xenophobia* as "a form of attitudinal, affective, and behavioral prejudice toward immigrants and those perceived as foreign." Xenophobia has been linked to jingoism, which refers to extreme chauvinism or nationalism, marked especially by a belligerent foreign policy and ethnocentrism, which is characterized by or based on the attitude that one's own group or culture is superior (Yakushko, in press). Xenophobia has also been defined as an attitudinal orientation of hostility against nonnatives in a given population, which can be viewed as a form of racism that does not use the concept of race as a defining element (Boehnke, Hagan & Hefler, 1998; Fry, 2001).

Over the past decade the negative attitudes toward immigrants and immigration in the United States may be best described as xenophobic (Gabaccia, 2002; Yakushko, in press). The United States has had a long history of mistreatment of immigrants in general, and women immigrants in particular (Foner, 2001). Public opinion polls continue to indicate the majority of Americans would like to either severely restrict or put a moratorium on immigration into the United States (DeLaet, 2000). Groups, such as the Federation for American Immigration Reform (FAIR), a national educational and lobbying network, are vocal in expressing their concern about "the adverse effects of out-of-control immigration" (National Council for Research on Women, 1995, p. 3). The 1986 Reagan-era Immigration Reform and Control Act (IRCA) sought to set limits on immigration with the rhetoric that immigration fuels U.S. unemployment, depresses wages, and that jobs of the native workers are lost to the low-wage, nonbenefits, nonnative laborers. The post–September 11th events ushered in an era of renewed anti-immigrant policies and attitudes, with immigrant employment being especially targeted by critics of immigration (Gabaccia, 2002; Yakushko, in press).

Women immigrants suffer negative consequences because of the xenophobic attitudes and policies (Yakushko, 2006; Yakushko & Chronister, 2005). Their career transitions and adjustment may be strongly influenced by these attitudes and policies. Women immigrants may perceive the labor market as closed to them because of the general attitude that immigrants are here to "get the jobs" of the native-born Americans. Immigrant women may be denied jobs or placed in the low-wage, unskilled labor workforce because of perceptions of their lower intellectual abilities due to their English skills or nonnative accent. If women choose to follow cultural practices around dress, holidays, or social interactions, employers may perceive the behavior as unacceptable for their companies and reject women's applications. These xenophobic reactions may further increase women's lack of career confidence and self-efficacy.

Racism is another force of oppression many women immigrants face. For immigrants of color, racism presents a new and painful reality. Around the turn of the century, the U.S. immigration policies were shaped by the dictate to control the "contamination by the inferior races" (Sinke & Gross, 1992, p. 68). Certainly, the nonwhite immigrants to the United States and the subsequent generations have suffered tremendous abuse and restrictions because of racist attitudes and policies (Sue, Ivey & Pedersen, 1996; Sue & Sue, 1999), and women immigrants in particular (see Comas-Diaz & Greene, 1994).

Immigrant women's career adjustment, similar to that of U.S.-born women of color, is likely to be negatively impacted by racism and racist stereotypes. McWhirter, Torres, and Rasheed (1998) stress that racism is one of the significant environmental barriers that women of color face in their career adjustment. Bingham and Ward (1994) provide an excellent overview of the impact of racism, both on the career development of minority women as well as the current status of career-focused research in this area.

Sexism is the force of oppression that impacts women globally (True, 2003). Patriarchy effects women in all parts of the world, and the process of immigration and its consequences will also be marked by women's struggle with societal sexism. Because women are often seen as the carriers of cultural norms and their continuation through their primary participation in childbearing and child-raising, the pressure on women to assume traditional gender roles in the new culture may be even greater than in their home environment (Espin, 1999; Narayan, 1997; Simons, 1999; Toren, 2001). Certainly, mail order brides, often coming from Asia and Eastern Europe, who are likely to be chosen for their submissive traditionally feminine behaviors and the widespread domestic violence against them, point to the intensity of patriarchal oppression of these immigrant women (Simons, 1999; Sinke & Gross, 1992). The dominant society's perceptions of immigrant women may contribute to an even greater impact of sexism on these women. Yeoh and Huang (2000) in their study of immigrant domestic servants found that immigrant women workers are often portrayed by the host culture as sexually predatory and promiscuous.

Women, however, may view immigration as an opportunity to redefine their gender roles (Espin, 1999; Prieto, 1992). A new location can be used as a place to renegotiate gendered relations, which may provide immigrant women a chance to escape the patriarchal constraints of their own cultures (Willis & Yeoh, 2000). The necessity of and opportunity for employment outside the home often serves as one such escape for immigrant women (see Simon, 2001; Willis & Yeoh, 2000). Pessar (1995) observed that women's opportunities to earn wages often gives immigrant women the right to greater autonomy and authority within the household, although the dynamics of how women assert these rights and what the rights mean within different cultures may differ.

The issues of *economic discrimination* and often *poverty* as well as employment discrimination have the most impact on immigrant women's well being in the United States. The majority of immigrant women must work in order to survive economically (Hogan, 1996; Menjivar, 1999; Simon, 2001; Yakushko, 2006). Ben-Sira (1997) suggests that "economic problems and problems of employment are among the most salient instrumental problems of immigrants" (p. 75). Immigrant women are continually over-represented in the lowest socioeconomic levels of U.S. society, and are likely to experience their work as oppressive (Yakushko, 2006).

The 2000 U.S. population census has provided important information about the employment status of the foreign-born population in the United States (Schmidley, 2001). This report suggests the unemployment rate is higher for the foreign-born population in the United States than for native-born individuals. Immigrant women who are either noncitizens or have been in the United States for less than ten years have the lowest reported labor participation. Foreign-born individuals are far less likely to occupy managerial or professional specialty occupations (i.e., jobs of the middle and higher social classes) and far more likely to work in unskilled labor and service-oriented jobs in comparison with native-born individuals. Immigrant women earn 59 cents of every dollar earned by U.S.-born males in similar occupations, and 83 cents of every dollar earned in a similar occupation by an average U.S.-born female. The poverty rate of foreign-born individuals is 16.8 percent versus 11.2 percent for native-born persons.

These census data also reveal further differences between immigrant individuals from various parts of the world, as well as immigrant men and women (Schmidley, 2001). For example, U.S. immigration policy has shaped the educational levels that are acceptable for employment. The highest percentage of high school completion is found in immigrants from Africa (94.9 percent), whereas it is 79.6 percent for immigrants from Central and South America, and 33.8 percent for Mexican immigrants. The poverty rate is the highest for Latin American immigrants—21.9 percent versus 11.2 percent for the nation as a whole. Individuals who migrated from Europe often have employment and educational levels closer to those of the native-born U.S. individuals. However, in each group, women immigrants appear to fair worse than men. For example, foreign-born men are far more likely than foreign-born women to have employment-based benefits, such as health insurance.

Historically, immigrant women from around the world have been employed in the United States as domestic workers (Chang, 2001; Messias, 2001). This trend toward hiring immigrant women for such jobs as domestic cleaning, laundry, childcare, and eldercare may have been spurred by the growing entrance of mostly white U.S.-born women into the workforce (Hondagneu-Sotelo, 1994). Immigrant women may be pushed into low-level domestic work because of their lack of English skills, as well as a lack of legal papers (Messias, 2001). However, for a great number of immigrant women, no matter what their background, language skills, or legal status, work after relocation is a downward shift to a low-wage, low-status, dead-end job (Foner, 2001; Hogan, 1996). Hogan (1996) states that "throughout American history, immigrant women often worked at unrewarding and difficult jobs, facing constant hazards, discrimination, exploitation, and even death" (p. 44). Immigrant women's qualifications based on their previous educational and work experience may be unrecognized because of language problems or difficulties with prerequisite educational and licensing exams in many fields (Foner, 2001).

The existence of sweatshops in the United States serves as the most vivid illustration of the types of employment discrimination and abuse experienced by immigrant women. U.S. sweatshops typically are based on forcing immigrant children and women to work in unsanitary conditions in virtual conditions of slavery. Branigin's (1995) report in the *Washington Post* describes the conditions of immigrant women who were garment workers in sweatshops throughout the United States, and states that these women found slavery instead of the paradise they hoped for. Pessar (2000) discussed why some immigrant women choose to work under such conditions. She studied the employment patterns of Dominican women in New York City and noted almost half of the women in her sample were employed by the garment industry with salaries of approximately $6,000 a year for full-time work. Pessar indicated that in addition to immigrant women's willingness to work in the sweatshop conditions because of money, women also perceived this work as providing them with more flexibility around time (i.e., shifting from daytime to nighttime work).

On the other side of the social class ladder in the United States, immigrant women from developing countries who have had distinguished academic careers in their homelands, have been able to receive special immigration privileges from the U.S. government. The experiences of immigrant women with advanced training, however, are often ones of downward shift in status as well as discrimination. Manrique and Manrique (1999) studied women scholars from non-European developing countries in American academia. The women professors in their study reported that both other faculty and students frequently experienced harassment because of their accent and the way they dressed. For example, one woman faculty member reported that "during one of her first job interviews, the male professor interviewing her derided her for wearing pants and proceeded to tell her that if this was common practice in her country of origin, she would be expected to wear something else if she were teaching in this institution" (p. 112). Manrique and Manrizue further highlight that immigrant women faculty, more than immigrant men, were questioned about their right to teach about *American* subjects. In their sample, women stated their standard of living, their social status, and the perceived support for their research was lower than that of their country of origin. Thus, even for the more privileged immigrant women, the experiences around employment often result in downward social and status mobility as well as discrimination.

According to the Census and scholarly publications, immigrant women are more likely to be employed than either native-born women or immigrant men (Espiritu, 1999; Hondagneu-Sotelo, 1999; Menjivar, 1999; Messias, 2001; Pessar, 1999; Schmidley, 2001). However, immigrant women are most likely to work at low-skills, low-level jobs that will offer them no opportunity for professional or personal growth (Espiritu, 1999; Hondagneu-Sotelo, 1999; Menjivar, 1999; Pessar, 1999). Furthermore, based on the empirical research on immigrant women's labor participation, it appears that immigrant women often view their employment as a means toward a *family investment*, and such investment is reflected in women not only working long hours but also taking care of all the domestic needs (Duleep, 2001).

Xenophobia, racism, sexism, and poverty or economic exploitation, are sociocultural forces that do not operate independently of each other. The multiple identities and their intersectionality in immigrant women's lives will mean they will often experience oppression and discrimination based on multiple sources of prejudice. Oppression for immigrant women may also come from their *religious affiliation, lesbian identity, age, physical ability*, and *appearance*.

Implications

Immigrant women's employment is central to their experience in the United States for reasons of economic survival and cultural integration. Thus, understanding the barriers immigrant women face in terms of their work experiences may be a key in helping immigrant women and their families adjust to their new environments. Those who work with immigrant women and families directly, such as case workers, counselors, and other human-service providers must begin to recognize the unique patterns of career development for this group of women, as well as the patterns of career and work transition they experience. Policy work that attends to issues of discrimination and oppression faced by immigrant women can further contribute to an environment that is welcoming rather than hostile to immigrants. Lastly, research on immigration, work, and gender continues to be limited. Culturally relevant scholarship in this area can elucidate immigrant women's experiences as well as provide information on theoretical and demographic trends in immigrant women's employment and career development.

Conclusion

Based on the U.S. Census estimates, one in ten women in the United States has recently immigrated to this country (Schmidley, 2001). Immigrant women, for many of whom employment in the United States is a survival necessity and a dream of a better life, seek to enter the U.S. workforce in greater numbers than U.S.-born women (National Science Foundation, 1997). Current literature has ignored the realities of immigrant women, although including them as part of the racial and ethnic diversity emphasis without recognizing the impact of migration. Greater attention must be given to the occupational realities of immigrant women and how career services can address these. Ecological systems in immigrant women's experience of work and career development in the United States must be taken into account. It is more likely that the macro-systemic factors such as xenophobia, racism, and sexism play a key role in restricting women from finding employment that is not low-level or dead-end. By focusing research on immigrant women, we may gain greater understanding of how the intersection of multiple identities influences career processes. We can also step out from the U.S.-centric scholarly focus toward a more global perspective. Lastly, the social advocacy that addresses immigrant women's rights toward fulfilling and meaningful employment in the United States can help serve the needs of one of the most disempowered groups.

References

Bemak, F., & Chung, R. C. (2002). Counseling and psychotherapy with refugees. In P. B. Pedersen, J. G. Draguns, W. J. Lonner & J. E. Trimble (Eds.), *Counseling across cultures* (2nd ed., pp. 209–232). Thousand Oaks, CA: Sage.

Ben-Sira, Z. (1997). *Immigration, stress, and readjustment.* Westport, CT: Praeger.

Betz, N. E. (1994). Basic issues and concepts in career counseling for women. In W. B. Walsh & S. H. Osipow (Eds.), *Career counseling for women* (pp. 1–41). Hillsdale, NJ: Erlbaum.

Betz, N. E. (2006). Basic issues and concepts in career counseling for women. In W. B. Walsh & S. M. J. Heppner (Eds.), *Career counseling for women* (2nd ed.). Hillsdale, NJ: Erlbaum.

Bingham, R. O., & Ward, C. M. (1994). Career counseling with ethnic minority women. In W. B. Walsh & S. H. Osipow (Eds.), *Career counseling for women.* Hillsdale, NJ: Erlbaum.

Boehnke, K., Hagan, J., & Hefler, G. (1998). On the development of xenophobia in Germany: The adolescent years. *Journal of Social Issues, 54,* 585–603.

Bowen, D. J., Carscadden, L., Beighle, K., & Fleming, I. (1992). Post-traumatic stress disorder among Salvadoran women: Empirical evidence and description of treatment. In E. Cole, O. M. Espin & E. D. Rothblum (Eds.), *Refugee women and their mental health: Shattered societies, shattered lives.* New York: Haworth Press.

Branigin, W. (1995 September 10). Sweatshop instead of paradise: Thais lived in fear as slaves at L.A. garment factories. *Washington Post,* p. A1.

Bronfenbrenner, U. (1979). *The ecology of human development.* Cambridge, MA: Harvard University Press.

Chang, G. (2001). Disposable domestics: Immigrant women workers in the global economy. *Women in Action, 1,* 62–63.

Chester, B. (1992). Women and political torture: Work with refugee survivors in exile. In E. Cole, O. M. Espín & E. D. Rothblum (Eds.), *Refugee women and their mental health: Shattered societies, shattered lives.* New York: Haworth Press.

Chittenden, V. (2000). Russian mail order brides. *TED Case Studies.* Washington, DC: American University. Retrieved on the world wide web on June 20, 2007, at www.american.edu/ted/bride.htm.

Comas-Diaz, L., & Greene, B. (Eds.). (1994). *Women of color: Integrating ethnic and gender identities in psychotherapy.* New York: Guilford Press.

Cook, E. P., Heppner, M. J., & O'Brien, K. M. (2002). Career development of women of color and White women: Assumptions, conceptualization, and interventions from an ecological perspective. *The Career Development Quarterly, 50,* 291–305.

DeLaet, D. L. (2000). *U.S. Immigration policy in an age of rights.* Westport, CT: Praeger.

Dillon, S. (2001 October 15). Mexican immigrants face new set of fears. *New York Times, Late Edition,* p. A14.

Duleep, H. O. (2001). The family investment model: A formalization and review of evidence from across immigrant groups. In R. J. Simon (Ed.), *Immigrant women*. New Brunswick, NJ: Transaction.

Espín, O. M. (1997). *Latina realities: Essays on healing, migration, and sexuality*. Boulder, CO: Westview Press.

Espín, O. M. (1999). *Women crossing boundaries: A psychology of immigration and transformation of sexuality*. New York: Routledge.

Espiritu, E. L. (1999). Gender and labor in Asian immigrant families. *American Behavioral Scientist, 42*, 628–647.

Foner, N. (1986). Sex roles and sensibilities: Jamaican women in New York and London. In R. J. Simon (Ed.), *International migration: The female experience*. Totowa, NJ: Rowan & Allenheld.

Foner, N. (2001). Benefits and burdens: Immigrant women and work in New York City. In R. J. Simon (Ed.), *Immigrant women*. New Brunswick, NJ: Transaction.

Friedman, A. R. (1992). Rape and domestic violence: The experience of refugee women. In E. Cole, O. M. Espin & E. D. Rothblum (Eds.), *Refugee women and their mental health: Shattered societies, shattered lives*. New York: Haworth Press.

Fry, B. N. (2001). *Responding to immigration: Perceptions of promise and threat*. New York: LFB Scholarly.

Gabaccia, D. R. (2002). *Immigration and American diversity: A concise introduction*. Malden, MA: Blackwell.

Garza-Guerrero, C. (1974). Culture shock: Its mourning and the vicissitudes of identity. *Journal of the American Psychoanalytic Association, 22*, 408–429.

Gold, S. J. (1989). Differential adjustment among new immigrant family members. *Journal of Contemporary Ethnography, 17*, 408–434.

Gonsalves, C. J. (1992). Psychological stages of the refugee process: A model for therapeutic interventions. *Professional Psychology—Research and Practice, 23*, 382–389.

Herbst, P. K. R. (1992). From helpless victim to empowered survivor: Oral history as a treatment for survivors of torture. In E. Cole, O. M. Espin & E. D. Rothblum (Eds.), *Refugee women and their mental health: Shattered societies, shattered lives*. New York: Haworth Press.

Hogan, D. G. (1996). Immigrant women in the U.S. and work. In P. J. Dubeck & K. Borman (Eds.), *Women and work: A handbook*. New York: Garland.

Hondagneu-Sotelo, P. (1994). *Gendered transitions*. Berkeley: University of California Press.

Hondagneu-Sotelo, P. (1999). Gender and contemporary U.S. immigration. *American Behavioral Scientist, 42*, 565–576.

Hovey, J. D. (2000). Acculturative stress, depression, and suicidal ideation in Mexican immigrants. *Cultural Diversity and Ethnic Minority Psychology, 6*, 134–151.

Hutchinson, E. (2001 September 14). Beware of backlash: The civil rights of Arab and Muslim Americans may become another casualty of the Sept. 11 terror attacks. *Mother Jones*, retrieved from world wide web on July 15, 2002 at www.motherjones.com/web_exclusives/commentary/opinion/backlash.html.

Itzhaky, H., & Ribner, D. S. (1999). Gender, values, and the work place: Considerations for immigrant acculturation. *International Social Work*, 42, 127–138.

Kosmarskaya, N. (1999). Post-Soviet Russian migration from the new independent states: Experiences of women migrants. In D. Indra (Ed.), *Engendering forced migration: Theory and practice* (pp. 177–199). New York: Berghahn Books.

Light, D. (1992). Healing their wounds: Guatemalan refugee women as political activists. In E. Cole, O. M. Espin & E. D. Rothblum (Eds.), *Refugee women and their mental health: Shattered societies, shattered lives* (pp. 297–308). New York: Haworth Press.

Manrique, C. G., & Manrique, G. G. (1999). Third world immigrant women in American higher education. In G. A. Kelson & D. L. DeLaet (Eds.), *Gender and immigration* (pp. 103–126). New York: New York University Press.

McWhirter, E. H., Torres, D., & Rasheed, S. (1998). Assessing barriers to women's career adjustment. *Journal of Career Assessment*, 6, 449–479.

Menjivar, C. (1999). The intersection of work and gender: Central American immigrant women and employment in California. *American Behavioral Scientist*, 42, 601–627.

Messias, D. K. H. (2001). Transnational perspectives on women's domestic work: Experiences of Brazilian immigrants in the United States. *Women and Health*, 33, 1–19.

Mulder, T. J., Hollmann, F. W., Lollock, L. R., Cassidy, R. C., Costanzo, J. M., & Baker, J. D. (2001). U.S. Census Bureau measurement of net international migration to the United States: 1990–2000. Washington, DC: Population Division U.S. Census Bureau. www.census.gov/population.

Narayan, U. (1995). "Male-order" brides: Immigrant women, domestic violence and immigration law. *Hypatia: A Journal of Feminist Philosophy*, 31, 104–126.

Narayan, U. (1997). *Dislocating cultures: Identities, traditions, and Third World feminism*. New York: Routledge.

National Council for Research on Women. (1995). Intervening: Immigrant women and domestic violence. *Issues Quarterly*, 1, 12–14.

National Science Foundation (NSF). (1997). Immigrant study provides new insights. Retrieved from the world wide web on July 15, 2002, at www.nsf.gov.

Office of the United Nations High Commissioner for Refugees. (1991). *Guidelines on the protection of the refugee women*. Geneva: The United Nations. Retrieved on July 15, 2002, at www.unhcr.ch.

Pedraza, S. (1991). Women and migration: The social consequences of gender. *Annual Review of Sociology*, 17, 303–325.

Pernice, R. (1994). Methodological issues in research with refugees and immigrants. *Professional Psychology: Research & Practice*, 25, 207–213.

Perry, M., Vandervate, B., Auman, L., & Morris, K. (2001). Evaluating components of international migration: Legal migrants. *Population Division Working Paper #59*. Washington, DC: U.S. Government. Retrieved from the world wide web on July 16, 2002, at www.census.gov/population.

Pessar, P. R. (1995). On the homefront and in the workplace: Integrating immigrant women into feminist discourse. *Anthropological Quarterly, 68*, 37–47.

Pessar, P. R. (1999). Engendering migration studies: The case of new immigrants in the United States. *American Behavioral Scientist, 42*, 577–600.

Pessar, P. R. (2000). Sweatshop workers and domestic ideologies: Dominican women in New York Apparel Industry. In K. Willis & B. Yeoh (Eds.), *Gender and migration*. Chetlenham, UK: An Elgar Reference Collection.

Prendes-Lintel, M. (2001). A working model in counseling recent refugees. In J. G. Ponterotto, J. M. Casas, L. A. Suzuki & C. M. Alexander (Eds.), *Handbook of multicultural counseling* (pp. 729–752). Thousand Oaks, CA: Sage.

Prieto, Y. (1992). Cuban women in New Jersey: Gender relations and change. In D. Gabaccia (Ed.), *Seeking common ground: Multidisciplinary studies of immigrant women in the United States*. Westport, CT: Greenwood.

Roe, M. D. (1992). Displaced women in setting of continuing armed conflict. In E. Cole, O. M. Espin & E. D. Rothblum (Eds.), *Refugee women and their mental health: Shattered societies, shattered lives*. New York: Haworth Press.

Rumbaut, R. G. (1991). The agony of exile: A study of the migration and adaptation of Indochinese refugee adults and children. In F. L. Ahearn & J. L. Athey (Eds.), *Refugee children: Theory, research, and services*. Baltimore: Johns Hopkins University Press.

Saldana, D. H. (1992). Coping with stress: A refugee's story. In E. Cole, O. M. Espin & E. D. Rothblum (Eds.), *Refugee women and their mental health: Shattered societies, shattered lives*. New York: Haworth Press.

Schmidley, A. D. (2001). Profile of the foreign born population in the U.S., 2000. *U.S. Census Bureau Current Population Reports, Series* (pp. 23–206). Washington, DC: U.S. Government. Retrieved from the world wide web on July 16, 2002, at www.census.gov/population.

Shepherd, J. (1992). Post-traumatic stress disorder in Vietnamese women. In E. Cole, O. M. Espin, & E. D. Rothblum (Eds.), *Refugee women and their mental health: Shattered societies, shattered lives*. New York: Haworth Press.

Simon, R. J. (1992). Sociology and immigrant women. In D. Gabaccia (Ed.), *Seeking common ground: Multidisciplinary studies of immigrant women in the United States*. Westport, CT: Greenwood.

Simon, R. J. (Ed.). (2001). *Immigrant women*. New Brunswick, NJ: Transaction.

Simons, L. (1999). Mail order brides: The legal framework and possibilities for change. In G. A. Kelson & D. L. DeLaet (Eds.), *Gender and immigration*. New York: New York University Press.

Sinke, S., & Gross, S. (1992). The international marriage market and the sphere of social reproduction: A German case study. In D. Gabaccia (Ed.), *Seeking common ground: Multidisciplinary studies of immigrant women in the United States*. Westport, CT: Greenwood Press.

Sue, D. W., Ivey, A. E., & Pedersen, P. B. (1996). *A theory of multicultural counseling and therapy*. Pacific Grove, CA: Brooks/Cole.

Sue, D. W., & Sue, D. (1999). *Counseling the culturally different: Theory and practice.* New York: John Wiley.

Toren, N. (2001). Women and immigrants: Strangers in a strange land. In R. J. Simon (Ed.), *Immigrant women.* New Brunswick, NJ: Transaction.

Toy, V. S. (April 28, 2002). Immigrant issues sprout like the daisies. *New York Times, Late Edition,* p. 1, Section 14LI.

True, J. (2003). *Gender, globalization, and postcolonialism.* New York: Columbia University Press.

U.S. Census Bureau (2000). *United States Census 2000.* Retrieved July 15, 2003, from www.census.gov/main/www/cen2000.html.

U.S. Department of Justice. (2002). *Immigration and Naturalization Services: Diversity Lottery.* Retrieved from the world wide web on July 15, 2002, at www.ins .usdoj.gov.

Weeks, K. A. (2000). The Berkeley wives: Identity revision and development among young temporary immigrant women. *Asian Journal of Women's Studies,* 2, 78–89.

Willis, K., & Yeoh, B. (Eds.). (2000). *Gender and migration.* Chetlenham, UK: An Elgar Reference Collection.

Yakushko, O., & Chronister, K. (2005). Immigrant women and counseling: The invisible others. *Journal of Counseling and Development, 83,* 292–299.

Yakushko, O. (2006). Career development of immigrant women. In W. B. Walsh & M. J. Heppner (Eds.), *Handbook of Career Counseling of Women.* Hillsdale, NJ: Erlbaum.

Yakushko, O. (In press). Xenophobia and prejudice against immigrants. *The Counseling Psychologist.*

Yee, B. W. K. (1992). Markers of successful aging among Vietnamese refugee women. In E. Cole, O. M. Espin & E. D. Rothblum (Eds.), *Refugee women and their mental health: Shattered societies, shattered lives.* New York: Haworth Press.

Yeoh, B. S. A., & Huang, S. (2000). Negotiating public space: Strategies and styles of migrant domestic workers in Singapore. In K. Willis & B. Yeoh (Eds.), *Gender and migration.* Chetlenham, UK: An Elgar Reference Collection.

Yoshihama, M., & Horrocks, J. (2002). Posttraumatic stress symptoms and victimization among Japanese American women. *Journal of Consulting and Clinical Psychology, 70,* 205–215.

Zlotnik, H. (2000). Migration and the family: The female perspective. In K. Willis & B. Yeoh (Eds.), *Gender and migration.* Chetlenham, UK: An Elgar Reference Collection.

About the Author

Oksana Yakushko, Ph.D., is an assistant professor in the Department of Educational Psychology at the University of Nebraska–Lincoln, 235 TCH, Lincoln, NE 68588-0345. Phone: 402-472-2119. Fax: 402-472-8349. E-mail: oyakushko2@unl.edu.

PARENTS AND CHILDREN III

Childcare Challenges of African Immigrant Families

10

An Inductive Thematic Analysis

SAYALI S. AMARAPURKAR AND M. JANICE HOGAN

Abstract

This qualitative study focused on exploring African immigrant parents' childcare experiences, including the barriers they face and the value they place on early childhood education and experiences. These immigrant families face many difficulties including low income, language, cultural barriers, navigation of the system, transportation, lack of family support, problems with childcare subsidies, and other issues. Their experiences were affected by the information they gathered, their values and child rearing beliefs, as well as the child's age, maternal employment, family income, availability of relatives, and childcare subsidy policies.

Keywords: Childcare, Thematic Analysis, African Immigrant Parents, Childhood Education.

> *At home [in Ethiopia] he was inside my family; they helped me take care of him, and I never worried a single day. After I came here, I was challenged to raise my child alone where I was new to everything in a new country.*

> —ETHIOPIAN, MOTHER OF TWO CHILDREN

Address all correspondence to Sayali S. Amarapurkar, Ph.D., e-mail: amar0011@umn.edu.

*I don't have much experience in this country, but what I
learned is keeping the child at childcare is important . . .
without childcare it is difficult to raise children and make them
ready for school. The childcare is a base for them.*

—ETHIOPIAN, FATHER OF THREE CHILDREN

THE ABOVE TWO QUOTES from Ethiopian immigrant parents bring out the essence of the two goals of childcare: supporting parents' employment and fostering children's development (Gennetian, Huston, Crosby, Eun Chang, Lowe & Weisner, 2002). One of every five children under the age of eighteen in the United States is an immigrant or has immigrant parents (Reardon-Anderson, Capps & Fix, 2002; Matthews & Ewen, 2006) and one in four low-income children is an immigrant's child (Fix, Zimmerman & Passel, 2001). Children of immigrant parents can benefit tremendously through participation in early education programs such as day care, Head Start, preschool, and prekindergarten, because these programs have the potential to equip the child with school readiness and language acquisition (Matthews & Ewen, 2006). However, characteristics such as poverty, two-parent households, low maternal education, and maternal unemployment that are associated with low levels of early education enrollment (National Institute for Early Childhood Education, 2006), are commonly found in immigrant families (Matthews & Ewen, 2006). Though immigrant parents may feel the need to use nonparental childcare, they may face several barriers to access good quality childcare and early education programs. To illustrate the childcare challenges faced by immigrant families, we use a case example of a qualitative research study of seven African immigrant families. A naturalistic inquiry paradigm and an inductive thematic analysis were used to explore the childcare challenges faced by families from Ethiopia, Nigeria, and Congo who immigrated from 1995 to 2000 to a midwestern metropolis in the United States. This study was based on secondary analysis of data from the Minnesota Child Care Partnership Research Project (MCCPRP). MCCPRP is a partnership among Minnesota state agencies, counties, childcare resource and referral agencies, and university researchers to foster sound research and policies on childcare issues at the state, local, and national level. This is the first qualitative study that focused on exploring the immigrant parents' childcare experiences in their own words. This study also reveals cultural practices and new behaviors they develop as they adjust to life in the United States. The chapter summarizes the experiences of the African immigrant parents in terms of their needs for childcare, and the barriers they face, as well as the value they place on early childhood education and care. It also discusses policy implications, makes recommendations for local administrators of early childhood centers and programs, and makes suggestions for future research.

Background and Significance

Though the research on childcare issues has been expanding rapidly with the trends of mothers' labor force participation, welfare reform, and a belief in the importance of healthy development in early years (Adams & Phillips, 2001), only a few of these studies have been conducted with immigrant families. A recent national population-based research study used nationally representative longitudinal data about childcare use among black, Asian, Mexican, and white immigrant and nonimmigrant families to provide valuable information about childcare arrangements (Brandon, 2002). However, this study did not represent the voices of the participants and the childcare experiences of individual families.

The African immigrant population has been growing (U.S. Census Bureau, 2000) with recent immigration from the nations of Ethiopia, Nigeria, and Congo. But despite demographic trends and policy significance, the research on children of African immigrant families is sparse. They have been largely excluded from research on issues confronting immigrants (Kamya, 1997).

In order to understand the childcare situation, research must take into account the complex context of immigrant families. They have to find employment, housing, learn the English language, adjust to the new culture, and maintain contact with family members and relatives in their native country. Many families may have endured great hardships and persecution in their native country and may have spent time in refugee camps before coming to the United States. Thus, like many other immigrant groups, members of African immigrant communities face a number of challenges simultaneously.

Rode (1999) suggested that childcare is one of the primary concerns immigrant African families face in Minneapolis-St. Paul. Their social support networks, such as family members, friends, and neighbors used for childcare in their home country, are disrupted due to migration. This isolation can have negative effects on the children's learning experiences as well as parenting experiences. African immigrant parents need to adjust to the new system of childcare, childcare subsidies, and most importantly, a culture very different from their own.

Childcare selection can be challenging for new African immigrant parents. Selecting childcare in the United States involves locating and examining options. Childcare costs are high compared to family income and government childcare subsidy programs available only for low-income parents who meet income guidelines. Once childcare is selected, the daily functional needs must be fulfilled, such as provision of lunch, clothing, diapers, blankets, and transportation (Leslie, Anderson & Branson, 1991; Uttal, 2002). Parents must make alternative arrangements when the child is sick or when the childcare setting is closed. These processes of selection and maintenance of a childcare arrangement require a parent who communicates with childcare providers and other adult members of the family, and makes timely decisions about whether to continue or end the childcare arrangement, which may result in starting a search for a new childcare setting (Uttal, 2002).

Ecological Contextual Framework

This research study followed Alejandro-Wright's (1982) three suggestions for conducting and interpreting research on minority families: (1) identify the areas which are relevant to the lives of ethnic communities; (2) conduct basic research which describes specific issues of their everyday lives, such as childrearing, without adopting an ethnocentric view; and (3) adopt an ecological perspective to inform minority research. Obtaining affordable quality childcare is one of the pressing needs of African immigrant families with young children (Rode, 1999). The current study carried out a basic descriptive thematic analysis about everyday childcare issues these families face. To maintain the ethnic perspective, the interviewers were the same ethnicity as the families and spoke both the Ethiopian dialect Oromiffia and English. Because the Nigerian and Congolese families spoke English, they were interviewed in English. Finally, an ecological perspective and its emphasis on contextual variables was adopted. The *ecological conceptual framework* guided the researchers' interpretations and understanding of the childcare experiences of African immigrant parents. From an ecological perspective, the need for childcare emerges at the interface between the family system and its environments (Bubolz & Sontag, 1993). Young children and their families directly and indirectly participate in multiple systems, which include the family, childcare environments, and parents' work environments. One family goal is to produce capable individuals through reproduction and socialization of offspring. When parents are not available to carry out the responsibility of day-to-day socialization because they have to earn a living, they draw on resources from multiple environments to help them implement their goals. Concepts from human ecology theory such as *family*, *needs*, and *values* emphasize the interdependence and interactions among people and their environments. They provide a framework for looking at ways in which intrafamilial processes are influenced by extra-familial conditions and environments (Bubolz & Sontag, 1993).

The Ecological Context of African Immigrants' Childcare Situation

Though the immigration status of research participants was not identified in this study, the childcare situation of African immigrant parents may be dependent on their *immigration status*, that is, whether they come to the United States as refugees, immigrants, or illegal aliens, as well as a number of *pre-migration* and *post-migration* factors. Pre-migration experiences are as-sociated with social integration processes, including the economic, social, political, and ideological experiences of immigrants and refugees (Jacob, 1994). This is especially true for refugees who come from countries such as Ethiopia where repressive regimes have been in place (Bertot & Jacob, 1991). Reasons for departure, such as fear of one's death or the death of a loved one, poverty, famine, and starvation, accompanied by persecution and trauma, may have a lasting impact on individuals. Post-migration ex-periences are influenced by factors that determine their ease of integration into the host society such as the age, gender, marital status, presence of children, and level of education of the individual (Jacob, 1994).

African Family Life and Childcare Preferences

The extended family structure, collectivist values, and gendered division of labor in their pre-migration environment are some of the important influences on the childcare preferences of African immigrant parents. The family is the cornerstone of Ethiopian, Nigerian, and Congolese cultures. In Ethiopia, the husband usually works and earns money for the family, while the wife cares for children at home (Rode, 1999). Nigerian extended fam-ily structure includes all persons related by blood over several generations and marriage; parenthood, two-parent families, and gendered division of responsibilities are highly valued (Nwadiora, 1996). Women have a strong influence on family decision-making within the domestic spheres, such as childrearing and childcare (Heitritter, 1999; Turtoe-Sanders, 1998). Nigerian mothers who work outside the home rely on family members, relatives, neighbors, or informal arrangements to care for their children and usually no money is exchanged (Turtoe-Sanders, 1998). In Ethiopia and Nigeria, physical proximity of relatives is common, resources are exchanged, and instrumental, social, or emotional support is sought from members of the community. Socialization of African children mostly takes place in the extended family (Turtoe-Sanders, 1998). Traditional family roles are also common in Congo where women are in charge of childcare and housework (Mitchell, 2006). These values and practices of Ethiopian, Nigerian, and Congolese families continue to be identified as important to their child rearing and child socialization. Collectivism is also expressed in terms of positive beliefs about childcare provided by relatives and friends, compared to Anglo parents who emphasize individualism and are not always happy about that option (Uttal, 2002).

Most of the African countries, including Ethiopia, Nigeria, and Congo, have experienced periods of war, famine, disease, and poverty leading to an increase in one-parent households where if the husband is separated or deceased, the wife is left on her own to take care of the children. In such conditions the physical proximity of the relatives is highly valued and relied upon for childcare. When such mothers migrate to the United States, they are faced with the dilemma of raising a child as well as working to support him.

Research Paradigm and Methodology

A qualitative research approach, elements of naturalistic inquiry, a holistic view, purposive sampling, and inductive analysis offer the opportunity to describe and interpret situations in childcare (Patton, 1980; Porter, 1982). Since this is an area about which not much is known, the researcher's aim was to listen to the informants' voices and build a picture based on their ideas (Glaser, 1992). In keeping with the methodological assumptions of qualitative research, the literature was examined inductively so that it did not direct the analysis of the researcher (Creswell, 1994). Relevant literature in the discussion section is included to compare and contrast with the results.

The current study adopted a naturalistic inquiry paradigm as described by Lincoln and Guba (1985, pp. 37–38), which emphasizes multiple constructed realities (Amarapurkar, 2004). Corbin and Strauss (1990), Dawson and Prus (1995), and Prus (1996) describe the characteristics of a naturalistic inquiry study.

Seven immigrant families from Ethiopia, Nigeria, and Congo, interviewed as a part of the Minnesota Childcare Policy Research Partnership—Quality of Childcare Sub-study (MCCPRP), were selected for the sample. The MCCPRP study examines the quality of childcare for 120 families from various economic and cultural backgrounds. While the original sample included both urban and rural families, the sub-sample selected for the current study lived in the urban area. While both parents were invited to participate in the interview process, most fathers were unwilling or unavailable. Hence, interview data used to understand childcare experiences came from the mothers in six families and a father in one family.

Sample Description

The sub-sample of families immigrated to the United States from two to six years ago (table 10.1). Five families emigrated from Ethiopia, one from Nigeria and one from the Congo. Four parents described themselves as married and living with a spouse and children, two mothers were divorced and received child support from their spouses, one mother was separated from her husband, who lived in Ethiopia. The families each had one to

Table 10.1. Descriptive Profile of Seven Participants

Participant	Country of Origin (Language)	Years in United States	Marital Status	Gender and Ages of Children	Type of Childcare/ School Grade	Childcare Subsidy
A	Ethiopia (Oromiffia)	3	Married	4 yrs—girl 16 yrs—boy 17 yrs—girl	Day care 10th Grade 11th Grade	No
B	Ethiopia (Oromiffia)	4½	Married	4 yrs—boy 6 yrs—boy	Day care 1st Grade	Yes
C	Ethiopia (Oromiffia)	2	Separated	11 yrs—girl	5th Grade/ Maternal care[a]	No
D	Ethiopia (Oromiffia)	5	Married	6 yrs—boy 11 yrs—girl	Day care 5th Grade Maternal care[a]	No
E	Ethiopia (Oromiffia)	3	Married	Infant—boy 17-mos—girl	Maternal care[a] Relative care	Yes
F	Nigeria (English)	3	Divorced	14-mos—girl	Relative care	Yes
G	Congo (English)	6	Divorced	20-mos—boy	Early Head Start Maternal Care	Yes

Note: [a]Maternal care after school.

three children between ages birth through seventeen years. All families had low income levels with monthly incomes ranging from $620 to $3,000. Two families received Minnesota Family Investment Program (MFIP) assistance; one also received Supplemental Security Income (SSI). Four families were on the Basic Sliding Fee Program (BSF). One family was above the income eligibility for childcare assistance.

The Research Question

The overall research question was: What are the childcare experiences of Ethiopian, Nigerian, and Congolese immigrant families in Minneapolis-St. Paul, who have infants through school-age children? Descriptive statements emerged through inductive thematic analysis to help understand the childcare challenges of these families.

Data Collection Procedures

Quarterly interviews were conducted over a two-year period (2001–2003). The MCCPRP team, in collaboration with county childcare assistance staff partners, developed interview questions and research scripts for the first four interviews and distributed them to community researchers. Based on the interviews and input from participants and interviewers, the next four interviews were designed to examine in-depth the research question.

Community researchers were of the same ethnicity of the respondents and conducted the interviews in languages most comfortable for the family (Oromiffia for Ethiopian families and English for Nigerian and Congolese families). Oromiffian interviews were translated into English by the same community researchers and the English translations were used for analysis. Only responses to open-ended questions and the demographic data from the eight interviews were used.

Data Analysis

Inductive thematic data analysis was used to describe and explain the essence of childcare experiences in participants' lives based on the data. The categories, themes, and patterns came from the data and were not imposed prior to data collection (Janesick, 1994). By using the participants' own words and actions, descriptive qualitative studies offer perspectives which quantitative, grouped data cannot (Porter, 1982). Moustakis's (1990) heuristic approach to inductive analysis was used through *five* phases. *First*, the inductive process started with the immersion in the data. *Second*, the incubation process allowed for thinking, becoming aware of nuances and meanings, and capturing intuitive insights to achieve understanding. *Third*, the phase of illumination allowed for expanding awareness. *Fourth*, the phase of explication included description and explanation to capture the experience of individuals in the study. *Finally*, creative synthesis was carried out to bring together each person's story as a whole, including the lived experience. The mechanical tasks of the analysis such as coding and identifying themes and patterns in the interview data were carried out by using a computer software program called NUDIST*Nvivo. Analytic work began with line-by-line coding of the first couple of transcribed interviews of parents, which included open coding and identifying themes. The initial coding was done to organize data and progressively it became interpretive as patterns and relationships between patterns emerged.

Constant Comparative Method of Analysis

This method of analysis allows for comparisons to be made continuously across cases and incidents in the research process. The constant comparative method was appropriate because each of the seven participants were considered as a separate data source. As eight interviews were carried out with each participant, there were enough data generated to make multiple comparisons of individual experiences. Within and across family comparisons allow for a comprehensive examination of how each parent's experience is both similar to and different from every other parent's experience (Snyder, 1992).

Results

Based on the overall analysis, the following thematic categories emerged as primary to the childcare experiences of these families. Themes were: seeking childcare, factors of childcare selection, experiences with childcare subsidies, value of childcare, and cultural dilemmas and discrepancies.

Seeking Childcare

This broad area explores why the need to seek childcare was felt, the sources of information about childcare, who were involved in childcare selection, and problems encountered in obtaining childcare as well as the type of childcare selected. The need to seek employment or to pursue education made all seven families consider nonparental childcare options. The parents received information about a particular facility, a childcare referral agency, or county support programs from a friend, a relative, a coworker, or a neighbor. An employment counselor, a social worker, or county caseworkers were the main sources of information for three families. Two families learned about childcare options from their child's school. Most parents called the childcare provider, received brochures from them, and subsequently learned there was an opening, and decided to use a childcare facility. Only two parents reported they visited the childcare site before making a decision. Parents considered only two options: home-based relative care or center-based childcare. Home-based nonrelative care was not an option considered by any of the seven parents.

A variety of reasons were given for putting their child in center-based care versus relative care. Childcare centers provided a safe environment, scheduled time, and flexibility. As one Ethiopian mother explained: "The childcare centers are programmed and ready to deliver the services. According to their schedule they are open; you can drop your children anytime in that schedule and go to your school or work." Another Ethiopian mother said: "For immigrant family like me, it helps me a lot; I can fly like a bird after I drop them in day care." One Congolese parent selected Early Head Start over a day care center because transportation was available and the parents could call the staff anytime.

Care by relatives was preferred either as the main or alternative type of care by most families. This was a continuation of the childcare practices from their original country where family members, friends and neighbors provided childcare. Parents preferred childcare by a family member, a relative, or a friend because of the trust that the relative would treat their child with love and would provide safety and security like the child's mother. A Nigerian mother said: "When I am at work, I feel so much better knowing that she is with her dad or with my nephew."

Parental care was the most preferred type of care when: (1) parents could not afford paid childcare, (2) parents did not trust neighbors or friends, and (3) parents were ineligible for a childcare subsidy due to income, unemployment, or part-time employment. Some problems identified by the participants in obtaining childcare were lack of: knowledge about childcare subsidies, transportation to the childcare center, eligibility for childcare subsidy due to unemployment, and backup childcare when their childcare was closed and when children were sick.

Factors of Childcare Selection

Parents directly or indirectly identified the factors they considered while selecting childcare:

1. *Safety and security consideration*: Most parents identified safety and security as the most important factor they considered in selecting their childcare. As the Nigerian mother stated:

   > I have heard too many scary stories about home-based care. I have been watching too many *Lifetimes*. It just seems like it's better for her to go to the center-based day care. I guess I feel more comfortable about it because there are actually other workers around. It's not just them and her. . . .

   Two families moved to another area of the city, which they perceived to be safer and hoped to find safe childcare there. Two other parents who used relative care had the safety of the child in mind. In general, parents made sure that the place was safe by either visiting the day care or asking questions to the provider and talking to other parents whose children went to the same place.

2. *Proximity of the day care or availability of transportation*: The second major factor that parents considered was the proximity of the childcare setting, as some did not have a car, use public transportation, or want to drive a long distance. An Ethiopian mother stated, "Generally I don't want to take risk in Minnesota weather driving far from my home with my child, my first criteria is the proximity and then the quality of program."

3. *Availability of a family member or a relative*: Whenever the mother was at home either due to unemployment or a leave from her job, the preference was given for care at home by the mother. If a relative was ready to provide childcare, then relative care was selected over day care. Reasons given were: they were a part of the family; they knew the behavior of the child; the child was exposed to their culture, language, and family values; there was no travel involved; and most importantly, they were available according to the mother's work schedule. An Ethiopian mother said:

   > Childcare at home is good, especially when the provider is one of the family members. I learned that keeping your children with a person with whom you share culture, language, and family values is important for the children. If your child is with the family member, you don't need to worry about your child's safety, security, food, health, and other things.

4. *Cost and availability of childcare assistance*: Cost of the childcare and availability of subsidies were two important factors that influenced the choice of childcare for almost all parents. An Ethiopian father shared:

> I changed [childcare settings] once. I used to get childcare assistance. The previous provider and all the facilities including the teachers were better than the current one. The diversity of the children was good, too. I was forced to change the day care because the assistance was stopped. I couldn't afford it.

5. *Other factors*: Some other factors that parents considered were: quality of the program, the presence of bilingual teachers, licensing, the child's comfort level and interest in the setting, sanitary conditions, staff qualifications, space for play and naps, facilities of the building such as air conditioning, availability of openings, child's need to socialize with other children, and ease of communication with the staff.

Experiences with Childcare Subsidies

Participants reported a range of problems in getting childcare subsidies. They were not aware of subsidies when they came to the Unites States. An Ethiopian mother said:

> For new immigrants there is no information available to apply for assistance. When I first arrived, I didn't know about the existence of childcare assistance . . . my friends were taking care of my child, but it was very difficult since they used to do it when they had time . . . not for pay. So they were not always available.

Most faced problems in the application process or had communication problems with caseworkers. A Congolese mother explained:

> They didn't treat me very good . . . the lady just sends me a letter saying that it's going to stop paying Head Start. I didn't know why. So I tried to contact her. I left messages. She never gets back to me. Then I went there. She didn't want to talk to me. I asked to talk to her supervisor. She told me that it's because of this, this. I told her . . . at least you should have sent me a warning. After that incident, I asked the supervisor to give me another caseworker.

Value of Childcare

Participants talked about the value of childcare in their lives by focusing on how it influences their lives, both positively and negatively, and how they are involved in the childcare setting. While talking about positive influences they referred to how their children benefit, as well as how they benefit as parents, and aspects of the childcare program they liked. The most important benefit of nonparental childcare was it allowed them to work, attend school, or carry out chores while their child was cared for in a safe, secure setting by the childcare provider, a relative, or Head Start school staff member.

A second benefit was seen as getting an opportunity to meet and get to know parents of other children in the childcare setting, to learn about their perspectives on childcare and child rearing, and to share their own views with them. This was seen as an important source of getting to know more about American culture and to understand the school system in the United States, which in turn helped them acculturate with the system better.

The negative influences they talked about were children's ethnic language development, since they did not learn their native language, problems with the childcare setting, such as lack of diversity in the classroom, and differences in the discipline policies at school versus home.

Those parents who chose home-based care by relatives talked about other benefits: trust, individual attention, open communication, and no transportation issues. Being able to keep their child *in the family* while they went to work was valuable to them.

Benefits to Children
The benefits children received from childcare were different for those who used formal childcare (center-based, Early Head Start) versus those who used informal care (relatives). A fundamental difference could be traced to the differences in value priorities. Parents who used formal care were happy the formal childcare settings exposed their children to American culture; they learned English, etiquette, and values to help them acculturate better. Whereas parents who used informal care were happy their children were with a relative who spoke their ethnic language, before their children were exposed to American culture.

Parents who used center-based care talked about the importance of childcare in terms of the educational input and social skills children gain making them ready for school. An Ethiopian mother said:

> Sending the child to childcare is important if the childcare provider and environment are good. They learn from each other, get exposed to a new environment and culture; the provider teaches them basic education for school. It is very easy if children are at childcare to join their first grade in school. Their interaction with other children and culture is good.

Children were perceived to learn a lot at the childcare setting that they would not learn at home. Almost all the participants reported their children learned creative skills, computer skills, social skills, intellectual skills, and physical skills in addition to the English language. Children enjoyed being at the childcare setting and expressed this as they talked about their day.

Negative Influences

Children in formal care did not learn their native language, and this was cited as a major disadvantage of formal care. An Ethiopian mother expressed her concern: "My children are not speaking our native language. When they go to day care they speak English. They spend most of their time at the day care, not with us. So, it is difficult for us to teach them our language." Another concern was the frozen food served in the center-based childcare setting, whereas at home they would eat freshly cooked food.

Parental Involvement in the Childcare Setting

All the parents who used formal childcare said they participated in parent counseling meetings; parent-teacher conferences; volunteered for various activities like picnics, book-reading for children, working on the school bus; took part in fundraising activities; donated toys; gave money for school purposes; and gave feedback to the school through feedback forms. They also took part in annual cultural and entertainment programs at the school.

They were involved by talking to the director and staff about concerns, in order to resolve problems. Parents interacted with other parents in the childcare center, exchanged ideas about issues related to childcare, and met outside the center in person or by phone to discuss concerns. While talking about the role male figures should play in childcare setting activities, most parents felt the mother and father should get equally involved. The father should take time off from his work to go on field trips, attend parent-teacher conferences, and be involved in other activities.

Cultural Dilemmas and Discrepancies

The participants made frequent references to the cultural conflicts they faced. Adjusting to a different childcare environment was one of the important components of acculturation. Important cultural conflicts were related to language, food, and values. An Ethiopian mother said:

> I don't have much time to spend with my children on other days; on my day off I prefer to stay with them. If I go out for recreation, I go with

them. In our culture we don't leave our children with someone and go to recreation alone. If it is mandatory to go alone, my husband takes a day off.

Participants who used formal childcare reported that their child learned English from staff and American children at the childcare setting. Some parents were concerned about the lack of diversity within the childcare setting, thinking their child may feel and be looked upon differently.

Discussion and Implications

This study increases our understanding of childcare among Ethiopian, Nigerian, and Congolese immigrant families in Minneapolis-St. Paul. The experiences of these seven immigrant families illustrate factors that determine choices of immigrant families about childcare such as age of the child, low-income, maternal employment, and the nature of immigrant employment (Matthews & Ewen, 2006; NIEER, 2006). In addition to many constraints usually faced by low-income parents, these immigrant families are challenged with language and cultural barriers, lack of information, and difficulty in navigating the system. Their jobs and incomes are not stable, which poses serious constraints on the childcare options available to them. Low-income families, in general, place importance on issues of safety and trust in the provider (Phillips, 1996), which was emphasized by the immigrant families in this study. Further lack of infant care, care for odd work hours, after-school care, and summer care serve as barriers in selecting quality childcare, which was supported in this study. Availability of childcare that fits parents' work schedules and provides assurance of their child's safety and well-being is a high priority. However, low incomes, the cost of childcare and difficulties accessing childcare subsidies create major barriers to the families' work efforts (Phillips, 1996; National Institute of Child Health and Human Development, 1997). Further, just like other low-income parents, these immigrant families experienced a loss of subsidies as parents moved to a higher paying job or were unemployed (NIEER, 2006).

The nonparental childcare arrangements in these seven African immigrant families can be better understood using the ecological perspective (Bronfenbrenner, 1986; Bubolz & Sontag, 1993). The childcare arrangements and the experiences associated with obtaining and maintaining childcare were found to be directly and indirectly influenced by a number of familial (e.g., parental beliefs, family income) and extra-familial (e.g., childcare subsidies, American culture) factors. Like other immigrant and nonimmigrant families they face the need to find childcare while juggling the demands of job and personal life. They interact with multiple environments like the work environment, childcare environment, and other government and social institutions as well as community organizations. They face a number of opportunities as well as constraints in obtaining high-quality nonparental childcare. Values held about childrearing and childcare influence their childcare decisions. They try to carry out responsible childrearing through exploring and decision-making. Their social and cultural environments are influenced by the decisions and actions of the individual family. Overall, their childcare arrangements were affected not only by the information they gathered, their values and childrearing beliefs, but also by factors such as child's age, mother's employment, family income, availability of relatives, and state and federal childcare subsidy policies.

A review of literature did not reveal any study that assesses the value or the positive and negative influences of nonparental childcare for immigrant or nonimmigrant families. Studies were found related to parental satisfaction with childcare arrangements (e.g., Atkinson, 1996; Kisker & Ross, 1997) and childcare as a pathway to help immigrant children acculturate (Brandon, 2002). This study contributes to our understanding of the positive and negative influences of childcare for immigrant families and how it benefits the parents and their children. The findings of the current study have implications in the areas of *theory*, *research*, *policy*, *education*, and *practice* as follows.

Theoretical Basis

This study confirmed the value of an ecological framework to understand the use of nonparental childcare by African immigrant families. A literature review shows that most of the past studies on childcare choices lack an explicit theoretical framework to support their research. A strong theoretical basis is essential for any study in order to enrich the understanding of findings and improve the quality of discussion, as well as to provide a more valid basis for application and action (Lavee & Dollahite, 1991). Theoretical frameworks need to be developed or theories like family systems theory and family ecological theory need to be applied in future studies to better reflect childcare experiences.

Research Implications

Most studies treat childcare as a women's issue and fathers and children are not represented. Preferences of fathers and older children, however, may also factor into decisions about childcare. In this study one father was included, and future research should include the voices of fathers and children, not adequately represented in the current study.

Most parents in this study identified interaction with center-based childcare, and American children and their parents as a means to acculturate better and faster with the American society. Future studies need to include multiple immigrant groups to strengthen this finding. Also, studies need to include larger samples that represent diverse family structures such as single parents, dual-earner parents, divorced parents, and stepfamilies and represent different geographical regions and socioeconomic classes. Since acculturation takes place over time, longitudinal studies are needed to capture the essence of people's experiences as they make choices, process information, and evaluate outcomes.

Whether families come to the United States as refugees, legal immigrants, or illegal immigrants determines their employment status, income level, access to government subsidies, and use of formal childcare settings. Future research should sample these various immigrant groups to look at the differences in their experiences. Also comparison of immigrant and nonimmigrant families to explore the differences due to poverty, nonstandard work hours, language barriers, parental values, preferences for kin care, and access to subsidies would help identify problems unique to the immigrant population.

Policy Recommendations

Public policies are needed that increase parents' access to high quality and affordable childcare programs. In Minnesota the childcare costs are particularly high. A recent survey found that quality infant care costs $12,000 per year, which makes Minnesota the second-least-affordable childcare state in the nation (Stassen-Berger, 2006). Higher costs are driving lower- and middle-income parents away from quality programs into less expensive and less effective options for their children. More government subsidies and tax breaks are needed so that low-income parents can afford quality childcare. If policies encourage the use of relatives, then immigrant parents may find this is a viable option (Kuhlthau & Mason, 1996). Accordingly, this relative-based policy could lower the cost of such care and benefit parents financially.

Long waiting lists, unavailability of openings, and lack of odd-hour care, sick-care, and infant care were cited as major issues by the parents in the current study. Efforts should be made to increase the supply of licensed day care facilities. Immigrant parents will consider the provider's trustworthiness, proximity, flexibility, and ability to accommodate odd work schedules as important factors in choosing nonparental childcare. Policy makers should try to increase the resources and support available to unlicensed providers so that they can offer more school readiness skills and socialization activities to children from immigrant families, while considering the cultural ideas and family wishes of different immigrant groups.

Educator and Practitioner Recommendations

Immigrant parents indicated a lack of knowledge about how to be good consumers of childcare. Resources about childcare available to most parents were informal, inadequate, and poorly distributed. Thus, on the one hand there is a need to enhance immigrant parents' abilities to be knowledgable consumers of childcare and on the other hand there is a need to educate all providers about issues of immigrant parents (Amarapurkar & Hogan, 2004) as follows:

1. Parent information resources that address the needs of immigrant families should be developed to be used by childcare referral centers, caseworkers, Extension educators, and other social service professionals who work with immigrant families (e.g., information about formal versus informal childcare, relative care, with advantages and disadvantages associated with each type of care). Brochures in languages spoken by different immigrant groups should be made available for parents.
2. Childcare counselors need to give ample time to immigrant parents to talk about childcare options and parental need, as well as time to help them negotiate the system.
3. Comprehensive coordinated services are needed for parents to be able to apply for childcare subsidies and obtain information about choosing childcare at the same time and at the same location.
4. Information dissemination through less formal channels, such as ethnic grocery store kiosks and community associations, can be used since these families show a higher tendency to use informal sources.
5. Staff working in the fields of childcare referral, government subsidies, teachers, and childcare providers need to develop *cultural competence*. This should increase the staff's ability to relate and communicate effectively with people belonging to different culture, ethnicity, or language groups. It is essential to understand

that each ethnically diverse family has its own cultural values and ideas about child rearing.

Conclusion

The seven African immigrant families resemble other low-income families in many of the considerations that guide their childcare choices. These include unstable jobs, unavailability of childcare openings, transportation concerns, lack of access to relatives, lack of sick care and odd-hours care, and problems with childcare subsidies. Further, these African immigrant families face language difficulties, cultural barriers, and lack of information and difficulties in navigating the system. Like other families, safety and trust in the provider are important for them. Overall, their childcare experiences were affected by the information they gathered, their values and childrearing beliefs, as well as ecological correlates such as child's age, maternal employment, family income, availability of relatives, and childcare subsidy policies. Implications for research, policy, childcare consumer education and practice are discussed in the context of understanding issues related to immigrant family life. The increasing diversity in the United States poses challenges to all parents but more so for immigrant parents who have issues of acculturation and multicultural socialization of their children in a foreign land.

Acknowledgments

We would like to thank Deborah Ceglowski, Ph.D., program coordinator at the Child and Family Studies in the Department of Counseling, Special Education, and Child Development, at the University of North Carolina, Charlotte, for permission to access the Minnesota Childcare Research Project dataset based on which this research was possible.

We are grateful to Dr. Paul Rosenblatt, professor in the Department of Family Social Science at the University of Minnesota for reviewing the manuscript.

References

Adams, G., & Phillips, D. (2001). Childcare and our youngest children. *The Future of Children, 11*(1). Retrieved from www.futureofchildren.org/information2826/information79342.

Alejandro-Wright, M. (1982). An intra-cultural perspective on research. *Childcare Quarterly, 11*(1), 67–78.

Amarapurkar, S. S. (2004). Childcare experiences of African immigrant parents in Minneapolis-St. Paul: An inductive thematic analysis of seven families. Unpublished Doctoral Dissertation, University of Minnesota.

Amarapurkar, S. S., & Hogan, J. M. (2004) The childcare experience of African immigrant parents. *National Council of Family Relations Report: Family Focus on International Perspectives, Issue FF24*, F8. Minneapolis: National Council on Family Relations.

Atkinson, A. M. (1996). Rural mothers' evaluation of strong and weak points of childcare. *Journal of Research in Rural Education, 12*(2), 83–91.

Bertot, J., & Jacob, A. (1991). *Integration of refugees: Two case studies: Salvadorans and Iranians*. Montreal: Meridian.

Brandon, P. D. (2002). The childcare arrangements of preschool children in immigrant families in the United States. *The Foundation for Child Development: Working Paper Series* (pp. 1–36). Retrieved December 15, 2003, from www .ffcd.org.

Bronfenbrenner, U. (1986). Ecology of the family as a context for human development: Research perspectives. *Developmental Psychology, 22*, 723–742.

Bubolz, M. M., & Sontag, M. S. (1993). Human ecology theory. In P. G. Boss, W. J. Doherty, R. LaRossa, W. R. Schumm & S. K. Steinmetz (Eds.), *Sourcebook of family theories and methods: A contextual approach* (pp. 419–448). New York: Plenum Press.

Corbin, J., & Strauss, A. (1990). Grounded theory method: Procedures, canons and evaluative procedures. *Qualitative sociology, 13*, 13–21.

Creswell, J. W. (1994). *Research design: Qualitative and quantitative approaches*. Thousand Oaks, CA: Sage.

Dawson, L. L., & Prus, R. C. (1995). Postmodernism and linguistic reality versus symbolic interactionism and obdurate reality. In N. K. Denzin (Ed.), *Studies in symbolic interaction: A research annual*, 17, 105–124. Greenwich, CT: JAI.

Fix, M. E., Zimmerman, W., & Passel, J. S. (2001). *The integration of the immigrant families in the United States*. Washington, DC: The Urban Institute.

Gennetian, L. A., Huston, A. C., Crosby, D. A., Eun Chang, Y., Lowe, E. D., & Weisner, T. S. (2002). *Making child care choices: How welfare and work policies influence parents' decisions*. MDRC. Retrieved January 28, 2006, from www .mdrc.org/publications/182/policybrief.html.

Glaser, B. G. (1992). *Emergence vs. forcing: Basics of grounded theory analysis*. Mill Valley, CA: Sociology Press.

Heitritter, D. L. (1999). *Meanings of family strength voiced by Somali immigrants: Reaching an inductive understanding*. Unpublished doctoral dissertation, University of Minnesota.

Jacob, A. G. (1994). Social integration of Salvadoran refugees. *Social Work, 39*(3), 307–312.

Janesick, V. J. (1994). The dance of qualitative research design: Metaphor, methodolatry and meaning. In N. K. Denzin & Y. S. Lincoln (Eds.), *Handbook of qualitative research*, (pp. 209–219). Thousand Oaks, CA: Sage.

Kamya, H. A (1997). African immigrants in the United States: The challenge for research and practice. *Social Work*, *42*(2), 154–165.

Kisker, E. E., & Ross, C. M. (1997). Arranging childcare. *The Future of Children*, *7*(1), 99–109. Retrieved May 6, 2004, from www.futureofchildren.org/information2826/information.

Kuhlthau, K., & Mason, K. O. (1996). Market childcare versus care by relatives: Choices made by employed and non-employed mothers. *Journal of Family Issues*, *17*(4), 561–578.

Lavee, Y., & Dollahite, D. C. (1991). The linkage between theory and research in family science. *Journal of Marriage and Family*, *53*, 361–373.

Leslie, L. A., Anderson, E. A., & Branson, M. P. (1991). Responsibility for children: The role of gender and employment. *Journal of Family Issues*, *12*(2), 197–210.

Lincoln, Y. S., & Guba, E. G. (1985). *Naturalistic inquiry*. Newbury Park, CA: Sage.

Matthews, H., & Ewen, D. (2006). *Reaching all children? Understanding early care and education participation among immigrant families*. Retrieved October 13, 2006, from www.clasp.org/publications/child_care_immigrant.pdf.

Minnesota Child Care Policy Research Partnership (MCCPRP). A wave III childcare policy research partnership. Project no. 90YE0010, Project years 2000–2003, Minnesota Department of Children, Families and Learning, Retrieved December 20, 2002, from www.acf.hhs.gov/programs/ccb/research/ccprc/partner/minesota.doc.

Mitchell, S. (2006). *Democratic Republic of Congo*. In Cultural Profiles Project funded by Citizenship and Immigration Center Canada. Retrieved September 5, 2007, from www.cp-pc.ca/english/congo/index.html.

Moustakis, C. (1990). *Heuristic research design, methodology and applications*. Newbury Park, CA: Sage.

National Institute of Child Health and Human Development (NICHD). Early child care research network. (1997). Poverty and patterns of childcare. In J. Brooks-Gunn & G. Duncan (Eds.), *Consequences of growing up poor* (pp.100–131). New York: Russell Sage.

National Institute for Early Childhood Education (NIEER). (2006). *Important predictors of early childhood education and care*. Retrieved October 13, 2006, from nieer.org/resources/facts/index.php?fastFactID=9.

Nwadiora, E. (1996). Nigerian families. In M. McGoldrick, J. Giordano & J. K. Pearce (Eds.), *Ethnicity and family therapy* (pp. 129–140). New York: Guilford Press.

Patton, M. Q. (1980). *Qualitative evaluation and research methods*. Beverly Hills, CA: Sage.

Phillips, D. (1996). *Childcare for low-income families: Summary of two workshops*. Washington, DC: National Academy Press. Retrieved March 21, 2002, from nccic.org/research/nrc_care/c_care.html.

Porter, C. J. (1982). Qualitative research in childcare. *Child Care Quarterly*, *11*(1), 44–54.

Prus, R. C. (1996). *Symbolic interaction and ethnographic research: Intersubjectivity and the study of human lived experience*. Albany: State University of New York Press.

Reardon-Anderson, J., Capps, R., & Fix, M. E. (2002). The health and well-being of children in immigrant families. *New federalism: National survey of American families*, Series B-52. Washington, DC: The Urban Institute.

Rode, P. (1999). *Ethiopian and Somali families in Minneapolis: A community study*. Minneapolis: Way to Grow.

Snyder, S. (1992). Interviewing college students about their constructions of love. In J. Gilgun, K. Daly & G. Handel (Eds.), *Qualitative methods in family research* (pp. 215–226). Newbury Park, CA: Sage.

Stassen-Berger, R. E. (2006). *Costly child care: Minnesota day care is second–least affordable in country*. *St. Paul Pioneer Press*. Retrieved February 21, 2006, from www.grandforks.com/mld/grandforks/news/13866661.htm?source=rss&.

Turtoe-Sanders, P. (1998). *African tradition in marriage: An insider's perspective*. Brooklyn Park, MN: Turtoe-Sanders.

U.S. Census Bureau (2000). *United States Census 2000*. Retrieved July 15, 2003, from www.census.gov/main/www/cen2000.html.

Uttal, L. (2002). *Making care work: Employed mothers in the new childcare market*. New Brunswick, NJ: Rutgers University Press.

About the Authors

Sayali S. Amarapurkar, Ph.D., is a research associate and lecturer in the Department of Family Social Science at the University of Minnesota, 290 McNeal Hall, St.Paul, MN 55108. E-mail: amar0011@umn.edu.

M. Janice Hogan, Ph.D., is an emeritus professor in the Department of Family Social Science at the University of Minnesota, 290 McNeal Hall, St. Paul, MN 55108. E-mail: jhogan@umn.edu.

Decisions about Child Rearing Practices in First Generation Asian Indian Immigrants

11

RUCHA LONDHE

Abstract

This research study explored the decision-making processes of immigrant Indian parents and measured the level of acculturation, stress, and social support experienced by these parents. The results of the study indicated parents drew from both cultures. Practices that were studied included sleeping arrangements, feeding practices, baby massage, toilet training, discipline, religious/social rituals, father participation in childcare, the role of the extended family, and day care arrangements. Some practices from the sending culture were completely retained, some practices were integrated, and some practices were adopted from the receiving culture.

Keywords: Child Rearing Practices, First Generation, Asian Indian Immigrants, Day Care.

WHILE RAISING THEIR CHILDREN, parents continuously make numerous decisions about child rearing and many of these decisions have important consequences. These decisions occur within the broader context of the parents' culture, which serves as a guiding framework for the parental decisions. When parents immigrate

Address all correspondence to Dr. Rucha Londhe, 135 Woodland Road, Southborough, MA 01772. Phone: 508-485-9160. E-mail: ruchalondhe@gmail.com.

to a different culture, however, they have to negotiate the conflicting demands and values of two cultures and then make new decisions about child rearing. The present study focused on the cultural dilemmas Asian Indian immigrant parents face while raising their children in the United States. The study focused not only on *what* choices the Indian immigrant parents make with regard to child rearing practices, but also on *how* they make those choices.

Cultural differences in caregiving practices are not arbitrary; they shape the specific experiences that parents structure for their children and the developmental outcomes of these experiences (Gaskins, 1996). The relationship between culture and child rearing has been explained by various theoretical and conceptual models (e.g., Bronfenbrenner, 1977; Lerner, 1978). These theories view parenting as a complex process; it goes beyond the parents providing mere food, shelter, and safety to their offspring to include dynamic and bidirectional interactions between the parent and the child. These interactions take place within the broader cultural context. Parents choose the settings in which the child resides, and these settings provide culture-specific experiences. The child rearing activities that take place in these settings are determined by cultural customs and parental ethnotheories (Super & Harkness, 1997).

Studies of culture and child development focus on various influences on the parenting styles and decisions of parents residing in a specific culture. They do not, however, address the parenting practices of immigrant parents who belong to one culture but raise their children in a foreign culture. One of the processes that helps to explain the practices of immigrant families is the process of acculturation. Acculturation is defined as the process of "accommodation to a host culture on the part of a member of a migrant culture" (Szapocznik, Scopetta, Kurtines & Aranalde, 1978, p. 114). Berry and Sam (1997) proposed a model of acculturation strategies that holds that immigrant families use approaches related to two main dimensions: cultural maintenance (the extent to which the family strives to maintain its original cultural identity) and contact and participation (the extent to which the family members participate in the host culture or remain away from it). Using these two dimensions the researchers have proposed four acculturation strategies: (1) assimilation occurs when the immigrant family does not want to maintain its original cultural identity and seeks to take on the new culture; (2) the exact opposite is separation, in which the family, not wanting to give up its original culture, withdraws from the host culture; (3) a lack of interest in either maintenance of the original culture or assimilation into the new one, is characteristic of marginalization; (4) finally, integration is a balance of retaining the original cultural identity to a certain extent and also participating in the larger social network. The particular acculturation strategy adopted by the immigrant parents' influences their child rearing decisions.

Research has indicated links among parenting stress, social support, and acculturation experiences in immigrant families (Short, 1996; Xu, 2004). Although national and class variations exist in the immigrant populations, most immigrants to the United States come from collectivistic societies that involve three-generational and extended family compositions (Falicov, 2003). Studies have shown that extended family members who are physically present for the immigrant families play a significant role in helping the family as it struggles through the challenges of finding continuity (Harwood, Miller & Irizarry, 1995). Similarly, social as well as cultural isolation and loss of social, interpersonal support can be sources of stress that affect parents in the immigrant families (Siantz, 1997).

The present research explored the decision-making processes of the immigrant Indian parents and measured the level of acculturation, stress, and social support experienced by these parents. It focused on three aspects of Indian parenting which include the following specific practices:

1. Physical care—sleep arrangements and regulation, feeding practices, baby massage, and toilet training.
2. Discipline and socialization—discipline techniques and religious/social rituals.
3. Childcare support—father participation, role of extended family, and day care arrangements.

Research has identified differences in American and Indian beliefs and practices with regard to the above-mentioned childcare areas. For example, in many countries including India, mothers and infants sleeping together is a common practice (Bhavnagri & Gonzalez-Menz, 1997). In contrast, for the most part co-sleeping is not considered desirable in the United States and American pediatricians discourage the practice (Bhavnagri & Gonzalez-Menz, 1997). In a study of Punjabi families in the United Kingdom, it was found that although the Indian immigrant parents tended to modify some of their child rearing practices, they retained the custom of co-sleeping (Dosanjh & Ghuman, 1996). In terms of the sleep regulation and routines of infants, medical opinion in India suggests that parents should try to put the child to sleep according to a fixed schedule but no fixed schedule should be followed for waking up the child (Devgan, 1998). Although more current research on the topic is not available, past research indicates that the majority of parents in India are not strict about sleep regulation (going to bed at a particular time) until the child is about three years old (Ojha & Pramanick, 1992). In contrast professionals in the United States recommend adopting a regular bedtime ritual as early as possible (Brazelton & Sparrow, 2003).

Another example is that of baby massage. Massage for infants is a common practice in most countries in south Asia, including India. Massage is described as rubbing the body of the infant with oil or some other ointment and then pressing one's hands, warmed over a fire, on the body of the infant with palms open so that the warmth is transferred to the infant. Reissland and Burghart (1987) have described in great detail the purposes of such massage, namely, "to clean, beautify, strengthen, limber up and fatten the baby as well as to instill in it positive mental-emotional qualities" (p. 231). Although baby massage is mentioned as a useful practice in some child rearing books in the United States (e.g., Eisenberg, Murkoff & Hathaway, 1989), it is not practiced commonly.

With regard to toilet training, research on medical professionals in India shows that the desired age for beginning toilet training is one year (Devgan, 1998) whereas books on parenting in the United States advise parents to begin toilet training by the age of two years (e.g. Spock, 2004; Ames, Meyerhoff, Mendelson & Mendelson, 1991). With regard to discipline, the ideas about individualism and collectivism play a role in parents' decisions about which discipline strategies to use. Although more recent studies are not available, older studies have indicated that Indian mothers tend to rely on persuasion and other internal control mechanisms (Kakar, 1978), whereas American mothers have been reported to use their power and authority for compliance from their children (Sinha, 1985).

Very few studies involving father participation in childcare have been conducted with Indian and Indian immigrant families (e.g. Jain & Belsky, 1997; Rajagopalan, 1989; Roopnarine, Lu & Ahmeduzzaman, 1989). Also, none of these studies has attempted to understand how the decisions about the level of father participation in Indian immigrant families are made. Similarly, there is also a dearth of research on the roles that grandparents and external day care facilities play in childcare in the immigrant Indian families in the United States.

Given these cultural differences in child rearing practices in India and the United States, this exploratory study focused on the following research questions:

1. In which domains of child rearing do first generation Asian Indian parents in the United States face cultural dilemmas while making decisions?
2. What child rearing decisions do the parents make? In what ways do their decisions reflect the traditional views? In what ways do they reflect Western views?
3. Is there a relationship between acculturation, social support, and the stress experienced by these parents?

In addition, the current study was designed to address a number of limitations in the literature on parenting in immigrant families. First, most of the research on parenting in Indian immigrant families has focused on identifying the differences/similarities in the parenting styles of immigrant and Western parents. In contrast, this study focused on the actual decision-making processes of these parents. Second, the present study extended the scope of the literature on immigrant parenting by including a variety of child rearing issues listed above. Third, the present study looked at the much-ignored fathers' role in child rearing in the Indian immigrant families. Fourth, unlike previous studies that have used questionnaires and parenting scales, the present study involved in-depth interviews, which facilitated the collection of richer information on the actual experiences of these parents.

Methodology

Sample
The sample for the present study consisted of Indian parents from mainland India, both mothers and fathers, of thirty preschool/kindergarten children between the ages of three-to-six years living in New England. For each couple, both the mother and the father were married, had been raised in India and had not migrated to the United States before the age of eighteen years. The participants, all Hindus, were recruited using a snowball sampling technique. The mean age of the mothers in the study was 33.3 years (range 26–41) and the mean number of years spent in the United States was 8.63 (range 4–15). The mean age of the fathers in the study was 36.4 years (range 31–45) and the mean number of years spent in the

United States was 11.3 (range 4–23). The sample for the present study was a highly educated sample with all the mothers and fathers having at least a bachelor's degree and 60 percent of the mothers and 83 percent of the fathers having a master's degree. All the fathers and 50 percent of the mothers were employed full time. The mean age of the children was 4.5 years. There were slightly more boys (nineteen) than girls (eleven). There were equal numbers of first-born and single children (twelve) and the remaining were second born. With regard to the extended family of the participants, all thirty couples reported that they were in touch with the paternal and the maternal grandparents of the child, who resided in India, through phone calls, e-mails, and regular visits. Except for one family, which chose English, all the other families reported some regional language of India as the primary language spoken at home.

Measures

INTERVIEW SCHEDULE. Semi-structured interviews, which took sixty to ninety minutes to complete, were conducted in English with both parents together at a location of their choice. An interview guide was designed to address the various areas of child rearing. A family information form, which helped to gather demographic information from the parents, was administered as a part of the interview. Using the instructions provided by Weiss (1994), initial codes were developed by the researcher through open coding of all thirty interviews. Parents' responses were initially indexed, based on the topic under which the response was given. Culturally relevant coding schemes for the content analysis of parents' open-ended responses were created inductively. Tree nodes were then used to create topical branches of coding categories. The factors involved in parental decision-making processes for each of the child rearing practices were analyzed separately. Mothers' and fathers' answers were combined during coding.

STEPHENSON MULTIGROUP ACCULTURATION SCALE. This instrument yields data on two separate scales for each individual: Ethnic Society Immersion (ESI) or the extent to which the family strives to maintain its original cultural identity, and Dominant Society Immersion (DSI) or the extent to which the family members participate in the host culture or remain away from it (Stephenson, 2000). The results on this scale were used to develop an overall profile of the sample on Berry and Sam's (1997) model of acculturation strategies. The scale has high reliability indexes (0.86 coefficient alphas for the entire scale and 0.97 and 0.90 for the two dimensions of ESI and DSI, respectively) and findings also have revealed that the two-dimension construction of the scale is consistent with the theoretical conceptualization of acculturation (Stephenson, 2000).

STRESS AND SOCIAL SUPPORT SCALES. The Parental Stress Inventory/ Short Form (Abidin, 1995a, 1995b) was used to assess parental stress and the Family Support Scale (Dunst, Trivette & Jenkins, 1994) was used to measure the social support experienced by the parents.

Results for Research Questions 1 and 2

Physical Care

SLEEP ARRANGEMENTS AND REGULATION. In terms of specific sleep arrangements, in 76.6 percent of the families studied the child slept in the same room as the parents (this included actual sharing of the same bed or simply placing the crib in the parents' room). Although there were a number of reasons that parents had for this particular arrangement, most common of those was that the children need the parents close to them at night for the reasons of security and attachment. In the words of one mother,

> I think some way the Indian parents are more emotionally attached with the child and we feel that if the child stays in separate room right from the beginning, the attachment, the emotional attachment, which is very strong in our culture, that will not be formed.

As is evident from this mother, the Indian parents also saw the specific sleep arrangements as a factor that helps boost the bonding between the parents and the infant:

> I think a lot of bonding occurs at the young age, in our culture that touch, the closeness is important, here holding is not so common, baby seat to car seat to crib, holding is so less. Even at night the touch, being near to the child is important to us.

These quotes also highlighted the fact that parents attribute their choices of sleep arrangements to their culture of origin. Many noted that they wanted to co-sleep with their children for the simple reason that it is the way they were brought up in India. When asked about the age at which they would like to transition the child to her or his own room 26 percent of the parents replied, "only when he/she is comfortable with the arrangement."

Thirty percent of the parents replied that they would do so when the child was about four or five years old. In the words of a mother,

> Seems like it [separate rooms] makes sense but when we grew up, [we were] sleeping in our parents' bed and that didn't mess us up and we don't do that when we are thirty. So we made a decision that only when he is ready we will do it [sleep separately].

The 23 percent of the children who did sleep in separate rooms were the older children in the sample. Also, out of these seven families, only in one did the parents seem to be following the practice on the advice of the pediatrician. Thus, sleep arrangements seem to be one of the child rearing practices where the parents' ideas were guided by what is considered traditional Indian thought.

It is not a common practice in India for parents to take special efforts to schedule the sleep of the child. The parents in the present study varied in their opinions related to scheduling. Although 80 percent of the parents said that scheduling the child's sleep is a good practice, their ideas about sleep schedule varied considerably with regard to whether parents should make any special efforts for the scheduling and if so, at what age of the child. A majority of the parents were of the opinion that the children need a sleep schedule around the time they start school and so that would be the ideal age to put them on a schedule. Again, parents seemed to believe that there were differences in the American and Indian ideologies on sleep scheduling, as is evident from the quote below from a family that chose the Indian way:

> We had not put any regulations till he was three. Since he was not in school, he would sleep sometime like midnight. Kids here sleep at 8–8:30 on weekdays but we didn't do anything like that. But when he started going to school we changed it so that he goes to bed at 8–8:30 so that he wakes up at a specific time. It has to be a routine on weekdays.

There were certain strong negative feelings expressed against scheduling. In the words of a father,

> no such thing as schedule . . . never thought about it. . . . He slept when he slept . . . and he was in bed with us . . . so there was no issue of nursing problems . . . don't know and don't care about the sleep schedule.

FEEDING PRACTICES. Parents in India tend to hand feed their children much longer than American parents do. Although the children in the present study were between the ages of three and six years, 97 percent of the parents replied that they hand fed their children during meals at home. The parents expressed the idea that if children are left on their own they would either not eat enough or would not eat the right types of food. They are often distracted and so need to be fed. Again, the parents were aware of the cultural differences in feeding habits, but tend to follow the Indian path. In the words of one of the fathers,

> In U.S. the kids eat on their own, even the parents don't force them . . . there is no compulsion . . . but I have not seen a single Indian parent who doesn't have problem with feeding his kid . . . they run behind the child. . . . The child rarely sits at one place and eats on his own . . . in India they will say, if the child is not eating you feed him . . . it's considered more motherly . . . good or bad I don't know . . . you will feed him . . . you will not like that he has not eaten properly . . . you will not be happy with that.

A few parents also mentioned that they made special efforts to keep the child vegetarian. These included informing the day care authorities about the type of food that the child can eat, talking and explaining to the child the nutritional facts about vegetarian food (especially for older children) and avoiding cooking meat at home. The parents were aware that the children may not always remain vegetarians but in the words of one mother, "maybe eventually she will make her decision to eat non-vegetarian food when she is older . . . but right now we have decided to stay vegetarian."

BABY MASSAGE. Massaging the infant before bath is a common practice in India. In the present sample, every family but one had implemented a baby massage routine for their infants. Although the parents gave a variety of reasons for continuing this traditional infant care practice, the most common reason (57 percent) was that the grandparents insisted that it be done. In a related question, 90 percent of the parents had reported that one set of the child's grandparents was present at the time of childbirth. So not only were the grandparents instrumental in advocating for the massage routine, but they were also actually present to teach it to the parents.

TOILET TRAINING. In India children are toilet trained at a much earlier age as compared to the norm in the United States. By twelve to fifteen months parents in India parents at least begin efforts to toilet train their child (Devgan, 1998), whereas in the United States the training usually does not begin before the age of two years (e.g., Spock, 2004; Ames, Meyerhoff, Mendelson & Mendelson, 1991). Parents in the present study were aware of these age differences and attributed them to a number of reasons, such as the easy availability and convenience of diapers in the United States, which tend to be extremely expensive in India; carpeted floors in the United States that allow for very few accidents during the training, compared to the cement flooring in India; and cold climatic conditions in the United States in contrast to the heat in India. Parents also linked the age of toilet training to the availability of support in India. The higher number of family members at home usually tends to include older cousins, and the presence of these older children facilitates toilet training of the younger children in the family. Another interesting factor contributing to the toilet training process in India, according to some parents, was the informal relations with the neighbors in India. In the words of a mother,

> in India your neighbor's child pees on the floor it's nothing that the parents or the neighbors will feel scandalized about, whereas in the U.S. even in the Indian families here, people are just taken aback . . . so you want to avoid accidents at all cost.

The immigrant parents, having recognized the differences in the toilet training ages in India and the United States, tend to follow the ideas of the host culture. In about 76 percent of the families, toilet training began only after the age of two years.

Discipline and Socialization

DISCIPLINE TECHNIQUES. In terms of the goals of discipline, the parents reported that there probably are not many differences between the two cultures. Parents in both cultures look at discipline resulting in responsible, good mannered, independent children, leading to good citizens of the world. The parents did mention the increased stress that they experience as they try to incorporate both Indian and American standards of behavior for their children. As a father put it,

> we came from India with rules X and learn in America rules Y . . . we are trying to teach the child rules $X+Y$ . . . we are doing too much . . . our children are doing too much . . . we have to reach a final ground of $X+Y-$ *something* so that it is manageable.

The parents identified a number of differences in the discipline styles of Indian and American parents. In their opinion, the American style of discipline treats the child as an adult, is consistent and methodical, and uses scolding and yelling at minimum. Although the parents accepted the advantages of these American techniques of discipline, they still maintained what according to them were the Indian ways of scolding, yelling, and spanking. The most common justification used by these parents was "that's the way we were brought up and so we know that it works." One third of the sample reported that they try to use both the techniques in a balance.

An interesting issue that came up was the link between social support, stress, and discipline. With the extended family in India some parents are able to cut themselves away from certain disciplinary situations, and this gives them breathing room as is indicated by this mother:

> I think there is reason to it . . . again it comes back to support. . . . Here it's only the two of you. First of all you are stressed out at the end of the day and then when he [the child] talks about watching TV and something like that . . . you are much more likely to break down here, whereas in India you have the support system of the people in the house so maybe if you don't want to deal with the situation at that time maybe the grandparents. . . . The grandparents always have a softer anger . . . they will say, "don't hit him, I will take care of it . . ." whatever . . . maybe they end up spoiling him . . . but just that diversion that is created helps.

RELIGIOUS AND SOCIAL RITUALS. There are a number of religious and social rituals associated with the birth of a child in an Indian family. Some of these include a traditional baby shower, an elaborate naming ceremony around the twelfth day, the first visit of the child to the temple, and the first intake of solid foods. Of these different events, the naming ceremony seemed to be the one practiced by most immigrant parents in the sample. The forty-day rule, which refers to the rule that the new mother and her infant do not leave the house until the child is forty days old, was in practice a difficult rule to follow, given the lack of social and domestic support in the United States. A considerable number of parents also chose to carry out a lot of traditional ceremonies during their month-long trips to India.

When asked about celebrating festivals, all the parents reported that they celebrated most of the Indian festivals. However, three specific themes came up with regard to festivals, namely (1) trying their best to celebrate the Indian festivals as celebrated in India, (2) feelings of loss because they cannot give the complete experience of the festival to their children, and (3) compensating by celebrating American festivals. Close to a third of the sample said that they try their best to celebrate the Indian festivals. These festivals usually include Diwali, Ganapati, Janmashtami, and Rakhi. The parents try to introduce the festivals to their children by putting up lights and making the special foods for Diwali, worshiping the idol of Ganapti for ten days during the Ganesh festival, performing the brother-sister Rakhi ceremony, attending various events at the cultural organizations during festivals, encouraging the children to participate in these cultural events, and other ways.

Although parents do try to celebrate the Indian festivals, a lot of them voiced regret that their children cannot get the complete experience of that festival here in the United States. A number of reasons were cited for this lack of a complete experience. First, Indian festivals are never a holiday in the United States. So it is not easy for the parents to celebrate these festivals to the fullest. The second reason, which stems from the first one, is that even though the parents create the festive atmosphere, it stays confined to their homes. The moment they step out of the house, it is no longer a festival time. So even if the children are involved in the celebrations they cannot make those cultural connections. Third, sometimes there are physical and weather constraints, for example, one cannot play with colors and water during Rangapanchami which falls in the month of March or one cannot get the complete experience of Diwali without the firecrackers. Finally, as a mother in the study put it,

> The problem is Christmas. Competing with Christmas is very hard thing to do, it's like Diwali at home.

So what do the parents do? A number of parents reported that they end up adopting the American festivals also. They send their children trick-or-treating for Halloween, invite family and friends for Thanksgiving dinner, and put up a tree and place gifts under it for Christmas. Finally, the parents realize that their children are born in the United States and have to lead their life here. As a mother put it,

> I really don't want my children to live in a bubble . . . you know, a bubble created by us . . . when they come home it's a bubble of *Indianness* . . . I don't want that . . . for them its confusing . . . with them we have to change . . . whether you like it or not . . . you change . . . we celebrate Halloween and Christmas . . . do what you were doing in India and also adapt to new things.

Related to learning about Indian culture and celebrations is the idea of sending the children to Indian school once they are a little older. These schools usually have two kinds of classes, one focused on the language and the second focused on the culture and history of India. A number of such organizations can be found in New England. The idea is that the children will learn Indian culture, history, and language from an early age. Along with celebrating each Indian festival within their families, the parents rely on these schools to elaborate on the significance of religious festivals and the cultural history of the country.

Childcare Support

FATHER PARTICIPATION. Two major themes emerged from parents' conversations on father participation in childcare. These were comparisons with the role played by fathers in India and the actual activities that the fathers undertook. With regard to comparison between fathers in India and the United States, 86 percent of the parents agreed that the immigrant fathers in the United States definitely play a greater parenting role than the fathers in India. This greater level of participation by fathers in the United States was attributed to two factors: lack of domestic help and lack of social support. In the absence of any other help, the parents have to divide childcare responsibilities and activities between the two of them.

The participation of the fathers in childcare in the United States begins right from the birth process. In India, fathers are usually not present during childbirth. Especially if it is the first child, the mother goes back to her parental home for the delivery and comes back only when the baby is about three months old. Even if it is the second or third child, there is always someone apart from the husband to help. Fathers in the present sample identified this as a disadvantage for the Indian fathers and they were glad to be a part of childcare right from childbirth.

ROLE OF GRANDPARENTS. Traditionally the grandparents in India, because of the joint family system, played a very crucial role in the life of the child. In spite of the diminishing number of joint families in India today, the grandparents still do contribute to childcare in the family. When asked if the grandparents play a role in childcare in spite of the physical distance between them, 40 percent of the parents said that they play a role whenever they visit them in the United States. This includes reading storybooks in regional languages for the children, telling them stories from Indian epics, making traditional Indian food for them, and playing with them. The parents suggested that when the grandparents visit them, they want the children to spend time with them; both the grandparents and the children need the interaction. To quote a father,

> There is something each generation gives to the next generation and when you are young, a lot of it comes from grandparents because you may not get along with parents, [you] may rebel from them but you always do get along with grandparents and they do things more traditionally than we do and he [child] learns those things . . . like speaking a second language, foodwise, religious stories, playing games like chess with them. . . . At the same time it is not just the child who is learning, the grandparent is also so involved in the whole process. It is actually great for both grandparents and children.

One third of the parents tended to consult the grandparents on issues related to the health of the child, especially seeking advice about simple home remedies. A few parents also sought advice on food (e.g., which Indian foods to introduce at what age) and child behavior (e.g., "Did I demonstrate this kind of behavior while I was growing up?"). Parents also agreed that the child's regional language would improve tremendously during their trip to India or grandparents' trip to the United States.

DAY CARE ARRANGEMENTS. Traditionally because of the presence of the joint family in India, the parents did not need to send children to day care facilities outside of home. Although today the scene is changing in India, parents still are conservative about the age at which children should be put in day care facilities. This conservatism also was reflected in the ideas of the parents in the present study. When asked about the ideal age at which the child should be put in day care, the parents unanimously agreed that it should not happen before the age of one year. Some parents used a different criterion to determine the readiness of the child, namely, the ability to communicate and express oneself, the idea was that the child should be able to report back to the parents about anything that happens at the childcare center. A couple of parents even mentioned the ideal arrangement would be to wait until the child was old enough to go directly to preschool.

When asked about the actual age at which their child was put in any kind of care outside of home, five parents (16.6 percent) reported that this happened before the age of one year. Of the remaining 83.3 percent, ten mothers made the conscious decision to be *stay-at-home* mothers and another six mothers quit their jobs after childbirth so that the child did not have to go to day care. The most common reason for not sending the child to day care before the age of one was that they were likely to catch infections easily because the immune system of the younger children is not optimally developed. In addition to these medical and health reasons, there were also strong psychological reasons. The parents felt that before the age of one year the child needs the one-to-one bonding with the mother. In short, with regard to the day care arrangements for the child, the immigrant parents in the study tended to follow the Indian practice of the *later the better.*

Results for Research Question 3

Analysis across the Acculturation, Parenting Stress, and Social Support Scales

The Stephenson Multigroup Acculturation Scale yields data on two separate scales for each individual: Ethnic Society Immersion (ESI) and Dominant Society Immersion (DSI). In the present sample, the mean score on ESI scale was 63.3 (range 49–68, SD = 4.0) and the mean score on DSI was 47.3 (range 29–58, SD = 6.6). The results on this scale were used to develop an overall profile of the sample on Berry and Sam's (1997) model of acculturation strategies. A scatter plot of these scores shows that the present sample was high on both the scales, indicating that the sample was "integrated" (see figure 11.1).

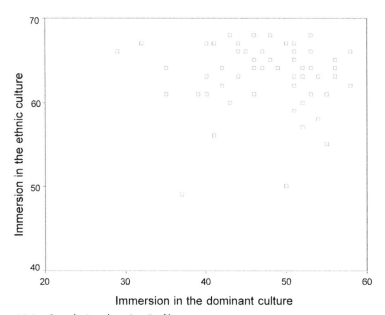

Figure 11.1.   Sample Acculturation Profile

The Family Support Scale includes eighteen items rated on a five-point scale from *not at all helpful* (1) to *extremely helpful* (5), yielding a range of eighteen through ninety on the total score. The mean score obtained on the scale was 35.4 (range 18–62, SD = 11.7). Among the individual items the highest mean score was obtained by *spouse* (mean 4.46) followed by *own friends* (mean 3.08) and *school and day care* (mean 3.05). These findings are in accordance with the findings from the interviews. As mentioned before, the data from the interviews identified the important role Indian immigrant fathers play in household and child-related chores. The support from friends and day care centers was also mentioned repeatedly for such child rearing issues as toilet training and discipline.

The Parent Stress Inventory—Short Form yields a total stress score between 36 and 180, with higher scores indicating higher levels of stress. The mean score obtained for the sample was 68.42 (range 42–101; SD = 12.2) indicating that the stress levels of the parents in the sample fell in the moderate range.

Although quantitative analyses of the data from these three scales showed no significant correlations among acculturation, social support, and the stress experienced by the parents, certain interesting connections came up through the interviews. For example, the presence of the extended family at home, grandparents and older cousins, helps during the toilet training process in India. The informal relationships with neighbors and friends in India also help the parents during the toilet training phase of their children. If the child has an accident at a neighbor's house, it does not bother the parent or the neighbor. Another example of interconnections between the various child rearing experiences is that the reduced social support and domestic help for Indian mothers in the United States is associated with the increase in the participation of the father in childcare activities.

Discussion

Results of the present study indicated that the Indian immigrant parents were aiming for a balance in the practices followed by both cultures, while making decisions about different aspects of child rearing. Using the model of acculturation strategies provided by Berry and Sam (1997), these parents could be categorized as an integrated population, striving to retain their original cultural identity to a certain extent, and at the same time also participating in the larger American social network. There are certain issues for which parents completely adhered to their Indian roots. These included sleep arrangements (parents favor co-sleeping), hand-feeding the older child, massaging the infant, the role of grandparents, and day care arrangements. The issues for which the parents seemed to adopt American thought were the age of toilet training (including the use of diapers), father participation in childcare beginning right from childbirth, and medical issues. Parents tried to strike a balance between the two viewpoints on issues such as disciplinary techniques and the socialization of the child. These various decisions seem to reflect certain underlying common themes described below.

Decisions Based on Indian Practices

CHILD-CENTERED PARENTING. Decisions about sleep arrangements and sleep schedule reflected the child-centered parenting of the Indian parents. Co-sleeping (the child sleeping in the parents' bedroom either in the same bed or her or his own crib near the parents' bed) was found to be a norm in the present study. Out of the various reasons put forth for these arrangements, the prominent one was the development of a bond and the feeling of security for the child through the proximity with parents during the night. These ideas of psychological comfort, security, and closeness to the child were also upheld by the Mayan mothers in the cross-cultural study by Morelli, Rogoff, Oppenheim, and Goldsmith (1992). According to these authors, decisions about the child's sleep arrangements reflect the values and goals of the community and culture of the parents. Most Eastern cultures, including India, aim to foster interdependence as a goal of parenting and the practice of co-sleeping serves as one of the means to achieve this goal.

Child-centered parenting of the immigrant parents was reflected also in the parents' feeding practices. The predominant goal of American parenting, namely to make the child independent is reflected in how early parents encourage self-reliance. One of the examples of this self-reliance is that the child is encouraged to eat on her or his own as early as possible. Indian parents in the study, however, placed more importance on the idea that the child should eat enough and should eat the right type of food, and so ended up hand-feeding the child. Folk wisdom in India suggests that the mother needs to take special efforts so that the child eats proper amounts, efforts that could involve even feeding the child, and the immigrant mothers seem to follow this principle.

Finally, the parents' ideas about day care arrangements for the child also reflected their child-centered parenting. In the present study, in 53 percent of the families the mothers either had taken the conscious decision not to work for the sake of their child or quit their job after the birth of the child. It needs to be mentioned here, though, that the sample in the present study comes from middle or higher-middle socioeconomic status. This educated group of immigrants was financially stable and could afford as a family to live on just one income. Given that the mothers did not *have* to work for financial reasons, they made the conscious decision to stay at home for their children.

CLOSE FAMILY TIES. Another idea underlying parents' choice of Indian ideologies is the effort to maintain close family ties. Consistent with Indian thought, the role of grandparents in the life of the grandchildren is upheld by the Indian immigrant parents. These parents realize the constraints of physical distance and so do not consult the grandparents for most of the child-related decisions, but definitely strive to help build a bond between the grandparents and the grandchildren. This is achieved through the grandparents' visits to the United States, parents' and children's frequent trips to India, and frequent phone calls to India.

RESPECT FOR INDIAN TRADITIONS. The immigrant parents also choose some of the Indian practices because of their faith in age-old Indian traditions, such as baby massage. Baby massage is seen in India not only as a good health practice that helps strengthen muscles (Reissland & Burghart, 1987) but also as a form of meaningful stimulation (Roopnarine, Hooper, Ahmeduzzaman & Pollack, 1993). Almost all the parents in the study followed some kind of a massage routine for their infant. For most parents it just followed naturally after the birth of the infant.

Decisions Based on American Practices

CONVENIENCE AS A FACTOR IN THE CHOICE OF CHILD REARING PRACTICE. The age of toilet training children is one of the dilemmas in child rearing where the Indian immigrant parents completely relied on American ideology. Medical opinion in the United States encourages parents to begin training by the age of two years (e.g., Spock, 2004; Ames, Meyerhoff, Mendelson & Mendelson, 1991) and the immigrant parents in the study followed this suggestion. These parents tended to rely on the pediatricians and the medical books as their sources for information on toilet training. The use of diapers is not common in India and so the extensive use of diapers by parents in the present study also indicated that they had accepted the American views on toilet training of children.

NECESSITY AS A FACTOR IN THE CHOICE OF CHILD REARING PRACTICE. Decisions about father participation in childcare reflected to some extent the role of necessity in decision-making. Traditionally, Indian society is a patriarchal society with the mother playing the nurturing parent role and father playing the roles of breadwinner and disciplinarian. The immigrant fathers in the present study, however, showed increased involvement in childcare, irrespective of the employment status of the mothers. These fathers contributed to the day-to-day life of the child because they *want to* and also because they *have to*. They have realized what their fathers missed out on by not being as emotionally involved with their children as they are.

Decisions Combining the Two Ideologies

BALANCING THE TWO IDEOLOGIES. The interviews revealed that the one area of child rearing in which the Indian immigrant parents seem to be aiming for a balance in *Indianness* and *Americanness* is that of socialization of the children. These parents do want their children to learn and understand the Indian culture. To achieve this goal they followed various practices such as celebrating Indian festivals, becoming a part of ethnic organizations, encouraging their children to participate in these organizations, keeping in regular contact with the local Indian community as well as the relatives in India, and enrolling their older children in ethnic schools. Yet the parents regretted that even these experiences do not help the children in comprehending some simple rules in the Indian culture such as, "You do not touch anything or anybody with your feet," "You do not walk in the house with your shoes on," "You do not drop or leave books on the floor," and "You do not eat with both hands." Also, even though the children celebrated all the Indian festivals with their parents, they could never get the complete experience of the festivals, as they are celebrated in India. That raised questions about *identity* and *Indianness* to the parents themselves. Parents found it difficult to answer the questions such as, "What does it mean to raise an Indian child?" or "What does it mean to raise an American child?"

COMBINING THE TWO IDEOLOGIES. Disciplining the child was one area where the parents were not completely in favor of either of the two ideologies and combined the two in practice. In India children are treated with indulgence and older studies have shown that Indian parents are more likely to tolerate the temper tantrums of their children (e.g., Sinha, 1985;

Ryback, Sanders, Lorentz & Koestenblatt, 1980). The parents in the present study showed the influence of the host culture while deciding their disciplinary techniques. The parents accepted what they called American ideas that children need to be treated as adults and need to be given the opportunity to make choices. At the same time they also held on to what they considered an Indian idea that children need to be inculcated in discipline and so practiced the techniques of scolding, yelling, and spanking.

Implications for Education and Practice

Immigration can imply a need to change parenting behavior and caregiving practices as these immigrant parents renegotiate their ideas and goals for parenting. Immigration challenges parents whose normative ideas of child rearing goals could be in contrast to those upheld by the host culture. Research has shown that intervention efforts then need to focus on solid knowledge of the particular values and practices of the immigrant parents to be successful (Kotchick & Forehand, 2002). The present study can contribute toward this effort. The information from the present study can be used for the enhancement of curricula for parent education and development of programs for immigrant parents in general and Indians in particular. Information obtained regarding the decision-making processes of immigrant parents can help parent educators write more appropriate curricula for them. In turn, better education programs can help the parents deal with the discrepancies in their traditional attitudes and ideas about child rearing and those in the United States. For example, the present study indicates the need for such parent education programs to focus on the discipline and socialization aspects of parenting, where parents are striving to maintain a balance between their own traditional ideologies and American practices.

In terms of education, the data obtained in the present study could also help write programs for childcare providers, teachers, heath care providers, and other professionals who work with immigrant groups to understand the cultural traditions in families from India and their parenting styles.

Implications for Research

Each year the United States receives more than one million immigrants, more than any other country in the world (Fix & Passel, 1994). The total number of Asian immigrants had risen to 7.2 million (one-quarter of the total foreign-born population) by the year 2000 and Indian immigrants (about a million) make up the third-largest immigrant group in the United States

(U.S. Census Bureau, 2000). Such high numbers warrant the study of the acculturation processes of these Asian Indian families in the United States.

The other implication relates to the scope of the data obtained from the present study. Studies on Indian immigrant parents have focused mostly on parenting styles, especially the discipline aspect of child rearing. However, the present study included a number of issues beyond discipline. The study thus extended the scope of the existing literature on culture and parenting. The scope of the literature was also extended by the inclusion of fathers as a part of the sample in the present study. Finally, unlike previous studies, the present study used a semi-structured interview and allowed an exploration of the decisions that immigrant parents make with regard to a number of child rearing practices.

The highly educated, middle class Asian Indian population that formed the sample of the present study presents some limitations regarding external validity. Further directions for research would include studying the Indian population from a different economic or educational background or from a different geographical location within the United States. Research could also be conducted to find similarities and differences between the child rearing experiences of the Indian immigrant parents and other immigrant groups. Finally, research could also focus on understanding the dilemmas and decision-making processes of Indian immigrant parents as their children grow older and move into adolescence.

References

Abidin, R. (1995a). *Parenting Stress Index professional manual* (3rd ed.). Odessa, FL: Psychological Assessment Resources.

Abidin, R. (1995b). *Parenting Stress Index Short Form test sheet*. Odessa, FL: Psychological Assessment Resources.

Ames, L. B., Meyerhoff, M. K., Mendelson, R. A., & Mendelson, L. M. (1991). *Complete book of parenting: The parent question and answer book*. Lincolnwood, IL: Publications International Ltd.

Berry, J. W., & Sam, D. L. (1997). Acculturation and adaptation. In J. W. Berry, M. H. Segall & C. Kagitcibasi (Eds.), *Handbook of cross-cultural psychology: Vol. 3. Social behavior and applications* (2nd ed., pp. 291–326). Boston: Allyn and Bacon.

Bhavnagri, N. P., & Gonzalez-Menz, J. (1997). The cultural context on infant caregiving. *Childhood Education, 74*, 2–8.

Brazelton, T. B., & Sparrow, J. D. (2003). *Sleep: The Brazelton way*. Cambridge, MA: Perseus.

Bronfenbrenner, U. (1977). Toward an experimental ecology of human development. *American Psychologist, 32*, 513–531.

Devgan, P. (1998). Ideal child rearing practices—A fuzzy approach. *Psycho-Lingua,* *28,* 159–166.

Dosanjh, J. S., & Ghuman. (1996). The cultural context of child-rearing: A study of indigenous and British Punjabis. *Early Child Development and Care, 126,* 39–55.

Dunst, C. J., Trivette, C. M., & Jenkins, V. (1994). Family support scale. In C. J. Dunst, C. M. Trivette & A.G. Deal (Eds.), *Supporting and strengthening families* (pp. 155–157). Cambridge, MA: Brookline Books.

Eisenberg, A., Murkoff, H. E., & Hathaway, S. E. (1989). *What to expect the first year.* New York: Workman.

Falicov, C. J. (2003). Immigrant family processes. In F. Walsh (Ed.), *Normal family processes: Growing diversity and complexity* (3rd ed., pp. 280–300). New York: Guilford Press.

Fix, M., & Passel, J. S. (1994). *Immigration and immigrants: Setting the record straight.* Washington, DC: Urban Institute.

Gaskins, S. (1996). How Mayan parental theories come into play. In S. Harkness & C. M. Super (Eds.), *Parents' cultural belief systems* (pp. 45–363). New York: Guilford Press.

Harwood, R. L., Miller, J. G., & Irizarry, N. L. (1995). *Culture and attachment: Perceptions of the child in context.* New York: Guilford Press.

Jain, A., & Belsky, J. (1997). Fathering and acculturation: Immigrant Indian families with young children. *Journal of Marriage and the Family, 59,* 873–883.

Kakar, S. (1978). *The inner world: A psychoanalytic study of childhood and society in India.* New Delhi: Oxford University Press.

Kotchick, B. A., & Forehand, R. (2002). Putting parenting in perspective: A discussion of the contextual factors that shape parenting practices. *Journal of Child and Family Studies, 11,* 255–269.

Lerner, R. M. (1978). Nature, nurture and dynamic interactionism. *Human Development, 21,* 1–20.

Morelli, G. A., Rogoff, B., Oppenheim, D., & Goldsmith, D. (1992). Cultural variation in infants' sleeping arrangements: Questions of independence. *Developmental Psychology, 28,* 604–613.

Ojha, H., & Pramanick, M. (1992). Religio-cultural variations in childrearing practices. *Psychological Studies, 37,* 65–72.

Rajagopalan, J. (1989). Current trends in infant care: An Indian experience. Unpublished master's thesis. New Delhi: Lady Irwin College, University of Delhi.

Reissland, N., & Burghart, R. (1987). The role of massage in south Asia: Child health and development. *Social Science Medicine, 25,* 231–239.

Roopnarine, J., Hooper, F. H., Ahmeduzzaman, M., & Pollack, B. (1993). Gentle play partners: Mother-child and father-child play in New Delhi, India. In K. MacDonald (Ed.), *Parent child play* (pp. 287–304). New York: State University of New York Press.

Roopnarine, J., Lu, M. W., & Ahmeduzzaman, M. (1989). Parental reports of early patterns of caregiving, play and discipline in India and Malaysia. *Early Child Development and Care, 50*, 109–120.

Ryback, D., Sanders, A. L., Lorentz, J., & Koestenblatt, M. (1980). Child-rearing practices reported by students in six cultures. *The Journal of Social Psychology, 110*, 153–162.

Short, K. H. (1996). Stress, maternal distress, and child adjustment following immigration: Exploring the buffering role of social support. *Dissertation Abstracts International Section B: The Sciences and Engineering, 57*(3-B), 2224. (UMI No. AAMNN06064).

Siantz, d. L. M. L. (1997). Factors that impact developmental outcomes of immigrant children. In A. Booth, A. C. Crouter & N. Landale (Eds.), *Immigration and the family* (pp. 149–164). Mahwah, NJ: Erlbaum.

Sinha, S. R. (1985). Maternal strategies for regulating children's behavior. *Journal of Cross Cultural Psychology, 16*, 27–40.

Spock, B. (2004). *Dr. Spock's baby and child care: The one essential parenting book* (8th ed.). New York: Pocket Books.

Stephenson, M. (2000). Development and validation of the Stephenson Multigroup Acculturation Scale (SMAS). *Psychological Assessment, 12*, 77–88.

Super, C. M., & Harkness, S. (1997). The cultural structuring of child development. In J. W. Berry, P. R. Dasen & T. S. Saraswathi (Eds.), *Handbook of cross-cultural psychology* (2nd ed., Vol. 2, pp. 1–39). Needham Heights, MA: Allyn & Bacon.

Szapocznik, J., Scopetta, M. A., Kurtines, W., & Aranalde, M. (1978). Theory and measurement of acculturation. *International Journal of Psychology, 12*, 113–130.

U.S. Census Bureau (2000). *Profile of the foreign-born population in the U.S.: 2000.* Washington, DC: U.S. Government Printing Office. www.census.gov/prod/2002pubs/p23-206.pdf.

Weiss, R. S. (1994). *Learning from strangers: The art and method of qualitative interview method.* New York: The Free Press.

Xu, L. (2004). Acculturation stress, social support and maternal satisfaction within immigrant Chinese families. *Dissertation Abstracts International Section A: Humanities and Social Sciences, 64*(9-A), 3498. (UMI No. AAI3104102).

About the Author

Rucha Londhe, adjunct faculty, Department of Psychology at Framingham State College, 100 State Street, P.O. Box 9101, Framingham, MA 01701-9101. Phone: 508-485-9160. Research associate, Goodman Research Group, Inc., 955 Mass Ave, Cambridge, MA 02139. E-mail: ruchalondhe@gmail.com.

Intergenerational Differences in Acculturation and Family Conflict among Korean Immigrant Families

12

C. RICHARD HOFSTETTER, PAULA M. USITA, MELBOURNE F. HOVELL,
VERONICA L. IRVIN, ANA MARTINEZ-DONATE, KYOUNG-RAE JUNG,
HAE RYUN PARK, HEE YOUNG PAIK, JOY ZAKARIAN, AND
JOOEUN LEE

Abstract

Using a sample of 494 parent-adolescent pairs drawn from a representative population-based probability sample of Korean adults throughout California, bilingual telephone interviews were completed in Korean or English based on respondent language preference, and 86 percent of the adults and 95 percent of the adolescents contacted completed surveys during 2001–2002. Reported family conflict was low. Parental and adolescent reports of conflict were correlated, as was level of parental and adolescent acculturation, adolescents reported higher levels of acculturation than their parents, and discrepancies in level of acculturation between parents and adolescents were associated with family conflict. Associations remained after multivariate statistical controls.

Keywords: Korean Families, Korean Adolescents, Parent-Adolescent Conflict, Acculturation

Address all correspondence to C. Richard Hofstetter, Ph.D., Center for Behavioral Epidemiology and Community Health, Graduate School of Public Health, San Diego State University, 9245 Sky Park Court, Suite 230, San Diego, CA 92123. Phone: 858-505-4770 ext. 146. Fax: 858-505-8614. E-mail: rhofstet@mail.sdsu.edu. Website: www.rohan-sdsu.edu/rhofstet or www.kahp.org.

WITH A POPULATION OF about three million, Asian/Pacific Islanders (AAPIs) are the second largest ethnic minority group in California, representing 11.5 percent of all residents (State of California, 2006). Korean Americans comprise the fifth largest subgroup of the fourteen major AAPIs in the state, and about one-third of them in the United States reside in California. Their numbers in California have increased 133 percent to 345,882 between 1990 and 2000 (Asian/Pacific Islander Data Consortium-ACCIS, 1992; Yu, Choe & Han, 2002).

Acculturation reflects the social reinforcers in the new nation that compete with prior reinforcers in the home nation and alter the values, beliefs, norms, and traditions of immigrants. Typically, behaviors include reading/writing preferences, food preferences, ethnic interactions, generational identities, and affinity and pride (Cuellar, Harris & Jasso, 1980; Suinn, Rickard-Figueroa, Lew & Vigil, 1987; Suinn, Khoo & Ahuna, 1995). Historically, acculturation has been employed in many studies as if it were merely an interesting demographic characteristic. Studies of acculturation also offer the possibility of specifying the role of cultures in encouraging or discouraging specific social practices. In concert with theory, studies of acculturation will inform possible culture-based interventions for immigrants as well as whole populations, in order to promote behaviors of public health benefit.

Although the familial relationships of Asian groups have been studied (Kwak & Berry, 2001; Usita & Blieszner, 2002), limited information is available about the acculturation effects on the quality of Korean parent-child relationships. This may be at least partially attributable to the relatively recent Korean immigration to North America (Kwak & Berry, 2001; Usita & Blieszner, 2002). Many studies about immigrants examine the difficulties with communication and language acculturation (Hofstetter et al., 2004; Usita & Blieszner, 2002) and are based on samples of students in universities.

With the continued growth in the numbers of new ethnic minorities in the United States, researchers are achieving a greater understanding of the psychological and social effects of intergenerational family conflicts (Lee, Choe, Kim & Ngo, 2000; Ying, 1999). Asian students often report elevated psychological distress due to relationships with their parents (Kim, 1996; Lee et al., 2000; Kang, 2000). Examination of the interplay between acculturation and family relations will enhance understanding of how immigrant families accommodate to disparate cultural values between parents and their adolescent children (Kwak & Berry, 2001; Matsuoka, 1990; Nguyen & Williams, 1989; Rosenthal, Ranieri & Klimidis, 1996). This study explored the degree to which ecological factors and intergenerational conflicts take place in the process of acculturation.

Conceptual Frameworks: Symbolic Interaction and the Behavioral Ecological Model

Symbolic interaction (SI) is a useful theory for understanding acculturation differences between immigrant parents and their offspring. SI posits that self meanings are developed through social interaction that arise through specific situations (LaRossa & Reitzes, 1993) and family, culture, and society are major sources of information about individual roles, expectations, and identities (Hall, 2006; Stryker, 1980). Immigrant parents and their offspring usually have different opportunities for social interaction with others. Monolingual immigrant parents, fluent in their native language, typically relate to other immigrants from their homeland. Bilingual offspring fluent in the mother language and that of the host society are exposed to bicultural messages-homeland messages upheld by their family, and are exposed to different messages passed on through schools, popular culture, and friends. Differences in acculturation between the generations is a common outcome; conflict between the generations may be one outcome of differing rates of acculturation.

The Behavioral Ecological Model (BEM) (Hovell, Wahlgren & Gehrman, 2002), a perspective that highlights the interlocking network of society (nationality, cultural values), community (laws, media, police), local networks (social services, friends, families), and the individual, sets a social context in which behavior (including interaction) occurs emphasizing reinforcers present in social interaction. The BEM maintains that members of the interlocking network influence each other through reinforcement, and is consistent with SI assumptions. Youth adoption of individualism values and individualistic behaviors may create dissonance between the generations and lead to episodes of family disharmony. The notion that interlocking networks influence self-identity is consistent with perspectives of SI (Stokes & Hewitt, 1976) and has received attention in studies of immigration (Foner, 1997; Szapocznik & Kurtines, 1993).

Acculturation and Family Conflict

Children of immigrants who reach adolescence in the United States often experience intergenerational conflicts of values with their parents due to differing levels and rates of acculturation (Asakawa, 2001; Baptiste, 1993; Chen, Greenberger, Lester, Dong & Guo, 1998; Drachman, Kwon-Ahn

& Paulino, 1996; Foner, 1997; Handal, Le-Stiebel, DiCarlo & Gutzwiller, 1999; Hauh, 1999; James, Kim & Armijo, 2000; Kwak & Berry, 2001; Lee et al., 2000; Matsuoka, 1990; Nguyen & Williams, 1989; Rosenthal et al., 1996; Szapocznik & Kurtines, 1993; Uba, 1994; Ying, 1999; Ying & Chao, 1996; Yoon, 2000).

Rate and magnitude of change in attitudes, beliefs, and behaviors that persons undergo are important sources of intergenerational differences. Adolescent immigrants acculturate more quickly than their parents (Baptiste, 1993; Lee et al., 2000). Rapid acculturation is apparent in adoption of Western lifestyles, values and attitudes, behaviors, and the acquisition of English as a primary language (Baptiste, 1993; Lee et al., 2000; Song et al., 2004). Adolescent immigrants may be more readily influenced by situational factors outside the family than by their parents (Baptiste, 1993; Kwak & Berry, 2001). An acculturation gap occurs when adolescents acculturate more quickly or differently than their parents (Uba, 1994). The acculturation gap was also a risk factor for depression among Korean American college students (Aldwin & Greenberger, 1987).

Immigrant families may deny the existence of transitional problems, partially due to cultural differences in the ways that family members perceive conflict, and partially due to more immediate survival needs that are a consequence of immigration (Baptiste, 1993). Stressors associated with the effects of immigration also include conflict between old and new values, identity confusion, language barriers, and racial prejudice (Tran & Des Jardins, 2000). Lack of appropriate job skills and employment opportunities (Espiritu, 1999), along with communication problems and discrimination, force some immigrant Korean males into a lower occupational status than they formerly enjoyed in Korea (Kim & Sung, 2000; Rhee, 1997). Although the women often must work to meet family financial needs, many immigrant Koreans, particularly men, still adhere to a traditional Korean family system in which males are valued and expected to govern the family (Kim & Sung, 2000; Rhee, 1997; Song-Kim, 1992). The diminished economic status of the male, in the context of traditional patriarchal values, marriage, and sex roles, may disrupt family tranquility (Min, 1995; Fuligni, 1998). These processes may lead to reversal or modification in traditional roles between male family leaders and their wives, daughters and, to a lesser degree, sons.

Acculturation may represent a breaking away from traditional Korean norms due to U.S. norms specific to gender in that Korean women are often exposed to more liberated views of life that influence health behaviors, while Korean men are subject to greater social pressures concerning similar behaviors than is traditional in Korea. For instance, the relative risk of smoking among California immigrants is less among men and greater among women relative to their gender counterparts in Korea (Hofstetter et al., 2004, Song et al., 2004).

Although a single common experience does not exist for each immigrant family in the United States, some shared transitional issues have been identified particularly among offspring (Baptiste, 1993). Such issues include a decrease of parental authority over children due to cultural conflicts in the performance of parental roles, changes in generational and familial boundaries, inadequate preparation for conflict, change brought on by the immigration experience, parental anxiety that their children will be lost to American culture, and extended family engagement–disengagement problems (Baptiste, 1993).

Intergenerational conflict is a risk factor for the development of mental health problems among migrant parents and their offspring (Lee et al., 2000; Lee & Liu, 2001; Ying, Coombs & Lee, 1999). There are few resources to help immigrant families adjust and mediate intergenerational and intercultural differences (Ying, 1999). Immigrant children may experience anxiety and depression, learning and behavioral problems, and some may join gangs as a substitute for family (Ying, 1999). Furthermore, stressors associated with the cultural transition of immigrants have been shown to affect family life and put families at risk for domestic violence (Kim & Sung, 2000).

The goal of this study was to describe the relationship between disparities in acculturation and intergenerational conflict between a sample of Korean adolescents and their parents.

Methods

The Sample
Data from this study were drawn from a larger study of health behaviors and acculturation among people of Korean descent conducted in California (Hofstetter et al., 2004), N = 2830. Sampling was designed to represent the California population of adults of Korean descent accessible by residential telephone. An electronic list of all residential telephones listed in California to persons with Korean surnames was purchased from a commercial firm, and then all non-Korean surnames were purged from the list. Persons whose first names were Asian but not Korean were then further purged from the list. This eliminated most non-Korean people with surnames that are common to Korea and to other nations (e.g., Ho, Cho, etc., who may be of Chinese descent). Persons with Korean surnames and Anglicized first

names were retained in the sample, and the list was then sorted into random order for interviewing. Potential respondents were filtered to insure Korean descent during the introduction to the survey. Stratified by gender, adult respondents were selected randomly in each household using the most recent birthday procedure (Frey, 1989). Parents were asked permission to interview the adolescent of Korean descent in the household aged twelve to seventeen with the most recent birthday. The most recent birthday procedure was again used in selecting a respondent when more than one eligible adolescent was present in households. Procedures were approved by the Institutional Review Board at San Diego State University.

Interviews were completed by 86.6 percent of all eligible respondents and by 95 percent of all eligible adolescents contacted. Up to seven callbacks were used and a specially trained interviewer attempted to convert refusals. After deleting cases with missing data on conflict and several other variables, a matched parent-child subsample was created for the following analysis (N=494). Initial contact was made in Korean and interviewers shifted to English if respondents indicated that preference (among the subsample in this analysis, 98.6 percent of adults and 21.5 percent of adolescents were interviewed in Korean). The survey was developed in English and translated into Korean and back translated with the advice of two study co-investigators from Myongi and Seoul National Universities in Korea. Interviewers were bilingual in English and Korean.

The Participants

Among the parent subsample 61.3 percent were female, mean age was 45.2 years (SD = 4.5), 95.9 percent were married or cohabiting, 3.6 percent were either widowed or divorced, and 0.4 percent were single or never married. The mean annual income was $60,600 (SD = $17,100). Nearly all (99.6 percent) of the adults were born in Korea, mean length of residence in Korea was 27.6 years (SD = 7.2) while mean length of residence in the United States was 17.3 years (SD = 7.2). Among the adolescent sample 54.7 percent were male, mean age was 14.6 years (SD = 1.7), and 70 percent were born in the United States.

Measurement

FAMILY CONFLICT. Adults and adolescents were asked to what extent (a great deal, some, not much, or no conflict at all) conflicts existed concerning dating, style of authority (parenting), cultural differences, school performance, relationships with friends, lack of communication, final decision making for the family, use of tobacco, and use of alcohol. Adult and adolescent subsamples were combined, items converted to standard form, and items factor analyzed and rotated to a simple structure using varimax procedures. This type of analysis insures that parents and adolescents are compared in the same factor space. Wording of items, loadings, and communalities are available from the senior author by request (see appendix 12B). A principal component, explaining 43.5 percent of the total variance, emerged from the analysis. A conflict scale was constructed by computing the mean of items (allowing up to three missing data points). Items in the scale reached a satisfactory level of reliability with Cronbach's $\alpha = .83$.

ACCULTURATION. Level of acculturation was measured using eleven items adapted from the Suinn-Lew Asian Self-Identity Acculturation Scale (Suinn, Rickard-Figueroa, et al., 1987; Suinn, Khoo, et al., 1995) to accommodate telephone interviews. Items among the adult and adolescent subsamples were first combined and then items were standardized (using Z-scores, with mean $= 0$, SD $= 1$). Items were analyzed using principal components procedures rotated to simple structure according to varimax criteria. Wording of items and associated statistics are available from the senior author by request (see appendix 12A).

An acculturation scale was operationalized by computing the mean of the eleven standardized items (mean $= 0$, SD $= 1$, and allowing up to three missing data points) that loaded most highly on the cultural background factor. Items included speaking and reading ability, language and music preference, language interviewed in, birthplace, ethnicity of friends and peers as a child (under age six) and as an adolescent (ages six to eighteen), food preferences at home and in restaurants, as well as preferred ethnic associations within the community. Differences in acculturation were measured by computing the absolute value of the difference between the adolescent factor score and the matching adult factor score.

Validity of the measures was supported by correlations between our acculturation scale and use of Korean language media parenting style, dietary patterns, and years lived in Korea were associated in the predicted direction with $r \geq .15$ to $.45$, $p < .001$.

Analyses

SPSS (version 6.1.3) was used in computations of t tests and multiple regressions analyses.

Findings

Level of Conflict Reported by Parents and Adolescents

Very low levels of conflict in the family were reported by the representative matched sample of parents and adolescents as reported in table 12.1. Less than 6 percent reported "a great deal" of conflict on any single item, and as many as 96.9 percent of parents and 95.1 percent of adolescents reported no conflict on alcohol, the least endorsed area of possible conflict. Consistent with other studies of mixed groups of Asian nationalities (Chung, 2001), the greatest areas of conflict reported by adults were style of authority, cultural differences, school performance, and communication, while the greatest areas of conflict reported by adolescents were school performance and communication.

Parents and adolescents rated conflict areas very similarly, since correlations between conflict ratings by parents and adolescents in dyads were positive (ranging from .20 to .37, P = .000). Correlations between parents

Table 12.1.   Extent of Conflict in Family Reported

	Amount Reported			
	Great Deal	Some	Little	None
Adults' Reported Conflict				
a. Dating	0.6	2.7	18.4	78.3
b. Style of authority	4.1	6.1	27.8	62.0
c. Cultural differences	3.9	12.2	47.6	36.3
d. School performance	3.1	5.9	24.0	67.0
e. Relationships with friends	1.6	4.3	15.7	78.4
f. Lack of communication	3.5	5.9	25.4	65.2
g. Final decision-making for the family	1.4	4.1	25.3	69.2
h. Use of tobacco	1.2	0.6	1.6	96.5
i. Use of alcohol	0.6	0.6	1.8	96.9
Adolescents' Reported Conflict				
a. Dating	1.8	5.9	16.1	76.2
b. Style of authority	2.2	7.8	27.8	62.2
c. Cultural differences	2.2	9.0	32.6	56.2
d. School performance	5.7	10.6	26.2	57.5
e. Relationships with friends	1.8	5.9	17.2	75.1
f. Lack of communication	3.0	7.9	16.8	72.3
g. Final decision-making for the family	1.4	6.3	16.9	75.4
h. Use of tobacco	1.2	1.6	2.8	94.3
i. Use of alcohol	1.0	1.4	2.4	95.1

Note: Numbers are the percentages of adults and adolescents reporting "To what extent do you have conflicts with your family in each of the following areas: A great deal, some, not much, or no conflict at all?"

and adolescents were strongest for dating (.37), communication (.31), and final family decision-making (.32). Older adolescents were more likely to mention a problem than younger adolescents (p < .05). Parents also mentioned style of authority, cultural differences, lack of communication, and final decision-making for the family as areas of conflict more often than adolescents, although differences only in dating ($t_{(486)}$ = −2.51), cultural differences ($t_{(486)}$ = 6.03), and school performance ($t_{(486)}$ = −4.38) were significant (P < .05).

Level of Acculturation and Intergenerational Differences

As hypothesized, the difference between the total acculturation scale, as well as the items on which it is based, among parents and matched adolescents, were statistically significant for both boys and girls (P = .000) with adolescents being more acculturated than their parents on all items (table 12.2, P < .05). Differences in restaurant food preferences were not significant but were in the same direction. As expected, parental and matched adolescent acculturation scores were correlated (r = .225 among boys and r = .204 among girls, P = .000).

Using raw data for items, t scores for the differences of paired means between adolescents and adults were computed to test whether adolescents were more acculturated than their parents. Each acculturation item differed significantly between adults and matching adolescents according to data reported in table 12.1 (P < .05). The difference between the total acculturation scale among parents and matched adolescents was also significant (t = −51.64, P = .000) with adolescents being more acculturated, and the correlation between parents and matched adolescents was positive, r = .25, P = .000. Thus, more acculturated parents are associated with more acculturated adolescents, although adolescents are usually at a higher level of acculturation than adults. The data show that adolescents were more acculturated than matched adults on each item in the scale. Findings were replicated among genders.

Adolescent-Adult Reported Conflict

Mean conflict differences between adolescents and parents are reported in table 12.2. Although adolescents reported greater conflict than adults concerning dating and school performance, they reported less conflict about cultural issues than adults (P < .05). No statistically significant differences were found on other items and no significant difference was found between adults and adolescents on the general conflict scale (P > .05). Adults and adolescents reported overall level of total conflict in the home similarly (r = .425, P = .000) as did boys and girls.

Multivariate Analysis

Larger differences in acculturation, older adolescent age, greater disparity in age between parents and adolescents, and lower levels of parental educa-

Table 12.2.   Differences between Paired Adults and Adolescents on Acculturation and Family Conflict

Item	Mean Difference	se	t	P=
Acculturation:[a]				
Speak Korean?	–1.164	.034	–34.35	.000
Which language do you prefer to speak? (Korean = 0; English = 1)	–.717	.021	–33.58	.000
Ethnic origin of the friends and peers up to age 6?	–1.790	.051	–35.09	.000
Prefer to associate with Korean/non-Korean?	–1.758	.046	–38.19	.000
Ethnic origin of the friends and peers age 6 to 18?	–.320	.042	–7.57	.000
Prefer Korean/non-Korean music?	–.888	.053	–16.89	.000
Read Korean/English?	–1.743	.031	–56.43	.000
At home prefer Korean food /American food?	–.207	.035	–5.99	.000
Food preference in restaurants Korean/American food?	–.103	.046	–2.23	.027
Where were you born? (Korea = 0 ; US = 1)	–.695	.021	–33.37	.000
Language of interview? (Korean = 0, English = 1)	–.774	.019	–40.13	.000
Acculturation Discrepancy	–1.132	.022	–51.64	.000
Family conflict:[b]				
Dating?	–.078	.031	–2.51	.012
Style of authority?	.018	.042	.44	.663
Cultural differences?	.263	.044	6.03	.000
School performance?	–.195	.045	–4.38	.000
Relationships with friends?	–.055	.037	–1.48	.140
Lack of communication?	.055	.041	1.36	.175
Final decision-making for the family?	.033	.034	.96	.338
Use of tobacco?	–.033	.023	–1.40	.161
Use of alcohol?	–.034	.020	–1.71	.088
Total Conflict Scale	–.004	.021	–1.40	.890

Notes: [a]Respondents were asked "In this set of questions we ask about your background that may be related to cultural identity." Verbatim wording is presented in appendix table 12A.1. Unless otherwise noted responses were coded as 1 "Exclusively Korean," 2 "Mostly Korean," 3 "Equal," 4 "Mostly English/American/Non-Korean," 5 "Exclusively/only English/American/Non-Korean."
[b]Respondents were asked "To what extent do you have conflicts with children in your home in each of the following areas: A great deal, some, not much, or no conflict at all?"

tion were associated with reports of greater conflict (P < .05) among parents (table 12.3). Higher adolescent grades in school were associated with less conflict reported by parents. Among adolescents, a similar pattern of bivariate correlations emerged, although the correlation between age difference and conflict reported by adolescents was not significant (P > .05). The greater the difference between adolescents and adults in acculturation, the more family conflict is reported by both parents and adolescents.

Reports of family conflict was regressed on difference in acculturation and selected demographic variables separately for adults and adolescents to ascertain whether statistical controls would eliminate associations between difference in acculturation and perception of conflict. Multicollinearity is an issue, since some associations were reduced after including controls. Neither difference in acculturation (P = .078) nor age difference (P = .068) were related to reported conflict among parents. Only grades in

Table 12.3. Regression of Parents' and Adolescents' Perceptions of Total Family Conflict on Differences in Acculturation among Matched Pairs of California Korean Parents and Adolescents

	B	se	β	P	r
Parents:					
Difference in total acculturation index	.068	.038	.081	.078	.124**
Child's age	.020	.010	.086	.052	.101*
Child's grades in school	−.111	.029	−.170	.000	−.203***
Age difference parent-adolescent	.008	.004	.087	.068	.089*
Child's gender	−.012	.037	−.014	.746	−.020
Adult's gender	.043	.039	.051	.277	.044
Adult's education	−.013	.008	−.077	.092	−.133**
(Constant)	−.280	.286		.326	
$R = .27, F_{(7,479)} = 5.47, P = .000$					
Adolescents:					
Difference in total acculturation index	.107	.041	.116	.010	.150***
Child's age	.046	.011	.174	.000	.189***
Child's grades in school	−.128	.031	−.178	.000	−.223***
Age difference parent-adolescent	.005	.005	.050	.279	.075
Child's gender	−.066	.040	−.073	.098	−.078
Adult's gender	−.019	.042	−.020	.650	−.018
Adult's education	−.015	.008	−.080	.073	−.136**
(Constant)	−.413	.307		.179	
$R = .33, F_{(7,482)} = 8.57, P = .000$					

Note: Numbers in columns are unstandardized regression coefficients, associated standard errors, standardized regression coefficients, and associated two-sided probabilities (except difference in acculturation is one-sided), and zero-order correlations between variables and family conflict.
*P < .05. **P < .01. ***P < .001.

school was negatively and significantly related to reported conflict among adults (P = .000) once controls were applied. The standardized regression coefficient, β, is nearly twice as large for grades in school as any other predictor in the equation.

Difference in acculturation and adolescent age are positively and grades negatively related to reports of conflict among adolescents (P < .05). Older adolescents, those with lower grades in school, and adolescents that were more acculturated than their parents were more likely to report conflict. In the case of adolescents, differences in ages between themselves and parents and adult gender were unrelated to reports of conflict. Adolescent gender and parent education did not quite attain statistical significance (P = .05). Analyses revealed that the associations were similar among boys and girls.

Discussion

Difference in acculturation between Korean American parents and their adolescent children is an important factor leading to adolescent reports of conflict within family life. The relationship is clear among adolescents if not among adults, as evidenced by consistency even after controlling for a number of variables. Korean American children appear to become acculturated much more quickly than parents, as is true among most groups of recent immigrants to the United States. The forces of mandatory free public schooling, mass media, peer pressure, and trying to get along in American society may lead children to learn the language, folkways, and mores of this society more quickly than their parents. This process also may reflect the degree to which parents have experienced many years of the traditional culture, compared to fewer (and qualitatively different) traditional influences on their children. This may lead parents to be more resistant to change in a new culture (a type of resiliency or inability to change). Most Korean American adolescents were either born in the United States or had very few years of exposure to the home culture prior to immigration. Adolescents who are members of relatively small groups in an urban setting, moreover, are more directly subjected to the ubiquitous reinforcing contingencies of American culture, such as television, peers, schools, and so on. These and the differential home cultural conditions set the stage for differential acculturation and for conflict.

Parents and adolescents reported what appear to be very low levels of conflict. In light of other studies of family relations involving somewhat older persons, these results are surprising, although very few population-based studies using representative probability samples have been conducted. Given differences and limitations in most of the literature, results from this representative sample may be more reliable.

The differences in levels of acculturation that do exist between adults and adolescents, however, have consequences for family life. Adolescents and parents report the overall level of conflict similarly. As in prior studies, dating, culture, and grades in school ranked high as a source of reported conflict. Some of these differences are likely to be exacerbated by differential acculturation, at least among adolescents.

It is also clear from these data that predictors of conflict are somewhat different between parents and adolescents. Much of the reported conflict by Korean adults is associated in one way or another with performance of adolescents in school, although differences in acculturation, adolescent age, age differences between parents and adolescents, and adult education may contribute. The traditional value placed on education and the pressure to excel placed on many Korean adolescents can easily give rise to conflict but is also consistent with success in American society. Among adolescents, school performance, age, and difference in acculturation with the parents are significant, and gender and adult education significant depending on exactly where the cut point of significance is.

Relationships among family members and family harmony are greatly valued in traditional Korean culture. The same is true of academic performance. Korean families are characterized by clearly defined gender roles, respect for the elderly, and duty to one's parents (Hurh & Kim, 1984; Min, 1995). Causes of dysfunction in Korean immigrant families may be associated with male domination and hierarchical authority (Shon & Ja, 1982), although that was not apparent in our data. Perhaps the explanation is that Korean immigrant adolescents may report a strict parenting style as rejection, parental hostility, and a source of family conflict (Kwak & Berry, 2001). About 38 percent of the adolescent sample reported some degree of conflict in the area of parental authority. However, a study examining high school students in Korea found that strict parental control was viewed as parental affection and evidence of low neglect by the adolescents (Rohner & Pettengill, 1985). This paradoxical view of parent caring may reflect the transitional processes involved in acculturation, where some features of the home culture are cherished (i.e., reinforcing) and some competing features of the new culture (e.g., independence) may be equally cherished (e.g., reinforcing), resulting in *approach approach* frustrations. Attitudes about parental authority are very likely to change as adolescents acculturate to U.S. society, while parents' attitudes may change less or not at all, contributing to increasing levels of family conflict (Kwak & Berry, 2001), at least until the adolescent moves into adulthood and/or moves from the family home. We found consistently positive correlations between adolescent age and reports of conflict by both adolescents and parents in these data, although not all associations among adults were statistically significant.

Symbolic Interaction and Social Reinforcers of Behavior

Symbolic interaction theory and the behavioral epidemiological model were helpful for conceptualizing the interlocking influences of individuals, local networks, communities, and culture/society. These two frameworks may be useful for future acculturation and family research in specifying the social contingencies that are responsible for the different levels of conflict within immigrant families. Future studies may specify the dynamics of Korean immigrants' lifestyle practices, the social contingencies within the family, and societal level contingencies that support low or high levels of family conflict.

Symbolic interaction theory views the acquisition of social norms as a function of learning through interaction with others. The behavioral eco-logical model seeks to identify social situations in which some behaviors are reinforced more than others. For example, we assumed that conflict might be viewed differently among male and female adolescents and male and female parents, and tested a series of associations among the subgroups. No subgroups were consistently different.

This study, like most studies of acculturation, provides a relatively ecological analysis of family conflict. Results from this and other studies confirm that differential acculturation contributes to reports of family conflict, especially among adolescents. However, it does not make specific the social contingencies responsible for conflict, nor does it isolate such contingencies for serious versus relatively mild levels of conflict. More research may reveal the dynamics of Korean immigrants' lifestyle practices and the social contingencies within the family and how these compete with differential contingencies that the adults and the adolescents experience from the larger community. Following the behavioral ecological model, future studies should measure more specific social interactions and the differential social contingencies derived from the larger society for conformance with the traditional Korean or new U.S. culture should be specified in order to understand the mechanism at the family and society level.

Limitations

These data are based on a cross-sectional survey that represents Korean adults in California and paired adolescents, and therefore are not a strong basis for assessing change in reports of family conflict, especially as adolescents age. Additional research using dynamic measures and longitudinal designs are needed to test the validity of our findings. Some of this differential might reflect the reluctance of Korean adults (if not also adolescents) to disclose sensitive information about the family. However, if low rates of conflict are confirmed by larger and multicultural comparisons, these results suggest unique features of the Korean culture might hold promise for decreasing the conflict between parents and adolescents from other cultures, including those from the U.S. culture.

The data were collected using telephone interviews, a procedure that provides cost-effective data but may be subject to limitations. Not all homes have telephones, and the change from landlines to cell phones is becoming a problem for researchers. Our surname sampling procedure may have failed to reach women who married males of other groups. However, sample demographic characteristics (age, gender, education) closely matched U.S. census data for all Korean adults residing in California that were collected shortly before the survey was taken.

Implications for Practice

Regularity of acculturative differences between immigrant parents and their adolescent offspring and possibility of future family conflict, presents practitioners with opportunities to help families. Drawing on empirical research, four approaches are discussed. First, emphasize acculturative differences and family conflict as normative experiences among Asian immigrant families (Chung, 2001). Normalization of conflict aids parents and children in accepting their own generational differences and conflicts, and in assigning more positive attributes to their own family (Usita & Blieszner, 2002). Second, educate families about the possibility that as parents become more acculturated to the host society, the degree of acculturative differences and ensuing conflict may lessen (Chung, 2001). Highly acculturated parent-child dyads report less conflict than moderate and low acculturated parent-child dyads (Chung, 2001). Third, emphasize immigrant families' strengths (McAdoo, Martinez & Hughes, 2005), including family generated strategies for curtailing schisms arising from acculturative differences. Family-identified workable relational strategies include reciprocal assistance, humor, and patience (Usita, 2001; Usita & Blieszner, 2002). Fourth, discuss importance of bicultural socialization (Nah, 1993; Szapocznik & Kurtines, 1993). One model, Bicultural Effectiveness Training, emphasizes detouring family conflict to cultural conflict and provides parents and children with strategies for becoming more comfortable with both cultures (Szapocznik & Kurtines, 1993). Korean immigrant families with high levels of family conflict are ideal candidates for family counseling services (Nah, 1993; Landau-Stanton, 1995).

Conclusion

This study focused on Korean immigrants to California. Similar research models might apply to immigrants from other countries who migrate to the United States. This study might also serve as a model for studying culturally specific groups moving to any new culture across or within a given nation. For such research to be promoted, however, new definitions of cultural groups will be needed as will new measures of "acculturation."

Acknowledgments

This research was supported by funds provided by the Tobacco-Related Disease Research Program, Grant Number 9RT-0073 to C. Richard Hofstetter. We thank the California Tobacco Related Disease Research Program and Korean study participants in California for their support in conducting this study.

Appendix 12A: Rotated Loadings for Measures of Acculturation among Adults and Adolescents in the Family

See the table on the next page.

Table 12A.1.

Item	Culture	Assimilation	h^2
When reading, do you read only Korean, read Korean better than English, read both Korean and English equally well, read English better than Korean, or read only English?	.908	.159	.819
Language of interview	.880	.101	.785
Which language do you prefer to speak?	.869	.129	.772
What was the ethnic origin of the friends and peers you had as a child up to age 6?	.849	.113	.734
Where were you born?	.825	.081	.687
What was the ethnic origin of the friends and peers you had as a child from age 6 to 18? Was it almost exclusively Korean, mostly Korean, equally Korean and non-Korean, mostly non-Korean, or almost exclusively non-Korean?	.801	.182	.675
In this set of questions we ask about your background that may be related to cultural identity. First of all, do you speak Korean only, mostly Korean with some English, Korean and English equally well, mostly English, or English only?	.796	.244	.693
At home do you prefer Korean food exclusively, mostly Korean food, about equally Korean and American food, mostly American food, or exclusively American food?	.516	.470	.521
With regard to music do you prefer only Korean music, mostly Korean music, equally Korean and non-Korean music, mostly non-Korean music, or non-Korean music only?	.108	.714	.487
What is your food preference in restaurants? Do you prefer Korean food exclusively, mostly Korean food, about equally Korean and American food, mostly American food, or exclusively American food?	–.038	.704	.497
If you could pick, whom would you prefer to associate with in the community? Would it be almost exclusively Korean, mostly Korean, equally Korean and non-Korean, mostly non-Korean, or almost exclusively non-Korean?	.239	.560	.370
Percent Total Variance Explained	52.4	11.8	64.2

Notes: Respondents were asked, "In this set of questions we ask about your background that may be related to cultural identity." Correlations are based on standardized item scores (mean = 0, SD = 1) within the parental and adolescents groups (computed separately) prior to merging parental and adolescent for the factor analysis). Internal consistency of items in the first factor using Cronbach's α was .93. Analysis of the second factor did not reveal a satisfactory level of internal consistency (α = .43) and was dropped from the analysis. When all items were scaled together, α was .89.
This table is not for publication but is available from the senior author on request.

Appendix 12B: Principal Component Loadings of Perception of Family Conflict among Adults and Adolescents in the Family

Table 12B.1.

Item	Conflict	h^2
Style of parenting	.733	.594
Lack of communication	.711	.561
School performance	.681	.513
Final decision-making for the family	.759	.580
Relationships with friends	.682	.489
Cultural differences	.571	.537
Dating	.632	.400
Use of alcohol	.564	.892
Use of tobacco	.569	.889
Percent Total Variance Explained		43.5

Notes: Respondents were asked: "To what extent do you have conflicts with children in your home in each of the following areas: A great deal, some, not much,
or no conflict at all?" Correlations are based on standardized item scores within
the parental and adolescents groups (computed separately) prior to merging parental and adolescent for the factor analysis. Internal consistency of items using
Cronbach's α was .83.
This table is not for publication but is available from the senior author on request.

References

Aldwin, C., & Greenberger, E. (1987). Cultural differences in the predictors of depression. *American Journal of Community Psychology, 15*(6), 789–813.

Asakawa, K. (2001). Family socialization practices and their effects on the internal-
ization of educational values for Asian and white American adolescents. *Applied Developmental Science, 5*(3), 184–194.

Asian/Pacific Islander Data Consortium, (ACCIS). (1992). *Our ten years of growth: A demographic analysis on Asian Pacific Islander Americans.* A CCIS Newsbrief. Asian and Pacific Islander Center for Census Information and Services. San Francisco, Fall 1992/Winter 1993.

Baptiste, D., Jr. (1993). Immigrant families, adolescents and acculturation: Insight for therapists. In B. H. Settles, D. E. Hanks III & M. B. Sussman (Eds.), *Families on the move: Migration, immigration, emigration, and mobility* (pp. 341–363). Binghamton, NY: Haworth Press.

Chen, C., Greenberger, E., Lester, J., Dong, Q., & Guo, M. (1998). A cross-
cultural study of family and peer correlates of adolescent misconduct. *Developmental Psychology, 34*(4), 770–781.

Chung, R. H. (2001). Gender, ethnicity, and acculturation in intergenerational conflict of Asian American college students. *Cultural Diversity & Ethnic Minority Psychology, 7*(4), 376–386.

Cuellar, I., Harris, L. C., & Jasso, R. (1980). An acculturation scale for Mexican American normal and clinical populations. *Hispanic Journal of Behavioral Science*, 2, 199–217.

Drachman, D., Kwon-Ahn, Y. H., & Paulino, A. (1996, December). Migration and resettlement experiences of Dominican and Korean families. *Families in Society*, 77, 626–638.

Espiritu, Y. L. (1999). Gender and labor in Asian immigrant families. *American Behavioral Scientist*, 42, 628–647.

Foner, N. (1997). The immigrant family: Cultural legacies and cultural changes. *International Migration Review*, 31, 961–974.

Frey, J. H. (1989). *Survey research by telephone* (2nd ed.). Newbury Park, CA: Sage.

Fuligni, A. J. (1998). Authority, autonomy, and parent–adolescent conflict and cohesion: A study of adolescents from Mexican, Chinese, Filipino, and European backgrounds. *Developmental Psychology*, 34, 782–792.

Hall, S. S. (2006). Marital meaning: Exploring young adults' belief systems about marriage. *Journal of Family Issues*, 27, 1437–1458.

Handal, P. J., Le-Stiebel, N., DiCarlo, M., & Gutzwiller, J. (1999). Perceived family environment and adjustment in American-born and immigrant Asian adolescents [Special Issue]. *Psychological Reports*, 85, 1244–1249.

Hauh, P.B. (1999). Korean-American adolescents' perspectives on conflictual issues with their parents. *Dissertation Abstracts International: Section B: the Sciences and Engineering*, 60(6-B), 3016.

Hofstetter, C. R., Lee, J., Hovell, M. F., Zakarian, J., Park, H., Paik, H. Y., et al. (2004). Tobacco use and acculturation among Californians of Korean descent: A behavioral epidemiological analysis. *Tobacco and Nicotine Research*, 6(3), 481–489.

Hovell, M. F., Wahlgren, D. R., Gehrman, C. A. (2002). The Behavioral Ecological Model: Integrating public health and behavioral science. In R. J. DiClemente, R. A. Crosby & M. Kegler (Eds.), *Emerging theories in health promotion practice and research: Strategies for improving public health* (pp. 347–385). San Francisco: Jossey-Bass.

Hurh, W. M., & Kim, K. C. (1984). Cohesive sociocultural adaptation of Korean immigrants in the U.S.: An alternative strategy of minority adaptation. *International Migration Review*, 18, 188–216.

James, W. H., Kim, G. K., & Armijo, E. (2000). The influence of ethnic identity on drug use among ethnic minority adolescents. *Journal of Drug Education*, 30, 265–280.

Kang, B. M. (2000). The relationship between differentiation of self and values in Korean immigrant church members in Los Angeles, California. *Dissertation Abstracts International Section A: Humanities & Social Sciences*. University Microfilms International, 61(4-A), 1634.

Kim, J. Y., & Sung, K. (2000). Conjugal violence in Korean American families: A residue of the cultural tradition. *Journal of Family Violence*, 15(4), 331–345.

Kim, S. (1996). The effects of parenting style, cultural conflict, and peer relations on academic achievement and psychosocial adjustment among Korean immigrant adolescents. *Dissertation Abstracts International Section A: Humanities & Social Sciences*. University Microfilms International, *57*(2-A), 0578.

Kwak, K. & Berry, J. W. (2001). Generational differences in acculturation among Asian families in Canada: A comparison of Vietnamese, Korean, and East-Indian groups. *International Journal of Psychology, 36*(3), 152–162.

Landau-Stanton, J. (1995). Adolescents, families, and cultural transitions: A treatment model. In M. Firkin & S. Komai (Eds.), *Handbook of adolescents and family therapy* (pp. 363–381). New York: Gardner Press.

LaRossa, R., & Reitzes, D. C. (1993). Symbolic interactionism and family studies. In P. G. Boss, W. J. Doherty, R. LaRossa, W. R. Schumm & S. K. Steinmetz (Eds.), *Sourcebook of family theory and methods: A contextual approach* (pp. 135–163). New York: Plenum Press.

Lee, R. M., Choe, J., Kim, G., & Ngo, V. (2000). Construction of the Asian American Family Conflicts Scale. *Journal of Counseling Psychology, 47*(2), 211–222.

Lee, R. M., & Liu, H. T. (2001). Coping with intergenerational family conflict: Comparison of Asian American, Hispanic, and European American college students. *Journal of Counseling Psychology, 48*(4), 410–419.

Matsuoka, J. K. (1990). Differential acculturation among Vietnamese refugees. *Social Work, 35*, 341–345.

McAdoo, H. P., Martinez, E. A., & Hughes, H. (2005). Ecological changes in ethnic families of color. In V. L. Bengtson, A. C. Acock, K. R. Allen, P. Dilworth-Anderson & D. M. Klein (Eds.), *Sourcebook of family theory and research* (pp. 191–212). Thousand Oaks, CA: Sage.

Min, P. G. (1995). Korean Americans. In P. G. Min (Ed.), *Asian Americans: Contemporary trends and issues* (pp. 199–231). Thousand Oaks, CA: Sage.

Nah, K. (1993). Perceived problems with service delivery for Korean immigrants. *Social Work, 38*, 289–296.

Nguyen, N., & Williams, H. (1989). Transition from East to West: Vietnamese adolescents and their parents. *Journal of the American Academy of Child and Adolescent Psychiatry, 28*, 505–515.

Rhee, S. (1997). Domestic violence in the Korean immigrant family. *Journal of Sociology and Social Welfare, 24*, 63–75.

Rohner, R. P., & Pettengill, S. M. (1985). Perceived parental acceptance-rejection and parental control among Korean adolescents. *Child Development, 56*, 524–528.

Rosenthal, D., Ranieri, N., & Klimidis, S. (1996). Vietnamese adolescents in Australia: Relationships between perceptions of self and parental values, intergenerational conflict, and gender dissatisfaction. *International Journal of Psychology, 31*, 81–91.

Shon, S. P., & Ja, D. Y. (1982). Asian families. In M. McGoldrick, J. K. Pearce & J. Giordano (Eds.), *Ethnicity and family therapy* (pp. 208–228). New York: Guilford Press.

Song, Y. J., Paik, H. Y., Park, H. R., Hofstetter, C. R., Hovell, M. F., Lee, J., et al. (2004). Acculturation and health risk behaviors among Californians of Korean descent. *Preventive Medicine, 39*, 147–156.

Song-Kim, Y. I. (1992). Battered Korean women in urban United States. In S. Furuto, R. Biswas, D. Chung, K. Murase & F. Ross-Sheriff (Eds.), *Social work practice with Asian Americans* (pp. 213–226). Newbury, CA: Sage.

State of California. Department of Finance. (2006). California Current Population Survey Report: March 2005. Sacramento, CA. Retrieved October 30, 2006, from www.dof.ca.gov/HTML/DEMOGRAP/ReportsPapers/documents/CPS_Extended_3-05.pdf

Stokes, R., & Hewitt, J. P. (1976). Aligning actions. *American Sociological Review, 41*, 838–849.

Stryker, S. (1980). *Symbolic interactionism: A social structural version.* Menlo Park, CA: Benjamin/Cummings.

Suinn, R. M., Khoo, G., & Ahuna, C. (1995). The Suinn-Lew Asian self-identify acculturation scale: Cross-cultural information. *Journal of Multicultural Counseling and Development, 23*, 139–148.

Suinn, R. M., Rickard-Figueroa, K., Lew, S., & Vigil, P. (1987). The Suinn-Lew Asian self-identity acculturation scale: An initial report. *Educational and Psychological Measurement, 47*, 401–407.

Szapocznik, J., & Kurtines, W. M. (1993). Family psychology and cultural diversity: Opportunities for theory, research, and applications. *American Psychologist, 48*, 400–407.

Tran, C. G., & Des Jardins, K. (2000). Domestic violence in Vietnamese refugee and Korean immigrant communities. In J. L. Chin (Ed.), *Relationships among Asian American women* (pp. 71–96). Washington, DC: American Psychological Association.

Uba, L. (1994). *Asian Americans: Personality patterns, identity, and mental health.* New York: Guilford Press.

Usita, P. M. (2001). Interdependency in immigrant mother–daughter relationships. *Journal of Aging Studies, 15*, 183–199.

Usita, P. M., & Blieszner, R. (2002). Immigrant family strengths: Meeting communication challenges. *Journal of Family Issues, 23*, 266–286.

Ying, Y., & Chao, C. (1996). Intergenerational relationships in Iu Mien American families. *Amerasia Journal, 22*(3), 47–64.

Ying, Y. W. (1999). Educational program for families on intergenerational conflict. In E. Kramer, S. Ivey & Y. Ying (Eds.), *Immigrant women's health: Problems and solutions* (pp. 282–294). San Francisco: Jossey-Bass.

Ying, Y. W., Coombs, M., & Lee, P. A. (1999). Family intergenerational relationship of Asian American adolescents. *Cultural Diversity & Ethnic Minority Psychology, 5*, 350–363.

Yoon, I. J. (2000). Korean immigration to the United States and intergenerational conflicts in Korean immigrant families. *Studies of Koreans Abroad, 9*, 5–44.

Yu, E. Y., Choe, P., & Han, S. I. (2002). Korean population in the United States, 2000: Demographic characteristics and socio-economic status. *International Journal of Korean Studies, 6,* 71–107.

About the Authors

C. Richard Hofstetter, Ph.D., is a professor of political science and adjunct professor of the Graduate School of Public Health, San Diego State University, 9245 Sky Park Court, Suite 230, San Diego, CA 92123. Phone: 858-505-4770 ext. 146. Fax: 858-505-8614. E-mail: rhofstet@mail.sdsu.edu.

Melbourne F. Hovell, M.P.H., Ph.D., is a professor in the Graduate School of Public Health, San Diego State University, 9245 Sky Park Court, Suite 230, San Diego, CA 92123. Phone: 858-505-4772. Fax: 858-505-8614. E-mail: mhovell@projects.sdsu.edu.

Veronica Lea Irvin, MPH, is a research associate at the Center for Behavioral Epidemiology and Community Health, Graduate School of Public Health, San Diego State University, 9245 Sky Park Court, Suite 230, San Diego, CA 92123. Phone: 858-505-4770 ext. 146. Fax: 858-505-8614. E-mail: vcramer@projects.sdsu.edu.

Kyoung-Rae Jung, M.S., is a doctoral student at the University of Minnesota, Duluth, Department of Psychology, 320 Bohannon Hall, 1207 Ordean Court, Duluth, MN 55812. Phone: 218-726-7117. E-mail: jungx068@umn.edu.

Jooeun Lee, M.A., is a doctoral student in the School of Public Health, Harvard University, 677 Huntington Avenue, Boston, MA 02115.

Ana Martinez-Donate, Ph.D., is an assistant professor in the Department of Population Health Sciences, School of Medicine and Public Health, University of Wisconsin–Madison, 610 Walnut Street, Room 605 WARF, Madison, WI 53726. Phone: 608-263-2880. E-mail: martinezdona@wisc.edu.

Hee-Young Paik, Sc.D., is a professor in the Department of Food and Nutrition, Seoul National University, San 56-1 Shillim-dong Kwanak-ku, Seoul, 151-742, Republic of Korea. E-mail: hypaik@yahoo.com.

Haeryun Park, Ph.D., is a professor in the Department of Food and Nutrition, Myongji University, Nam-dong San 38-2, Yongin City, Kyunggi-do, 449-728, Republic of Korea. E-mail: hrpark@mju.ac.kr.

Paula Usita, Ph.D., is an associate professor in the Graduate School of Public Health, San Diego State University, 9245 Sky Park Court, Suite 230, San Diego, CA 92123. Phone: 619-594-5868. Fax: 858-505-8614. E-mail: usita@mail.sdsu.edu.

Joy Zakarian, MPH, is a research associate at the Center for Behavioral Epidemiology and Community Health, Graduate School of Public Health, San Diego State University, 9245 Sky Park Court, Suite 230, San Diego, CA 92123. Phone: 858-505-4770 ext. 119. Fax: 858-505-8614. E-mail: jzakarian@projects.sdsu.edu.

"Lost Boys" Finding Their Way 13
Challenges, Changes, and Small Victories of Young Sudanese Refugees in the United States

TOM LUSTER, DEBORAH J. JOHNSON, AND LAURA BATES

Abstract

The researchers provide detailed information on the Sudanese war and resulting displacement of millions of Sudanese children and youth. The research focuses on the experiences of the "Lost Boys" (and girls) of Sudan who lived in peer groups without parents and often adult supervision for nearly a decade before being relocated to the United States. Data comes from two groups (unaccompanied minors and young adults) who were resettled in mid-Michigan. Challenges and accomplishments of both groups are discussed as they transitioned into American culture.

Keywords: Lost Boys, Sudan, Sudanese Civil War, Africa, Refugee, Resettlement

Most young refugees resettle in their new homeland with their parents, and prior research has established that parents' adjustment in their new country has important implications for how well their children adapt to their new surroundings (Caplan, Choy & Whitmore, 1991). But what happens to adolescents and young adults who have to make their way in a new country without the support of their biological parents? What happens to refugee youth who have lived apart from their parents in refugee camps for a decade, and instead, lived in peer groups which functioned much like surrogate families? In this chapter, we attempt to shed light on these questions by discussing the experiences of young refugees from southern Sudan who resettled in mid-Michigan. These youth were called the "Lost Boys of Sudan" by the media and workers from relief agencies; they were named for the orphans in the Peter Pan story who lived in peer groups in Neverland (Barrie, 1967).

Our study began in 2001 when the Sudanese refugees were resettled in the United States and a partnership was formed between Michigan State University and two resettlement agencies responsible for the care of the unaccompanied minors (Lutheran Social Services of Michigan and Refugee Services of St. Vincent Catholic Charities, Inc.) and the young adults who were in their late teens or early twenties. Based on reports written about the experiences of these youth in Africa (Duncan, January 2000, April 2000) and numerous resettlement interviews conducted in the Kakuma refugee camp by a member of our research team, we were aware that the "Lost Boys" had experienced extraordinary adversity but were also viewed as being remarkably resilient. Thus, a risk and resilience theoretical framework guided our research (Luthar & Zelazo, 2003).

Through focus groups and individual interviews with the youth, we began by investigating refugees' perceptions of the risks they experienced in Africa and the protective factors that helped them to cope with chronic adversity and traumatic events. In addition, we interviewed the youth about their perceptions of the risks or challenges they experienced in the six to eighteen months after resettlement, their accomplishments to date in the United States, and individual and contextual factors that helped them to cope successfully with these new challenges. Another goal of the research was to increase our understanding of how the Sudanese refugees' experiences in Africa related to their resettlement experiences. To add to our understanding of their adjustment process since resettlement, we also collected data from those who worked with the unaccompanied minors— foster parents and caseworkers.

The Effects of War on Children

Although the Sudanese youth differ from most refugee groups studied to date, many children suffer similar fates in conflicts throughout the world. Recent changes in the nature of warfare have increased the risks for children. In the decade 1986–1996, UNICEF estimates that two million children were killed in wars, one million orphaned or separated from their parents at least temporarily, and twelve million displaced from their homes (UNICEF, 1996). A particularly vulnerable group is children separated from their parents and other adult relatives during conflict. In 2003, 12,800 unaccompanied refugee children applied for asylum in developing countries—4 percent of total asylum applicants (UNHCR, 2004).

Children caught in conflict are exposed to many risk factors that can undermine normal development. Deleterious outcomes include posttraumatic stress disorder (PTSD), anxiety, depression, and other forms of psychopathology, poor health and disfigurement, behavioral disorders, substance abuse, delinquency, and low academic achievement (Joshi & O'Donnell, 2003; Shaw, 2003). Far less is known about resilience among victims of war and protective factors that contribute to resilient outcomes, particularly for unaccompanied and separated children. Research on protective factors for children exposed to war has focused on how parental adjustment and behavior affects the children (Garbarino, Kostelny & Dubrow, 1991; Shaw, 2003), and thus has limited applicability to the unaccompanied children.

Although the twentieth century abounds with examples of children separated from their parents by war, few studies exist that systematically examine the issues of risk, resilience, and adaptation of these children over time. Literature on unaccompanied children tends to focus on documenting trauma experiences and assessing initial adjustment and service needs among recently separated and relocated children; few researchers were able to follow children beyond the initial adjustment period (e.g., Ingleby, 2005; Sourander, 1998). In addition there are a few retrospective descriptive studies of the unaccompanied refugee group's perceptions of their experiences and their adjustment as adults (e.g., Conde, 1999; Moskovitz, 1985). Many retrospective studies have limitations as well. For example, studies of the *Pedro Pan* children of the Cuban Revolution (Conde, 2003), the Kindertransport of World War II (Harris & Oppenheimer, 2000), and Basque children sent abroad during the Spanish Civil War (Legarreta, 1984) have limited applicability to the majority of separated children, because these groups were evacuated with the consent of parents to protect them from harm and experienced less of the violence and deprivation directly associated with the conflict. Many had the opportunity to communicate with parents, at least occasionally, and some were reunited with parents over time.

Thus, the circumstances of the Sudanese youth provided a rare opportunity to study the resettlement experiences of unaccompanied minors and young adults; not only did they arrive in the United States without their parents, most of these youth had lived apart from their parents throughout the decade of the 1990s. Of particular interest to us were the challenges faced by this atypical group of new arrivals during resettlement and factors that contributed to successful outcomes among these young refugees.

Method

The findings described in this chapter reflect analyses across a series of investigations conducted by the authors (Bates et al., 2005; Luster, Bates & Johnson, 2006). We used a mixed-methods approach to study the resettlement experiences of the Sudanese refugees and to explore their experiences in Africa.

Data Sources

In all, our research included five components: (1) seventy refugee youth (forty-four minors and twenty-six adults) completed questionnaires regarding current employment, educational progress, social support, and behavioral adjustment (Lambert & Rowan, 1999); (2) forty-nine refugee Sudanese youth participated in nine focus groups; (3) two focus groups with ten foster parents; (4) five interviews conducted with caseworkers from Lutheran Social Services of Michigan; and (5) one case study of a twenty-four-year-old Sudanese male adult including forty hours of videotaped interviews with one of the investigators.

Data Analysis

Use of mixed methods for the analysis of trauma experienced by the youth proved particularly advantageous. For example, using the quantitative and qualitative components of these data we could assess the effects of trauma with an established PTSD measure (Foa, Johnson, Feeny & Treadwell, 2001) and address how individuals recalled and processed traumatic events during focus groups and individual interviews.

Overlapping themes were assessed across the parent, caseworker interviews, and youth focus groups from transcribed audiotapes. In this paper the case study provided confirmatory support to themes assessed as cutting across the central data sources. Transcripts for youth were initially analyzed for themes of resilience and coping by an investigator and three assistants (two Kenyan and one other international). Each reviewer independently identified themes, and then themes and evidence were discussed. Overlapping themes were given higher priority for inclusion. Three investigators then reviewed these themes again and consensus on key themes was achieved. The parent focus groups were conducted by a family therapist. Investigators reviewed a synopsis of the interviews by the investigator/therapist and themes distilled from transcripts by another investigator to determine final themes. Subsequently, investigators analyzed the youth, parent, and caseworker transcripts again focusing on family relations. Themes of resilience, initial and long-term adjustment, identity, and family relations that emerged from these analytic processes are presented in this chapter.

Results

The Background of the Sudanese Refugees

We will begin by describing the circumstances that led to their separation from their parents, and their experiences in refugee camps in Ethiopia, displacement camps in Sudan, and the Kakuma refugee camp in Kenya. Focus groups and individual interviews about their experiences in Africa provide a rich context for understanding their resettlement experiences.

In 1983, a civil war began in Sudan between the army of the government of Sudan, based in Khartoum in the northern half of the country, and the rebel forces of the Sudanese People's Liberation Army (SPLA), based in the south. The conflict involved differences in religion, ethnicity, political agendas, and a desire to control resources, including oil. This round of fighting began when the Islamic government in the north imposed *Sharia* (i.e., Islamic) law on the country. The Black Africans of the south, who practiced Christianity and tribal religions, resisted this change and demanded more political power, especially in governmental matters that concerned the south. The civil war, war-related famine, and disease claimed the lives of over two million people and led to the displacement of hundreds of thousands of others. Among those who fled their villages during the fighting were thousands of children (mostly boys), who made their way to displacement camps in Sudan or to refugee camps in neighboring countries. In the late 1980s, thousands of youth walked great distances across grasslands, swamps, and deserts on their way to refugee camps in Ethiopia.

Ethiopia was controlled by the Mengistu regime, a Marxist government that received support from the Soviet Union. The regime provided space for refugee camps and the SPLA bases. When the Soviet Union fell in 1991 and support for the Mengistu regime disappeared, a rebel army gained control of Ethiopia and violently expelled the SPLA and the refugees because of their links to the old regime (Hecht, 2005). As the Sudanese fled back to Sudan, many became trapped between the Gilo River at flood stage and the Ethiopian army that was driving the SPLA out of their country. Survivors estimated that 2,000 refugees drowned or were shot trying to cross the Gilo River.

Back in Sudan, the youth teetered on the brink of starvation in displacement camps. Living on the border of Ethiopia and Sudan, the youth lived in fear of attacks by both the Ethiopian and Sudanese armies. Eventually the youth were attacked and began another long trek—this time to Kenya. Again, they had to forage for food and drink water from rivers, streams, and puddles; the lack of purified water resulted in disease and parasites. Because of aerial bombardment, sniper attacks by local tribesmen, animal attacks, and disease, many youth never reached Kenya.

The Kakuma Refugee Camp

Those who made it to Kenya were eventually resettled in the hot, dry, and sparsely populated area near the city of Kakuma in northwest Kenya. Located near the equator, the temperatures in Kakuma routinely topped 100 degrees Fahrenheit and desert winds blew sand unrelentingly through the encampment. Many of the youth helped build their own houses out of mud bricks with grasses, plastic, and poles provided for the roofs. Most occupied these homes with three to five peers in a section of the camp set aside for the minor group; a small number of adults were hired by the UN to serve as caretakers. Mostly the peers looked to each other and to religion for comfort.

There were no schools when they arrived. The first classrooms were under the trees that lined a riverbed that was dry much of the year. Sometimes class sessions were cut short because dust storms made it impossible to see the chalkboards that teachers had set up under the trees. Eventually, schools were built. Often the teachers were fellow refugees who had a high-school education but little training in teaching. Textbooks were few and many children shared one book; one youth recalled sharing a book with fifteen other students and getting to take it home to read about twice a month. After school, the youth spent time with their peers who became surrogate family members. Some played soccer, others used chess sets, dominoes, and playing cards that were eventually provided as diversionary activities by relief agencies. Older youth took turns grinding grain and cooking the grains with lentils in water over a wood fire. In Sudanese culture, males were not expected to cook, but the alternative was to go hungry. As dark descended, the youth gathered in their homes to pray with their housemates that God would protect them through the night. News of raids by local tribesmen during the night and inter-tribal violence in the section of the camp set aside for adults and families made sound sleep next to impossible at times.

In the mid-1990s, because of budget constraints, the youth's food rations were reduced. The ration, which had to stretch across two weeks, was often completely consumed days before their next ration was distributed. The resulting inadequate nutrition made it difficult to attend school or concentrate on school material. Some of the youth dropped out while others pushed themselves up the educational ladder, believing that education was their only hope for a better future. With no parents to meet their needs, the youth were guided by the proverb, "Education is my mother and father." However, even those who managed to complete high school in Kakuma had few opportunities. The refugees were not permitted to work outside the camp in Kenya, and there were very few jobs inside the camp. A very small number of youth were fortunate enough to be selected for jobs as teachers shortly after completing high school. Like their predecessors, they were thrown into the role of educating their younger peers with little training; while on the job, they received some instruction on educational methods from certified teachers during weekend seminars. One former teacher told us his best training for teaching was the time that he spent in the drama club in the camp; his acting experience helped him to play the part of the teacher in his eighth grade science classes until the certified teachers could provide him with some pedagogical training.

With no employment opportunities, most of the youth had to cope with the monotony of camp life where one day seemed the same as the next. Some youth struggled with sadness, others struggled with feelings of hopelessness because there was no reason to believe that conditions would improve. But hopefulness returned in the late 1990s, when word spread through Kakuma that the "Lost Boys" would get a chance to resettle in the United States. Youth who had arrived in Kakuma before 1994, and whose parents were deceased or untraceable, began the interview process with officials from the United States.

Julianne Duncan (January, 2000), who conducted 174 *Best Interest Determination* interviews, shared her observations of the youth: "Virtually every child interviewed is suffering from symptoms of unresolved trauma" (p. 4). The symptoms include disturbed sleep, nightmares, and startle reactions. However, Duncan (May, 2001) also described the youth as remarkably

resilient and identified three factors that may have contributed to their resilience: (1) religious faith, (2) a strong desire for education, and (3) a desire
to contribute in a positive way to eventually rebuilding Sudan after the
war. Some of the youth also had developed relationships with adults in the
camp, who functioned as surrogate parents providing advice, encouragement, admonishment for violations of cultural norms, and help finding basic
necessities such as food and medical care.

With regard to the female minors, Duncan (April, 2000) noted that
they had been taken in by families in the camp, in part because of the
bride wealth the families would obtain when the girls married. However,
they were treated much like domestic servants doing household chores
for long hours and serving as nannies. Although UN policy was that both
boys and girls should attend school in the camp, girls were often kept out
of the classroom to perform household duties. Many of the females were
exploited in other ways, including sexual and/or physical abuse. Duncan
(April, 2000) noted more symptoms of depression among the females, and
attributed this to the abuse they experienced.

As a result of the interview process, about 3,800 Sudanese youth were
approved for resettlement in the United States. In November 2000, the
first of 135 youths who were eventually resettled in the mid-Michigan
area, boarded a plane in Kakuma headed to a place about which they knew
very little. Each month a few more youth arrived until the events of 9/11
sharply curtailed the flow of refugees into the United States. Several of the
youth commented that terror seemed to follow them across the ocean.

Resettling Adults and Minors: Catholic and Lutheran Social Services

Once they arrived, the refugees who were eighteen or older received
services from Refugee Services of St. Vincent Catholic Charities, Inc.
Youth younger than eighteen entered through the unaccompanied minors
program of Lutheran Social Services of Michigan, and were placed in the
refugee foster care program.

REFUGEE SERVICES. Sudanese young adults received the package of
resettlement services provided to all adult refugees who enter the United
States (i.e., assistance with obtaining housing, employment, medical care,
and in some cases, help with English-language skills). During the first
month, the young men received a cultural orientation—a *crash course* on
how to function effectively in the United States. Part of the course focused

on using unfamiliar household technology (e.g., stoves, microwave ovens, flush toilets, and telephones). Other skills included shopping and preparing food, using the bus system, filling out employment applications, and learning about employer expectations. Within four months of arrival, they were expected to be economically self-sufficient. To supplement what was provided by Refugee Services, the youth were assigned volunteer mentors whose job description was to be an American friend who assisted the refugees in adjusting to their new life in the United States. Mentors were asked to help the refugee they were assigned for six months, and to meet with the refugee every week for at least two hours.

LUTHERAN SOCIAL SERVICES OF MICHIGAN (LSSM). Sudanese minors were resettled through the Unaccompanied Refugee Minor Program. Children in this program are placed in foster homes and receive services until the age of twenty-one to help them adjust to U.S. life and transition into independent living. Youth and foster parents receive financial assistance, monitoring, and services such as case management, counseling, and mental-health services.

The youth learned much about American culture by being embedded in an American family, with foster parents and foster siblings acting as cultural brokers (Pipher, 2003). Caseworkers also worked with the youth to help them understand their new country and culture. Most of the minors enrolled in public high schools or middle schools, which offered another vehicle for learning about the culture. LSSM assisted with academics by providing tutors for many youth.

Challenges, Changes, and Accomplishments

Some challenges were common to the adults and the minors. For example, everyone had to adjust to Michigan winter weather after living near the equator in east Africa. During the first year that they were in Michigan, it was not unusual to see the Sudanese refugees wearing winter coats while they were inside their homes, until late spring. Everyone also had to learn how to use unfamiliar technology, ranging from computers to telephones. There was also the common obstacle of understanding a new culture and the cultural expectations for individuals in each new setting, such as homes, schools, restaurants, and other businesses. For youth reared in the United States, learning the *scripts* for how to go about routine tasks in these various settings are acquired through years of mundane experiences. The Sudanese youth noted that one of the most taxing challenges for them was that everything was new, and they were constantly trying to understand how they were expected to behave in each setting; they missed being able to do routine things without having to think about them during the first year. Other challenges varied for the adults and the minors because of their differing circumstances, and females faced unique challenges based on their past experiences and differing cultural expectations. Thus, we discuss the challenges and accomplishments of the three groups separately.

The Challenges Faced by the Adults

The challenges associated with moving to a markedly different country and culture were discussed in the focus groups (held six to eighteen months after the refugees arrived). The challenges that were noted changed somewhat over this time period; as one challenge was mastered, new ones emerged. However, one of the consistent challenges for the adults involved work and income.

WORK AND INCOME. Most of the young adults had no work experience prior to coming to the United States. In addition, most of them had little or no experience paying bills or managing money. After their initial month of cultural orientation, they were eligible for welfare support for only three more months. To help us appreciate their circumstances, one youth noted, "If an American had to go to another country and did not know the culture, and had to take care of himself after three months, it would not be easy."

With the assistance of Refugee Services, most of the youth found jobs before their welfare benefits ran out. These were entry-level jobs that paid the minimum wage and often were for less than forty hours per week. Few included health benefits. Health care was provided by Medicaid for their first eight months. After that they had to hope that they found a job with health insurance or never had a serious illness or injury.

The entry-level jobs available to the Sudanese men were often viewed as inappropriate for men in their culture. For example, cooking hamburgers at a fast-food restaurant or working in a hospital laundry were viewed as tasks normally carried out by females. However, the young men took jobs that they were not particularly comfortable with until they were able to change jobs several months later.

The tax system in the United States was unfamiliar to the Sudanese. In anticipation of their first paycheck, they calculated their hourly wage times the number of hours worked and expected to receive the full amount.

They were surprised to learn that their paycheck was about one-third less than what they expected. In our first focus group, one of the participants ticked off each of the taxes taken out of his check and concluded:

> We decided that the reason America brings us here is only to pay the taxes. When we go to the job, at the end of the week when we get the money, we find that most of the money was taken by the taxes.

In addition, when they first arrived, the Sudanese had a different approach to time than most Americans. Based on information provided at the cultural orientation, most of the Sudanese understood that arriving late did not go over well in the workplace. However, some of them struggled with the cultural demands for punctuality. "Some employers when you arrive late for work they say: 'Go home.' That's a thing I don't understand. Is it most of Americans that say that or just some of them?" Having grown up without electric lights near the equator where the sun rose and set at nearly the same time year round (twelve hours of daylight), the youth were accustomed to being active from 6 a.m. to 6 p.m. and then resting. Obviously, the time when people worked in the United States was not dictated by available sunlight. One youth saw second and third work shifts as being out of line with what God intended:

> Where I come from we don't work nights. It is God's agreement to put a difference between day and night. There is a time when God wants you to do everything, and there is a time when God wants you to rest. When I came to the United States there is no rest for the night [laughter from the group]. So it is like Americans are also contradicting themselves what God plans to do. Working at night and working daytime is hard. For example, I have to work at night and then go to school during the daytime.

EDUCATION. The Sudanese refugees came to the United States with a strong desire to obtain further education. When asked about his decision to come to the United States, one refugee explained, "I needed to fill my empty head. I did not leave Kakuma because of the lack of food, heat, or dust. I had learned to live with those conditions by then. But I could not get more education in Kakuma."

Several expressed a desire to acquire knowledge and skills that could be used to help rebuild southern Sudan once the civil war ended. A generation of youth growing up in southern Sudan had few opportunities to attend school because of the fighting and lack of funding for schools and teachers. The elders who saw the "Lost Boys" off at the Kakuma airport often reminded them that with this special opportunity to study abroad came special responsibilities to help those who were left behind.

Although the motivation to further their education was strong, there were challenges as well. Because of the low-paying, entry-level jobs that most of the Sudanese refugees had, it was difficult to save money for college expenses. This problem was compounded by the frequent requests they received for money from friends and relatives who remained in the refugee camps. Knowing full well what the refugees were experiencing, the Sudanese in the United States sent as much money as they could back to Africa. Sometimes this meant deciding between sending money back for food or paying for tuition at the community college. Because they were under no legal obligation to support these friends and relatives, these contributions could not be considered when making financial aid awards to the youth.

Once they made it into the classroom, there were challenges related to their educational background in the camps. Although they had learned to converse in English, they had almost no experience writing in English. Thus, their English writing skills were well behind their speaking skills. Fortunately, Lansing Community College had a series of classes designed to improve English composition and a multicultural advising center to help the refugees enroll in courses commensurate with their skills. Although many of the refugees were reluctant to delay taking courses in their major, they found the English classes not only useful for improving their writing skills, but also for acquiring basic information about college courses, such as how to use a syllabus or prepare for final exams.

Another challenge for some of the youth was dealing with symptoms of post-traumatic stress disorder (PTSD). Twenty-six adults and forty-four minors completed a PTSD measure and about two-thirds of them reported nightmares and upsetting thoughts or images. One refugee described difficulties concentrating in class because he would suddenly recall the attack on his village or picture friends screaming for help as they were swept away by the Gilo River.

STRENGTHS AND ACCOMPLISHMENTS: VICTORIES BIG AND SMALL. Given the challenges, we were struck by the resilience and adaptation of the young adults. Navigating the unfamiliar world of work and becoming economically self-sufficient was difficult, but they did it. Succeeding in an unfamiliar educational system with less than optimal educational preparation was difficult, but many of the refugees are attending community college, several of them have advanced to four-year colleges, and a few from the original study group are already college graduates.

Many of the personal strengths and supports that were important to their survival in East Africa have been important for their adaptation in the United States. For example, the belief that God has a plan for them has helped the youth weather the difficulties involved in the transition to a new culture and to believe that things will work out as intended in the end. Similarly, the support of the peer group that was so important to their survival in the refugee camps is also important in the current context. Typically the young adults live in apartments with three or four house-mates. They share living expenses and household tasks. If one of them is laid off from work or loses a job, the peer group picks up the financial slack, covering expenses until a new job can be found. The peer group also supports its members through sharing information. It was evident that when one youth learned useful information from a mentor or Refugee Services (e.g., how to fill out a financial-aid application), other refugees benefited from this information. The peer group also seemed to carry out some functions that may have been carried out by parents if they were available. For example, the youth shared advice, provided encouragement during difficult times, and even admonished members of the group who behaved inappropriately.

Challenges Faced by the Minors

Because of differences in resettlement policies affecting minors and young adults, their adjustment experiences were somewhat different. Because minors received financial and personal support and services over several years, they had a significant advantage in achieving their educational goals over those who came in as young adults. However, they faced different challenges as a result of their foster-placement experiences.

Initial placement in foster homes with American families was both an asset and a challenge. Foster families provided a high level of material sup-port, such as food, shelter, transportation, and assistance with schoolwork, allowing youth to concentrate on school. Living in an American house-hold gave them invaluable experience in American culture. On the other hand, foster families were spread throughout the metropolitan area, and youth were dependent on busy foster families for transportation. Many youth, accustomed to daily intimate contact with their Sudanese peers, felt socially and culturally isolated. To maintain contact, some youth spent many hours on the telephone with friends here in Lansing and even in

Africa. Large telephone bills and calls from Africa that frequently came in the middle of the night, causing disruption to family life, were major points of contention in some homes. By purchasing phone cards, parents were able to limit telephone charges.

Cultural and language barriers created situations where misunderstandings and hurt feelings could easily occur. Initially many problems centered on food and food preparation. Youth were accustomed to having a freshly prepared meal of Sudanese food at each meal time. Because refrigeration was not readily available in the camps, leftover food was never served, so some youth feared that the families might *poison* them by serving leftovers. Cultural etiquette about food was different, and so youth and families frequently misinterpreted the comments of the other. For example, youth refused food when parents asked them if they wanted to eat, because in Sudan it would be considered rude or greedy to say yes. In Sudanese culture one just serves the food, and people eat if they are hungry.

Families and youth had different expectations of what the fostering relationship would be and these differing expectations sometimes led to disappointment or conflict. Foster parents often expected that youth would easily become part of their families and relationships would be long lasting. In many cases, emotional bonds took longer to form or did not form at all. Because these youth were older and had little experience with traditional family life in any culture, they did not know what to expect from American family life. While many foster parents were looking for a child who would become a permanent part of their family, many youth were looking more for mentors than for parents. Cultural differences in the relationships between parents and children and among siblings also created misunderstandings and conflicts in some homes. Youth had different cultural expectations of how parents and children would interact. In Sudanese homes, the oldest boy and the oldest girl have specific roles and responsibilities in relation to younger siblings. One Sudanese caseworker explained this as:

> like the relationship of a husband and a wife in terms of who is calling the shots and who had to decide. . . . The girl come[s] as advice to the man [the older brother] and the man . . . is responsible for the family. When they came here everything was different. Everybody is responsible to the head of the family [the father].

Some foster families experienced these cultural differences played out in their homes as power struggles between them and the older adolescents about who was in charge of the family. In addition some youth were suffering from unresolved trauma, leading to acting out and other resistive behavior.

Many conflicts in families were resolved successfully; however, in some key instances problems were insurmountable. For example, hostility expressed toward the Sudanese by American siblings or grandchildren created some conflicts. When issues could not be resolved, youth were moved into new placements. After years of making their own decisions, some youth were unwilling or unable to submit to parental authority and chose to move into independent living at the earliest possible opportunity.

School also presented both rewards and challenges for the youth. Although going to public schools provided daily lessons in American youth culture, adjusting to the school environment was a major challenge. Youth went to school in the home district of the foster family, encompassing urban, suburban, and rural school districts. Schools with large immigrant populations had English as a Second Language (ESL) classes but others had no such supports. In addition, youth who had not received a good basic education in the refugee camps struggled in secondary-school classes that assumed basic literacy. Caseworkers and foster parents spent much of the early resettlement period negotiating with schools for more appropriate services to assist students who were struggling. Many of the schools they attended had virtually no ethnic or cultural diversity, and some youth reported harassment from other students based on language, race, or cultural differences. The boys tended to shrug off these insults, dismissing them as not important to their central purpose in being here. As one boy said, "even in Africa we have some kind of stupid kid[s]; they don't understand people some time."

Dating was a major concern for the boys, given the vast cultural differences in male-female relationships. Some males were shocked by female assertiveness among their adolescent school peers. As one commented, "Like here, ladies, they chase boy[s] around—in front of people. . . . [In Africa] the boys are the ones who chase ladies."

Meeting the academic challenges of high school was difficult for some, although many students rose to the challenge. Students who entered in their junior or senior years had to struggle to meet the requirements for graduation. Some students took six or seven classes a semester to graduate on time. Those who graduated and enrolled in college benefited greatly from an educational voucher program that the resettlement agency obtained. It provided additional financial support to the youth while they attended college, thus enabling them to cut back on the number of hours they had to work.

Like most American teens, the Sudanese were exposed to the risky behaviors of high school—drugs, alcohol, and early sex. According to case-workers, remarkably few youth got into trouble during their high-school careers; however, many did suffer from depression or other effects of un-resolved trauma, even if they appeared to be functioning well. The agency offered counseling, but cultural differences in attitudes about mental health made youth reluctant initially to use these services. Only two of the mi-nors, one girl and one boy, had children as unwed parents; three youth had attempted suicide during their second year, and a few were in treatment for serious mental-health problems. Two minor youth had been identified as having substance abuse problems and were receiving treatment.

STRENGTHS AND ACCOMPLISHMENTS OF THE MINORS: CREAT-ING VICTORIES. Like the young adults, the minors have done remark-ably well in spite of the many challenges they've faced. At the time of the caseworker interviews, most male minors were continuing their education, either through community colleges or four-year universities. For example, one young man, who had struggled in his first foster home, found the right fit with his second foster father and really flowered. He graduated as valedictorian of his class at a private high school and is currently attending a major state university. A few who were younger when they came to the United States are still in high school.

Under the refugee foster care program, the minors had the opportunity to *transition* out of foster care by first going into supervised independent living. As they moved into independent living, they faced new challenges, such as caring for themselves and working part-time to meet expenses. Some foster parents adapted to the changes by maintaining contact after the child left the foster home and continuing to offer support.

While demonstrating progress in other areas, many youth were also negotiating one of the major developmental tasks of adolescence—identity formation. Separated from their home culture as young as four years of age, living in refugee camps with little adult guidance for years, many had only second-hand experience with Sudanese culture. Resettled in a vastly different culture while making the transition to adulthood, these young people were faced with the challenge of sorting out their cultural identity. Are they Sudanese, American, or some combination? A variety of solu-tions emerge. Some identify primarily with Sudanese culture and remain heavily involved in Sudanese activities and politics. Some have turned to Sudan to choose marriage partners, and by observing the traditions and rituals of marriage in their own tribe, have helped to form their identity as

Sudanese living in America. Most appear to be settling into some form of bicultural identity. A few young people have totally immersed themselves in American culture, complete with the overt indicators of youth culture. According to the agency caseworkers, finding an identity that they are comfortable with has been a major accomplishment for many youth.

The Sudanese Girls

The experience of Sudanese girls is unique among unaccompanied minors, despite some overlap in their experiences with the male youth. Sudanese girls entered into foster care with their male counterparts, often in sibling groups of two or three, which was sometimes unexpected by foster families. Moreover, longstanding sibling groups were organized, and entrance into the foster care setting meant that this organization and the associated roles of male and female children were disrupted. For most girls the new living situation marked the loss of their traditional caregiving role toward the males of their group, but also of male authority over the girls. Caseworkers were aware of these challenges. A Sudanese caseworker remarked, "It's because she feels she's playing the role of the mother. . . . And that role she's still supposed to be playing, and they come here and they find somebody who's a mother all of a sudden. It's a conflict." Unlike boys who embraced aspects of the new culture quickly, the girls were slower to take on aspects of the new culture, particularly around independence and youth culture. However, some girls perceived the lack of household duties as new freedom and a relief.

Resettlement in the United States allowed the girls to redefine gender roles, including their view of education. Educational opportunities were perceived as a different kind of chance at life. One adolescent girl remarked, "When I was in Kenya the women and you can't go to school like the guys." Another girl agreed saying, "But now [here in the United States] we can go to school. . . . Nobody can say . . . I need you to go cook, go wash dishes, go clean my house."

Although school represented new opportunities and experiences, there were many challenges. Because their time in school had been truncated by other duties and roles in Africa as well as other types of cultural imperatives, such as socialization toward marriage, education had not been especially valued for girls. As a consequence, missed time in school, paired with its lower value for them, had limited their preparation. Many were far behind the boys in their educational and English-language skills. Moreover, sometimes they felt that teachers were not as helpful to them as they could be.

While studying and making sense of American education required an enormous effort on the part of girls, the context of the school was not always hospitable in their view. Some girls had very harsh experiences with harassment and prejudice. One young girl described an incident during one of the first days of school, "When I was in middle school they write on the board that we don't want black people in this school." The girls described a variety of hurtful experiences from being physically assaulted, to being cursed at, and being told they did not belong in the United States. While ongoing harassment was rare, one adolescent girl reported numerous experiences with harassment by a group of boys, which ended when the police were called to school.

However, the girls also had positive experiences in the schools and developed good friendships as well. "I thought the kids would not like me or something . . . but they are really nice to me." Like the boys, a few have excelled at sports, especially track, and enjoyed the status associated with athletic skill in high school. Moreover, they see the advantages of their opportunities, with one girl noting, "I'm in school now. I do not [have to] pay my [way] . . . college and bills and things like that myself."

Cultural imperatives and remnants of role assignments influenced the transition from foster homes to adult independent living for the girls. Caseworkers, particularly Sudanese caseworkers, and Sudanese community members were not supportive of these young women living on their own. Still, several of the girls were excited to strike out on their own and live in an apartment without adult authority figures, as many of the boys had done. Several of the girls managed to obtain jobs but often struggled with the financial management of their households. For most girls, these arrangements ended, and the imperative to be absorbed into households with male relatives reemerged. According to several caseworkers, these arrangements allowed the girls to fare better, and the Sudanese community was more comfortable with these arrangements. Still, their dreams of independence were put on hold.

Certainly the path for the refugee girls is replete with many more disadvantages, cultural imperatives, and constraints than among the male refugees. Despite these imposed limitations, the girls are tenacious in their attempts to make the promise of America work for them while balancing cultural continuity. At least one youth has started college and others have completed high school and are continuing to increase their work skills. When asked, the girls talk about their aspirations to teach, model, pilot, or enter engineering fields; yet they also express their marital objectives.

Adversity has been a common experience but they seem willing, perhaps driven, to make it work and triumph over the many stumbling blocks.

Conclusions and Implications for Practice

As Rutter (2001) noted, youth who are successful in dealing with adversity over time may deal more effectively with subsequent stressors than youth who have little experience coping with stressors or who have been unsuccessful in coping with past stressors. We and other investigators also have noted that strong religious beliefs helped the youth interpret their experiences and find reasons to go on struggling. In addition to personal characteristics that contributed to their resilience, we have learned that although they were without parents, they were not without relationship supports. Many youth told us of adults who helped them in Africa and sometimes acted as surrogate parents—families who took them in temporarily when they fled to Ethiopia, workers in the refugee camps, religious group leaders, and elders of their respective tribes who provided guidance. In the United States, the refugees found caring allies among caseworkers, foster parents, mentors, and interested community volunteers. The peer group was perceived by the youth as a critical support—a constructed family of siblings, cousins, and other youth. In many cases older siblings became the *parent* for younger siblings and cousins. These peer relationships became a key source of support in making the adjustment to life in the United States.

Practitioners working with at-risk youth in the United States are beginning to apply concepts of resilience to develop services that build on individual and community assets (Tableman, 2002). In the case of the Sudanese youth, their principal assets are these strong relationships. An understanding of the importance of peer support and other constructed family relationships that youth had developed in the refugee camps points to the importance of considering those relationships in arranging resettlement plans. Every effort should be made to identify these relationships and to keep them intact during the resettlement period. In addition, agencies must find ways to build supportive relationships in their new homes in ways that are culturally acceptable to the youth and the larger immigrant community in which they reside (Luster, Bates & Johnson, 2006).

Once these refugees arrived in their new homes, it was particularly important to provide opportunities to maintain peer support systems during the adjustment. In Lansing, the resettlement agencies and Michigan State

University developed a group support/education program that was well attended by the minors, who were more socially isolated in foster homes. Caseworkers viewed this program for maintaining established friendships with Sudanese peers as especially important as the youth coped with so much that was unfamiliar following resettlement.

The youth in foster care experienced special challenges in adjusting to American foster families and the American educational system. These issues are discussed in detail in a recent paper by the authors and our agency partners (Bates et al., 2005). Some of the characteristics the youth developed that were adaptive in the refugee camps, such as autonomy and taking responsibility for their own needs and the needs of younger family members, created problems with some foster parents who expected to step into a traditional parenting role. The resettlement agency learned that foster parents who were more flexible in their views on parenting and were willing to adopt a role more like tribal elders—that is, a mentoring role—had fewer conflicts with the youth and more success in helping them adapt to their new homeland.

Because of the unusual developmental histories of the Sudanese youth, we hope to continue to learn from them about human resilience and adaptation as the youth take on new roles such as marital partners and parents. In addition, we are following the youth's search for surviving family members in Sudan. How do the youth cope with ambiguous loss when they do not know if their parents and siblings are dead or alive (Boss, 2006)? How do those who are successful in locating family members reestablish relationships with parents or siblings who gave up hope that the youth were still alive more than a decade ago? Sometimes tragic circumstances provide unique opportunities for learning about human development and family relationships. We are grateful to the Sudanese refugees for allowing us to learn from them as they cope with the many consequences war has for children.

Acknowledgments

Support for this research was provided by the Michigan Agricultural Experiment Station, Families and Communities Together (FACT) Coalition, and University Outreach and Engagement at Michigan State University. We would like to thank the Sudanese refugees, foster parents, and caseworkers who participated in this study. In addition, we are grateful to the two resettlement agencies—Refugee Services of St Vincent Catholic Charities, Inc., and Lutheran Social Services of Michigan—who were our community partners in this project.

References

Barrie, J. M. (1967). *Peter Pan*. Harmondsworth, Penguin.

Bates, L., Baird, D., Johnson, D. J., Lee, R. E., Luster, T., & Rehagen, C. (2005). Sudanese refugee youth in foster care: The "Lost Boys" in America. *Child Welfare, 84*(5), 631–648.

Boss, P. (2006). *Loss, trauma, and resilience: Therapeutic work with ambiguous loss*. New York: Norton.

Caplan, N., Choy, M. H., & Whitmore, J. K. (1991). *Children of the boat people: A study of educational success*. Ann Arbor: University of Michigan Press.

Conde, Y.M. (1999). *Operation Pedro Pan*. New York: Routledge.

Duncan, J. (2000, January). Overview and mental health findings for UAM and separated children: Interviews as part of the UNHCR best interest determinations Kakuma Refugee Camp.

Duncan, J. (2000, April). Sudanese girls in Kakuma. Unpublished report.

Duncan, J. (2001, May). Sudanese "Lost Boys" in the United States: Adjustment after six months. Paper presented at the United States Catholic Conference, Washington, DC.

Foa, E. B., Johnson, K. M., Feeny, N. C., & Treadwell, K. R. H. (2001). The Child PTSD Symptom Scale: A preliminary examination of its psychometric properties. *Journal of Clinical Child Psychology, 30* (3), 376–384.

Garbarino, J., Kostelny, K., & Dubrow, N. (1991). *No place to be a child: Growing up in a war zone*. Lexington, MA: Lexington Books.

Harris, M. J., & Oppenheimer, D. (2000). *Into the arms of strangers: Stories of the Kindertransport*. London: Bloomsbury Publishing Plc.

Hecht, J. (2005). *Journey of the Lost Boys*. Jacksonville, FL: Allswell Press.

Ingleby, D. (Ed.). (2005). *Forced migration and mental health: Rethinking the care of refugees and displaced persons*. New York: Springer.

Joshi, P. T., & O'Donnell, D. A. (2003). Consequences of child exposure to war and terrorism. *Clinical Child and Family Psychology Review, 6*(4), 275–292.

Lambert, M. C., & Rowan, G. T. (1999). *Behavioral assessment for children of African descent: Self-report for ages 12 to 18*. East Lansing: Michigan State University.

Legarreta, D. (1984). *The Guernica generation: Basque refugee children of the Spanish Civil War*. Reno: University of Nevada Press.

Luster, T., Bates, L., & Johnson, D. J. (2006). Risk and resilience. In F. Villarruel & T. Luster (Eds.), *Disorders in adolescence* (Vol. 2). In H. E. Fitzgerald, R. Zucker & K. Feerark (Eds.), *The crisis in youth mental health*. Westport, CT: Praeger.

Luthar, S. S., & Zelazo, L. B. (2003). Research on resilience: An integrative review. In S. S. Luthar (Ed.), *Resilience and vulnerability: Adaptation in the context of childhood adversities* (pp. 510–549). New York: Cambridge University Press.

Moskovitz, S. (1985). Longitudinal follow-up of child survivors of the Holocaust. *Journal of the American Academy of Child Psychiatry, 24* (4), 401–407.

Pipher, M. (2003). *The middle of everywhere*. New York: Harcourt.

Rutter, M. (2001). Psychosocial adversity: Risk, resilience and recovery. In J. R. Richman & M. W. Fraser (Eds.), *The context of youth violence: Resilience, risk, and protection* (pp. 14–41). Westport, CT: Praeger.

Shaw, J. A. (2003). Children exposed to war/terrorism. *Clinical Child and Family Psychology Review, 6*(4), 237–246.

Sourander, A. (1998). Behavior problems and traumatic events of unaccompanied refugee minors. *Child Abuse & Neglect, 22*(7), 719–727.

Tableman, B. (2002). Validating the assets approach to achieving outcomes for children and youth. Best Practice Brief No. 25. East Lansing: Outreach Partnerships at Michigan State University. Retrieved on April 20, 2007 from outreach .msu.edu/bpbriefs/issues/brief25.pdf.

UNICEF. (1996). The state of the world's children. Retrieved on April 20, 2007, from www.unicef.org/sowc96/.

United Nations High Commissioner for Refugees (UNHCR). Trends in unaccompanied and separated children seeking asylum in industrialized countries, 2001–2003. Retrieved online September 20, 2006, from www.unhcr.org/statistics.

About the Authors

Laura Bates, M.A., is a research assistant in University Outreach and Engagement at Michigan State University, 110 Human Ecology, East Lansing, MI 48824-1030. Phone: 517-353-6617. Fax: 517-432-3320. E-mail: bateslau@msu.edu.

Deborah J. Johnson, Ph.D., is a professor in the Department of Family and Child Ecology at Michigan State University, 103 Human Ecology, East Lansing, MI 48824-1030. Phone: 517-432-9115. Fax: 517-432-2953. E-mail: john1442@msu.edu.

Tom Luster, Ph.D., is a professor in the Department of Family and Child Ecology at Michigan State University, 13 Human Ecology, East Lansing, MI 48824-1030. Phone: 517-432-3323. Fax: 517-432-3320. E-mail: luster@msu.edu.

Distant Relations between Migrant Adult Children and Their Older Parents

14

PUSPARANI PANDA AND GREGORY F. SANDERS

Abstract

The purpose of the research reported in this chapter was to learn about the relationships between migrant adult children and their parents who remain in the home country. The respondents were adult children from thirty-five different countries currently living in the United States. The authors describe the participants' contact with older parents; perceptions of parental satisfaction; relationship stress; support given to parents; and benefits and barriers adult children experience in relation to their distant parents. Further, the relations between these variables and the quality of the parent-child relationship were analyzed. Overall, adult children experienced both benefits and barriers from living in a different country, and a number of stressors were prevalent among the participants. Variance in relationship quality was explained by perceived disadvantages of being at a distance, relationship stress, and parents' satisfaction with the help provided.

Keywords: Migrant Adult Children, Parent-Child Relationship Quality, Distant Relations, Relationship Stress, Parental Satisfaction

Address all correspondence to Gregory F. Sanders, Ph.D., Department of Child Development and Family Science, North Dakota State University, 255 EML, Fargo, ND 58105. Phone: 701-231-8272. E-mail: greg.sanders@ndsu.edu.

PEOPLE HAVE MIGRATED to other countries for study, jobs, and a better life. Often they have left behind family members in their home countries, creating potential problems for maintaining relationships (Lin & Rogerson, 1995). Adjustment of international students, for example, has been related, in part, to family pressures (Heggins & Jackson, 2003). Gupta (2000) stressed the importance of understanding the structural and cultural factors related to support for older parents among immigrant adults, so that culturally sensitive care could be provided. Even the definition of old age, or the status of the elderly in society, varies by culture. For example, in one culture, the status of elderly might be identified on the basis of age, while in another it is identified by some event in the life cycle (Cowgill, 1986).

Glaser, Agree, Costenbader, Camargo, Trench, Natividad, and Chuang (2006) noted that demographic transitions, such as declining fertility rates in some parts of the world, has had an impact on the availability of family support to older adults. In addition, the increasing rate of intergenerational migration has created a separation between family members (Crimmaons & Ingegneri, 1990; Schoonover, Brody, Hoffman & Kleban, 1998). This decline in availability of adult children has occurred at the same time that there has been an increase in the number of older parents who need care. McCabe (2006), for example, pointed to the increase in the prevalence of dementia in one area of India that resulted from an increase in the older population. The combination of decreased family size, aging populations, and migration of some adult children makes distant parent-adult child relations a concern to migrant children.

For parents who have needed care, providing it has been found to be a most difficult task when the children live thousands of miles from their parents (Stewart, 2002) and, even within the same country, emotional, physical, and financial effects of giving care from a distance have been noted (Smith, 2006). In her qualitative study of cross-national parent-child relations, Baldock (2000) noted that caregiving incorporated both attachment and emotions. She found that it was difficult to keep in contact regularly over the phone and often impossible to visit each other frequently. Climo (1992) found the frequency of visits depended upon how far the son or daughter lived from their home country. According to Climo, distant caregivers felt that they were a partial help to their parents and worried about their siblings who were the immediate caregivers. Climo also indicated that the emotional factors applied to elderly parents as well, because they often were negatively affected by the absence of their own children and grandchildren.

Silverstein and Litwak (1993) noted that certain kinds of support were not possible from great distances. Valle (1998) found adult children who were living closer more often provided physical help to their elderly parents, and distant-living adult children provided financial help. The frequency of assistance also decreased when adult children lived far away from their homeland (Valle, 1998). Baldock (2000) noted that immigrant children often provided care through letters, telephone calls, and return visits to the home country.

Some researchers also considered the positive aspects of geographical separation among elderly parents and their adult children (Bengston, Rosenthal & Burton, 1996; Cicirelli, 1995), emphasizing modern communication technology could enhance closeness among the family members.

Although distance has been considered as an important variable in the relationship between older parents and their adult children, especially in the context of caregiving, few researchers have explored the dynamics of these relationships among immigrants whose older parents live in the country of origin. Baldock's (2000) qualitative study has been the most notable exception. The current study adds to the work of Baldock by taking a quantitative approach to cross-national relations of adult children and their parents.

The focus of the current study was on discovering barriers, stresses, and benefits of living in another country to the relationship between adult children and their parents. The research questions for the focus of this study were:

1. What types and levels of contact and exchanges do migrant adult children's relationships have with their parents who remain in the home country?
2. What are the barriers migrant adult children face while providing support to and exchanges with their parents?
3. What are the benefits of living in another country on the exchanges between adult children and their parents?
4. What are the cultural, emotional, and financial issues relevant to exchanges with parents across national boundaries?
5. What are the stresses adult children encounter in having a relationship with a parent who lives in another country?

6. What are the relative effects of contact, exchanges, barriers, benefits, cultural experiences, and stresses on the quality of the parent–child relationship?

While this descriptive study is not a direct test of theory, the symbolic interaction perspective was used as a framework for interpreting the results and suggesting future research. The concepts of meaning, role, and role strain (White & Klein, 2002) are particularly relevant to the issue of migrant adult children and their relationships with their parents, and these concepts are discussed relative to the study findings.

Methodology

Selection of Participants

Participants for this study were migrant adult children (sons, daughters, sons-in-law, and daughters-in-law) age twenty and above currently living in the United States who have parents or parents-in-law age fifty-five or older living in the home country. Age twenty was used as a minimum age in order to include participants with more experience on their own. Age fifty-five was used as the minimum for parents to include those from late middle age through the oldest old. The participant group included people who migrated permanently to the United States, and people who were living in the United States for a certain period of time without having citizenship or a green card. These adult children were asked to complete a questionnaire about the relationship they have with the parent or parent-in-law with whom they had the most contact and to whom they were providing the most support. If they provided equal support to more than one parent, participants were asked to choose one. Personal contacts and snowball sampling were used for data collection. In total, 241 of 300 surveys were returned.

Data Collection Procedures

Potential participants were given a letter explaining the nature of the study and other relevant information, and a survey to return in a self-addressed, stamped envelope. The letter also explained participation was voluntary, and respondents were given assurance their answers would be confidential. There were no names attached to the returned surveys. The researchers contacted potential respondents through e-mail, phone, personal contacts, and letters. Other contact groups included an Indian association and a center for refugees. Letters and surveys were provided in person, by mail, or through contact groups.

Demographics

Checklist items were used to collect information from the participants regarding gender, marital status, income, occupation level, educational status of the adult children, their reasons for staying abroad, age of their parents, their age, and their family types (nuclear or extended). Items on nationality, occupation, and parent's occupation were open-ended questions.

Respondents for this study came from India, China, Bangladesh, Nepal, Japan, Malaysia, Indonesia, Turkey, Jordan, Philippines, Kenya, Yugoslavia, Vietnam, Thailand, Egypt, Sri Lanka, Yemen, Poland, Pakistan, Ukraine, Dominican Republic, Sudan, Germany, Australia, Portugal, Russia, France, Brazil, Korea, Cameroon, South Africa, Iran, Ivory Coast, Croatia, and Bosnia. Forty-seven percent of the adult children were from India. The other most-represented countries included China (13 percent), Bangladesh (7 percent), and Nepal (6 percent). A total of 2 percent or fewer of the respondents came from each of the other countries. Table 14.1 indicates the demographics of the sample. More than half of the participants were males and 83 percent were under age thirty-nine.

More than half (62 percent) of the respondents were married; 33 percent were never married. Fifty-six percent of respondents were sons; 36 percent were daughters, and the remaining participants were either daughters- or sons-in-law to chosen parents. Although respondents were asked to indicate one person as the target parent, 48 percent of adult children chose more than one parent. The remaining chose one parent, 32 percent (of the total) chose mothers, 17 percent chose fathers, and 3 percent chose fathers- or mothers-in-law.

The adult children were highly educated on the average, and 59 percent were currently students. It is suspected that many of those who indicated Ph.D. under education were actually Ph.D. students. Thirty-four percent of adult children had incomes of less than $10,000, and only 11 percent made more than $50,000. Forty-two percent of the adult children came from an extended family system, and 55 percent from a nuclear family system. Most were staying abroad for education, though 39 percent were staying for employment or a better life. The majority of parents were in the fifty-five to sixty-four age group (67 percent); 21 percent were between sixty-five and seventy-four; 10 percent were seventy-five to eighty-five; and 1 percent were eighty-five or older.

Table 14.1. Demographic Characteristics of the Distant Adult Children and Their Elderly Parents

Characteristics	Adult Children n = 241
Gender	
Male	58% (141)
Female	41% (100)
Age of the adult children	
20–29	48% (116)
30–39	35% (85)
40–49	13% (32)
50+	3% (7)
Educational status of the adult children	
Less than high school	2% (5)
High school	9% (21)
Associate degree	1% (1)
Bachelor's degree	20% (49)
Master's degree	33% (80)
Ph.D. degree	35% (84)
Age of the parents	
55–65	67% (161)
65–75	21% (51)
75–85	10% (24)
85+	1% (2)
Adult Children's occupation	
Students	59% (142)
Teacher	13% (32)
Engineer	3% (7)
Housewife	9% (23)
Nurse	2% (5)
Business	3% (7)
Other (caregiver, retired, doctor, baker, journalist, accountant, geographer, station leader, federal job) (1% each)	9% (11)
Marital status	
Never married	33% (80)
Currently married	62% (149)
Separated	2% (4)
Divorced	2% (6)
Widowed	1% (2)
Family types	
Extended family	43% (101)
Nuclear family	57% (133)
Government employee	23% (55)
Private employee	11% (26)
Retired	35% (83)
Running own business	10% (24)
Farmer	7% (17)
Other	13% (32)

Characteristics	Adult Children $n = 241$
Adult children's income	
Less than $10,000	34% (76)
$10,001–$15,000	26% (58)
$15,001–$30,000	16% (35)
$30,001–$40,000	11% (25)
$40,001–$50,000	3% (6)
More than $50,000	11% (25)
Reason for staying abroad	
Education	65% (156)
Employment	20% (48)
For a better life	19% (47)
Political reasons	2% (4)
Religious conflicts	2% (4)
Other reason	5% (13)
Staying with spouse	2% (6)
Stay permanently	1% (1)
Refugee	1% (1)

Measurements

Relationships with parents, purposes of visits to the home country, frequency of visits, frequency of telephone calls, and contact with the parent through letters and e-mail were the contact variables used in the study. Participants were asked how satisfied they thought their parents were with the support they provided. Respondents rated their answers from *very satisfied* to *very dissatisfied* (5-point scale).

Participants were asked whether they were the major care provider (yes/no) and, if not, who (relationship to the respondent) was providing the most care for their parent. Respondents were also asked to respond *yes* or *no* to "Do you arrange any type of care through siblings or other family members?"

Building on qualitative work by Baldock (2000), the authors created seven items to measure migrant adult children's experience of barriers to providing support to their elderly parents due to distance, using five-point rating scale items (*strongly agree* to *strongly disagree*). Items reflected barriers related to time, travel costs, distance, and politics. The seven items were combined to create a barriers scale. However, because of low reliability (alpha=.424) this scale was not used in the regression analysis. Respondents were also asked what types of benefits (financial, educational, and cultural) they received from living at a distance and how those benefits related to parent care. Responses to questions on benefits were measured on a five-point rating scale (*strongly agree* to *strongly disagree*).

Items in areas of cultural issues, emotional issues, and financial issues were rated on a five-point rating scale (*strongly agree* to *strongly disagree*) and were based on both qualitative findings by Baldock (2000) and informal discussions with migrant adult children. Regarding cultural issues, participants were asked to rate two items on how they maintained cultural functions from a distance and how they were able to provide culturally sensitive care to their elderly parents. Participants were also asked to rate six items pertaining to emotional issues they experienced from a distance, (i.e., missing homemade food and cultural events, getting homesick, getting scared when they receive late-night calls, and how distance makes both the adult children and their family members sad). Regarding financial issues, respondents rated six items about providing financial support from a distance, helping parents afford better health care, helping financially during crises, and whether their education is the key to their financial strength. Items in these three areas were analyzed individually.

Respondents were asked to rate (from *very important* to *very unimportant*; five-point scale) four reasons for visiting the home country, including to see parents, to help with home maintenance, to give physical assistance, and to help make major family decisions. The responses are described for each individual item in the results.

Stress of the adult children was rated using a sixteen-item scale, including items adapted from the Caregiver Index Strain Questionnaire (Robinson, 1983; Deimling & Bass, 1986) and new items developed to reflect the distant nature of these relationships. The new items were based on anticipated stresses and Baldock's (2000) qualitative study on migrant adult children. The responses of adult children were measured on a five-point rating scale (*strongly agree* to *strongly disagree*). The reliability coefficient alpha obtained for the 16-item scale using the current sample was 0.84.

Analyses

Expanding on previous qualitative work by Baldock (2000), a descriptive approach was used in this study. The lack of research on cross-national parent–adult child relations warrants such an approach. A regression analysis was also conducted to explore the relation of support and relationship variables to the quality of these parent–adult child relationships. Age of parent, frequency of providing financial support to parent, experience of stress in providing support to parents, frequency of visits with parent, perceived satisfaction of parent with support given, perceived advantages/disadvantages of living at a distance, frequency of phone contact, and current health of parent were selected as independent variables based on Baldock's research and research related to family caregiving (Townsend & Franks, 1995).

Results

Contact and Supports in the Distant Adult Children's Relationship with Their Elderly Parents

Adult children who migrated from other countries rated the purposes for returning to the home country. Nearly all (95 percent) of adult children indicated it was very important or important that they visited their home country for the purpose of seeing their parents and/or in-laws. A total of 41 percent of participants indicated it was important or very important to visit in order to help with home maintenance and 24 percent indicated this was unimportant/very unimportant. Fifty-three percent of adult children responded that providing physical assistance to their parents was an important or very important purpose for visiting, and 52 percent indicated an important/very important purpose for visiting was to make major family decisions.

The adult children indicated the most frequent contacts with their elderly parents were through telephone calls. Fifty-three percent of participants had telephone contacts every week, and 26 percent of respondents called more than once a month. Regarding in-person visits, 35 percent of adult children visited their parents/in-laws every two years, 30 percent visited once a year or more, and 34 percent visited every three years or less. Fifty-seven percent of the adult children sent letters to their home several times a year or more. There were also 37 percent of adult children who contacted their parents/in-laws through e-mail every week, and 73 percent used e-mail to contact parents sometime during the year. Twenty-nine percent of the adult children perceived their parents were very satisfied with distant support; 42 percent thought they were satisfied, 24 percent said they were neither satisfied nor dissatisfied, and only 6 percent responded that their parents were dissatisfied or very dissatisfied.

Adult children were asked about the various ways they provided care when needed. More than half (53 percent) helped by making care arrangements by phone, 38 percent sent money, 41 percent made care arrangements with siblings, 32 percent tried to visit, and 13 percent made other arrangements. Most (73 percent) adult children strongly agreed or agreed they felt good when they provided financial help to their parents or in-laws. Most (88 percent) indicated they felt good as a care provider when visiting their parents (agreed or strongly agreed) and 54 percent of adult children strongly agreed or agreed that sending medical care from a distance made them feel good. Seventy-four percent of adult children agreed or strongly agreed they felt good sharing advice for family problem solving.

Barriers Migrant Adult Children Face while Providing Support to Their Older Parents

For most adult children, the high cost of air travel (79 percent) and/or lack of time (65 percent) were causes of less frequent visits to their home country. Seventy-seven percent could not provide physical help due to distance. For some (26 percent), relationship strains had occurred between adult children and their parents due to distance. Forty-nine percent of the adult children indicated distance caused them to be less informed about their parents' condition, and some indicated they could not return home due to political conflict (6 percent) or a high rate of crime, war, or terrorism (7 percent) in their home countries.

Benefits of Supporting Older Parents while Living in Another Country

About half (51 percent) of respondents strongly agreed or agreed that the ability to provide financial help to their elderly parent was a benefit of being at a distance. Other benefits to staying abroad were they could afford better health care for their parent (36 percent), improve their parent's standard of living (39 percent), and better provide support in a crisis (47 percent). Most (88 percent) indicated their parent felt happy about their opportunity for higher education. Adult children perceived their higher education helped them to better understand their parent's health conditions (46 percent), find better solutions when a parent got sick (50 percent), and make major family decisions (52 percent). Many viewed education as the key to their financial strength (65 percent).

Cultural, Emotional, and Financial Issues

CULTURAL. Forty percent of participants strongly agreed or agreed their interaction with and exposure to different cultures helped them to provide better support for their parents, whereas 17 percent disagreed or strongly disagreed with this statement. A total of 40 percent of distant children indicated they could provide culturally sensitive services to their elderly parents from a distance (agree/strongly agree), but 13 percent disagreed or strongly disagreed with this statement. Most (69 percent) of the adult children agreed/strongly agreed they managed to maintain cultural traditions and roles from a distance. However, 76 percent of them responded that they did miss cultural events because of being abroad.

EMOTIONAL. Respondents were also asked how they shared emotions with their parents from a distance. In total, 87 percent of participants agreed or strongly agreed they shared their feelings by telephone. Most (81 percent) of the adult children responded they tried to provide emotional support during the times of crisis. Sixty-eight percent of participants strongly agreed or agreed their departure from home made both them and their parents sad; only 7 percent disagreed or strongly disagreed with this statement. Thirty-six percent of adult children indicated their parents felt that the adult child would not be able to see them due to distance. Forty-seven percent of respondents replied that, if they stayed abroad longer than planned, their parents would be unhappy, but 26 percent disagreed or strongly disagreed that this was the case. Nearly half (49 percent) of adult children agreed or strongly agreed they got scared when they received late-night phone calls, and 57 percent of participants indicated they got homesick when they stayed apart from parents for a long period.

In total, 58 percent of participants strongly agreed or agreed they missed important family events like attending the marriages of siblings because of distance. A large proportion of adult children (83 percent) indicated they missed homemade food, 58 percent missed not providing physical care, and 88 percent of adult children missed not seeing their parents.

FINANCIAL. Nearly half (47 percent) of adult children strongly agreed or agreed they provided major financial help to their elderly parents during a crisis, and 51 percent provided general financial support. Fifty-seven percent of participants sent money several times a year; 9 percent sent money monthly, 28 percent sent money yearly or less, and 33 percent did not send money at all. Participants were also asked about their reasons for sending money. More than half of adult children (57 percent) indicated they provided money for general living expenses; 21 percent sent money for medical care, and 22 percent of adult children sent money for other purposes. The other purposes included traveling expenses for parents, money for house construction, purchasing gifts, festival expenses, savings, and paying back loans from parents.

Stress of Providing Support to Parents

The immigrant adult children in the study experienced stress in a number of areas. Because of the importance of stress as an issue for caregivers, these findings are presented in detail in table 14.2. Most (72 percent) of the respondents strongly agreed or agreed that caregiving from a distance is not convenient because they were not able to provide physical care. Eighteen percent strongly agreed or agreed that their sleep was disturbed because of late-night phone calls, and 56 percent of respondents indicated that caring from a distance was a psychological stress. Most adult children (77 percent) expressed that staying abroad was stressful because they could not reach their parents in an emergency. Twenty-eight percent of adult children thought

Table 14.2. Stressors from a Distance

Stressors	SD*	D*	N*	A*	SA*
Unable to provide physical care due to distance	3%	3%	23%	42%	30%
	(6)	(7)	(53)	(96)	(69)
Sleep is disturbed because of late night	26%	33%	24%	11%	7%
phone calls	(60)	(76)	(55)	(25)	(16)
Caring from distance is a psychological stress	3%	18%	24%	42%	14%
	(6)	(41)	(56)	(96)	(32)
Children may not be able to reach their parents	3%	4%	16%	40%	37%
on emergency	(6)	(10)	(37)	(92)	(85)
Financial strain	14%	29%	29%	21%	7%
	(31)	(67)	(66)	(49)	(15)
Parent behaviors are sometimes upsetting	32%	29%	25%	11%	3%
	(73)	(66)	(56)	(25)	(6)
Relationship with parent maybe strained	41%	28%	21%	6%	3%
	(94)	(65)	(49)	(14)	(7)
Adult children may resent parents	39%	27%	25%	6%	4%
	(87)	(59)	(55)	(13)	(8)
Elder care negatively affects other	45%	24%	23%	6%	2%
family relations	(104)	(56)	(53)	(13)	(4)
Adult children may feel manipulated	50%	26%	18%	5%	2%
	(115)	(59)	(41)	(11)	(4)
Parent may be demanding	46%	26%	19%	6%	3%
	(105)	(59)	(44)	(14)	(6)
Stressful to fulfill the personal requirements	18%	14%	28%	30%	9%
of the parent	(42)	(33)	(64)	(69)	(20)
Stressful to fulfill cultural requirements of parent	16%	15%	29%	32%	8%
	(36)	(34)	(66)	(73)	(18)
Stressful to fulfill emotional requirements	13%	13%	29%	32%	13%
of parent	(31)	(29)	(66)	(74)	(29)
Caring is stressful because parent depends upon	32%	27%	24%	12%	5%
the adult child	(74)	(63)	(54)	(27)	(11)
Parents poor health condition causes adult	14%	12%	22%	31%	21%
children worry	(33)	(27)	(51)	(70)	(48)

Note: *SD = strongly disagree; D = disagree; N = neither agree nor disagree; A = agree; SA = strongly agree.

caring from distance was a financial strain. Interpersonal issues seemed to create less stress: 14 percent indicated their parent's behavior was upsetting, 9 percent of respondents experienced strained relationships with their elderly parents, and 10 percent of adult children felt resentful toward them.

Very few respondents (8 percent) strongly agreed or agreed that parent care had negatively affected their other family relationships. Only 6 percent of adult children strongly agreed or agreed that their parents sometimes manipulated them, and 9 percent responded that their parents could be demanding. In total, 39 percent of participants expressed it was stressful to fulfill all of the personal requirements of their elderly parents from a distance. Participants were also asked whether it is stressful to fulfill the cultural requirements of elderly parents from abroad, and 40 percent of participants strongly agreed or agreed it was stressful. Forty-five percent of adult children indicated it was stressful to fulfill the emotional requirements of their parents, and 17 percent of participants agreed that caring from a distance was stressful because their parent depended upon them the most. Fifty-two percent of adult children indicated the poor health condition of their parent caused them worry.

Impact of Distance Issues on Relationship Quality

A multiple regression analysis was conducted with family strengths as the dependent variable and age of parent, frequency of providing financial support to parent, experience of stress in providing support to parents, frequency of visits with parent, perceived satisfaction of parent with support given, perceived advantages/disadvantages to living at a distance, frequency of phone contact, current health of parent, and perceived barriers to providing support from a distance (see table 14.3). The independent variables

Table 14.3. Results of Regression Analysis of Support and Relationship Variables with Family Strengths for Cross-National Parent-Adult Child Relationships

Predictors	Beta
Stress	$-.374*$
Disadvantages to distant care	.161*
Current health of parent	$-.076$
Giving money	.065
Frequency of visits	.039
Perceived parental care satisfaction	.321*
Parent's age	$-.057$
Frequency of phone contact	.005
Stress	$-.368***$
F	$6.20***$
Adjusted R Squared	.207

Notes: $*p < .05$; $**p < .01$; $***p < .001$

were entered as a block. A total of 20.7 percent of the variance in family strengths was accounted for by these variables (SE = .86). Significant betas were found for perceived disadvantages (.194; p = .15), stress (−.304; p = .001), and parental satisfaction with support (.334; p = .000). Family strength was higher when perceived disadvantages of being at a distance was greater, stress of giving support was lower, and perceptions of parental satisfaction with support was higher.

Discussion

This study focused on how adult children experienced their relationships with elderly parents living in another country and the different areas of exchanges that adult children engaged in with their parents during their stay abroad. While adult children were able to support their parents in various ways and maintain their relationships from a distance, there were also a variety of barriers and stresses related to this type of family situation.

In symbolic interaction theory, the meaning of behavior must be understood in order to understand the behavior (White & Klein, 2002). Meaning is influenced by the social and cultural context of the individual. The meanings of the adult child and caregiver roles are particularly relevant to this study. Efforts to fulfill these roles while living far away and in a different culture could be especially challenging if these roles are considered of great importance in the individual's culture and if the person's family standing (such as first-born son) gives even greater meaning to the role. The finding that the stress of giving support was relatively high, even though the parents were fairly healthy as a group, would suggest that the expectations of fulfilling the role of adult child could be an important source of stress, independent of the physical and emotional challenges of actually providing care. According to Burr, Leigh, Day and Constantine (1979), role strain would be influenced by both role consensus and diversification. The adult children in the current study, living at a great distance and in a new culture, may be unsure of how to meet the traditional expectations of their parents under the current conditions. In addition, diverse roles, including adapting to a different culture, may further add to role strain.

Glaser et al. (2006) noted that both national and regional demographic factors affected the availability of kin for older adults. In addition to those trends, Stewart (2002) found adult children often live far from their family-of-origin because of opportunities for employment, career advancement, and better living conditions. The current study also found that adult children stayed abroad for jobs and better lives. Most of the participants were students who were staying abroad to pursue their education. Research by Rogerson (1995), who found the higher the educational level, the greater the distance between elderly parents and their adult children, would suggest many of these current students will remain at a geographic distance from their parents. Relevant to symbolic interaction, both increased education and influences of a different culture could decrease role consensus and increase role strain.

Contact

Similar to the findings of Baldock's (2000) qualitative study, many adult children in the current study felt visiting their home country was very important because they could see their parents, provide physical assistance, and help with home maintenance. The majority of participants in this study also reported it was very important for them to visit their parents in order to feel good about themselves. However, because of the high price of airline tickets, some of the adult children in this study had not been able to visit their parents for more than four years. Because this study consisted mostly of students who may have been living on a fixed budget, the high cost of airfare would be more of a barrier.

Bengston et al. (1996) suggested modern technology could enhance close relationships among family members. Most of the participants in the current study had telephone contacts every week, and e-mail contacts, though less frequent, occurred to some degree for a majority of respondents. Baldock (2000) also found the use of modern technology to be helpful in keeping family members connected even though they lived far from one another. Her research showed telephone and e-mails were the most frequent and convenient way to keep contacts with distant parents.

Benefits of Living Abroad

Financial support was the main source of help to parents from a distance. More than half of the adult children sent money several times a year. The majority of the participants were from Asian cultures where the son's responsibilities are to look after the elderly parents and to provide help with major financial expenses (Jamuna, 1997). However, Baldock (2000) found that male and female distant-care providers were equally responsible for providing care to their elderly parents or in-laws living in another country.

Baldock, (2000) also found distant adult children were able to provide financial support to the siblings who live close to their parents and are providing the physical support when needed. The results suggest the adult children in the current study were not alone in helping their parents, but rather found opportunities to play an important part in the extended family system. This included giving financial support, which was seen as an important benefit of living in the United States. In addition, giving emotional support and information on things such as health care were other ways in which these distant adult children worked with family members and others to fill gaps where parents needed help.

They had siblings, friends, and relatives look after elderly parents. Most of the adult children made suitable arrangements through telephone contacts when a parent got sick. Further study is needed to determine the impact of the availability of other family members on the performance of and satisfaction with the adult child role. For example, an only child may be less comfortable performing a supportive role from a distance because there are no siblings with whom to collaborate. From a symbolic interaction perspective, such a lack of resources to enact a role would lead to role strain (White & Klein, 2002).

Participants reported they were able to provide better health care for their parents due to their stay abroad. Whereas this related, in part, to the ability to send money to cover health-care costs, it also reflected access to information and, in a few cases, the ability to bring the parent to the United States for medical care. Adult children in this study also indicated their education helped them to better understand their parents' health-care needs.

Barriers

Valle (1998) suggested that it is difficult to receive care from distant adult children because their presence is essential for physical support. In the family situations in the current study, distance was an obvious barrier to providing physical assistance. Almost all of the participants also mentioned distance kept them from being as informed as they wished to be about their elderly parents. Time and money were also barriers to visiting their parents frequently, and a small number of respondents indicated that war, terrorism, and getting a visa were also barriers to interacting with and providing support to parents.

Distance also created barriers to practicing cultural traditions for some; one-third of the adult children mentioned they could not attend important cultural events. However, most of the adult children participated in cultural functions or events by celebrating them where they currently lived.

Interactions with another culture were seen as beneficial; respondents indicated their interactions with different cultures helped them to learn from others about advanced medicines and health-care techniques they could then share with parents.

Regarding the emotional issues of these international relations, the majority of the adult children felt sad because of being away from family members. Some adult children indicated that they worried when they received late-night phone calls because they might have to hear some bad news from their family members.

Stress

The parents of these adult children were relatively young and only 32 percent of adult children identified themselves as major care providers. In addition, when support was needed, most of the participants indicated they had other family members to take care of their elderly parents back home. It is somewhat surprising, therefore, that the experience of stress related to issues in regard to parent care was fairly high for participants. Distance was felt as an obstruction for the adult children as they felt less informed of their parents' health issues and could not reach their parents quickly during an emergency.

The present study used an adaptation of Robinson's (1983) caregiver strain index with additional questions added related specifically to distance care. Therefore, the scores cannot be directly compared to previous studies. Because physical care is often a major stressor, it was interesting the majority of respondents experienced stress because they were *not* able to provide physical care. However, this again makes sense from a symbolic interaction perspective. The meaning of the role for the individual and how she or he defines that role would influence performance expectations and role strain (Burr et al., 1979). Those who saw direct, hands-on care as key to a supportive role for parents would be stressed if their role performance were limited to distant support.

Ungerson (1990) stated that caregivers for elderly parents face extreme burdens while providing care. Immediate family members caring for the elderly parents faced more physical stress compared to distant care providers (Baldock, 2000). According to Baldock, migrant care providers experienced stress for different reasons. In her study, participants took leave to visit home not to relax, but to provide care for their elderly parents. Baldock suggested that migrants with family obligations in other countries sometimes experienced emotionally painful concerns about who they were and where they belonged. Although the current study did not directly compare distant caregivers with the parent in the United States versus abroad, the travel costs and time alone appears to constitute a considerable added stressor for many whose parents live out of the country.

The level of stress was related to the quality of the parent–child relationship in the regression analysis. While stress could have a negative impact on the relationship, it is also possible that some adult children experienced more stress because of the demands of a parent with whom they have a less strong relationship. The relation between perceived parental satisfaction with support and family strengths may reflect the appreciation of help received or better communication about needs parents have. Greater perceived disadvantages of being at a distance corresponded to higher family strengths. The makeup of these questions focused on issues such as missing parents, missing homemade food, and being homesick. It is not surprising such feelings would be experienced more intensely when family strengths are higher. Burr et al. (1979) proposed that individuals who perform well in a role (such as parental support) would be more satisfied with that relationship. The findings in the current study regarding the impact of both stress and perceived disadvantages support this symbolic interaction perspective.

Implications for Practice and Research

Some of this stress might be alleviated by being prepared for emergency situations, such as illness of a parent. Those with family members living in other countries should have their passport and visa ready to travel immediately. Because there are many others who have also left family behind in another country, support groups may help reduce the emotional stress as well as provide opportunities to share ideas about how to deal with distant parental relationships and care. Universities and work settings could provide information and referrals that enhance the benefits and decrease the stress and barriers of this family situation.

Generalizability of this study is limited because the sample was not randomly selected and because of the particular demographic group of adult children who participated. While many cultures were represented, there were not enough participants from many groups to make comparisons. A limitation with the survey was participants were asked to discuss their relationship with one parent, however, many participants indicated more than one parent. While this may not have influenced the overall experience they shared in completing the survey, it may have influenced some responses to specific items.

Future research on cross-national family relations should include the following:

1. Comparisons by the age and health of parent need to be made. Ideally, longitudinal studies could be conducted to determine changes in parent-child relationships across national borders over time.
2. The parents in these families need to be included in future studies to gain their perceptions about having children living in other countries.
3. Qualitative studies need to be conducted to gain a more in-depth understanding of these relationships. Such work will also further inform future quantitative efforts.
4. Comparisons are needed by nationality and cultural group to clarify how these factors influence distant parent-child relations and influence support to parents.
5. Although this study did not focus on the grandparent-grandchild relationship, some respondents commented on it, and further research is needed to learn about how grandparents maintain relationships with their grandchildren who live in another country. Studies such as one by Yi, Pan, Chang, and Chan (2006) in Taiwan point to the impact on grandchildren in relation to care by grandparents. How the experience of grandchildren (and grandparents) differs when grandchildren are raised in another culture has not been explored.
6. Future research should attempt to gain greater insight into the match between role expectations and role performance, and how that match related to stress and relationship quality. Level of acculturation may be expected to influence role expectations and should also be measured in further research.

References

Baldock, C. V. (2000). Migrants and their parents. *Journal of Family Issues, 21,* 205–224.

Bengston, V., Rosenthal, C., & Burton, L. (1996). Paradoxes of families and aging. In R. H. Binstock & L. K. George (Eds.), *Handbook of aging and the social sciences* (4th ed., pp. 253–282). San Diego: Academic Press.

Burr, W. R., Leigh, G., Day, R., & Constantine, J. (1979). Symbolic interaction and the family. In W. R. Burr, R. Hill, F. I. Nye & I. Reiss (Eds.), *Contemporary theories about the family* (Vol. 2, pp. 42–111). New York: Free Press.

Cicirelli, V. G. (1995). *Sibling relationships across the life span*. New York: Plenum.

Climo, J. (1992). *Distant parents*. New Brunswick, NJ: Rutgers University Press.

Cowgill, D. O. (1986). *Aging around the world*. Belmont, CA: Wadsworth.

Crimmaons, E. M., & Ingegneri, D. G. (1990). Interaction and living arrangements of older parents and their children. *Research on Aging, 12*, 211–213.

Deimling, G., & Bass, D. (1986). Symptoms of mental impairment among elderly adults and their effects on family caregivers. *Journal of Gerontology, 41*, 778–784.

Glaser, K., Agree, M., Costenbader, E., Camargo, A., Trench, B., Natividad, J., & Chuang, Y. (2006). Fertility decline, family structure, and support for older persons in Latin America and Asia. *Journal of Aging and Health, 18*, 259–291.

Gupta, R. (2000). A path model of elder caregiver burden in Indian/Pakistani families in the United States. *International Journal of Aging and Human Development, 51*(4), 295–313.

Heggins, W., & Jackson, J. (2003). Understanding the collegiate experience for Asian international students at a midwestern research university. *College Student Journal, 37*, 379–391.

Jamuna, D. (1997). Stress dimensions among caregivers of the elderly. *Indian Journal of Medical Research, 106*, 381–388.

Lin, G., & Rogerson, P. A. (1995). Elderly parents and the geographic availability of their adult children. *Research on Aging, 17*, 303–331.

McCabe, L. F. (2006). The cultural and political context of the lives of people with dementia in Kerala, India. *Dementia, 5*, 117–136.

Robinson, B. C. (1983). Validation of a caregiver strain index. *Journal of Gerontology, 38*, 344–348.

Rogerson, P. A. (1995). Elderly parents and the geographical availability of their adult children. *Research on Aging, 17*, 303–331.

Schoonover, C. B., Brody, E. M., Hoffman, C., & Kleban, M. H. (1998). Parent care and geographically distant children. *Research on Aging, 19*, 472.

Silverstein, M., & Litwak, E. (1993). A task-specific typology of intergenerational family structure in later life. *The Gerontologist, 33*, 258–264.

Smith, C. (2006). Engaging the emotional, financial and physical ramifications of long-distance caregiving. *Home Health Care Management and Practice, 18*, 463–466.

Stewart, C. T., Jr. (2002). Migration as a function of population and distance. *American Sociological Review, 25*, 347–356.

Townsend, A. L., & Franks, M. M. (1995). Binding ties: Closeness and conflict in adult children's caregiving relationships. *Psychology and Aging, 10*, 343–351.

Ungerson, C. (1990). *Gender and caring*. Hemel Hempstead, UK: Harvester Wheatsheaf.

Valle, R. (1998). *Caregiving across cultures: Culture and the acculturation continuum.* New York: Taylor & Francis.

White, J. M., & Klein, D. M. (2002). *Family theories* (2nd Ed.). Thousand Oaks, CA: Sage.

Yi, C., Pan, E., Chang, Y., & Chan, C. (2006). Grandparents, adolescents and parents: Intergenerational relations of Taiwanese Youth. *Journal of Family Issues, 27,* 1042–1067.

About the Authors

Pusparani Panda, M.S., completed her master's degree at North Dakota State University and lives at 5054 Lancashire Court, Flowery Branch, GA 30542. E-mail: puspapanda@hotmail.com.

Gregory F. Sanders, Ph.D., is a professor in the Department of Child Development and Family Science at North Dakota State University, 255 EML, Fargo, ND 58105. Phone: (701) 231-8272. E-mail: greg.sanders@ndsu.edu.

Co-residence in Chinese Immigrant Families

15

XIAOLIN XIE AND YAN XIA

Abstract

This chapter describes results of a qualitative study designed to explore co-residence among Chinese immigrants and their adult children in the United States. Data were collected from seniors through either a focus group or an individual interview. Results focus on family dynamics created by co-residential patterns in the United States, and especially on the mutual aid/benefits and challenges associated with this particular type of living arrangement.

Keywords: Co-residence, Adult Children, Living Arrangement, Inter-generational, Mutual Aid Model

CONFUCIANISM HAS INFLUENCED Chinese families for thousands of years. Confucianism emphasizes social and family harmony, and family hierarchy (Ho, 1981; Hsu, 1985). Inherent in Confucianism is the notion of filial piety that conveys respect and obligation to seniors in the country, and an emphasis on group harmony (Wong, 1998). Filial piety includes authority, power hierarchy, and family lineage (Chow, 1997). That is, children are supposed to defer to their seniors, to conform to their expectations and requests, and to provide financial support (Ishii-Kuntz, 2004). The ultimate goal of filial piety is to achieve a cohesive and harmonious family that shares mutual obligations and minimizes overt conflicts. Therefore, to achieve harmony, family tends to take precedence over the individual (Hsu, 1985). One practice of subordinating individuals to the larger social group is seen in the way Chinese write their names. The family name, being more important, precedes the personal name (Wong & Lai, 2000).

One way to demonstrate filial piety is through the traditional living arrangement, mainly, co-residence among three or more generations, to display a reciprocal support network for the young and for the old. However, the dynamics of Chinese families in the United States may be shifting. Assimilation to the main culture may play a role in alternating this practice among Chinese immigrant families. Family living arrangements in New York's Chinatown were at best described as heterogeneous. More educated, middle-class professionals placed greater emphasis on husband-wife relationships over the father-son dyad, and as such, preferred living with their spouse rather than in multigenerational households. The latter was a common practice among the less acculturated Chinese immigrant families (Wong, 1985). Similarly, Kamo, and Zhou (1994) found consistent results in their study. The more assimilated seniors became, the more likely they were to adopt the mainstream pattern of living arrangements, and less likely to co-reside with their adult children. Even in China today, co-residence may not be as popular as it once was. Unger (1993) found that parents with more resources, such as pension or work income, were more likely to maintain their own residence. By the same token, researchers found that the majority of the seniors and their adult children preferred to live apart, but near each other, and the exchange of support between parents and their nonco-resident children was high (Bian, Logan & Bian, 1998). A survey that involved twenty-seven provinces in China revealed that only 22 percent of parents expressed a desire to live with their adult children and only 24 percent of children favor co-residing with their parents (Pan, Logan, Bian, Bian, Guan & Lu, 1997).

Though co-residence between adult children and their aging parents is not a new phenomenon, research on co-residency in Chinese immigrant families remains patchy. Therefore, literature review on co-residence in China and in the United States would shed some light on this topic. Levy (1949), a family sociologist, predicted over five decades ago that modernization and urbanization would decrease the traditional patrilineal family living arrangement in China. Co-residence among generations would decline in frequency and it would become more responsive to adult children's needs rather than parents' wishes. Recent studies yielded divided results regarding the greater beneficiaries of this living arrangement—seniors or adult children. A 1993 survey of two large cities in China found that the proportion of aging parents living with their adult children remained high at 67 percent, compared to 71 percent in 1984 (Logan, Bian & Bian, 1998). The researchers concluded from this survey that co-residence was influenced mainly by parental needs, not child needs. Also, co-residence tended to be patrilocal, referring to the fact that adult children and the son's parents would be co-residing, independent of parents' or adult children's socioeconomic status. Some researchers attributed the high rate of co-residence to the Chinese government's lack of support and interest in expanding urban housing markets between the 1950s and early 1980s (Chen, 1996; Unger, 1993).

In contrast, some studies argued that co-residence served the needs of adult children mainly (Aquilino, 1990; Davis-Friedmann, 1991). Knodel and his colleagues' (1992) study revealed similar results that co-residence in Thailand was largely child-centered. In the United States, researchers have found the usual path of assistance (by a ratio of approximately two to one) from parents to children (Aquilino, 1990). In China, the older generation was regarded as an important resource by their adult children. The former would provide temporary housing for their married children till the latter acquired their own. The seniors would give financial help to their noncoresidential children, and assisted with housework and children for coresidential children (Sheng, 1991). In some cases, the older generation, with more resources and in better health, volunteered to provide free housing and childcare to the younger generation to augment the grandchild's care (Settles & Sheng, 2002). A more recent study indicated that this co-residence pattern in China changed over parents' life course, from child-centered to parent-centered as parents age (Zhang, 2004).

Among newly arrived senior immigrants in the United States, co-residence is more of a necessity than a voluntary decision due to age, resources, and English proficiency level. Wilmoth, Dejong, and Himes (1997) found that senior immigrants had a greater tendency to co-reside with adult children than their native-born counterparts. Their study also indicated that senior immigrants who spoke little English or were sixty or older when they came to the United States were more likely to have a co-residing living arrangement than other immigrants. In 1990, 11.2 percent of Chinese seniors lived alone, 26 percent lived with their spouse only,

51.5 percent lived with at least one child, 9.4 percent lived with other related or unrelated persons, and 1.7 percent were institutionalized. In contrast, 25.7 percent of the native born seniors lived alone, 45.1 percent lived with spouse only, 16.7 percent lived with their child, 8.2 percent lived with other related or unrelated persons, and 4.2 percent were institutionalized (U.S. Bureau of the Census, 1990).

However, co-residence does not always warrant satisfactory relationships. Treas and Mazumdar (2002) conducted interviews with twenty-eight senior immigrants and found that these immigrants experienced loneliness, residential and geographic constraints, and isolation within the family. Many of these seniors were disappointed that the values they brought along from their collectivist cultural background, such as respect for the senior, family closeness, and companionship, may not be highly valued in the new land. Luescher and Pillemer (1998) suggested that intergenerational family relationships were inherently prone to generate conflict and ambivalence. They pointed out three areas of possible sources of conflicts as conflicting norms, dependency/autonomy, and solidarity.

Corporate Group/Mutual Aid Model

As mentioned earlier, Chinese families are under the influence of Confucianism that dictates the structure and function of intergenerational relationships. Families remain the cornerstone of all types of support. For many decades, Chinese families adopted the corporate group/mutual aid model that allows family members to be interdependent and to offer assistance when in need (Sun, 2002). One example of this mutual aid model was for grandparents to take care of their grandchildren, at least when the latter were still young.

Chinese immigrant families continue to adopt this corporate group/ mutual aid model when they come to the United States by inviting their parents to take care of their own children. In recent decades, when Chinese young adults come to the United States to pursue higher education, and eventually, to start a family, it is a common practice that their parents are called upon to provide childcare to youngsters. The free childcare is sought after among adult children who struggle between work and child-rearing. As soon as they are in the United States, seniors are quick to integrate into the family network and contribute to family care and support. They are more likely to reside with their kin than their white counterparts (Burr & Mutchler, 1993).

In their qualitative study, Treas and Mazumdar (2004) revealed that immigrant elderly were valuable resources to their adult children in America and they contributed to the family corporate group in various ways. First, they provided physical care to the family members, such as taking care of grandchildren. Second, they had domestic duties, such as housekeeping and kinkeeping, and third, they took on the responsibilities of maintaining culture and preserving family, such as teaching traditions, preparing ethnic foods, and teaching their own languages to the younger generations. Seniors with a few children in the United States spent years moving between homes to care for a succession of youngsters (Treas, 1995).

Taking care of small children is, understandably, a demanding job. Many foreign-born elders take on full-time responsibility as the *involved* grandparents, a practice that is not so common in the main culture (Cherlin & Furstenberg, 1986). On the other side of the mutual aid model, seniors received satisfaction from their involvement in their adult children and grandchildren's lives. They found their current lives, with challenges, were more interesting and less lonely and isolated. In fact, many Chinese seniors competed among themselves to nurture and care for their grandchildren (Sheng & Settles, 2006). Despite the fact that they gave up their comfortable retirement in China, left their homes and their friends behind, many seniors did not regret the decision. Their caregiving is "remarkably selfless, but it is also inherently self-serving" (Treas & Mazumdar, 2004, p. 116). Because seniors will need to be cared for in their old age, and unlike their white counterparts, their major resource would be their kin (Treas & Mazumdar, 2004).

In summary, these seniors continued to remain involved in their adult children's lives after retirement. At the request of their adult children who were juggling between work and family in the United States, many seniors left their home country to help with childcare and other domestic work, and reinforced a new sense of family by becoming kinkeepers between countries. However, co-residing families can pose conflicts in many areas, such as ways to run the household, and deference to adult children. Older people who fail to negotiate the loss of authority over their children have difficulty adjusting to life in the United States (Treas, 1995).

Despite the increasing rate of co-residency between Chinese American adult children and their parents, scant attention has been focused on this topic. Therefore, the purpose of this study was two-fold: (1) to identity the main reasons behind this co-resident living arrangement among Chinese immigrant families via seniors' perspectives, and (2) to identify themes that delineate strengths and conflicts germane to this living arrangement.

Methodology

Sample

In this convenience sampling, forty-one seniors (twenty-six females, fifteen males) who were currently co-residing with their adult children in western suburbs of Chicago, Illinois, participated in this study. Their ages ranged from fifty-eight to seventy-six with a mean age of sixty-six. All had at least one grandchild residing at the same place. All of their adult children held at least a college degree, and were working outside of the home or studying for a master's or Ph.D. at the time of the interview. All adult children were the head of the households. The co-resident living arrangements lasted between six months to seventeen years by the time of the interview in the fall of 2005. All interviews lasted from forty-five minutes to two hours. Directors of the Asian Community Center were contacted to help organize the two focus groups, and interviews were conducted on Saturday afternoons on a local community college campus where activities such as English learning classes or *tai chi* classes were held. Participants for individual interviews were recruited through snowball sampling methods. Interviews were conducted in Chinese schools, Chinese churches, the Asian Community Center, or at the interviewees' homes. Out of the forty-one participants, twenty-five were individual interviews, and there were two focus groups with eight persons each. Information about the twenty-five seniors is provided in table 15.1. (All names are pseudonyms.)

Procedures

Due to the "transient and difficult-to-reach" nature of this population group, a quantitative study was not feasible (Treas & Mazumdar, 2004, p. 4). Instead, a semi-structured interview, and a qualitative research method was used for this study. This research method aims at understanding experience as closely as possible as its participants' feel or live it (Sherman & Webb, 1988).

Qualitative research is largely an investigation process in which the researcher gradually makes sense of a social phenomenon by building, comparing, and classifying the objects of study (Miles & Huberman, 1984). Qualitative research is well suited to discover meanings within the private realm of family life (Daly, 1992).

This study was not intended to investigate co-residence among Chinese American families in its entirety. Instead, the aim of this study was to provide insight into the interactional and interpretive meanings of forty-one

Table 15.1.   Information about the Twenty-five Seniors in Co-resident Households

Names	Length of U.S. Stay (Years)	Green Card Holder/ U.S. Citizen	Grandchildren's Age (Years)	College Education
Mr. and Mrs. Hong	4	Green card holders	8 and 1	Yes
Mr. and Mrs. Yang	17	Citizens	16 and 8	No
Mrs. Xiao	11	Citizen	9 and 4	Yes
Mr. and Mrs. Lin	4	Green card holders	7 and 1	Yes
Mr. and Mrs. Zhou	15	Citizen	5 and 1	Yes
Mr. and Mrs. Zhang	5	Green card holders	16	Yes
Mr. and Mrs. Zhou	6	Green card holders	6 and 3	Yes
Ms. Wang	6	Green card holder	4	Yes
Mr. and Mrs. Bao	1	Neither	1	Yes
Mrs. Yie	.5	Neither	One month	Yes
Mr. and Mrs. Mei	.5	Neither	15	Yes
Mr. and Mrs. Zhang	1	Neither	12 and 2 months	Yes
Mr. and Mrs. Zhu	1	Neither	6 and 1	Yes
Mrs. Zhu	1	Neither	8, 4, and 1	Yes
Mrs. Hua	1.5	Neither	7 and 5	Yes

seniors who co-resided with their adult children at the time of the interview and to elaborate on their experiences.

General questions for the elderly parents included: What are the reasons for co-residing with your adult children? How would you describe your living arrangement? And what are some pros and cons about this arrangement? By encouraging the participants to share their stories, the research aimed at shedding light on many *invisible* meanings and perspectives surrounding this issue. All interviews were recorded and transcribed verbatim.

An issue-focused strategy (Weiss, 1994) was used during these interviews in order to uncover major themes in co-resident living arrangements between adult children and their parents. All interviews were read and reread, and similar co-resident experiences were grouped together to extract patterns and themes. These patterns and themes from the interview were introduced and analyzed using brief illustrations from the transcripts without revealing much information about the interviewees. For example, seniors reiterated the importance of being there for their children in times of major events, such as childbirth, despite the sacrifices they made. They emphasized the meaning and function of a family. At the same time, during their narration, they also disclosed, albeit hesitantly, some adjustment and accommodation when living under the same roof with adult children. Many also shared how they coped with their lives in the United States by being actively involved in community activities organized for seniors and even volunteering their services when opportunities arose.

Results

A New Sense of Family—Caring Transnationally

Though their adult children emigrated thousands of miles away, when they were needed during critical time periods, these seniors came to their children's rescue. That critical time period was usually the birth of their grandchildren. It was a common practice in many parts of China to have grandparents take care of grandchildren, reinforcing the family mutual aid model and intergenerational interdependency. Many seniors took on the responsibilities naturally. After all, some had retired from their work and this allowed them to give back to society. Since the event highlighted one major landmark in their lives and an important identity—grandparent-hood—they by no means would miss the occasion to get involved. One grandma shared, "I have been in the U.S. twice. Each time when my daughter gave birth to a child, I came here to help her." At times, it was a choice between work and family and often involved serious thinking and decision-making. One retired father commented, "After retirement from my career, I was offered a teaching position that paid 5,000 yuan a month in a university, but I turned it down because my daughter asked me and her mother to come over here to help with childcare. Of course, we see it as our duty to help." In this case, duty as parents and grandparents took precedence over financial benefits. Another father concurred, "I was still supervising graduate students before I came. My wife said, 'Let's go supervise our grandchildren instead.' We have been here for five years now."

Many adult children sent out invitation letters as soon as they found out they were pregnant in order for their parents to have ample time to apply for visas and for other preparations. Sometimes, parents and parents-in-law rotated coming to the United States to help with childcare.

Many of these seniors had more than one adult child in the United States, and in some cases, all their adult children were residing in the United States. Therefore, they redefined what families were. They relished spending time with their adult children after years of separation, but as time went by, they started to miss their own routine in China. They missed their friends and the convenience of moving around. In the United States, they did not necessarily have much mobility due to their inability to speak English or to drive. Yet, returning to China with their children and grandchildren all in the United States was not totally appealing either.

One retired father explained, "The first time I went back to China with my wife, I got sick. When I was in the hospital, nurses asked me where my children were, and how come only my former colleagues came to visit me. I did not have an answer. My two children were all in the U.S., I did not even have a family here to care for me when I was sick."

Some seniors have other relatives in China that required their care and attention. At times, they were caught between the roles they played and felt the dilemma about their decision. But it seemed like parental obligation was the top priority. One retired schoolteacher shared, "At the time when my daughter gave birth to her girl, my son was about to become a father in China. My father was sick and my husband was all alone in a new job. I came to help my daughter and asked my in-law to help my son." Before her visa in the United States expired, she flew back to help her son with childcare. Another retired schoolteacher in her early seventies echoed a similar sentiment, "My mother is in her nineties and she is living with my sister in China. My help was needed here to help my son with his children. He has two boys under seven years old. He and his wife both work, so we could not turn down his request to help. I can only help my mom by giving my retirement income to my sister who is taking care of her at the moment." She also commented that she would fly back to visit her aging mother at least once a year.

Obviously, the definition of family has acquired new meaning for these seniors. In some ways, they became a transnational family—a family that has kin and roots in both China and the United States. Staying in one place for long periods of time would mean losing connection with the other, something that seniors did not wish to happen. As such, they adopted the transnational stay and visit to maintain kinship in both places, at an age that still allowed them to do so. They realized that their resources (i.e., services and time) were needed in both places.

Mutual Support between Adult Children and Seniors

It was obvious that many adult children were relieved from childcare when their parents came over. Their parents' presence and caring for their offspring were welcome and appreciated. Many of these seniors played the role of *involved parents* or even *surrogate parents* since they were with the grandchildren day and night. One grandma poured out her detailed responsibilities at her daughter's house, "My youngest granddaughter has diabetes. I give her injections twice a day. My daughter and her husband have a very busy work schedule, so I cook, clean, and take care of my two granddaughters. I even teach them piano for awhile." Obviously, she was shouldering the lion's share of childcare. Another grandma was excited to have two grandsons, but she concurred that she worked "seven days a week." On weekends, she and her husband took care of one grandson while her son took classes to finish his master's degree, and her daughter-in-law would be driving the other grandson to swimming and Chinese lessons.

Sometimes, these seniors acted as crisis managers as well. One senior was invited to come during a time when her son's marriage was falling apart. With her son's busy travel schedule and her daughter-in-law's frequent absence from the house, she was often the only caregiver for her grandchildren, both under ten.

Despite the amount of work these seniors were undertaking at the time of the interviews, they did not seem to complain, and instead felt their responsibility was to help their children in the United States who had demanding work. One senior stated, "I think my son has a harder life here in the U.S. His job is not very secure here, so he has to work long hours to keep it. Now that I can still help, I will help him out as much as I can." Another mother, a retired physician in her sixties, concurred, "My daughter changed jobs a couple times. Now, she is teaching in a middle school. Since the school is so far away, and she just started her job and is required to take more classes, some nights, she does not get home till ten."

At the time of the interviews, though this living arrangement served the adult children's needs more so than the seniors, many seniors also reported what their adult children had done for them. This included installing Chinese TV in the house and having a Chinese newspaper, and driving them to weekend Chinese community activities, such as health checkups, English classes, singing and dancing classes for seniors, and Chinese holiday parties, such as the Chinese New Year party and the mid-autumn festival celebration organized by Chinese associations. Since some of these seniors could not speak English, they gravitated toward any Chinese community activities that were available. One senior said, "The Asian American Community Center offers a free healthcare check-up twice a year. My son would drive an hour to take us there so we can check our blood pressure and other things." With the widespread use of the Internet, many seniors appreciated some tutoring lessons from their adult children that helped them get on the Internet to read their local news in Chinese. The Chinese TV that their children installed for them allowed them to watch their favorite programs that they used to watch in China. Though many were unable to drive and move around town, the Internet and television provided them a window to the outside world, especially to the world that they were so familiar with prior to coming to the United States.

Some seniors were invited to go for a cruise or for a family vacation in Florida or Hawaii. Others returned to China after their visa expired and waited patiently for their permanent resident cards to arrive so they could reunite with their adult children in the United States.

Though this phenomena of co-residency between adult children and their parents in this study was more adult child-centered than senior-centered, many seniors may consider this to be an investment in their own security, as some of them had lived with their adult children for over ten years and decided to make the United States their permanent residence. As the average age of this group of seniors was sixty-six, many of them would need elder care in the not-too-distant future. Meanwhile, several seniors found that a busy life in the United States was better than a slower pace of life in China where they could not visit their children and grandchildren as often as they desired. Therefore, it can be concluded from this study that seniors were providing, mainly, instrumental support to their adult children by taking care of their grandchildren and doing household chores, whereas their adult children provided emotional support, and possibly, old-age security to some. Seniors relished having their adult children close by, and welcomed the fact that they were still needed after retirement. As one grandpa put it, "I like being around with small children. I don't feel so lonely this way." In sum, these co-resident households demonstrated the interdependency among generations—the exchange of emotional and instrumental support.

For those seniors who have been in the United States for a long period of time, and decide to make the United States their home, the adult child-centered co-resident households may become senior-centered. One grandma who was currently co-residing with her daughter shared, "My husband and I have been here seventeen years. We are not going back to China now. We have even bought our tombs here." Another senior said, "I will just follow wherever my daughter goes." However, in this study, the majority of the seniors were still actively involved in childcare for their grandchildren. It is beyond the scope of this study to investigate elder care among Chinese immigrants, although this would be an important topic for future investigation.

Caregiving Stress, Co-residential Household Tension, and Adaptation

Chinese immigrant families in this study faced many challenges related to immigration (Xie, Xia & Zhou, 2004). Migration is a multifaceted event, even if it means reunion with family members. It impacts seniors socially, emotionally, and physically. Many seniors leave their familiar environment—their support network, their freedom to move around town—to live with their adult children in America. The reunion entails much excitement and joy, at least at the beginning, but tension may ensue. As mentioned earlier, intergenerational relationships are innately structured to create ambivalence and conflict (Luescher & Pillemer, 1998). It may be related to the intensity of caregiving responsibilities, conflict norms, the lack of freedom for elders to walk around places, their inability to speak English, or loss of authority over adult children. One grandpa who wanted to go back to China as soon as he could shared, "I feel like a kid here—not able to walk because I can't drive, not able to talk because I can't speak any English."

Some seniors had not seen their children for several years before coming to share their residence with them. Upon arrival, they may experience culture shock as well as the shock to see their children not deferring to them as much as when they were together in China. Some clashed in the areas of money management and child rearing practices. Others realized that they were here to help their adult children, and careful not to take control over how to run the household or how to discipline the youngster(s). One older woman could not quite understand the amount of money her children spent on family vacations. To her, the money would be put to better use if it were sent to China to help other siblings. She brought this issue up with her co-resident child, but was met with some disagreement and unpleasant reactions. With her spouse's help, she finally realized that her grown-up child was not likely to defer to her as much as in the past. After all, this was her adult child's household. She explained, "My husband reminds me that we are here to help, and should not intrude into our children's financial situations." She was certainly not alone. Some found it difficult to defer to their own children or children-in-law, but they realized they were only staying for one year or so, so they learned not to be vocal about their expectations. Others found that different lifestyles could generate stress. At times, these lifestyles were merely related to bedtime and wakeup time. One mother shared: "I make breakfast in the morning, and at weekend, my children like to sleep in, and not knowing exactly what time they would get up, so I just reheat the breakfast from time to time. It can get very annoying." Other minor arguments involved how much to dress the grandchildren, and what to feed their grandchildren.

In some cases, the intensity of childcare took a toll on seniors' health. Some expressed the desire to return to China earlier than planned due to illnesses. One grandma in her late seventies commented: "I am so tired. I can't go to bed till after 11 p.m. when I put my granddaughter to bed first and wash all the laundry. There is always work to do. The house needs to be cleaned all the time." Another senior echoed: "I just had to take a break. I went to China for several months."

Another source of stress was isolation. Since these seniors' adult children all worked or took classes during the daytime, they were often left alone to take care of the youngsters. Seniors with spouses around faired better, but in a few cases, seniors who came to the United States alone found it hard to fend off the loneliness and isolation. Some seniors got disheartened when their efforts and help did not seem to get recognized enough.

Lack of mobility also engendered stress in seniors' lives. Some seniors, unable to read and speak English, found it difficult to make a connection with the community. However, some decided to solve this issue in a constructive manner—they became involved actively in English-learning classes on weekends or volunteered to teach dance classes or tai chi classes to their fellow country folks, and being professionals in China, many volunteered their services as physicians and counselors. One couple in their sixties, both physicians prior to their retirement in China, decided to offer free counseling classes to seniors on weekends.

To deal with their lack of mobility, some relatively young seniors, who had some English proficiency and planned to stay in the United States for longer periods of time, decided to learn how to drive. One sixty-one-year-old senior joyfully shared, "I met an elderly woman in her seventies when I first came. I was surprised to learn that she could drive. I told my husband right afterward that we should learn how to drive. That was several years ago. Now, I have my own *feet*."

Discussion

This study reveals that Chinese immigrant families, interdependent in nature, model corporate group/mutual aid practices by emphasizing caring for the welfare of their family members. Seniors provide instrumental support to their adult children by taking care of the grandchildren and doing some household chores, while adult children reciprocate with emotional support and, possibly, some old age support by applying for permanent residence status for their parents. The majority of participants were retired professionals in China. Prior to coming to the United States, they all maintained their own independent household. Therefore, coming to live in a co-residential household with their adult children required some adaptation and accommodation, as intergenerational family relationships are intrinsically prone to generate ambivalence and tension due to conflicting norms, and difficulties finding a balance of dependency and autonomy. However, understanding and respect from family members, connection to ethnic community activities, and a positive attitude helped to alleviate conflict and strengthen intergenerational relationships.

Many seniors also took an active role in combating their isolation, they would not allow themselves to only stay inside the house and run errands. Many managed to have some time for themselves despite their busy schedules. Attending weekend classes was one favorite activity in which they participated. These classes not only provided them an opportunity to learn the language, but also gave them an opportunity to replenish themselves physically and emotionally and to socialize with people of their own age group.

Local community can play a role in facilitating their adjustment to the United States. The city in which these interviews were conducted has a relatively large Asian population—12 percent. It also housed a recently established Asian American Community Center where many activities were held for younger and older generations. The spectrum of activities includes weekend English classes to biannual health checkups and various Chinese holiday celebrations. Along with this, the city is also close to downtown Chicago where numerous multicultural activities take place. This has certainly helped make the seniors' stay in their adult children's homes more attractive and enjoyable.

It can be concluded from this study that these seniors form an invisible National Guard for Chinese immigrant families, contributing their resources to their adult children so the latter can balance work and family, and indirectly contributing to American society. Helping them adapt to their lives in the United States requires support at the micro and macro levels. The micro level refers to the individual families, and in this case, their children's families. Appreciation and reciprocal support is one way to pay back what their parents contribute to them. The macro level refers to the community support network where seniors can have some respite from their caregiving activities, have time for their own interests and hobbies, and more importantly, develop some social support groups among people their own age so as to restore themselves physically and emotionally.

This study reiterates the importance of adopting an emic perspective in studying Chinese immigrant families. The cultural background and practice emphasizes the interdependent relationship among generations. Therefore, when working with this unique population, practitioners and social workers should be aware of their family dynamics, and family system, which often includes the grandparent generation. With the increasing number of Chinese immigrants, some of whom are elderly, support should be culturally sensitive, and multileveled. At the local community level, age-oriented and needs-sensitive programs and activities should be implemented, such as recruiting medical health professionals to provide free workshops and health check-ups, offering *tai chi* classes to adults and ethnic language learning classes to youngsters, recruiting volunteers to provide transportation for the elderly, and setting up local hotlines in case of emergency. Since many of these recent immigrants are professionals themselves, resources can be enlisted from them to set up weekly or monthly groups for family activities. Policy makers, social service professionals, and local businesses should support their ethnic cultural activities, such as the celebration of New Year, the mid-autumn festival, and other holidays. In sum, these family support programs at various levels will help facilitate immigrants' entry into the United States, lessen their migration stress, and protect their mental health in times of transition and transnational living.

References

Aquilino, W. (1990). The likelihood of parent-child coresidence effects of family structure and parental characteristics. *Journal of Marriage and Family, 52,* 405–419.

Bian, F., Logan, J. R., & Bian, Y. (1998). Intergenerational relations in urban China: Proximity, contact, and help to parents. *Demography, 35,* 115–124.

Burr, J., & Mutchler, J. (1993). Nativity, acculturation, and economic status: Explanations of Asian American living arrangements in later life. *Journal of Gerontology, 48,* 55–63.

Chen, J. (1996). *Old age support and intergenerational relations in urban China: Maintenance of obligations between older parents and children.* Ph.D. dissertation, Department of Sociology, University of Michigan, Ann Arbor.

Cherlin, A. J., & Furstenberg, F. (1986). *The new American grandparent: A place in the family, a life apart.* New York: Basic Books.

Chow, N. S. W. (1997). *The policy implications of the changing role and status of the elderly in Hong Kong.* Hong Kong: University of Hong Kong.

Daly, K. (1992). The fit between qualitative research and characteristics of families. In J. Gilgun & K. Daly (Eds.), *Qualitative methods in family research.* Newbury Park, CA: Sage.

Davis-Friedmann, D. (1991). *Long lives: Chinese elderly and the communist revolution.* Cambridge, MA: Harvard University Press.

Ho, D. Y. F. (1981). Traditional patterns of socialization in Chinese society. *Acta Psychologica Tawanica, 23,* 81–95.

Hsu, J. (1985). The Chinese family: Relations, problems and therapy. In W. Tseng & D.Y. H. Wu (Eds.), *Chinese culture and mental health* (pp. 95–112). Orlando, FL: Academic Press.

Ishii-Kuntz, M. (2004). Asian American families: Diversity history, contemporary trends, and the future. In M. Coleman & L. W. Ganong (Eds.), *Handbook of Contemporary Families*. Thousand Oaks, CA: Sage.

Kamo, Y., & Zhou, M. (1994). Living arrangements of elderly Chinese and Japanese in the United States. *Journal of Marriage and Family, 56*(3), 544–558.

Knodel, J., Chayovan, N., & Siriboon S. (1992). The impact of fertility decline on familial support for the elderly: An illustration from Thailand. *Population and Development Review, 18,* 79–103.

Levy, M. (1949). *The family revolution in modern China*. Cambridge, MA: Harvard University Press.

Logan, J. R., Bian, F., & Bian, Y. (1998). Tradition and change in the urban Chinese family: The case of living arrangements. *Social Forces, 76,* 851–882.

Luescher, K., & Pillemer, K. (1998). Intergenerational ambivalence: A new approach to the study of parent-child relations in later life. *Journal of Marriage and Family, 60,* 413–425.

Miles, M. B., & Huberman, A. M. (1984). *Qualitative data analysis: A sourcebook of new methods*. Beverly Hills, CA: Sage.

Pan, Y., Logan, J., Bian, F., Bian, Y., Guan, Y., & Lu, H. (1997). Housing and family structure in Chinese cities. *Sociological Research, 6,* 69–79.

Settles, B. H., & Sheng, X. (July, 2002). *Rethinking the one child policy: Challenges confronting Chinese families in the 21st Century*. Paper presented at the 15th World Congress of Sociology, Brisbane, Australia.

Sheng, X. (1991). The family life of urban Chinese elderly. In R. Hu, S. Yao & B. Liu (Eds.), *The study of aging issues in urban China*. Tiangjin, China: Jianjin Educational Press.

Sheng, X., & Settles, B. H. (2006). Intergenerational relationships and elderly care in China: A global perspective. *Current Sociology, 54*(2), 293–313.

Sherman, R., & Webb, R. (1988). *Qualitative research in education: Focus and methods*. London: Falmer Press.

Sun, R. J. (2002). Old age support in contemporary urban China from both parents' and children's perspectives. *Research on Aging, 24*(3), 337–359.

Treas, J. (1995). Older Americans in the 1990s and beyond. *Population Bulletin, 50,* 1–48.

Treas, J., & Mazumdar, S. (2002). Older people in America's immigrant families: Dilemmas of dependence, integration, and isolation. *Journal of Aging Studies, 16,* 243–258.

Treas, J., & Mazumdar, S. (2004). Kinkeeping and caregiving: Contributions of older people in immigrant families. *Journal of Comparative Family Studies, 35*(1), 105–122.

Unger, J. (1993). Urban families in the eighties. In D. Davis & S. Hareel (Eds.), *Chinese families in the post-Mao era*. Berkeley: University of California Press.

U.S. Bureau of the Census (1990). *Census of population and housing summary tape files 3 and 4, technical documentation*. Washington, DC: U.S. Department of Commerce.

Weiss, R. S. (1994). *Learning from strangers: The art and method of qualitative interview studies*. New York: The Free Press.

Wilmonth, J. M., DeJong, G. F., & Himes, C. L. (1997). Immigrant and non-immigrant living arrangements among America's white, Hispanic, and Asian elderly population. *International Journal of Sociology and Social Policy, 17*(9/10), 57–82.

Wong, B. (1985). Family kinship, and ethnic identity of the Chinese in New York City, with comparative remarks on the Chinese in Lima, Peru and Manila, Philippines. *Journal of Comparative Family Studies, 16*, 231–254.

Wong, I., & Lai, P. (2000). Chinese cultural values and performance at job interviews: A Singapore perspective. *Business Communication Quarterly, 63*(1), 9–22.

Wong, M. G. (1998). The Chinese American family. In C. H. Mindel, R. W. Habenstein & R. Wright (Eds.), *Ethnic families in America*. Paramus, NJ: Prentice Hall.

Xie, X., Xia, Y., & Zhou, Z. (2004). Strengths and stress in Chinese immigrant families: A qualitative study. *Great Plains Research, 14*(2), 203–218.

Zhang, Q. F. (2004). Economic transition and new patterns of parent–adult child coresidence in urban China. *Journal of Marriage and Family, 66*(5), 1231–1245.

About the Authors

Yan Xia, Ph.D., is an assistant professor in the Department of Child, Youth, and Family Studies at the University of Nebraska–Lincoln, 235 MABL, Lincoln, NE 68588-0236. Phone: 402-472-4086. Fax: 402-472-9170. E-mail: rxia2@unl.edu.

Xiaolin Xie, Ph.D., is an associate professor in the area of Family and Child Studies in the School of Family, Consumer, and Nutrition Sciences at Northern Illinois University, 122 G Wirtz Hall, FCNS, DeKalb, IL 60115. Phone: 815 753-6335. Fax: 815-753-1321. E-mail: xiaolinx@niu.edu.

COMMUNITY AND PROGRAMMATIC ISSUES

IV

Stress, Status, and Sociability   **16**
Exploring Residential Satisfaction in the Rural Midwest following Rapid Immigration

JAMES J. POTTER, RODRIGO CANTARERO, AND AMY E. BOREN

Abstract

This investigation examined predictors of residential satisfaction among newly arrived residents (NAR) and long-term residents (LTR) of a rural community following a rapid influx of immigrants into the community. The physical environment, social/cultural aspects of life, and resources and public services were hypothesized to affect perceptions of residential satisfaction. Both LTR and NAR were pleased with environmental attributes, sociocultural attributes, and public services. An inverse relationship was revealed between stress and residential satisfaction. The primary sources of stress for LTR related to economics and social status issues, whereas the primary sources of stress among NAR involved issues concerning family and friends.

Keywords: Latino, Rural, Residential Satisfaction, Environmental Attributes, Newly Arrived Residents, Stress

Address all correspondence to Dr. James J. Potter, 239 Architecture Hall, College of Architecture, University of Nebraska–Lincoln, Lincoln, NE 68588-0107. Phone: 402-472-9240. Fax: 402-472-3806. E-mail: jpotter2@unl.edu.

ROM 1990 TO 2000 the United States showed a considerable increase in its Latino population (Census Bureau, 2000). Interestingly, during that time many Latino immigrants diverged from their traditional destinations on the East and West Coasts and opted instead to settle in the midwestern and southern regions of the country. In the Midwest, some regions found their Latino populations growing by more than 100 percent (Census Bureau, 2000). This remarkable increase in the Latino population is clearly seen in Nebraska where over one half (n = 56) of the state's ninety-three counties experienced significant growth (> 100 percent) in their Latino populations (Census Bureau, 2000).

Due to these dramatic increases in immigrant populations, many small, rural communities in the Midwest have seen significant increases in the size and scope of their citizenry. These historically homogeneous communities have found their population changing from an almost entirely Anglo populace to a diverse blend of ethnic groups (Census Bureau, 2000). The vast majority of this change in the Midwest is due to the large influx of Latino immigrants that has come to these communities in search of work in the local food-processing plants (Baker & Hotek, 2003; Dalla & Christensen, 2005; Grey, 1999; Grey & Woodrick, 2002; Stull, Broadway & Griffith, 1995). While this surge in immigration has injected life into sluggish, rural economies, many of these small communities find themselves struggling socially and culturally with the rapid changes they are experiencing (Baker & Hotek, 2003; Dalla, Villarruel, Cramer & Gonzalez-Kruger, 2004). As Anehensel (1992) has noted, increased levels of perceived personal and interpersonal stress are endemic among the residents of areas undergoing dramatic change.

A number of qualitative studies have been done to explore community residents' individual perceptions of, and responses to, this rapid in-migration (Dalla et al., 2004; Dalla & Christensen, 2005; Grey & Woodrick, 2002; Hernandez-Leon & Zuniga, 2000). In a study conducted by Dalla and colleagues (2004), they explored perceptions of long-term community residents concerning community change related to immigration; however, the views of the newly arrived community residents were not examined in this study. In a separate study, Dalla and Christensen (2005) examined the community perceptions of the immigrant residents in rural communities, but there was no comparison done between the views of these more newly arrived community residents and the long-term community residents.

While these studies have been helpful in providing information about the feelings and opinions of individual community residents, a more objective measure of community residents' perceptions concerning community changes is necessary to lay a foundation for future research. At present, there is a dearth of quantitative studies exploring both newly arrived and long-term rural community residents' perceptions of their communities following massive immigration. Additionally, except for Dalla, Cramer, and Stanek (2002), previous studies have not compared the similarities and differences in the perceptions of the newly arrived community residents and the long-term community residents regarding the quality of life in their community. Although Dalla et al. (2002) suggest that long-term community residents and immigrant newcomers are more alike than different; we suspected there might be some significant differences in perception, as well. Therefore, the purpose of the study was to examine perceptions of residential satisfaction to gain insight into how immigration affects newly arrived residents and long-term residents differently.

Residential Satisfaction

Defining and measuring residential satisfaction has been the subject of much research since the concept's inception in the 1940s (Anderson & Weidemann, 1997; Barcus, 2004; Davies, 1945; Galster & Hesser, 1981; Marans, 2003; Sikorska-Simmons, 2001; Sirgy, Rahtz, Cicic & Underwood, 2000). As a measure, satisfaction taps into the perceived well-being of an individual and, as such, has been examined from many diverse perspectives. It has been defined as an attitude (Francescato, Weidemann & Anderson, 1986), and as a measure has been considered as affective (Andrews & Withey, 1976; Marans & Rodgers, 1975), cognitive (Andrews & Withey, 1976; Rapoport, 1977), and behavioral (Fishbein & Ajzen, 1975). In light of these interpretations of satisfaction, it is suggested that residential satisfaction should be understood as a multifaceted construct that incorporates affective, cognitive, and behavioral components (Anderson & Weidemann, 1997).

It is important to note the subjectivity of satisfaction as a measure. Since satisfaction is a measure of *perceived* well-being, it is critical to point out that perceptions are not always congruent with objective measures. In fact, several variables have been found to influence people's perceptions of residential satisfaction, including: culture (Deshmukh, 1995; Smith &

Krannich, 2000), life satisfaction (Amerigo, 1990; Pruitt, 1978; Rohe & Basolo, 1997; Theodori, 2001), neighborhood, as well as house and neighbors (Amerigo & Aragones, 1990; Basolo & Strong, 2002; Taylor, 1993; Taylor, 1995), social factors (Filkins, Allen & Cordes, 2000; Goudy, 1977), and race (Painter, Gabriel & Myers, 2001). As noted in the literature cited above, an individual's sense of satisfaction is easily influenced by contextual factors, thus compromising its objectivity as a measure. However, it is important to point out that satisfaction is contingent upon the *meaning* an individual assigns to it; therefore, it is critical to evaluate what the physical, social, and psychological climate of a community means to its residents (Andrews & Withey, 1976; Campbell, Converse & Rodgers, 1976).

Since the measure of satisfaction is subject to the individual perceptions of diverse members of a community, it is imperative to address residents' perceived well-being on several different levels in order to more accurately gauge their perceptions (Andrews & Withey, 1976; Rapoport, 1977). As previously stated, the measure of satisfaction has been identified as affective, cognitive and behavioral in scope (Andrews & Withey, 1976; Fishbein & Ajzen, 1975; Marans & Rodgers, 1975; Rapoport, 1977). Since satisfaction is comprised of several dimensions, many methods of evaluation have been devised to address those different dimensions (Andrews & Withey, 1976; Campbell et al., 1976; Francescato et al., 1986). The method proposed by Francescato et al. (1986) is incorporated into the model used in this study. Francescato et al. (1986) suggested a list, or index, of four questions to encompass affective, cognitive and behavioral aspects of overall satisfaction. These four questions are as follows: (1) How satisfied are you with living here? (2) How long do you want to live in this community? (3) If you move again, would you like to live in another place like this? (4) Would you recommend this place to one of your friends?

Francescato et al. (1986) suggest that since an individual's interpretation of and responses to questions reflect affective, cognitive and behavioral elements, many different questions containing these same elements should be used throughout an assessment. In this way, each dimension of satisfaction is addressed in several different ways, thus producing a more accurate representation of the individual's sense of satisfaction (Francescato et al., 1986).

The model proposed by Francescato et al. (1986) also describes a six-domain taxonomy of predictor variables for residential satisfaction including: environmental attributes, individual characteristics, behavioral and normative beliefs, perceptions, emotions, and behavioral intentions. These variables address much more than mere environmental perception; they touch on the underlying issues that influence a resident's perceived well-being (Andrews & Withey, 1976; Francescato et al., 1986).

The Question at Issue

The hypothesis of this study is that community residents' perceived residential satisfaction is affected by at least three major factors and that the importance of these factors will be different for long-term residents (LTR) of a rural community versus newly arrived residents (NAR). The three influencing factors are: the physical environment, social and cultural aspects of life, and the availability of resources and public services (Marans, 2003). A model of the relationships between these three factors and perceived quality of life is shown in figure 16.1.

Definitions for each factor included in the model are as follows: physical environmental attributes include variables such as neighborhood and housing conditions, noise level, and crowding; the sociocultural attributes in the model address issues such as family relations, feelings about neighbors, as well as a sense of affiliation and belonging to the community; the services and resources attributes deal with topics such as employment, retail conditions, access to police and fire protection, recreation, and

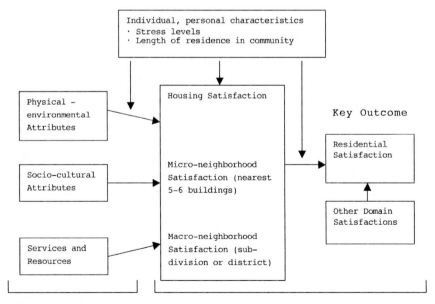

Figure 16.1. Model of the Relationship between Physical Environment, Sociocultural Attributes, and the Availability of Resources

transportation. The level of importance that each of these factors holds for individual community residents is different; thus, it is the aggregate combinations of these factors that impact the overall perceived satisfaction with housing, immediate neighborhood, area of residence, and the community as a whole. The manner in which an individual perceives the objective attributes of the model will be mediated by the personal characteristics of that individual which result in subjective evaluations of satisfaction. The individual, personal characteristics which mediate this relationship include such things as the person's length of residence in the community and level of stress. It is important to reiterate that individual differences in perception exist. Although these perceptions reflect the reality experienced by each individual community member, they may vary from the actual conditions in the community itself.

Method and Procedure

This study examined the perceived quality of life in a fast-changing rural community that had been impacted by a large influx of immigrants, a community located in sparsely populated east-central Nebraska, boasting a population of just slightly more than 4,000 residents. At the time of this study, roughly 800 of the community's 4,000-plus residents had recently moved to town; the majority of those newcomers were Latino (66.7 percent). This rapid influx of residents to the community was primarily due to the availability of employment with the town's expanding meat-processing plant. Meat processing is not typically a job sought after by many members of the Anglo population (Dalla et al., 2004; Grey & Woodrick, 2002; Massey, Durand & Malone, 2002; Stull et al., 1995). In order to fill these jobs, meat processing plants had been hiring more and more non-Anglo workers (Dalla et al., 2004; Grey & Woodrick, 2002; Massey et al., 2002). From 1995 through 1996, a group of architectural and planning researchers at the University of Nebraska–Lincoln conducted a survey study to learn about the impact of this population influx on the perceived quality of life of the community residents. The methodology used in this study involved three stages. The goal of the first stage was to identify issues related to immigration, population influx, life quality, housing, city services and infrastructure, and city planning. In order to obtain the information, the research team conducted meetings with two focus groups; one with fourteen LTR and the other with eight NAR. LTR were defined as those who had lived in the community for at least fifteen years, and NAR were defined as those who moved into the city within the last five years. All information was provided in English and Spanish.

Based on the findings of the study's first stage, a questionnaire was developed and the research team conducted face-to-face interviews with residents of eighty-five households in February of 1996. Respondents of the LTR and NAR were selected by targeting specific areas of residential neighborhoods, that is, those that concentrated LTR and those that concentrated NAR, using census-block data, supplemented by local key informants. From the targeted areas individual households were randomly selected and surveyed. Fifty-five percent (n = 47) of those surveyed were LTR and 45 percent (n = 38) were NAR. Fifty-four percent of the respondents were male and 46 percent were female.

The survey questionnaire included nearly one hundred questions. Most of the questions used a five-point Likert scale. Consistent with Marans's (2003) model of residential satisfaction, the survey questions addressed issues regarding residents' satisfaction with, as well as perceptions of: (1) aspects of their physical environment, (2) the city's sociocultural environment, and (3) community services and resources. Marans (2003) suggested that the physical environment is comprised of both natural and built attributes. In line with Marans's (2003) definitions, the current study included housing and neighborhood quality, crowding, and noise levels. The sociocultural attributes of Marans's (2003) model were addressed in this study through items concerning relationships with family and neighbors, and the general sense of community. Consistent with Marans's (2003) definition of services and resources, this study included items addressing fire and police protection, education, financing, recreation, and healthcare. The potential mediators of residential satisfaction—including length of residence and level of stress—were addressed following Anehensel's (1992) discussion of change-related stress. Researchers tapped into these variables by examining the types of changes taking place in the community and the sources of stress that residents experienced in their daily lives.

Findings

In the first stage of analysis, the questions from the survey were grouped together based on which topic they were addressing: changes in the community, housing, services, sociocultural issues, stress, and so on. Cronbach's Alpha was then used to test the reliability of the twelve topical areas. The combination of variables that produced an alpha above 0.7 was

Table 16.1.   Cronbach's Alpha

Index Variable	Total Population	LTR	NAR
Changes in the Community	.89	.76	.89
Stress Factors	.77	.78	.79
Service Issues	.76	.79	.74
Housing Concerns	.72	.63	.80

considered to be reliable (see table 16.1). The other topical areas that were deemed unreliable for determining residential satisfaction were dropped from subsequent analyses. The questions that were considered reliable were collapsed into composite scores (means) or indexes. Four indexes were created. In addition to an index variable of *residential satisfaction*, four other index variables were used in the subsequent analysis of residential satisfaction. They were *Changes in the community*, *Stress Factors*, *Service Issues*, and *Housing Concerns*. Although the *Housing Concerns* index was considered reliable for the total population, it was not as reliable for measuring residential satisfaction among LTR. We felt that the alpha value was close enough and the index was important enough to warrant including it in the subsequent analysis.

After determining the indexes to be used in further investigation, a stepwise multiple regression analysis was performed to predict residential satisfaction for each of the following groups: the total population of the community, the NAR, and the LTR (see tables 16.2 and 16.3).

Gender and age were also included since prior research has suggested they influence quality of life (Garrison, 1998; O'Brien, McClendon & Ahmed, 1989) and subjective well-being (Diener, 1988).

The stepwise regression analysis revealed some significant similarities and differences in residential satisfaction between the LTR and NAR. For the total population of the community, stress had a significant ($p = .001$) inverse relationship with residential satisfaction. In other words, for both

Table 16.2.   Stepwise Regression—Total Population

Index Variable	Beta
Changes in the community	−.03
Stress Factors	−.50**
Service Issues	.01
Housing Concerns	.19
Gender	.12
Age	.04
Resident Type (long/short term)	−.07

Note: **$p < .01$

Table 16.3. Stepwise Regression—Newly Arrived Residents (NAR) and Long Term Residents (LTR)

Index Variable	NAR Beta	LTR Beta
Changes in the community	.04	−.04
Stress Factors	−.43*	−.41**
Service Issues	.13	−.01
Housing Concerns	.03	.37**
Gender	−.02	.20
Age	.07	.02

Note: *p < .05, **p < .01.

LTR and NAR, higher levels of stress were indicative of lower levels of residential satisfaction. For the NAR, stress had a significant ($p = .013$) inverse relationship with residential satisfaction; for the LTR, stress also had a significant ($p = .002$) inverse relationship with residential satisfaction.

In addition, the results indicate that for LTR of the community, issues concerning housing were significantly ($p = .006$) related to residential satisfaction. In other words, as satisfaction with housing increased, so did residential satisfaction. Surprisingly, housing issues were not significantly correlated with residential satisfaction for the NAR of the community.

Since stress was a factor that influenced the residential satisfaction of both LTR and NAR, the individual items in the stress index were analyzed to determine what significant relationships, if any, existed between them and the residential satisfaction index. For the LTR, insufficient income ($r = -.370$), having a residence which provides a healthy environment ($r = .297$), economic differences in the neighborhood ($r = -.466$), living in a residence which undermines social status ($r = -.424$), struggling for a better house ($r = -.511$), social and cultural differences of people in the neighborhood ($r = -.339$), and recommending the neighborhood to a friend ($r = .379$) were all significantly related to the residential satisfaction index (see table 16.4).

Table 16.4. Correlations for Residential Satisfaction Index and Stress Items—LTR.

Items from Stress Index	Sig.
Insufficient income	−.37*
Residence is healthy environment	.30*
Economic differences in neighborhood	−.47**
Current residence undermines status	−.42**
Struggle for a better house	−.51**
Social/cultural differences in neighborhood	−.34*
Recommend neighborhood to friend	.38**

Notes: *p < .05, **p < .01

Table 16.5.   Correlations for Residential Satisfaction Index and Stress Items—NAR.

Items from Stress Index	Sig.
Tension with neighbors	−.60**
Living in the community is good for my family	.46**
Very happy to live in the community	.37*

Notes: *p < .05, **p < .001

For the NAR, tension with neighbors (r = −.601), living in the community is beneficial for family (r = .460), and being happy to live in the community (r = .366) were all significantly related to the residential satisfaction index (see table 16.5).

Interestingly, the sources of stress for LTR appeared to be related more to economic and social status issues than to other issues. Sources of stress for NAR seemed to be based more on issues concerning family and social relations.

Discussion

According to the findings of this study, residents' perceptions of their quality of life differed only slightly by length of residence in the community. The total population seemed to be basically pleased with environmental attributes, sociocultural attributes, as well as the services and resources available in the community. One important difference between the LTR and NAR was the salience of housing concerns. LTR felt that housing issues concerning quality and maintenance of housing were closely tied to their perceived residential satisfaction. This may seem odd taken at face value, since the vast majority of the NAR were of Latino ethnicity and housing for ethnic minorities in rural communities usually tends to be insufficient (Whitener, 2001). However, since LTR may tend to feel that their neighborhoods are being compromised by the presence of an ethnic minority group (see Dalla & Christensen, 2005), it is possible that issues of integration caused them to perceive housing quality and maintenance as salient concerns. As a point of clarification, in such a small community, "neighborhoods" and "neighbors" may need to be interpreted in the broadest sense of these words. The community is like one big neighborhood, and neighbors probably mean other community members.

Though the LTR and NAR perceived housing issues differently, both groups did believe that the most critical issue influencing residential satisfaction and quality of life in the community was stress. When considering

Anehensel's (1992) discussion of change-related stress, the high levels of stress found in both the LTR and NAR of the community are very understandable. High stress levels are quite common among people who are experiencing major changes in their lives (Anhensel, 1992). In light of the immense changes that the community was experiencing due to its rapid population growth and collision of cultures, the elevated stress levels are not surprising. What is surprising, however, is the difference between the perceived sources of stress for each resident group. The LTR struggled with issues concerning social status in the community. It appears as though the economic, social, and cultural differences between people in their neighborhoods created a great deal of anguish among the LTR. Perhaps having to share a neighborhood with people of a different ethnic background was considered to be a threat to the social status of LTR in the community. A definitive feature of many small, rural towns is their sense of community, or corporate identity (Burton, 2002; Salamon, 2003). Much of what binds small, rural community members together is a shared history—cultural roots—that provides them with an understanding of themselves and their neighbors that often spans generations (Burton, 2002; Flora, Flora & Tapp, 2000; Salamon, 2003). This shared, social identity has made it easy for many members of small communities to *otherize* newcomers to their towns (Salamon, 2003). Newcomers who are drastically different from the traditional members of the community may be perceived as a threat to the community identity which could result in stereotyping and discrimination (Tajfel, 1982). The perception of threat may induce the *fight or flight* response in community members, thus resulting in elevated levels of stress. Future research could examine this phenomenon in greater detail.

The sources of stress for NAR were vastly different from those of the LTR. Tension with neighbors appeared to be the most stressful aspect of life for NAR of the community. Though the NAR are happy to live in the community and believe that living there is good for their families, they seem to struggle in their relationships with their neighbors. As discussed previously, some of this may be explained by the strong sense of corporate identity found in rural communities, which often leads to the rejection of newcomers (Obsr, Smith & Zinkiewicz, 2002; Salamon, 2003). This problem may be exacerbated by the cultural dissimilarity between the LTR and the NAR, resulting in racial tensions (Dalla et al., 2004; Lausch, Heuer, Guasaco & Bengiamin, 2003; Supples & Smith, 1995; Wirth & Dollar, 2004). Additionally, language barriers between the two groups have been found to magnify their differences and foster more tension (Dalla & Christensen, 2005; Dalla et al., 2004). The tension with neighbors experienced by the NAR is clearly a complicated issue that needs to be addressed. Future research which addresses this issue from the view of both LTR and NAR is needed.

Conclusion

The findings of this study underscore the importance of examining the perceptions of both newly arrived residents and long-term residents in rural communities in order to assess the issues important to each group more accurately. This study unearthed a critical difference in perceived sources of stress for each group, as it relates to residential satisfaction. Long-term residents find issues that are related to their status within the community as their primary sources of stress. Newly arrived residents' sources of stress are related to relational issues, particularly tension with their neighbors. These findings highlight some key sociocultural issues which should be of concern for community leaders who wish to effectively address the needs of all members of their communities. The findings suggest the importance of education in the area of language acquisition by newcomers (which also suggests a service component of adult ESL classes). In addition, in the area of social-cultural familiarization with each other, for both newcomers and long-term residents, there need to be programs to help break down barriers created by the fear/mistrust arising from mutual cultural unfamiliarity. This could be addressed through the local school system (involving school children and parents), and by organizing community events that attract and involve both community groups (e.g., food festivals, recreational sports leagues).

Further research with other communities would increase the sample size and reduce the limitations imposed by the small sample size of this study, thus enhancing our ability to generalize the findings that would contribute to policy action. Also, there has been a dearth of research examining the impact on the sending communities, which would greatly contribute to a better understanding of the ongoing national immigration policy debate. Finally, we recognize that tackling these issues poses a significant challenge to local community leaders and community members, but it is a good first step toward fostering goodwill between neighbors of all ethnicities.

References
Amerigo, M. (1990). The perception of residential environment and environment role. In H. Pamir, V. Imamoglu & N. Teymur (Eds.), *Culture, Space and History* (Vol. 5). Ankara, Turkey: M.E.T.U.

Amerigo, M., & Aragones, J. (1990). Residential satisfaction in council housing. *Journal of Environmental Psychology, 10,* 313-325.

Anderson, J., & Weidemann, S. (1997). Developing and utilizing models of resident satisfaction. In G. Moore & R. Marans (Eds.), *Advances in Environment, Behavior, and Design* (Vol. 4, pp. 287–314). New York: Plenum Press.

Andrews, F. M., & Withey, S. B. (1976). *Social indicators of well-being: The development and measurement of perceptual indicators.* New York: Plenum Press.

Anehensel, C. S. (1992). Social stress: Theory and research. *Annual Review of Sociology, 18,* 15–38.

Baker, P. L., & Hotek, D. R. (2003). Perhaps a blessing: Skills and contributions of recent Mexican immigrants in the rural Midwest. *Hispanic Journal of Behavioral Sciences, 25*(4), 448–468.

Barcus, H. R. (2004). Urban-rural migration in the USA: An analysis of residential satisfaction. *Regional Studies, 38*(6), 643–657.

Basolo, V., & Strong, D. (2002). Understanding the neighborhood: From residents' perceptions and needs to action. *Housing Policy Debate, 13,* 83–105.

Burton, O. V. (2002). Reaping what we sow: Community and rural history. *Agricultural History, 76,* 631–658.

Campbell, A., Converse, P. E., & Rodgers, W. L. (1976). *The quality of American life: perception, evaluations and satisfactions.* New York: Russell Sage.

Census Bureau. (2000). Difference in diversity, 1990 to 2000: Hispanic or Latino origin and all races. Mapping Census 2000: The geography of U.S. diversity. Retrieved August 9, 2005, from www.census.gov/population/cen2000/atlas/censr01-104.pdf.

Dalla, R. L., & Christensen, A. (2005). Latino immigrants describe residence in rural Midwestern meatpacking communities: A longitudinal assessment of social and economic change. *Hispanic Journal of Behavioral Sciences, 27*(1), 23–42.

Dalla, R. L., Cramer, S., & Stanek, K. (2002) Economic strain and community concerns in three meat packing communities. *Rural America, 17*(1), 20–25.

Dalla, R. L., Villarruel, F., Cramer, S. C., & Gonzalez-Kruger, G. (2004). Rural community change, strengths, and challenges: LTR describe impacts of rapid immigration. *Great Plains Research Journal, Special Issue/New Immigrants in the Great Plains: Strengths and Challenges, 14*(2), 231–252.

Davies, V. (1945). Development of a scale to rate attitudes of community satisfaction. *Rural Sociology, 10,* 246–255.

Deshmukh, R. (1995). Housing satisfaction: a cross cultural study of married student housing. *Environmental Design Research Association Proceedings, 26,* 169.

Diener, E. (1988). The influence of financial stressors upon farm husbands' and wives' well-being and family satisfaction. In R. Marotz-Baden, C. B. Hennon & T. H. Brubaker (Eds.), *Families in rural America: Stress, adaptation, and revitalization* (pp. 32–39). St. Paul, MN: National Council on Family Relations.

Filkins, R., Allen, J. C., & Cordes, S. (2000). Predicting community satisfaction among rural residents. *Rural Sociology, 65*(1), 72–86.

Fishbein, M., & Ajzen, I. (1975). *Belief, attitude, intention, and behavior: An introduction to theory and research.* Reading, MA: Addision-Wesley Publishing.

Flora, C. B., Flora, J. L., & Tapp, R. J. (2000). Meat, meth, and Mexicans: Community responses to increasing ethnic diversity. *Journal of the Community Development Society, 31,* 277–299.

Francescato, G., Weidemann, S., & Anderson, J. R. (1986, July). Residential satisfaction and residential quality: An overview of recent applications. Paper presented at the 21st International Congress of Applied Psychology, Jerusalem, Israel.

Galster, G., & Hesser, G. (1981). Residential satisfaction. Compositional and contextual correlates. *Environment and Behavior, 13,* 735–758.

Garrison, B. M. E. (1998). Determinants of the quality of life of rural families. *The Journal of Rural Health, 14*(2), 146–153.

Goudy, W. J. (1977). Evaluations of local attributes and community satisfaction in small towns. *Rural Sociology, 42,* 371–382.

Grey, M. A. (1999). Immigrants, migration, and worker turnover at the Hog Pride Pork Packing Plant. *Human Organization, 58*(1), 16–27.

Grey, M. A., & Woodrick, A. C. (2002). Unofficial sister cities: Meatpacking labor migration between Villachuato, Mexico, and Marshalltown, Iowa. *Human Organization, 61*(4), 364–376.

Hernandez-Leon, R., & Zuniga, V. (2000). "Making carpet by the mile": The emergence of a Mexican immigrant community in an industrial region of the U.S. historic South. *Social Science Quarterly, 81*(1), 49–66.

Lausch, C., Heuer, L., Guasaco, C., & Bengiamin, M. (2003). The experiences of migrant health nurses employed in seasonal satellite nurse-managed centers: A qualitative study. *Journal of Community Health Nursing, 20*(2), 67–80.

Marans, R. W. (2003). Defining and measuring residential quality: Opportunities through quality of life studies. Paper presented to EDRA Residential Environments Network, May 21, 2003. Available online at www.tcaup.umich.edu/workfolio/DAS2001/EDRA03.pdf.

Marans, R. W., & Rodgers, W. (1975). Toward an understanding of community satisfaction. In M. Janowitz & G. Suttles (Eds.), *Metropolitan America in contemporary perspective.* New York: Sage.

Massey, D. S., Durand, J., & Malone, N. J. (2002). *Beyond smoke and mirrors: Mexican immigration in an era of economic integration.* New York: Russell Sage.

O'Brien, D. J., McClendon, M. J., & Ahmed, A. (1989). Neighborhood community and quality of life. *Journal of the Community Development Society, 20*(2), 59–71.

Obsr, P., Smith, S. G., & Zinkiewicz, L. (2002). An exploration of sense of community, part 3: Dimensions and predictors of psychological sense of community in geographical communities. *Journal of Community Psychology, 30*(1), 119–133.

Painter, G., Gabriel, S., & Myers, D. (2001). Race, immigrant status, and housing tenure choice. *Journal of Urban Economics, 49,* 150–167.

Pruitt, L. (1978). The influence of residential domain satisfactions and life domain satisfactions on overall satisfaction with quality of life. *Environmental Design and Research Association, 9*, 226–238.

Rapoport, A. (1977). *Human aspects of urban form: Toward a man-environment approach to urban form and design.* New York: Pergamon Press.

Rohe, W., & Basolo, V. (1997). Long-term effects of home ownership on the self-perceptions and social interaction of low-income persons. *Environment and Behavior, 29*(6), 793–819.

Salamon, S. (2003). *Newcomers to old towns: Suburbanization of the heartland.* Chicago: University of Chicago Press.

Sikorska-Simmons, E. (2001). Development of an instrument to measure resident satisfaction with assisted living. *Journal of Applied Gerontology, 20*(1), 57–73.

Sirgy, M. J., Rahtz, D. R., Cicic, M., & Underwood, R. (2000). A method for assessing residents' satisfaction with community-based services: A quality of life perspective. *Social Indicators Research, 49*(3), 279–316.

Smith, M., & Krannich, R. (2000). "Culture clash" revisited: Newcomer and longer-term residents' attitudes toward land use, development, and environmental issues in rural communities in the Rocky Mountain West. *Rural Sociology, 65*, 396–421.

Stull, D. D., Broadway, M. J., & Griffith, D. (1995). *Any way you cut it: Meat processing and small town America.* Lawrence: University Press of Kansas.

Supples, J. M., & Smith, M. C. (1995). East and west of Main Street: Racism in rural America. *Public Health Nursing, 12*(4), 235–241.

Tajfel, H. (1982). *Social identity and intergroup relations.* Cambridge: Cambridge University Press.

Taylor, P. (1993). Geographical scales of residential satisfaction for older adults: a comparison of dwelling and neighborhood satisfaction. *Environmental Design Research Association Proceedings, 24*, 114–118.

Taylor, P. (1995). Social and environmental contexts of aging in place. *Environmental Design Research Association Proceedings, 26*, 107–112.

Theodori, G. (2001). Examining the effects of community satisfaction and attachment on individual well-being. *Rural Sociology, 66*, 618–628.

Whitener, L. A. (2001). Housing poverty in rural areas greater for racial and ethnic minorities. *Rural America, 15*(2), 2–7.

Wirth, J. B., & Dollar, S. C. (2004). Concerns of Hispanics and service providers in southwest Missouri. *Great Plains Research, 14*(2), 253–270.

About the Authors

Amy E. Boren, Ph.D., is a lecturer in the Department of Agricultural Leadership, Education, and Communications, Institute of Agriculture and Natural Resources, University of Nebraska–Lincoln, 300 Agriculture Hall, Lincoln, NE 68583-0709. E-mail: aboren2@unl.edu.

Rodrigo Cantarero, Ph.D., is an associate professor in the Community and Regional Planning Program, College of Architecture at the University of Nebraska–Lincoln, 314 Architecture Hall, Lincoln, NE 68588-0107. E-mail: rcantarero1@unl.edu.

James J. Potter, Ph.D., is a professor in the Architecture Program, College of Architecture at the University of Nebraska–Lincoln, 239 Architecture Hall, Lincoln, NE 68588-0107. Phone: 402-472-9240. Fax: 402-472-3806. E-mail: jpotter2@unl.edu.

Rural Latino Immigrant Families
Hunger, Housing, and Social Support

17

KIMBERLY GREDER, CHRISTINE C. COOK, STEVEN GARASKY,
YOSHIE SANO, AND BRUCE C. RANDALL

Abstract

Qualitative and quantitative methods were used to gather data from forty-eight Latino immigrant mothers. Data focused on food secure versus insecure families, housing, and social support. Data were collected in three rural communities in two states (Iowa and Oregon). Type (e.g., emotional, practical) and source (e.g., friends, family, formal service providers) of social support differed by context (e.g., state and community) as well as by food secure versus insecure families.

Keywords: Social Support, Food Insecurity, Housing, Spacial Isolation, Resource Sharing, Rural, Latinos

THE EXPONENTIAL GROWTH of the Latino immigrant population in rural America is a focal point of policy makers, professionals, and local residents (Kandel & Newman, 2004). However, this growth is not uniform, but rather highly concentrated in a few states (U.S. Census

Address all correspondence to Dr. Kimberly Greder. This project has been funded in part by the USDA, Agricultural Experiment Station through North Central research projects NC-223 and NC-1011: "Rural Low-Income Families: Tracking their Well-Being and Functioning in the Context of Welfare Reform."

Bureau, 2006) and a few counties within these states (Kandel & Newman, 2004). This source of population growth has prevented net population loss in these select rural communities that would otherwise occur as a result of chronic population decline from natural decrease (more deaths than births) and out-migration. Nevertheless, the population growth of Latino immigrant families in rural communities may cause stress to local resources as they are more likely to be unable to meet their food (Long, 2003; Nord, Andrews & Carlson, 2005) and housing needs.

Recently, it has been common for Latino immigrants to live in crowded housing conditions and in spatial isolation from non-Latinos (Kandel & Newman, 2004). As a result of this isolation and lack of knowledge and availability of housing and food resources, new Latino immigrants often do not access available community food and housing resources (Delgadillo, Sorensen & Coster, 2004). In addition, they often have few or no financial resources, no credit history, and a mistrust of financial institutions (Quinn, 2001). Furthermore, language barriers and limited skills result in low wages and seasonal employment (Kandel & Newman, 2004).

It is not known how the interactions between individual and family social support, social networks, knowledge and use of community services, and public assistance buffer families from hardship in meeting basic needs. Few investigations have focused on indicators of family strengths among rural low-income Latinos; that is, how and to what extent they are able to overcome challenges and rebound from adversity (Parra-Cardona, Bulock, Imig, Villarruel & Gold, 2006). Previous research among low-income families has suggested that multiple forms of social support contribute to their economic and social well-being and ability to "make ends meet" (Greder & Brotherson, 2002; Henley, Danziger & Offer, 2005). In addition, a lack of social networks has been shown to negatively impact employment and earnings and increase reliance on welfare (Harknett, 2006; Lin, 2001).

In this study, we examined food insecurity, housing hardships, and the role of multiple forms of social support in the lives of low-income Mexican immigrant mothers with young children. In addition to understanding their strengths and challenges, we considered their knowledge and use of community resources to feed and shelter their families. Pressure is mounting to identify policy initiatives and to create or enhance service programs that will assist Latino immigrants in meeting their basic needs and smoothing their integration into their new home communities. Our objective was to fill some of the research gaps identified previously while providing implications for future research, policy, education, and service provision.

Guiding Conceptual Framework

Social Support Networks

Social networks composed of family and friends are linked to improved well-being. Social support aids households in meeting their food (Greder & Brotherson, 2002) and housing needs (Myers et al., 1995). Furthermore, social support networks, especially those that include kin, have been linked to improved self-management of chronic health conditions (Gallant, 2003), decreased depression and better general health among women (Umberson, 1992). In other words, "those who have diverse and resourceful social networks tend to do better" (Harknett, 2006, p. 173); those without such networks are more likely to experience poverty and welfare dependence (Wilson, 1987).

Building on prior research, we expected to observe that family and friends are particularly relevant to recent Latino immigrants. Social and geographic isolation, however, may mean that knowledge of community resources or social networks composed of non-Latinos may be limited. Furthermore, the individuals who make up their social networks often face poverty themselves and commonly have few financial resources to share. A lack of documentation compounds the situation of immigrants by making some program benefits unavailable. We expected that family and friends who also have recently immigrated face similar circumstances compared to Latino immigrants who have been in the United States for several years (e.g., ten or more years). Longer residency may improve well-being by the existence of more opportunities to become proficient in English, aware of how to access local resources, and gain citizenship. Additional skills, knowledge, and documentation may enable immigrants to provide a different level of support to others, as well as to better meet their own food and housing needs.

Latino immigrants often sustain complex linkages and patterns of resource-sharing through intercommunity and international connections. The most important network relationships are based upon kinship, friendship, and commonality in country of origin (Massey, Alarcón, Durand, & González, 1987). These networks also facilitate the processes of immigration and accommodation by providing social and economic support (Haymes & Medina, 1999). The commonality of the immigration experience creates ethnic communities in a relatively short time (Portes, 1995).

It is common among Latino immigrant families to have extended family members living together in the same household. In general, the economic and job-related effects of extended family members and social networks are positive and contribute to economic opportunity, job acquisition, and tenure and pay (Aguilera, 2005). However, ethnic-based informal social networks tend to channel immigrants—especially those who are undocumented—into the rapidly growing informal economy.

Food Security

In 2004, 11.9 percent of United States households were food insecure at some point in the previous year (Nord, Andrews & Carlson, 2005); they did not have access at all times to enough food for an active, healthy life. The negative health, behavioral, and educational consequences of food insecurity have been well established (Cook et al., 2004).

Twenty percent of all food insecure households in the United States are headed by a Latino person (Nord et al., 2005). However, studies that have sought to understand this high rate of food insecurity have revealed conflicting answers. Some studies have found that food insecurity among Latinos is partly attributed to factors that are more common among Latino households (e.g., low income and low education) than among non–Latino white households. Latino households are at a higher risk of food insecurity even after controlling for income. Kaiser and colleagues (2002) found that Mexican American families in California who had higher parental education and income and who were more linguistically acculturated were less likely to be food insecure. However, other studies revealed income as a mediating factor between linguistic acculturation and food insecurity (Mazur et al., 2003). In other words, a higher degree of acculturation partially compensates for socioeconomic disadvantage.

Housing

Previous research has emphasized that poor rural families face more severe housing deprivation relative to those in urban areas (Fitchen, 1992; HAC, 1997). Overcrowding is a problem among rural Latino households that occupy one-quarter of all crowded housing units in non-metropolitan areas. Census data confirm that the age and condition of housing stocks in rural communities and the limited number of rental units affect nonwhite and Latino rural households more than their white counterparts (HAC, 2002).

The latest wave of Latino immigrants has increased the magnitude of the housing shortage in small and mid-size communities. "What frequently happens is that substandard housing, which may have stood vacant, is pressed into use. [Units] may not meet minimum health and safety codes and landlords may fail to make needed repairs" (Quinn, 2001, p. 2). Unscrupulous landlords take advantage of new residents by charging rates per person rather than per unit. Although the cost of housing is substantially lower in rural communities than in the metropolis, "more than four of every ten rural poverty-level households pay over 50 percent of their meager incomes for housing" (Housing Assistance Council, 1997, p. 2).

The lack of affordable housing can be an important structural barrier to achieving economic self-sufficiency for low-income families (Shlay, 1993, 1995). Affordable rental units in rural areas are often older mobile homes or trailers that are in poor condition. Government-assisted housing such as public housing and Section 8 certificates can provide important housing stability and thwart chronic mobility. Yet, families are often faced with either doubling up with other family members or friends, or trading quality for affordability (Bartlett, 1997). For example, unmanageable energy costs associated with substandard housing can precipitate chronic mobility that can undermine social networks and simply result in exchanging one costly housing problem for another (Colton, 1996). Cook et al. (2002) found that informal subsidies and provision of housing by family and friends were important to low-income rural families in Iowa.

Nutrition and health risks among families without adequate housing benefits are substantial (Myers et al., 1995; Sharfstein, Sandel, Kahn & Bauchner, 2001). The link between substandard housing and poor health has been corroborated with findings on "allergen and asthma, lead paint and neurological damage, deteriorating conditions and fatal fires, and unaffordable rent and inadequate nutrition and growth" (Sharfstein et al., 2001, p. 1191). In addition, nutritional outcomes have been linked to unaffordable housing energy costs. Bhattacharya and colleagues (2003) found that families reduced their expenditures on food in response to cold weather. Low-income families use food subsidies to partially meet their food needs, yet they continue to be burdened by having to spend a large share of their budget for housing. However, little is known about housing hardship and food security among rural Latinos or how recently arrived immigrants strategize to obtain and afford available housing while meeting their families' food needs.

Methodology

The data used in this study were from Rural Families Speak, a seventeen-state research project aimed at assessing the circumstances of rural low-income families (Bauer, 2004). Qualitative and quantitative data were drawn from two project states, Iowa and Oregon, which specifically interviewed forty-eight Latino mothers (thirty-one in Iowa, seventeen in Oregon) who had immigrated to the United States within the last fifteen years. Common challenges, strengths, and strategies of these families as they strive to meet their food and housing needs were identified.

Participants

Interviews were conducted in three counties: two in Iowa (Linden and Dogwood) and one in Oregon (Manzanita). (All county names are pseudonyms.) Bilingual Mexican women who resided in the counties were trained to recruit and interview participants. Purposive sampling was used to identify mothers age eighteen and older with at least one child twelve years old or younger, and whose family incomes were at or below 200 percent of the federal poverty line. Contact was made with potential participants through public assistance and education programs.

Data Collection

A qualitative-quantitative protocol was developed for conducting face-to-face interviews. Survey instruments administered during the interviews specific to this study included: CES-D (Center for Epidemiological Studies Depression Scale) (Radloff, 1977), Life Skills Assessment, Knowledge of Community Resources (Richards, 1998), and Food Security Module (Nord & Andrews, 1999). Open-ended questions pertaining to each topic area (i.e., social support, food security, housing, parenting) were asked. A Mexican graduate student majoring in linguistic studies translated the protocol and survey instruments from English to Spanish. University institutional review boards in both states reviewed the translations for accuracy, and approved the study.

Almost all of the interviews were conducted in Spanish in the mothers' homes. Interviews were audio-taped and transcribed verbatim. In Iowa, interviews conducted in Spanish were translated to English and then transcribed by the same student who translated the protocol and instruments. In Oregon, transcripts were translated by bilingual, bicultural undergraduate students. Translations were compared to one another in order to verify consistency and accuracy.

Study Communities

Manzanita County, Oregon, is the largest of the three study counties with 24,590 people in 2003 compared to Linden (20,205) and Dogwood

(17,876) in Iowa (Census Bureau, 2005c). Linden has the largest Latino population (3,486) (Census Bureau, 2005b), accounting for almost one-fifth of their population. Manzanita County has almost half as many Latinos (1,578) with Dogwood having the fewest (755). Between 2000 and 2003, the Latino population grew in Linden by over one-third, in Manzanita by more than one-fourth, and in Dogwood by one-eighth.

The economic picture in each county is strikingly unique. The employment situation deteriorated in each county between 2000 and 2003, but at different rates. Unemployment edged up in Linden to 2.8 percent, increased by nearly 2 percentage points in Manzanita to 6.6 percent, and skyrocketed to 10.2 percent in Dogwood (Bureau of Labor Statistics, 2005). Poverty among all persons was about 11 percent in all three counties (Census Bureau, 2005a). However, the percentage of children living in poverty was much higher in Manzanita (18 percent) than in the other counties (12 percent).

Housing markets differed considerably across counties (Census Bureau, 2005a). While homeownership rates were loosely similar, the median values of owner-occupied housing units in Manzanita ($143,900) was more than double that of Linden ($64,900) and Dogwood ($64,200) in 2000. Rents were higher in Manzanita, as well. In 2000, the median year of construction for all housing structures was 1973 in Manzanita, 1951 in Linden and 1943 in Dogwood (Census Bureau, 2005a). Unfortunately, food insecurity rates were not calculated at the county level (Nord et al., 2005).

Analyses

Interview responses were examined to understand the challenges and strengths experienced by rural Latino families in meeting their food and housing needs. Since the ability to feed one's family is critical to its well-being, and since housing expenditures can deprive families of money for food (Long 2003), we initially examined the food security status of families. By examining housing strategies by food security status, we were able to identify the role of social support in providing food and shelter.

Families were sorted by their food security and food insecurity status based on quantitative responses to the Food Security Module (Nord, 2004). Transcripts were read multiple times to develop sub-codes related to housing and social support. This coding process was guided by grounded theory as outlined by Strauss and Corbin (1998), as well as by the writings of experts in the field of qualitative research (Berg, 1997; Lincoln & Guba, 1985). The research team then reviewed the coded data several times using the process of constant comparative analysis (Strauss & Corbin, 1998) in order to identify emerging themes and discrete ideas. This process enabled the team to identify types (e.g., cash, emotional support, food) and sources (e.g., family, friends, agency/organization, government) of support received by families. Emerging themes were examined and organized by predominant patterns of social support and housing issues by food security status.

Results

Latino Immigrant Families in Oregon and Iowa

In analyzing the data, it was clear that family experiences are place bound. That is, location "creates and limits individual and collective opportunities and outcomes" (Tickamyer, 2000, p. 807). Specific to this context, spatial dimensions affect the availability and affordability of food, housing, and community resources that shape family decisions about meeting needs.

Demographics

Table 17.1 shows the socioeconomic characteristics of the study families. The average age of the mothers ranged from thirty-one to thirty-four years. All but two of the women (n = 48) were married and/or living with a partner and, on average, had three children living in their household. Manzanita households were the largest with an average of six members. Over half of the mothers in each county had less than an eighth-grade education. Only one mother was employed in Dogwood, while more than 60 percent of their counterparts in Linden and Manzanita were employed. Among employed mothers, Manzanita mothers earned the least, only $6.79 per hour on average. Reflecting the mothers' unemployment rate, Dogwood families had the least annual income ($22,677) compared to Linden ($27,748) and Manzanita ($25,505). More than half (58 percent) of the households were food insecure (45 percent in Iowa and 82 percent in Oregon); they did not have access at all times within the past year to enough food for an active, healthy life.

Food Security and Social Support

A prominent strength of the families in this study was their access to and use of social support to meet their food needs. Almost all of the households reported accessing some form of social support (e.g., money, food, transportation) from family, friends, or community agencies to help them

Table 17.1. Household Demographics

| | Iowa | | | | Oregon | | | |
| | Dogwood (N = 15) | | Linden (N = 16) | | Manzanita (N = 17) | | Total (N = 48) | |
Variables	M	SD	M	SD	M	SD	M	SD
Household information								
Mother's age at the time of interview	31.22	5.25	33.86	6.43	30.87	3.98	31.98	5.35
Partner's age at the time of interview	35.37	6.85	37.14	7.15	32.80	3.37	34.99	6.06
Number of children living in the household	3.27	1.28	3.31	1.74	3.29	1.36	3.29	1.44
Age of youngest child of a household	3.71	3.64	4.79	2.64	2.94	1.95	3.78	2.84
Number of children living away from home	0.00	0.00	.19	.54	.18	.53	.13	.44
Number of other household members	.40	.91	.19	.40	1.18	1.33	.60	1.05
Total number of household members	5.47	1.30	5.44	1.75	6.47	1.66	5.81	1.63
Annual income[a]	$22,677	$5,151	$27,748	$9,497	$25,505	$7,643	$25,366	$7,802
Employment (based on employed participants/partners)[b]								
Mothers								
Number of jobs	1.0	—	1.18	.60	1.0	.00	1.09	.42
Wage per hour[a]	$11.20	—	$7.25	$2.75	$6.79	$2.03	$7.22	$2.48
Total working hours per week	40.00	—	37.80	13.78	34.50	11.05	36.33	11.99
Partners								
Number of jobs	1.0	.00	1.08	.28	1.0	0.0	1.02	.15
Wage per hour[a]	$10.40	$2.19	$10.64	$3.14	$8.87	$1.51	$9.93	$2.40
Total working hours per week	41.64	6.12	40.58	3.03	45.47	11.90	42.82	8.44

(continues)

Table 17.1. (continued)

Variables	Iowa Dogwood (N = 15) N	%	Iowa Linden (N = 16) N	%	Oregon Manzanita (N = 17) N	%	Total (N = 48) N	%
Employment								
Mothers								
Employed	1	6.7	11	68.8	11	64.7	23	47.9
Not employed	14	93.3	5	31.3	6	35.3	25	52.1
Partners								
Employed	15	100.0	13	81.3	17	100.0	45	93.8
Not employed	0	0.0	1	6.3	0	0.0	1	2.1
Marital status of mothers								
Married	15	0.0	14	87.5	16	94.1	45	93.8
Living with partner	0	0.0	0	0.0	1	5.9	1	2.1
Separated	0	0.0	2	12.5	0	0.0	2	4.2
Mothers' current education level								
8th grade or less	11	73.3	9	56.3	12	80.6	32	66.7
Some high school	3	20.2	3	18.8	2	11.8	8	16.7
High school or GED	0	0.0	1	6.3	3	17.6	4	8.3
Some college including associate degree	0	0.0	2	12.5	0	0.0	2	4.2
Bachelor's degree	1	6.7	1	6.3	0	0.0	2	4.2

Notes: Data were collected in 2000–2001 for Oregon and 2004–2005 for Iowa. Missing data range from 0 to 5.
[a]Values were adjusted to dollar values of 2004.
[b]Data about employment were based on the number of participants/partners who were employed.

acquire food. However, the sources and types of social support they accessed varied. A strength of food secure families was their knowledge of community resources and money management skills. For example, 65 percent of food secure families knew how to get help paying heating bills, compared to only 35 percent of food insecure families. Similarly, 85 percent of food secure families knew how to make a family budget compared to 50 percent of food insecure families.

Key themes related to food security and social support were: (1) multiple forms of social support were more prevalent among food insecure than food secure households; (2) financial support from family members was accessed more often by food insecure than by food secure households; and (3) tangible social support from community agencies (e.g., food from food pantries, food vouchers from WIC) was used more often by food secure than by food insecure households.

MULTIPLE FORMS OF SOCIAL SUPPORT. Food insecure mothers commonly received several types of support (i.e., shared housing, childcare, transportation, food, money for medical bills, rent, utilities) from multiple sources (i.e., family, friends, church, agencies), as illustrated below:

> When we didn't have money to pay the light bill . . . one time they even shut it off on us because we didn't have any money to pay, and well my husband asked [a friend] to borrow money to put it back on.

FINANCIAL SUPPORT FROM FAMILY MEMBERS. Food insecure mothers accessed financial support from family members as demonstrated by one participant who stated, "Yes, right now it [paying rent] has been hard. My sister let us borrow [money]." When families borrowed money ($100–$700), they quickly paid it back with their next paycheck. In contrast, food secure mothers more often reported that they could ask family members for financial support, however, many reported they did not need assistance from family members with meeting bills, purchasing food, and so on. They were able to meet their basic necessities.

TANGIBLE SOCIAL SUPPORT FROM COMMUNITY AGENCIES. While both food secure and food insecure mothers accessed support from community agencies (e.g., WIC), food secure mothers accessed community social support more often. One noted, "Yes, during the winter they [community action agency] help us [electricity]." And another stated, "When my husband loses jobs we go to [community action agency]." In Iowa, more food secure households (71 percent, n = 12) received WIC benefits, as compared to food insecure households (64 percent, n = 9).

Housing

The housing portion of the interviews began with a question "about your house" and its "adequacy." Most mothers said "yes, the house is adequate" because "it has everything I need" or that "it is fine for now." However, often a single probe about the size of the home or its condition quickly uncovered housing inadequacies including concerns about lead paint, moisture from roofs that needed repair, plumbing problems, vermin and rodents, leaky windows, and furnaces that didn't work. Families experienced "serial housing inadequacy"; that is, moving from place to place that results simply in exchanging one housing quality problem for another. These conditions often are taken in stride: "that's normal [for an old house]" said one Iowa mother. Families may alter their belief systems in order to make meaning of adversity. Previous research has suggested that, despite economic limitations and discriminatory practices, recent Latino immigrants recognize opportunities available to them in the United States that were not available in their home country (Parra-Cardona et al. 2006).

HOUSING AND SOCIAL SUPPORT. Whether food secure or insecure, nearly all families indicated that they had lived with relatives when they first arrived in the United States. Furthermore, housing reciprocity endured after arrival when families moved from one state to another; families relied on their extended family networks to *get started*. Basic necessities, including sharing housing and providing loans for food, utilities, and transportation were commonly reported. To ease the transition to the U.S. culture, other Latinos, often relatively new arrivals themselves, helped kin to identify job opportunities, learn English, and navigate the community.

Families adjust their housing in response to deficits by moving to a new home, remodelling their current home, or restructuring their household—someone moves in to help pay the rent or someone moves out to reduce space shortages (Morris & Winter, 1978). Many low-income families rent so usually few alterations to the home are permitted. Residential mobility is the preferred strategy to reduce housing deficits. Moving is motivated by changes in family size, such as the birth of a new baby. However, sometimes new family members arrive and more space is needed, as illustrated below.

Before living there I lived with my sister . . . [I moved] because an uncle of mine arrived from Mexico and came to work here and then we left my sister's place and we moved to the apartment . . . we left because the rent was too high and it only had two bedrooms.

The Latino mothers in this study provided evidence of moving from place to place to improve family well-being, as well as the role of family and friends in making transitions. Reciprocal help in which a family living in the United States hosts others making the transition from Mexico was also noted.

HOUSING AFFORDABILITY AND HOMEOWNERSHIP. Although social support from kin is a strength that helps families find shelter, there are several contextual issues (e.g., quality of housing stock, affordability, lack of public assistance) that present challenges to meeting housing needs for the families we interviewed, as well as the kin with whom they are integrally involved. Two key themes related to housing were identified: (1) affordable housing and *downsizing* to improve affordability; (2) home ownership as an important goal among study families.

Unaffordable housing is when housing expenses (rent or mortgage payments plus utilities) exceed 30 percent of household income. Unaffordable housing reduces the resources available for other necessities. Families can, and do, identify varied strategies to ease the strain of paying excessive housing costs. For example, knowledge and use of community support programs can help families manage housing costs, however, mothers in this study rarely indicated either knowledge or use of such supports. As indicated in table 17.2, food insecure mothers were less likely to have knowledge of getting help with heating bills (36 percent) or applying for subsidized housing (14 percent), compared to food secure mothers (65 percent and 20 percent, respectively). Food insecure mothers were more likely to know how to locate temporary housing (32 percent), compared to food secure mothers (20 percent). None of the mothers were likely to receive housing, energy, or fuel assistance. Possible reasons for this included a lack of knowledge and being undocumented.

Evidence from the mothers in this study suggested that they choose to pay lower rents (table 17.2) at the expense of meeting family space needs. Furthermore, the data suggest that families often move to secure housing that is less expensive and downsize to reduce housing costs. Though we can only conjecture regarding motives, one might argue that reducing housing costs is part of an overall strategy families have to stretch limited

Table 17.2. Comparison of Food Secure and Food Insecure Families

Variables	Food Secure Families (N=20)		Food Insecure Families (N=28)	
	M	S.D.	M	S.D.
Total number of children living in household	3.25	1.21	3.32	1.61
Total number of other household members	0.60	1.19	0.61	0.96
Total number of household members	5.70	1.56	5.89	1.71
Proportion of rent to monthly income	16.61%	6.94	21.22%	7.64
	N	%	N	%
Type of housing				
Rent	9	45.0	23	82.1
Own	10	50.0	2	7.1
Trailer house	0	0.0	0	0.0
Other	1	50.0	3	10.7
Receiving assistance				
WIC	14	70.0	17	60.7
Housing assistance	0	0.0	1	3.6
Energy/fuel assistance	2	10.0	3	10.7
Medicaid	7	35.0	18	64.3
Income adequacy				
Not at all adequate	1	5.0	3	10.7
Can meet necessities only	6	30.0	14	50.0
Can afford some of the things we want but not all we want	10	50.0	10	35.7
Can afford about everything we want	1	5.0	1	3.6
Can afford about everything we want and still save money	1	5.0	0	0.0
Missing value	1	5.0	0	0.0
Knowledge of community resources: Know how to . . .				
Get help on heating bills	13	65.0	10	35.7
Apply for subsidized housing	4	20.0	4	14.3
Find temporary housing	4	20.0	9	32.1
Apply for Medicaid	18	90.0	19	67.9
Apply for welfare	14	70.0	18	64.3
Apply for food stamps	16	80.0	19	67.9
Apply for WIC	20	100.0	26	92.9
Life skills: Know how to . . .				
Manage bills	17	85.0	19	67.9
Make a family budget	17	85.0	14	50.0
Stretch groceries to the end of the month	18	90.0	21	75.0
Prepare a well-balanced meal for the family	20	100.0	25	89.3
Work with the landlord to improve housing	15	75.0	17	60.7

resources to meet all needs, including housing and food. The mother below indicates that her family moved from a place that cost nearly $1,100 per month for rent and utilities to a smaller place to stretch their budget:

> And so we are nine. And there are only two small rooms, and, well, the children sleep in the living room and we are all right on top of each other . . . But, well yes, it is okay in terms of what we pay . . . It's $450 . . . It will never be as comfortable, right? But yes, yes we are comfortable. Above all because one pays less and what one earns goes a little farther.

Reliance on cash transactions was evident among the mothers, unlike previous research in which low-income families were found to use informal subsidies as much as federal assistance to secure affordable housing (Cook et al., 2002). Informal subsidies included renting homes from kin and friends at below market rents, and/or irregular payment schedules, shared housing arrangements, and receiving cash assistance for food or utilities to divert money to other housing expenditures. At least seven of the mothers received informal subsidies with sharing housing being more common than cash gifts or loans. In Oregon, another four families received housing from their employers. One mother indicated that they paid no rent because the boss owned the unit. Employer subsidies were not common among Iowa respondents.

Half of the families who were food secure were homeowners, compared to only 7 percent of food insecure families. Characteristically, home ownership is an important goal of U.S. families. One might expect that because of cultural differences families from Mexico might not subscribe to the same housing tenure norms, but that is not evidenced in these data. It is clear that the desire for home ownership is strong among Latino immigrants; in fact, for some participants housing adequacy is synonymous with homeownership as evidenced in the following dialogue:

> I: Is your house adequate for your needs and your family's?

> R: No . . . because it's not ours

And conversely:

> I: Is your house adequate for your needs and your family's?

> R: Yes, because it's ours.

In other words, food acquisition and housing challenges faced by the rural immigrant families in this study are numerous and complex. The strategies they employ to meet their needs are multifaceted as well. Nevertheless, as is apparent in the dialogue above, throughout this study it was clear that participants see their current circumstances as the next stop on their quest to attain a better life for themselves and their families.

Conclusions

This study examined challenges and strengths of new Latino immigrants in three rural communities. Past research has suggested that these families arrive with few resources (Quinn, 2001), weakened social networks (Long, 2003), limited knowledge of available social services (Delgadillo et al., 2004), and multiple barriers to employment (Kandel & Newman, 2004). As a result, food and housing hardship often arises. This study adds to this base of knowledge by examining how a purposive sample of forty-eight low-income, recently immigrated Latino mothers with children met food and housing needs through the use of social support networks. In addition, we examined the effects of community context on food security and housing adequacy. Understanding how these new immigrant families provided for themselves will equip researchers, policy makers, educators, and service providers with important insights for future work related to helping Latino immigrants achieve economic self-sufficiency.

Families in this study faced economic challenges that influenced their ability to meet their food and housing needs. The prevalence of high food insecurity rates suggest that food needs often went unmet. Families often chose substandard, deteriorating, inadequate housing, chose housing that was small with too few bedrooms to accommodate family members, and/or moved to cheaper housing as it became available in order to meet their housing needs, while simultaneously stretching resources to meet other needs. Other studies focused on low-income (Nord et al., 2005), rural (Cook et al., 2002; Quinn, 2001), and Latino (Mazur et al., 2003) households found similar results. Clearly, housing costs affect the ability of families to meet their food needs.

Social support contributed substantially to the economic and social well-being of the families in this study. Consistent with Massey and colleagues (1987), most study families accessed social support networks predominantly of kin to acquire shelter and to make ends meet. However, the type and source of support varied among families. For example, while nearly all families in this study reported accessing some form of social support, families who were food secure were more likely to know how to access financial support from public assistance programs to help meet food and housing expenses compared to food insecure families. Food secure families compared to food insecure families also reported relying on fewer sources of social support and were less likely to report needing financial assistance from family members.

Contextual conditions (e.g., local public assistance program eligibility rules, outreach efforts, local labor and housing market conditions) create barriers for some families in meeting their food and housing needs despite available social support. For example, lower housing costs created greater opportunities for families in Linden and Dogwood counties to be food secure, compared to families in Manzanita County. Individual characteristics also impacted the ability of families to be economically self-sufficient. Knowing how to access community resources (e.g., WIC, utilities assistance) and manage household resources (e.g., develop a budget, manage bills) were more common among food secure families than among food insecure families. Families that needed the most help more often relied on informal social support and were less likely to meet their basic needs.

Implications

Implications for Future Research

This study represents an important first step in understanding the strengths, challenges, and strategies employed by rural Latino immigrants in meeting their food and housing needs. Additional research is needed on a variety of fronts. For example, these data hint that home ownership may be instrumental in the acculturation process. Other evidence suggests that acculturation may partially compensate for socioeconomic disadvantage (Kaiser et al., 2002). Additional information about social capital formation—attending school functions, friendships with non–Latinos, and church membership—may increase understanding of Latino immigrant acculturation. Examinations of social capital and acculturation, distinct from social support and community integration, would be fruitful next steps in understanding how immigrant families face the challenges of living in a new community.

Future research is needed to carefully examine housing quality and affordability. Previous research has demonstrated that adequate housing is in limited supply in rural areas for low-income and newly immigrated families (Fitchen, 1992; HAC, 1997, 2002; Quinn, 2001). Families in this study frequently experienced housing problems regarding overcrowding and structural issues such as lead, moisture, and dampness. Some families were concerned for children's safety outdoors, as well as indoors. Previous research also revealed that housing quality and affordability impact family health, and psychological and economic well-being (Myers et al., 1995; Sharfstein et al., 2001). The U.S. Department of Agriculture over the last decade made considerable effort in trying to assess and understand household food needs (Nord et al., 2005). Future research is needed that examines housing hardship and insecurity in a similar way.

Immigration is a vital component of rural life for a variety of reasons highlighted in this research and elsewhere (Kandel & Newman, 2004). Yet, the data in this study and most other studies did not identify which families were undocumented. Future research is needed to understand how the immigration status of a family affects its ability to meet basic needs. It is well-known that undocumented residents are not eligible for many public assistance programs (i.e., Food Stamps, TANF, subsidized housing). Future research is needed to identify the unique challenges faced by undocumented immigrants and the strategies they employ to obtain adequate food and housing. Findings regarding the similarities and differences experienced by documented and undocumented immigrants can inform public policy designed to help ensure that all U.S. residents receive support to meet their basic needs.

Implications for Policy Makers

Often, first perceptions of Latino immigration on a community are negative (Kandel & Newman, 2004). However, the positive impacts of immigration need recognition. Without the influx of Latino immigrants, many rural communities would be doomed to die (Kandel & Newman, 2004). Immigrants often help address labor shortages (Iowa Workforce Development, 2001) and contribute to the local economy through paying taxes and consuming goods.

This study indicates that newly immigrated Latino families need assistance in meeting their basic needs. Policies and systems need to be put in place to help them have adequate housing and enough food so that they can make greater contributions to their communities. Given the frequency with which support from kin was sought among the study families, it appears that such support is vital among Latino immigrants. With this in mind, it is important to shape policies that help families maintain and strengthen kin connections. At the local level, housing zoning policies that do not restrict residency to immediate family members, but rather are sensitive to the need for extended family members to share housing in order to manage scarce resources, would be beneficial. In addition, given that newly immigrated families often face housing challenges, efforts are needed to create and enforce policies for monitoring and ensuring that rental housing meets basic living standards.

Implications for Education

New Latino immigrants offer rural communities a chance for resurgence. Education plays a key role in allowing these families to maximize their community contributions. A vast majority of the mothers in this study did not have a high-school education. Inadequate education and other human capital limitations are significant barriers for immigrant families (Delgadillo et al., 2004). Many adults in this study did not understand or speak English. Seamless opportunities should be developed for immigrants to learn English at locations in which they interact with community members, such as worksites, schools, and churches. Education regarding local laws and regulations, assistance program rules, and how to advocate for family needs also is vital. An example of how these objectives could be achieved locally is through Iowa Community Voices, an Iowa State University Extension program designed to (1) open dialogue between new immigrants and the established community; (2) give new immigrants the knowledge and confidence; to actively participate in community, school, and government activities; and (3) help immigrants connect with each other and explore the feasibility of joining together in new civic and/or neighborhood organizations (Iowa State University Extension, n.d.). Such a program can also educate the established community (e.g., local residents, service providers, retailers, policy makers) about how Latino culture can enhance the community.

Implications for Service Provision

The Latino families in this study required services unique from and beyond those needed by long-time community residents. Support services such as finding a local physician, enrolling children in school, setting up a checking account, and understanding available public transportation options were needed by study families. Immigrant families often required other more unique services related to language barriers and legal issues that surround immigration. In addition, differences were detected in service needs across the three study locations. This suggests that understanding the community context of new immigrant families is important. Strategies for providing services must be relevant to the local community and its residents.

In conclusion, it is evident that rural Latino immigrant families play a key role in the long-term existence of their communities, and that social support networks are important to the vitality of these families. Educators, service providers, and policy makers need to work with immigrant families to jointly establish social support networks that meet the needs of families and are feasible from a community perspective. Consistent with current strategies for identifying and addressing service needs in other areas (Garasky, Greder & Brotherson, 2003), an idea is to involve Latino immigrant families in shaping services and policies that impact them. Doing so will assist communities in developing and delivering services that are socially acceptable to Latino immigrant families, as well as policies that promote Latino family well-being. In short, a joint and multifaceted effort is essential for rural communities to thrive with the arrival of these new residents.

References

Aguilera, M. B. (2005). The impact of social capital on the earnings of Puerto Rican migrants. *The Sociological Quarterly, 46*, 569–592.

Bartlett, S. (1997). The significance of relocation for chronically poor families in the USA. *Environment and Urbanization, 9*(1), 21–131.

Bauer, J. W. (2004) Basebook report: Low income rural families: Tracking their well-being and functioning in the context of welfare reform. North Central Region, Multi State Project NC223.

Berg, B. (1997). *Qualitative research methods for the social sciences* (3rd ed.). New York: Allyn & Bacon.

Bhattacharya, J., DeLeire, T., Haider, S., & Currie, J. (2003). Heat or eat? Cold-weather shocks and nutrition in poor American families. *American Journal of Public Health, 93*(7), 1149–1154.

Bureau of Labor Statistics, United States. (2005). *Local area unemployment statistics.* Accessed December 21, 2005, from www.bls.gov/lau/.

Census Bureau, United States. (2005a). *American fact finder.* Accessed December 21, 2005, from factfinder.census.gov/home/saff/main.html?_lang=en.

Census Bureau, United States. (2005b). *Hispanic population of the United States.* Accessed December 21, 2005, from www.census.gov/population/www/socdemo/hispanic.html.

Census Bureau, United States. (2005c). *Population estimates.* Accessed December 21, 2005, from www.census.gov/popest/estimates.php.

Census Bureau, United States. (2006). Race and Hispanic origin in 2004. *Population profile of the United States: Dynamic version.* Accessed February 25, 2006, from www.census.gov/population/www/pop-profile/profile.html.

Colton, R. D. (1996). A road oft taken: Unaffordable home energy bills, forced mobility and childhood education in Missouri. *Journal of Children and Poverty, 2*(2), 23–40.

Cook, C. C., Crull, S. R., Fletcher, C. N., Hinnant-Bernard, T., & Peterson, J. (2002). Meeting family housing needs: Experiences of rural women in the midst of welfare reform. *Journal of Family and Economic Issues, 23*(3), 285–316.

Cook, J., Frank, D., Berkowitz, C., Black, M., Casey, P., Cutts, D., et al. (2004). Food insecurity is associated with adverse health outcomes among human infants and toddlers. *Journal of Nutrition, 134*, 1432–1438.

Delgadillo, L., Sorensen, S., & Coster, D. C. (2004). An exploratory study of preparation for future care among older Latinos in Utah. *Journal of Family and Economic Issues, 25*(1), 51–78.

Fitchen, J. M. (1992). On the edge of homelessness: Rural poverty and housing insecurity. *Rural Sociology, 57*(2), 173–193.

Gallant, M. P. (2003). The influence of social support on chronic illness self-management: A review and directions for research. *Health Education and Behavior, 30*(2), 170–195.

Garasky, S., Greder, K., & Brotherson, M. J. (2003). Empowerment through involvement: Iowa's experience with welfare reform. *Journal of Family and Consumer Sciences, 95*, 21–26.

Greder, K., & Brotherson, M. J. (2002). Food security and low income families: Research to inform policy and programs. *Journal of Family and Consumer Sciences, 94*(2), 41–47.

Hanson, G. (2005). *Emigration, labor supply and earnings in Mexico.* NBER Working Paper No. 11412. New York: National Bureau of Economic Research.

Harknett, K. (2006). The relationship between private safety nets and economic outcomes among single mothers. *Journal of Marriage and Family, 68*, 172–191.

Haymes, M., & Medina, I. (1999). *Latino culture, child welfare, and family support: Engaging informal supportive cultural practices.* Family Resource Coalition Report, Empowerment and Latino Families, Fall/Winter 1994–1995, Chicago.

Henley, J. R., Danziger, S., & Offer, S. (2005). The contribution of social support to the material well-being of low-income families. *Journal of Marriage and Family, 67*, 122–140.

Housing Assistance Council (HAC). (1997). *Rural housing and welfare reform: Housing Assistance Council 1997 report on the state of the nation's rural housing.* Washington, DC: HAC.

Housing Assistance Council (HAC). (2002). *Taking stock: Rural people, poverty, and housing at the turn of the 21st century.* Washington, DC: HAC.

Iowa State University Extension. (n.d.). *Iowa community voices: A community development and leadership program for minority residents of Iowa.* Accessed May 22, 2007, from www.extension.iastate.edu/communities/voices/.

Iowa Workforce Development. (2001, March). *Barriers to employment: Central Iowa Latino laborforce survey.* Des Moines, IA: Iowa Workforce Development.

Kaiser, L. H., Melgar-Quiñoz, C., Lamp, M., Johns, J. S., & Harwood, J. (2002). Food security and nutritional outcomes of preschool-age Mexican-American children. *Journal of the American Dietetic Association, 102*, 924–929.

Kandel, W., & Newman, C. (2004). Rural Hispanics: Employment and residential trends. *Amber Waves, 2*(3), 38–45.

Lin, N. (2001). *Social capital: A theory of social structure and action.* Cambridge: Cambridge University Press.

Lincoln, Y., & Guba, E. (1985). *Naturalistic inquiry.* New York: Sage.

Long, S. K. (2003). *Choosing among food, housing, and health insurance.* No. B54 in Series, New Federalism: National Survey of America's Families. Accessed August 22, 2005, from www.urban.org.

Massey, D. S., Alarcón, R., Durand, J., & González, H. (1987). *Return to Aztlan: The social process of international migration from Western Mexico.* Los Angeles: University of California Press.

Mazur, R., Marquis, G., & Jensen, H. H. (2003). Diet and food insufficiency among Hispanic youths: Acculturation and socioeconomic factors in the Third National Health and Nutrition Examination Survey. *American Journal of Clinical Nutrition, 78,* 1120–1127.

Morris, E. W., & Winter, M. (1978). *Housing, family, and society.* New York: John Wiley.

Myers, A., Frank, D. A., Roos, N., Peterson, K. E., Casey, V. A., Cupples, L. A., & Levenson, S. M. (1995). Housing subsidies and pediatric undernutrition. *Archives of Pediatrics & Adolescent Medicine, 149*(10), 1079–1085.

Nord, M. (2004). *Food security in the United States: Measuring household food security.* Accessed November 15, 2006, from www.ers.usda.gov/Briefing/FoodSecurity/measurement.htm.

Nord, M., & Andrews M. (1999). Six-item short form of the food security survey module. USDA Economic Research Service Briefing Room. Accessed February 24, 2006, from www.ers.usda.gov/Briefing/FoodSecurity/surveytools/index.htm#questionnaire.

Nord, M., Andrews, M., & Carlson, S. (2005). *Household food security in the United States, 2004.* Economic Research Report No. 11. Washington, DC: U.S. Department of Agriculture.

Parra-Cardona, J. R., Bulock, L. A., Imig, D. R., Villarruel, F. A., & Gold, S. J. (2006). "Trabajando duro todos los dias": Learning from the life experiences of Mexican-origin migrant families. *Family Relations, 55,* 361–375.

Portes, A. (1995). Children of immigrants: Segmented assimilation and its determinants. In A. Porters (Ed.), *The economic sociology of immigration* (pp. 248–279). New York: Russell Sage.

Quinn, T. (2001). *Housing Issues of New Hispanic Residents in Iowa.* Accessed September 8, 2003, from www.ncrcrd.iastate.edu/spanishconf/ses3a-housing-handout.html.

Radloff, L. S. (1977). The CES-D Scale: A self report depression scale for research in the general population. *Applied Psychological Measurement, 1,* 385–401.

Richards, L. N. (1998). *One step at a time: A report on the outcomes of Oregon's 1996/1997 Even Start Programs prepared for Oregon Even Start Programs and Department of Community Colleges & Workforce Development.* Corvallis, OR: College of Home Economics and Education, Oregon State University.

Sharfstein, J., Sandel, M., Kahn, R., & Bauchner, H. (2001). Is child health at risk while families wait for housing vouchers? *American Journal of Public Health, 91*(8), 1191–1192.

Shlay, A. B. (1993). Family self-sufficiency and housing. *Housing Policy Debate*, *4*(3), 457–495.

Shlay, A. B. (1995). Housing in the broader context in the United States. *Housing Policy Debate*, *6*(3), 695–720.

Strauss, A., & Corbin, J. (1998). *Basics of qualitative research: Techniques and procedures for developing grounded theory* (2nd ed.). Thousand Oaks, CA: Sage.

Tickamyer, A. R. (2000). Space matters! Spatial inequality in future sociology. *Contemporary Sociology*, *28*(6), 805–813.

Umberson, D. (1992). Relationships between adult children and their parents: Psychological consequences for both generations. *Journal of Marriage and Family*, *54*(3), 664–674.

Wilson, W. J. (1987). *The truly disadvantaged: The inner-city, the underclass, and public policy*. Chicago: University of Chicago Press.

About the Authors

Christine C. Cook is an associate professor in the Department of Human Development and Family Studies at Iowa State University, 4380 Palmer Building, Room 2330, Ames, IA 50011. Phone: 515-294-8695. Fax: 515-294-2502. E-mail: cccook@iastate.edu.

Steven Garasky is an associate professor in the Department of Human Development and Family Studies at Iowa State University, 4380 Palmer Building, Room 2330, Ames, IA 50011. Phone: 515-294-9826. Fax: 515-294-1765. E-mail: sgarasky@iastate.edu.

Kimberly A. Greder, Ph.D., is a Family Life Extension State Specialist and associate professor in the Department of Human Development and Family Studies at Iowa State University, 4380 Palmer Building, Room 2330, Ames, IA 50011. Phone: 515-294-5906. Fax: 515-294-5507. E-mail: kgreder@iastate.edu.

Bruce C. Randall is a former graduate student in the Department of Human Development and Family Studies at Iowa State University.

Yoshie Sano is an assistant professor in the Department of Human Development at Washington State University, Vancouver, 14204 NE Salmon Creek Avenue, Vancouver, WA 98686. Phone: 360-546-9124. Fax: 360-546-9076. E-mail: sano@vancouver.wsu.edu.

Parental Stress among U.S. Mexican Heritage Parents

18

Implications for Culturally Relevant Family Life Education

M. ELISE RADINA, STEPHAN M. WILSON, AND CHARLES B. HENNON

Abstract

Parents in immigrant families not only must cope with the everyday stresses of being a parent but are also faced with unique stresses as immigrants (e.g., language barriers, access to healthcare). This chapter presents a general theoretical model regarding what can precipitate and diffuse parenting stress. Based on this general model and available empirical research, the authors present an alternative model that reflects potentially unique stress that Mexican heritage parents face. Using this alternative model, the authors make recommendations for culturally relevant family life education intended to meet the needs of Mexican heritage parents as they cope with parenting stresses.

Keywords: Parenting, Parenting Stress, Family Life Education, Mexican Heritage, Parental Empowerment

Address all correspondence to Dr. M. Elise Radina, Department of Family Studies and Social Work, Miami University, 101E McGuffey Hall, Oxford, OH 45056. Phone: 513-529-3639. Fax: 513-529-6468. E-mail: radiname@muohio.edu.

BEING A PARENT in the United States in the twenty-first century can be uniquely stressful given the new influences on how Americans live their daily lives (e.g., the increase in access to and use of communication technologies, the threat of terrorism, and economic uncertainty). For immigrant families, these stresses are compounded by other factors such as linguistic isolation, the acculturation process, healthcare issues, and uncertainty about the future prospects for illegal immigrants—particularly given recent discussions at all levels of government about this issue (California Immigrant Welfare Collaborative, 2006). In this chapter we introduce a general model of parenting stress based on the common ideas of risk and protective factors, and how these relate to family stress and thus parental stress. From there, we present an adapted version of this model that can be used with Mexican heritage families. The discussion of this model involves a review of research specific to risk and protective factors characteristic of this population and the additional construct of acculturation. We conclude by highlighting the unique role of culturally relevant and specific resource delivery and intervention in reducing stress among Mexican heritage parents. The ultimate goal of this adapted model is to allow for transformative learning and the empowerment of these parents in order to reduce both family and parental stress, which will lead to more optimal outcomes for parents and children.

Focusing on parents of Mexican heritage, particularly those who have recently immigrated with their children, is essential considering that family life education (FLE) and other resources may not be culturally relevant, fail to meet the needs of this population, and are not always effective with Mexican heritage parents (Hennon, Peterson, Polzin & Radina, 2006). Latinos are the largest (12.5 percent: U.S. Census, 2000) and fastest growing U.S. ethnic minority population. About 9 percent of the U.S. population and 63 percent of all Latinos are of Mexican ancestry (U.S. Census, 2003b).

Family Stress Theory and Parental Stress

Figure 18.1 depicts the basic process and contributing factors to family stress and its relationship to parenting stress. Specifically, a combination of risk and protective factors influences the level of family stress. This influence increases when a resource shortfall occurs due to a family's lack of resources, lack of awareness of resources, or limitations in access to resources.

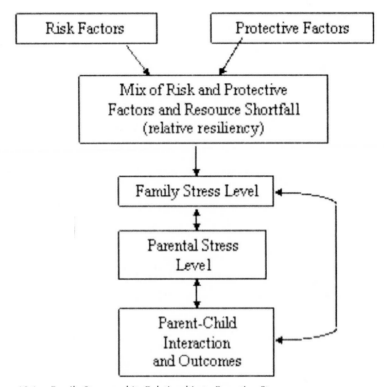

Figure 18.1.   Family Stress and Its Relationship to Parenting Stress

These factors can contribute to stress experienced by the family system and the resulting impact on parent-child interactions and child outcomes that influence (in a reciprocal manner) the degree of parental stress. The level of parental stress influences parent-child interaction and child outcomes, and the overall level of family stress in a cyclic manner. Without the application of an internal or external method to suppress the level of stress and distress, these cyclical processes can continue to spiral and accelerate to problematic levels.

Parental stress is an aversive reaction (e.g., felt emotional, psychological, and physical) resulting from caring for, socializing, disciplining, and nurturing children (Crnic & Low, 2002). These ideas focus on the individual as the unit of analysis, and thus are limited in contrast to system level perspectives such as family stress theory. According to family stress theory, parental stress is conceptualized as *distress*, an individual-level experience resulting from social stress occurring when family systems are strained and structural change is necessary. Thus, parental stress is a felt pressure or tension to change interaction patterns or family organization and functioning (Peterson & Hennon, 2005). Included in this conceptualization is the notion that parents can jointly negotiate a *view* of a situation and organize a *team* response. A systems approach considers the context of families (Kuczynski, 2003), which includes geographic location, characteristics of the community, the sociopolitical conditions (e.g., discrimination), economic factors, cultural values and norms (e.g., religion), as well as the more general sociohistorical period. Consequently, understanding parental stress requires that the individual, relationship (e.g., parental subsystem and parent-child relationship), the total family system, and community levels be considered. At all levels, stress is a pressure to change current, less functional patterns of parenting and child behavior (Boss, 2002).

From a systems perspective, parental stress is a multidirectional process involving connections among systemic components that affect other family members (Kuczynski, 2003). Common sources of difficulty that lead to parental stress come from a variety of circumstances faced by parents, based on their connections with children and other individuals, both within and beyond the immediate family, including marital issues, problems with other relatives (e.g., extended family members meddling in parental affairs), school and work environments (e.g., achievement; employment security worries), and healthcare (Peterson & Hann, 1999; Peterson & Hennon, 2005).

Parents' distressed responses can have social and emotional consequences on well-being for parents and children. Highly distressed parents are inclined to be anxious and emotionally reactive, preoccupied with adult-centered goals, and less likely to monitor children and to maintain child-centered parenting goals. Hence, parental stress contributes to being less responsive and affectionate, or perhaps neglectful, punitive, or even abusive. Negative outcomes may result, such as less effective social skills, lower self-esteem, displaying disruptive and aggressive behaviors, becoming socially withdrawn, and experiencing psychological distress (Crnic & Low, 2002; Peterson & Hann, 1999).

Less-distressed parents are inclined to be more responsive, warm, rational, and moderate in the kinds of control used with children. They are likely to use firm control, reasoning, consistent rule enforcement, and monitoring (Crnic & Low, 2002). Child characteristics associated with such behaviors include sound school achievement, better social skills, effective peer adjustment, good self-esteem, and a balance between conforming to parents and progress toward autonomy, all key aspects of social competence within a variety of cultures (Peterson & Hann, 1999).

Risk and Protective Factors

Resiliency, a vital component of healthy family systems, encompasses how families endure in the face of adversity, navigate their way through transitions and tragedies, and flourish in the face of life's hardships (Walsh, 2002). Resiliency involves, in part, the complex interplay of risk and protective factors over time, and includes individual, relationship, family, and larger sociocultural influences. Frameworks that conceptualize this complex interplay of risk and protective factors have advanced the analysis of stress-moderating or stress-enhancing processes (Voydanoff & Donnelly, 1998). *Risk factors* are social-psychological elements that endanger adaptive functioning, well-being, health, and social performance (e.g., parenting). *Protective factors* are conditions or resources that minimize or manage stress, buffer the influence of risk factors, foster adaptive functioning, and maintain effective social performance at the individual, family, and extrafamilial levels (Voydanoff & Donnelly, 1998).

Resource Delivery and Shortfalls

This resiliency approach encompasses the idea that parental stress often results from resource shortfalls that can be overcome by service delivery systems (formal and informal) aimed at providing needed resources so that families feel supported (Briar-Lawson, Lawson, Hennon & Jones, 2001). *Resources* include material goods, emotional support, practical help, important knowledge, and a sustainable social support network. A resource shortfall, therefore, can be viewed from the standpoint that all parents and families have strengths upon which to build, rather than relying on deficit models that result in parents being blamed for deficiencies. Ineffective parental responses that are based in excessive stress can then be viewed as resulting from insufficient but possibly only temporary shortages of resources (i.e., a transitory lack of knowledge, skills, attitudes, or other parenting resources) rather than some trait that is relatively permanent. This conceptualization emphasizes the *potential* of parents and leads to empowerment models in which the goal is to help parents/families learn to overcome barriers to enhancing the quality of family life. The key is enhancing parental resiliency by using the expertise of more experienced parents and empirically based professional knowledge about parenting and stress management to build resource capabilities using appropriate delivery systems.

Parental Stress among Mexican Heritage Families

Our goal in the subsequent sections is to elaborate upon the framework discussed above as it relates to parental stress for Mexican heritage parents, introducing the *Culturally Relevant and Specific Resource Delivery for Parental Empowerment Model* (CRPE: figure 18.2).

Mexicans in the United States are a diverse group. Some families have ancestors who became U.S. citizens after the territory above the current U.S.-Mexican border was annexed in the mid 1800s. Many of these families have a unique culture that blends Mexican, American Indian, and Spanish influences (Becerra, 1998). Other families and individuals are living in the United States because of subsequent legal and illegal migration (Phillips & Massey, 2000). Some Mexicans are in the United States for only a short period, perhaps for economic gain. Some are native-born citizens, immigrants who are long-term residents seeking naturalization,

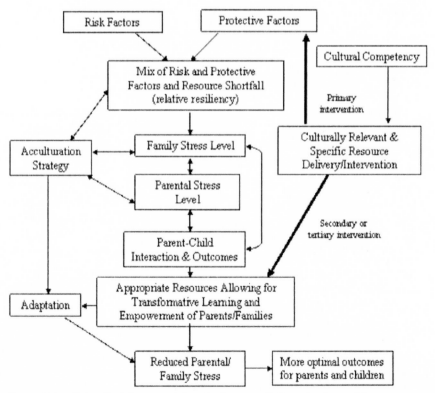

Figure 18.2.   Culturally Relevant and Specific Resource Delivery for Parental Empowerment Model

or undocumented immigrants who are living in the United States for extended periods but are not pursuing citizenship (Haskins, Greenberg & Fremstad, 2004).

The average income of Hispanic households in the United States in 2001 was $33,565, with 20 percent of Mexican heritage families living in poverty (U.S. Census, 2003a). Mexican heritage family members tend to have blue-collar occupations (U.S. Census, 2003a) and relatively high rates of unemployment (8.4 percent in 2002, Ramirez & de la Cruz, 2002). Poor education and English proficiency contribute to lower wages (Haskins et al., 2004) and individuals of Mexican heritage are disproportionately represented among school dropouts (Martínez & Mehan, 1997).

Close to 70 percent of Hispanic households have children under the age of 18 living in the home, compared to about 50 percent for non-Hispanic households. Mexican heritage families are twice as likely, compared to white non-Hispanic families (40 percent and 21 percent, respectively), to have children under age six (Becerra, 1998). Mexican heritage parents value their roles, attach importance to their children, and experience parenting as a source of satisfaction and meaning in their lives. Maternal views of child development and actual child rearing behaviors indicate a complex diversity and a broad range of styles (Becerra, 1998; Hildebrand, Phenice, Gray & Hines, 2000; Valentine & Mosley, 2000). Evidence suggests that many Mexicans in the United States have child development expectations and interactional processes that differ from those of the majority culture (Martínez, 1993; Sanchez, 1997). However, studies have been inconsistent about child rearing practices and attitudes (Martínez, 1993). Some research has concluded that parents of Mexican heritage in the United States exhibit permissive child rearing while other research indicated that strong traditional values and authoritarian parenting were also characteristic. Data from self-reports suggest than child rearing is warm, affectionate, and nurturing within a context of a patriarchal, authoritarian family structure with high respect for males and the elderly (Hildebrand et al., 2000; Martínez, 1993).

Observational studies of parenting (e.g., Parke et al., 2004; Sanchez, 1997) have pointed toward different findings regarding parenting style. These studies have indicated relatively equal numbers of authoritative and authoritarian parents, with few being permissive (Sanchez, 1997). Some studies have even pointed to mothers exhibiting harsh or hostile parenting behaviors (Parke et al., 2004). Overall such parenting tends to focus on the child learning that obedience will lead to being an esteemed member of society. This focus stands in contrast to parenting focusing on obedience as a natural conclusion and more important than autonomy.

The *traditional* structure of Mexican families tends to be patriarchal, hierarchical, and with a set role structure and value orientation (Becerra, 1998; Esteinou, in press; Hildebrand et al., 2000). The concepts of *machismo/marianismo* that are prevalent in Mexican and other Latino cultures reflect expectations surrounding gender-role differentiation (Esteinou, in press). According to the cultural value of *machismo*, husbands are the head of the wife and the household. The father/husband is provider and protector and is charged with monitoring and controlling family members' participation with the world beyond the home. Thus, families often operate in a patriarchal fashion with the male assuming responsibility for the family's material well-being. Men are expected to be strong and protective of the women in their lives (Cox & Monk, 1993; Esteinou, in press). The cultural value of *marianismo* suggests that women consider their personal needs after their family and take on responsibility for care of the home and the children (Cox & Monk, 1993; Esteinou, in press). Mexican heritage wives/mothers are to be submissive and obedient, self-sacrificing, self-effacing, serving their husbands, and nurturing their children. She is to be the overseer of the family's children. These various duties are often at the expense of her wishes, needs, and desires. While the father might be aware and controlling of the activities of the children, his more limited involvement in day-to-day family life places the mother in the position of more continuous interaction with, and responsibility for, children (Hildebrand et al., 2000).

Culturally Relevant and Specific Resource Delivery for Parental Empowerment Model

The CRPE posits that parental stress is a result of risk and protective factors and resource shortfalls that may be managed by appropriate FLE. Building upon the preceding discussions of parental stress (see core model, figure 18.1) and research regarding Mexican heritage families, the following additional constructs are added to the core conceptual model: the family factors of acculturation strategy, acculturative stress, and adaptation along with the programmatic factor of cultural competency as the basis for culturally-relevant and specific resource delivery. The result of these additions is the CRPE.

The CRPE is a family-centered approach to FLE for the development of appropriate resources and appropriate, culturally sensitive, and responsive resource delivery. This perspective gives priority to families (versus organizations or social services) in order to assist them in gaining the skills to overcome barriers and factors contributing to parental stress. Educators must have a good understanding of parenting and parental stress theory and research, as well as comprehension of the target population's cultural heritage, factors that might make their family life distinctive, and the diverse acculturation strategies they might be employing given their life goals. The aspiration is to offer appropriate resources and services in a timely and effective manner with the intent of these allowing for the building of resiliency, facilitating empowerment and transformative learning, and thus reducing parental/family stress. The goal is more optimal outcomes for parents and children.

Using the CRPE can help family life educators to reduce parental stress through two pathways: delivery of such resources that address the family/parents' balance of risk and protective factors (*primary intervention*), and introduction of such resources in situations where family/parental stress, parent–child interactions, and child outcomes have already reached critical levels and attempts are then made to restore adequate family functioning (*secondary* or *tertiary intervention*). Doing this requires the educator/programmer to acquire a high degree of cultural competency in order to interact with these families. Professionals and organizations develop cultural competence as they become proactive in acquiring understanding and effective in working with a broad range of family types, ethnicities, and cultures (Allen & Blaisure, 2003).

Risk Factors

Economic hardships that pressure Mexican wives/mothers to seek employment outside the home have resulted in sometimes unwelcome changes within their families. Economic pressures appear to *push* mothers and children into gainful employment, even if values concerning the central role of mothers within the family are violated. Mexican families, and particularly mothers, can become significantly stressed as these demands requiring the reorganization of parental roles are faced at the same time that pressures exist to maintain traditional family role obligations (Hildebrand et al., 2000). The notion of *machismo* has been challenged in the United States, both as women are often employed and thus increase their relative power, and as families have become more assimilated. One consequence of *marianismo*, mothers' suppression of personal wishes in favor of family wishes and responsibility for children, could be that mothers experience more parental stress than fathers.

For Mexican heritage families, the expectation is that marriage is stable and long lasting, and women are especially expected to play their part to help the marriage stay strong. Integration or assimilation often is accompanied by more marital problems and marital distress, as values associated with traditional Mexican family roles erode (Parke et al., 2004). Marital dynamics, particularly lower marital quality, are associated with the degree of parental stress. However, hostile parenting seems to decrease when couples adopt more equalitarian power sharing and individualistic tendencies (Parke et al., 2004). This is especially the case as maternal acculturation proceeds and results in a growing awareness of alternative parenting strategies (e.g., privilege loss, withdrawal of love, reasoning).

Mexican heritage fathers have somewhat limited involvement with, especially, younger children. As children age and reach adolescence, however, fathers are often called upon to exert authority, especially in matters of discipline. Given a lack of earlier involvement, this change may prove difficult for fathers and unacceptable to adolescents leading to conflict. Some (Hildebrand et al., 2000; Sanchez, 1997) argue that persistent father-adolescent conflict may be one reason Mexican youth join gangs.

Rather than an emphasis on early achievement and attainment of developmental milestones, Mexican heritage parents place greater emphasis on developing their children's sense of dignity and proper demeanor. It is unclear how these expectations and cultural values influence parental stress, parental-child interactions (e.g., discipline), or the developmental outcomes of children. This is, in part, because people of Mexican heritage have been excluded or underrepresented in many studies of early environmental and biological influences on the development of infants and children (Kolobe, 2004). Mexican immigrant families hold children to greater accountability. Consequently, what may be viewed as harsh or hostile parenting might in fact be behaviors to promote the parents' goal of accountability.

The overall need for childcare may be great in immigrant communities. Immigration and the resulting distance from extended family networks reduce the availability of kin to assist with childcare, especially for those migrating without an already existing kin network in the United States. Hispanics prefer to leave their preschool-age children in the care of a spouse or relative more so than do other mothers. However, other arrangements must be made when working outside the home. Childcare arrangements (i.e., increasing use of extra-familial childcare) and satisfaction with such arrangements may be related to the acculturation process, the acculturation strategy utilized, and the resulting level of parental stress (Buriel & Hurtado-Ortiz, 2000). Considering that an internalized expectation of Mexican heritage mothers is to care for and nurture their children, it is not surprising that when in the labor force they experience distress, or role conflict, and have concerns about the well-being of their children. It may be possible to reduce stress if a kin member is in charge of the children. However, kin are often not available or are themselves employed (Hildebrand et al., 2000). Families could then rely on informal care by nonfamily members, but many could also be employed and unavailable for childcare services. Families are left with the use of licensed childcare arrangements in the absence of relatives and available nonfamily members (Buriel & Hurtado-Ortiz, 2000).

Children of immigrants are at increased risk of poor developmental outcomes (Hernandez, 2004) due to a greater likelihood than nonimmigrants of living in single-parent households, living in linguistically isolated households, having mothers without high school diplomas, and economic deprivation. Close to 70 percent of children born to immigrants live with one or more of these risk factors, and almost 20 percent have three (Hernandez, 2004). There is a correlation between children who are more academically able and parental education level, the ability of parents to help their children academically, parental monitoring, and parental support of their children. Foreign-born youth have less chance than native-born youth to succeed academically because they may lack the language skill; youth who speak more Spanish than English at home have lower academic motivation and educational aspirations (Plunkett & Bámaca-Gómez, 2003). Parents can become stressed due to their inability to help their children with school-related achievement and the consequences of dropping out of school. At the same time, Mexicans in the United States have the highest fertility rate of Hispanic groups. This reality, when coupled with lower education, is correlated with poverty (Valentine & Mosley, 2000). For some, economic hardships, high fertility, and other risk factors for non-optimal child outcomes all contribute to parental stress, which in turn contributes to poorer child outcomes.

Protective Factors

Family is a source of security and emotional strength for people of Mexican heritage. These families are especially known for practices that keep family members close, both emotionally and geographically (Niemann, Romero, Arredondo & Rodriguez, 1999). Traditional Mexican culture emphasizes the sanctity of family and more recent immigrants, in particular, have strong family orientations. Individual goals are often subordinated to family needs (Freeberg & Stein, 1996), sometimes resulting in children dropping out of school to help the family financially. As assimilation with the dominant U.S. culture occurs, levels of familism decrease in later generations of Mexicans, but family support stays relatively constant across generations (Perez & Padilla, 2000).

Familism is an important aspect of Mexican family life (see Lugo Steidel & Contreras, 2003). Among Mexicans, the concept of *compadrazgo* within familism refers to relationships involving *fictive kin*. This idea includes *padrinos y ahijados* (godparents and children) and parents and godparents who become *compadres* or co-parents (Zinn, 1998).

Acculturation

Berry (2005) defines acculturation as "the dual process of sociocultural, institutional and psychological change that takes place as a result of contact of a group and its individual members with another that is external to it. . . . At the group level, it involves changes in social structures and institutions and in cultural practices, and at the individual level, it involves changes in a person's behavioral repertoire" (p. 3). At the individual level, this is psychological acculturation. This process can involve diminished identification with the home culture, loss of contact with family back home, decreased loyalty to traditional cultural values, and improved English-language proficiency.

Acculturation strategies are how people go about engaging in the process of acculturation, and there are great variations. Two components of the strategies are attitudes or preferences about how to acculturate and the goal to be achieved, and behaviors or what people actually due to achieve the goals. These are exhibited in people's day-to-day intercultural encounters and while there is a correspondence between the two, constraints can be imposed by the dominant culture. The strategy used is a function of many antecedent factors (cultural and personal) and there are variable outcomes (cultural and personal) of the different strategies (Berry, 2005). For some people, acculturation is reactive, or a rejection of the dominant group's cultural influences; it can also be a creative process of developing a merger of ways of living, speaking, and thinking.

An important consequence of acculturation that may have an impact on parental stress is the experience of acculturative stress. Acculturative stress occurs when cultural conflict is experienced by the acculturating individual, and the experiences are perceived to be "problematic but controllable and surmountable" (Berry, 2005, p. 20). Research suggests that elevated acculturative stress is negatively related to psychological as well as physical well-being (Berry, 2005).

Acculturation occurs at a variable pace in different families and for individual family members. Thus, child rearing practices and parenting roles often differ in substantial ways for newly immigrated parents of Mexican heritage, compared to parents of other ethnic groups and to Mexican parents who are long-term U.S. residents. Also, some observers have argued that the acculturation experiences of Mexicans are different from other immigrant/ethnic groups (Becerra, 1998; Hildebrand et al., 2000). Specifically, families of Mexican heritage often maintain more continuous interaction with first-generation immigrants who reinforce traditional family values and practices. This influences acculturation (i.e., acculturation strategies) among those who remain in highly concentrated Mexican communities where some traits stay relatively unchanged. The practice of living in close proximity to their original homeland also encourages visits, extended family ties, and support for traditional Mexican family values (Becerra, 1998; Hildebrand et al., 2000). This preservation of native culture may be a risk factor as traditional family values, while important, may cause both difficult and stressful adaptation to the United States. An added factor potentially leading to parent–child conflict and parental stress is that children often have different acculturation strategies than adults (Perez & Padilla, 2000).

Acculturation progress is associated with adaptation and types of risk factors for parental stress. Adaptation refers to relatively stable changes of individuals and families to the demands of their new society. Adaptation is an outcome that can be more or less positive. Berry (2005) indicates four adaptation possibilities of acculturation strategies (integration, assimilation, separation, and marginalization). Integration is achieved through bicultural accommodation in which values and traditions from the home country are maintained, while skills for interacting with the host culture are developed simultaneously. In some ways, this might be an optimal strategy. Pursuing assimilation (shedding heritage culture while becoming absorbed into the dominant society) could also prove useful if all in the family agree to this major transformation. Mexican heritage parents who pursue strategies of separation (rejecting involvement with the dominant culture, and clinging to their heritage culture) or marginalization (when there is minimal interest in heritage cultural maintenance or in relating to the dominant culture perhaps due to exclusion or discrimination) often experience hostility, rejection, or discrimination. Such parents might experience greater economic hardship that can lead to parental stress, more hostile parenting, and child adjustment problems (Berry, 2005; Hildebrand et al., 2000; Parke et al., 2004). Parents who are less adaptive to U.S. society tend to use stricter and authoritarian parenting strategies (Buriel, 1993). Mexican heritage children who speak Spanish tend to have mothers who use more hostile controlling behaviors than children who speak English (Hill, Bush & Roosa, 2003).

Conclusions and Implications for Culturally Relevant Service Delivery

This chapter specifies and explains the CRPE model of community-based FLE education. The CRPE suggests that parental stress is a result of both risk and protective factors that may be overcome by appropriate service delivery systems. This is a culturally sensitive and responsive approach to the creation of FLE programs relying on parental expertise and empirically based professional knowledge to develop the necessary resources and appropriate FLE delivery systems.

Considering family stress theory and the family-centered empowerment model, the strategies presented require that FLE be culturally sensitive, family-centered, effective, and timely (Hennon & Peterson, 2006). The CRPE indicates that resource shortfalls are critical factors in intensifying family and parental stress, thus enriching families' cache of resources that increase protective factors and reduce risk factors is critical. Further, the CRPE indicates that families should be helped to develop effective and efficient stress management strategies. In order to build capacity for family resiliency, FLE should address the various components listed by Hennon and Peterson (2006) as well as the additional factors listed by Walsh (2002). However, the educator should be mindful of presenting information in such ways that it can be incorporated into parents' preexisting paradigms. While there is great diversity within any ethnic minority group, culture does play some role in how parents parent, and the cultural competency of family life educators is a necessary component of good programming. At the same time, caution must be maintained to not overgeneralize and thus *type* parents of a particular ethnic group as being like-minded and similar in parental concerns and practices.

Implications

Consistent with a systems approach, family life educators should work at various system levels to affect change and advocate for families. For example, at the community level, working for economic development and job creation, helping establish language programs, facilitating the creation of community resource centers offering one-stop service delivery services, promoting a childcare cooperative or other system, facilitating home-school relations, and working to reduce discrimination and acceptance of diverse families would all be important targets of interventions. Another often-useful resource is parental support groups, especially when composed of parents facing similar challenges (e.g., learning disabilities, acculturation issues, chronic illnesses, addictions) (Smith, Cudaback, Goddard & Myers-Walls, 1994). At the family level, improving parent-child communication, understanding child development and normative versus risky behaviors, developing effective parenting behaviors and attitudes, and assisting in the evaluation of potential resources would be empowering. Helping to develop knowledge of childcare options might be useful, and endorsing good home-school relations could be valuable. At the individual level, enhancing self-esteem, developing academic skills, and facilitating acquisition of human and social capital could prove important. Helping obtain knowledge of laws, regulations, healthcare systems and eligibility, norms of behavior, and customs of the dominant society might be especially helpful for immigrant and ethnocultural communities. FLE should address various resiliency components at the family and individual levels

Overall, parents may become more knowledgeable about protective and risk factors that influence the lives of children and youth, as well as parental responses and thus parental stress. Parents can also learn more effective disciplinary skills, communication techniques, the appropriate amount of monitoring of their children, the difference between necessary quests for autonomy by their children versus potentially dangerous or risky actions, and the like. Knowing how to deal more effectively with stressors is of major importance (Boss, 2002). Development of this knowledge and understanding can be facilitated when appropriate resources such as FLE are available.

FLE intended for U.S. Mexican immigrants requires sensitivity to influences of familism and extended family pressures and resources; cultural conditioning of gender, marital, and parenting roles, parental behaviors, child rearing values, and concerns about childcare; and other sources of parental stress such as economic pressures and difficulties with schools. Sensitivity should be given to degrees of assimilation/integration, and how acculturation creates stress, as there is pressure to change family roles and other aspects of life. FLE should be structured in ways that do not violate the vital role of ethnicity in living a fulfilling family life. Programmers should not assume that all people of Mexican heritage are alike in values, behavioral patterns, family organization, socioeconomic status, and sources of and ways of dealing with stress.

Good educators are sensitive to how essential knowledge and skills are transferred to learners in a manner that offers dialogue and respect for differences (Jacobson, 2003). Programs offered by members of the targeted population, or in a team approach with some members being of the same ethnicity and by native Spanish speakers as necessary, are desirable (Jacobson, 2003; Martínez, 1993). Programs could be offered in a non-formal manner with informal learning experiences, rather than more structured classroom-like activities, as Martínez (1988) suggested that people of Mexican heritage are less likely to participate in general parent education classes and such classes are less likely to retain them. Family centered approaches with professionals as facilitators rather than experts who know what parents need are desirable (Briar-Lawson et al., 2001; Jacobson, 2003). This approach involves parents in the identification of the need for parent education and the necessary content, as well as parental involvement in the design, implementation, and evaluation of programs.

For example, one study showed that teaching strategies such as the use of praise and directives believed to promote learning in children were associated with greater gains in task performance in Anglo American children, but not in Mexican American children (Moreno, 1997). Other research has indicated that ethnic minority families demonstrate inconsistent, less predictable, or less favorable outcomes (Kolobe, 2004). Assumedly, these outcomes are measured against the parenting values and behaviors of ethnic majorities. This difference in programmatic outcomes is perhaps due to programs not being culturally sensitive and specific (Wiley & Ebata, 2004). In one intervention designed for Mexican American mothers, maternal nurturing behaviors, parent-child interaction, and quality of the home environment were positively correlated with the infants' cognitive development (Kolobe, 2004). (Examples of FLE and other intervention resources for Mexican American families are available; see Hennon et al., 2006.)

Becoming a Culturally Competent Professional

Cultural competency, a valued expertise for family life educators, is an acquired skill and attitude that can be continuously updated. Cultural competency helps in realizing that not all families are alike, simply because they share some characteristic such as ethnic heritage, and they may differ in many ways including their goals for acculturation, experience with acculturative stress, and risk and protective factors faced. While it is difficult to become completely competent, approximations to this ideal are possible.

This bicultural/multicultural outlook helps the educator better grasp the worldview of populations targeted for programs, who might see and understand the world with a different paradigm than the one originally adhered to by the family life educator, while creating motivation and skills for designing and implementing appropriate FLE. We assume that culture is a factor in determining parenting schema for both family life educators and parents. For educators wanting to affect change in parental stress, this means realizing that parents are likely to attempt or resist change based on if the new information is in harmony with their culturally, ethnically, religiously, or socioeconomically based parenting scheme (Kolobe, 2004). The extent to which newly presented knowledge and skills are compatible with held values helps parents achieve desired cultural and family goals, and will determine the program's success.

Good FLE programming is research-based with valid information about the conditions of families and the determinants of parental stress. Finding such information about Mexican heritage immigrant families can be difficult. In addition to the relative lack of research grounded in theory and suitable cultural experience to ask relevant questions (and aptly interpret results), some information could present an idealized or proscriptive version of what families should be rather than the lived experience of such families (Anderson & Sabatelli, 2007). This typical view makes it difficult to consider the diversity found among, and the complexity of dynamics within, families.

Comparative research, the basis for much of the information on culture and child rearing, indicates how groups differ and are similar. However, these findings can obscure within-group variations (Kolobe, 2004) when relying on measures of central tendencies and describing the average ethnic heritage family. This is even truer when people of diverse origins are lumped together as Latinos or Hispanics and considered as a homogeneous group. Family life educators need to beware of committing an ecological/ethnic fallacy as they attempt to be culturally competent and design relevant programs. That is, just because a family is living in an area (ecology) or is ethnic and such families can be described as having certain characteristics (e.g., family size, income, or parenting practices) does not mean that *this* family will have the same characteristics. It is a fallacy to say that all families of a particular ethnic heritage will be alike. In an area distinguished as impoverished or membership in a group characterized by strict patriarchal power, educators might find families with adequate income or rather egalitarian decision-making. While families can derive meaning from cultural, ethnic, religious, geographical or other identifications, one cannot know to what extent these factors influence particular families and parenting without direct information from these families (Anderson & Sabatelli, 2007).

All Mexican heritage families are unique, and no family might match perfectly the model as represented through an amalgamation of divergent research. Family life educators should not reify the concept of the Mexican immigrant family or the generalizations about these families to the extent that they become the Mexican immigrant family. What are real are the everyday lives of people as they are living and being family. There are many ways of being family. Not all diversity, all uniqueness, all idiosyncratic variations can be described in a book, article, or book chapter, including this one.

It is important that research continues to investigate the sources of parental stress and how it can be prevented or remedied among ethnic minority immigrants, the pathways by which culture influences parental stress and child rearing practices, how this is impacted by acculturation and acculturative stress, how stress and child rearing practices are related to optimal/nonoptimal child development, and if these practices can be advantaged through FLE leading to more positive developmental outcomes and less parental stress. A review of literature to form the foundation for programming should indicate factors that might lead to parental stress as well as important sources of family strength or resiliency. As research accumulates, it is imperative that family life educators keep up to date with this literature and modify programming in necessary ways. Factual knowledge changes with time and becomes outdated. However, there are enduring understandings important for learning about and understanding Mexican heritage families (Wiggins & McTighe, 1998).

Enduring understandings are transferable ideas to help in being a lifelong learner of family diversity and being a culturally competent professional. Such understandings include: (a) interpreting family behavior from the point of view of its culture; (b) knowing where a family lives (e.g., culture, political system, available resources geography) because these influence how they live; (c) understanding that cultures are complex, not static, and vary in homogeneity or pluralism; (d) being aware that culture is dynamic and what is true at one time may not be true in another time, or what is true of that culture in one context may not hold for that culture in another context (e.g., after migration, urban compared to rural area); (e) knowing that not all families sharing a given culture or ethnicity will be alike nor will they necessarily share the same acculturation strategies or adapt to a new culture in a like manner; (f) understanding that some aspects of family life appear to be rather universal, while others are rather specific to certain groups; (g) being aware that more knowledge leads to better, more culturally appropriate programming; and (h) knowing that increased understanding can both lead to greater cultural-sensitivity and acceptance by reducing naive or provincial attitudes or beliefs, but can also lead only to enhanced awareness that can reinforce stereotypes, prejudice, and intolerance.

We believe that while people are often not able to function well within multiple groups, they can still develop awareness of, sensitivity to, and appreciation of other cultures that is meaningful and authentic. This can be termed enlightenment. With this level of sophistication, one still might not *fit in* or necessarily feel comfortable functioning in diverse cultures. A professional might not have the language skills or enough opportunities to "feel natural," and thus the cultural identity might still be indigenous to one's upbringing. However, cultural competency requires educating oneself and becoming enlightened to the family patterns of ethnic minorities to reduce naive or provincial attitudes or beliefs.

Conclusion

This chapter offered suggestions for a family centered, resiliency-based approach to the creation of culturally relevant education to empowering Mexican heritage, especially immigrant families, for preventing or reducing parental stress. FLE should be empirically grounded and theoretically informed. Good pedagogy is, of course, required. We believe that family centered approaches with participants as codevelopers of the design, content, and evaluation of the programming are best. We also caution the interventionist to be alert to a tendency to overgeneralize about ethnic groups.

References

Allen, W. D., & Blaisure, K. R. (2003). Family life educators and the development of cultural competency. In D. J. Bredehoft & M. J. Walcheski (Eds.), *Family life education: Integrating theory and practice* (pp. 10–21). Minneapolis: National Council on Family Relations.

Anderson, S. A., & Sabatelli, R. M. (2007). *Family interaction: A multigenerational developmental perspective* (4th ed). Boston: Allyn and Bacon.

Becerra, R. N. (1998). The Mexican-American family. In C. H. Mindel, R. W. Habenstein & R. Wright Jr. (Eds.), *Ethnic families in America: Patterns and variations* (4th ed., pp. 153–171). Upper Saddle River, NJ: Prentice Hall.

Berry, J. W. (2005, June). *Acculturation: Social, cultural, and psychological change among immigrants.* Paper presented during workshop Agency and Human Development under Conditions of Social Change, Jena, Germany.

Boss, P. G. (2002). *Family stress management* (2nd ed.). Mountain View, CA: Sage.

Briar-Lawson, K., Lawson, H. A., Hennon, C. B., & Jones, A. R. (2001). *Family-centered policies & practices: International implications.* New York: Columbia University Press.

Buriel, R. (1993). Childrearing orientations in Mexican American families: The influence of generation and sociocultural factors. *Journal of Marriage and Family, 55,* 987–1000.

Buriel, R., & Hurtado-Ortiz, M. T. (2000). Child-care practices and preferences of native- and foreign-born Latina mothers and Euro-American mothers. *Hispanic Journal of Behavioral Sciences, 22,* 314–331.

California Immigrant Welfare Collaborative. (2006). *Immigrants and the U.S. health-care system.* Sacramento, CA: Author.

Cox, C., & Monk, A. (1993). Hispanic culture and family care of Alzheimer's patients. *Health & Social Work, 18,* 92–100.

Crnic, K., & Low, C. (2002). Everyday stresses and parenting. In M. H. Bornstein (Ed.), *Handbook of parenting: Vol. 5: Practical issues in parenting* (2nd ed., pp. 243–267). Mahwah, NJ: Erlbaum.

Esteinou, R. (In press). Mexican families: Sociocultural and demographic patterns. In C. B. Hennon & S. M. Wilson (Eds.), *Handbook of families in cultural and international perspectives.* Binghamton, NY: Haworth Press.

Freeberg, A. L., & Stein, C. H. (1996). Felt obligations toward parents in Mexican-American and Anglo-American young adults. *Journal of Social and Personal Relationships, 13,* 457–471.

Haskins, R., Greenberg, M., & Fremstad, S. (2004). Federal policy for immigrant children: Room for common ground? *The Future of Children, 14*(2), 1–6.

Hennon, C. B., & Peterson, G. W. (2006). Estrés parental: Modelos teóricos y revisión de la literatura [Parenting stress: Theoretical models and a literature review]. In R. Esteinou (Ed.), *Fortalezas y desafíos de las familias en dos contextos: Estados Unidos de America y México* [Strengths and challenges of families in two contexts: The United States of America and Mexico]. México, DF: Centro de Investigaciones y Estudios Superiores en Antropología Social (CIESAS) y Sistema Nacional para el Desarrollo Integral de la Familia (DIF).

Hennon, C. B., Peterson, G. W., Polzin, L., & Radina, M. E. (2006). Familias de ascendencia mexicana residentes en Estados Unidos: recursos para el manejo del estrés parental [Resident families of Mexican ancestry in United States: Resources for the handling of parental stress]. In R. Esteinou (Ed.), *Fortalezas y desafíos de las familias en dos contextos: Estados Unidos de America y México* [Strengths and challenges of families in two contexts: The United States of America and Mexico]. México, DF: Centro de Investigaciones y Estudios Superiores en Antropología Social (CIESAS) y Sistema Nacional para el Desarrollo Integral de la Familia (DIF).

Hernandez, D. (2004). Demographic change and the life circumstances of immigrant children. *The Future of Children, 14*(2), 17–48.

Hildebrand, V., Phenice, L. A., Gray, M. M., & Hines, R. P. (2000). *Knowing and serving diverse families* (2nd ed.). Upper Saddle River, NJ: Merrill.

Hill, N. E., Bush, K. R., & Roosa, M. W. (2003). Parenting and family socialization strategies and children's mental health: Low-income Mexican-American and Euro-American mothers and children. *Child Development, 74,* 189–204.

Jacobson, A. L. (2003). Parent education and guidance. In D. J. Bredehoft & M. J. Walcheski (Eds.), *Family life education: Integrating theory and practice* (pp. 110–116). St. Paul, MN: National Council on Family Relations.

Kolobe, T. H. A. (2004). Childrearing practices and developmental expectations for Mexican-American mothers and the developmental status of their infants. *Physical Therapy, 84,* 439–453.

Kuczynski, L. (2003). Beyond bidirectionality: Bilateral conceptual frameworks for understanding dynamics in parent-child relations. In L. Kuczynski (Ed.), *Handbook of dynamics in parent-child relations* (pp. 3–24). Thousand Oaks, CA: Sage.

Lugo Steidel, A. G., & Contreras, J. M. (2003). A new familism scale for use with Latino populations. *Hispanic Journal of Behavioral Sciences, 25,* 312–330.

Martínez, E. A. (1988). Child behavior in Mexican American/Chicano families: Maternal teaching and child rearing practices. *Family Relations, 37,* 275–280.

Martínez, E. A. (1993). Parenting young children in Mexican American/Chicano families. In H. P. McAdoo (Ed.), *Family ethnicity: Strength in diversity* (pp. 184–195). Newbury Park, CA: Sage.

Martínez, E. A., & Mehan, H. (1997). *Contextual factors surrounding Hispanic dropouts.* Washington, DC: National Center for Bilingual Education. Retrieved July 26, 2004, from www.ncbe.gwu.edu/ miscpubs/hdp/1.

Moreno, R. P. (1997). Everyday instruction: A comparison of Mexican American and Anglo mothers and their preschool children. *Hispanic Journal of Behavioral Sciences, 19,* 527–539.

Niemann, Y. F., Romero, A. J., Arredondo, J., & Rodriguez, V. (1999). What does it mean to be "Mexican"? Social construction of an ethnic identity. *Hispanic Journal of Social Sciences, 21,* 47–60.

Parke, R. D., Coltrane, S., Duffy, S., Buriel, R., Dennis, J., Powers, J., French, S., & Widaman, K. F. (2004). Economic stress, parenting, and child adjustment in Mexican American and European American families. *Child Development, 75,* 1632–1656.

Perez, W., & Padilla, A. M. (2000). Cultural orientation across three generations of Hispanic adolescents. *Hispanic Journal of Behavioral Sciences, 22,* 390–398.

Peterson, G. W., & Hann, D. (1999). Socializing children and parents in families. In M. B. Sussman, S. K. Steinmetz & G. W. Peterson (Eds.), *Handbook of marriage and the family* (2nd ed., pp. 327–370). New York: Plenum.

Peterson, G. W., & Hennon, C. B. (2005). Conceptualizing parental stress with family stress theory. In P. C. McKenry & S. J. Price (Eds.), *Families and change: Coping with stressful events and transitions* (3rd ed., pp. 25–48). Thousand Oaks, CA: Sage.

Phillips, J., & Massey, D. S. (2000). Engines of immigration: Stocks of human and social capital in Mexico. *Social Science Quarterly, 81*, 33–48.

Plunkett, S. W., & Bámaca-Gómez, M. Y. (2003). The relationship between parenting, acculturation, and adolescent academics in Mexican-origin immigrant families in Los Angeles. *Hispanic Journal of Behavioral Sciences, 25*, 222–239.

Ramirez, R. R., & de la Cruz, G. P. (2002). *The Hispanic population in the United States: March 2002.* Retrieved November 21, 2004, from Current Population Reports, P20-545 Website: www.census. gov/prod/2003pubs/p20-545.pdf.

Sanchez, Y. (1997). Families of Mexican origin. In M. K. DeGenova (Ed.), *Families in cultural context* (pp. 61–81). Mountain View, CA: Mayfield.

Smith, C. A., Cudaback, D., Goddard, H. W., & Myers-Walls, J. A. (1994). *National extension parent education model.* Manhattan: Kansas Cooperative Extension Service.

U.S. Census. (2000). *Race and Hispanic or Latino: 2000.* Retrieved July 13, 2005, from factfinder.census.gov.

U.S. Census. (2003a). *Hispanic Heritage Month 2003: Sept. 15–Oct. 15.* Retrieved September 29, 2004, from www.census.gov/Press-Release/www/2003/cb03-ff14.html.

U.S. Census. (2003b). *Pct006. Hispanic or Latino by specific origin—universe: Total population.* Retrieved September 29, 2004, from factfinder.census.gov.

Valentine, S., & Mosley, G. (2000). Acculturation and sex-role attitudes among Mexican Americans: A longitudinal analysis. *Hispanic Journal of Behavioral Sciences, 22*, 104–113.

Voydanoff, P., & Donnelly, B. W. (1998). Parents' risk and protective factors as predictors of parental well-being and behavior. *Journal of Marriage and Family, 60*, 344–355.

Walsh, F. (2002). A family resilience framework: Innovative practice applications. *Family Relations, 51*, 130–137.

Wiggins, G. P., & McTighe, J. (1998). *Understanding by design.* Alexandria, VA: Association for Supervision and Curriculum Development.

Wiley, A. R., & Ebata, A. (2004). Reaching American families: Making diversity real in family life education. *Family Relations, 53*, 273–281.

Zinn, M. B. (1998). Adaptation and continuity in Mexican-origin families. In R. L. Taylor (Ed.), *Minority families in the United States: A multicultural perspective* (2nd ed., pp. 77–94). Upper Saddle River, NJ: Prentice Hall.

About the Authors

Charles B. Hennon, Ph.D., CFLE, is a professor in the Department of Family Studies and Social Work and Associate Director, Center for Human Development, Learning, and Technology at Miami University, 101 McGuffey Hall, Oxford, OH 45056. Phone: 513-529-4908. Fax: 513-529-6468. E-mail: hennoncb@muohio.edu.

M. Elise Radina, Ph.D., CFLE, is an assistant professor of Family Studies in the Department of Family Studies and Social Work at Miami University, 101 McGuffey Hall, Oxford, OH 45056. Phone: 513-529-3639. Fax: 513-529-6468. E-mail: radiname@muohio.edu.

Stephan M. Wilson, Ph.D., CFLE, is a professor in the Department of Human Development and Family Studies and associate dean for the College of Health and Human Services at the University of Nevada, Reno, Mail Stop 136, Reno, NV 89557. Phone: 775-682-7496. Fax: 775-784-6979. E-mail: swilson@unr.edu.

The Impact of Latino Immigrants and Bicultural Program Coordinators on Organizational Philosophy and Values

19

A Case Study of Organizational Responsiveness

LYNET UTTAL

Abstract

The author discusses how organizations serving Spanish-speaking immigrant Latinos can be more responsive to the culturally specific philosophies immigrants bring with them. This is accomplished through the use of a case study developed over the first two years of the creation of the Latino Family Childcare Project, a family childcare provider certification program. Challenges to achieving full organizational responsiveness to Latino worldviews and organizational cultural competency are discussed.

Keywords: Latino Immigrants, Program Effectiveness, Organizational Change, Cultural Competency, Bicultural Program Coordinators

SERVING THE LATINO IMMIGRANT population poses important questions concerning cultural competency and resource allocation for agencies. Although previous academic literature has emphasized how developing cultural competency is important for understanding cultural diversity, establishing relationships with clients, and culturally adapting programs, the exploration of how organizations respond when met with cultural differences has been limited. The area of cultural competency has focused more on program adaptations and the interpersonal style between service providers and clients, than on how organizational philosophies and operating principles can change in order to incorporate the worldviews of ethnically different populations. This chapter presents, from the perspective of Latina immigrant women and a researcher involved in action-oriented, community-based research, the changes that participants brought with them to an organization that had not previously served Latino immigrants. I use both my observations at workshops and my informal discussions with the bilingual/bicultural program coordinators and planning team to illustrate how Latino immigrants challenge organizations to be more culturally responsive and competent.

As the numbers of Spanish-speaking immigrants requiring social services has increased in the United States, the need to develop culturally informed programs has become a major concern of social service agencies. To establish more culturally competent services, services are altered to fit with the values and practices of the intended audience (Malley-Morrison & Hines, 2004). There are several ways to make these modifications. First, individual staff practice greater cultural competency in their interactions with clients (Weaver, 2005). Second, program curriculum are adapted to the culture of the populations being targeted (Cheng Gorman, 1996; Malley-Morrison & Hines, 2004). Third, accessibility is also encouraged by providing incentives for people that may be unfamiliar with and reluctant to participate in programs, such as conducting raffles and providing childcare, meals, and transportation at meetings (Gross, Julion & Fogg, 2000). And despite many good intentions, the stories of cultural conflicts continue.

Cultural misunderstandings are not unexpected, given that different cultural groups not only hold different philosophical views, but also the words that are used to describe these views are not easily translatable and explainable from one language to another. The same word in one language may have a different meaning in another, requiring careful attention to word choice (Erkut, Alarcon, Garcia Coll, Tropp & Vazquez Garcia, 1999). Misunderstandings occur, for example, when a Spanish-speaking immigrant says that she values "educación" and this is translated as "education," what is lost in translation is that the immigrant does not mean only formal K–12 education, as assumed by the listener from the United States, but rather something broader that has to do with how the individual is in relationship to their community. According to Latino cultures, an educated person is someone who has awareness of others around oneself, not just a person who has achieved a higher level of classroom education.

While *translation* is a necessary modification, translated materials alone are not sufficient to make a program culturally competent and effective (Cheng Gorman & Balter, 1997). Even if the program is in the language of the target group, the examples used to teach the curriculum may not reflect the practices of the target group (Cheng Gorman & Balter, 1997). Going one step further, programs need to be culturally *adapted*. In culturally adapted programs, the examples that are used to teach the main lessons are transformed to respect the target culture's practices. For example, in a culture that does not verbally express self-emotions, the expectation for people to talk about themselves is dropped. By replacing *I* statements exercises with *other* discussions, such as scenarios, the original lessons of a program are left in tact but change the style of learning.

However, cultural adaptations of elements of the program curriculum may still not go far enough. Cheng Gorman (1996) makes another important distinction between culturally adapted programs and those that are culturally specific. In *culturally specific* programs, the transformations go beyond adding culturally adapted components within a predefined program curriculum. To make a program culturally specific, the philosophy and underlying assumptions of the program integrate the target group's values and beliefs. This change requires that the assumptions of the overall program are critically examined and the program philosophy is altered to reflect the worldview of the target population. For example, conventional parent education programs that are child-centered and emphasize the individual child's development may not work with participants who come from family-centered cultures. Latino immigrant parents may find the child-centered notions of child development in the United States strange and offensive. To become culturally specific, a program would incorporate the value of family and community into its philosophy of parenting.

What has received less attention in research and practice is how organizations may need to develop not only the cultural competency of the content of their programs or interpersonal staff-client communication styles, but also the cultural competency of their organizational philosophy. Organizations also develop their own particular set of values and operating principles. The current and past assumptions that demarcate the commonly held organizational views, beliefs, and values define organizational culture (Bernard, 1998). Organizational values are delineated by its governing board, staff and community, its mission statement about the agency's values, the fiscal state of the agency, attitudes toward equity-related initiatives, the ethnic composition of the staff, and its relationship with traditionally un-derrepresented groups. According to Bernard (1998), organizations need to adapt and let go of outmoded assumptions and operating principles in order to more effectively work with new populations.

Organizational cultural competency is typically measured by several characteristics, including the racial and ethnic diversity of its staff, whether an organization's mission statement acknowledges and supports the im-portance of cultural diversity, if staff are expected to receive training in cultural competency, and if the organizational environment is perceived as welcoming by the clients who use it (Geron, 2002). In addition to special program services and adaptations for clients, which include such changes as the provision of interpreter services for all services, coordination with community workers and traditional caregivers, and immersion knowledge of another culture, changes in the administrative and organizational prac-tices can also increase the cultural competency of an agency's staff and its programming (Geron, 2002). Not surprisingly, the beliefs that clients have about how services work may not be the same as the way the organization intends that they should be carried out.

Building on these ideas, this chapter suggests that the philosophy and assumptions of an organization need to be reconsidered in order to achieve organizational cultural competency. In this example, I will show how one agency responded to serving a new Latino immigrant population. While it took the first steps of changing its staffing and culturally adapting one of its programs, it did not fully respond by transforming the overall service philosophy of the organization within which the program was embedded. However, what is instructive from this case study is how organizational philosophy, and not just specific programs or staffpersons, also need to be-come more culturally specific. There are lessons that can be learned from this case about how the foundational philosophy of organizations also need to be transformed to take into account the community-based philosophy of new Latino immigrants.

First, I introduce the case study and the methods used to develop the interpretative analysis. Then I present examples of where the Latina im-migrant program participant's values and practices conflicted with the program's expectations, and how these were resolved by adaptations made by the program coordinators. I examine how the misunderstandings went deeper than program content and design. In the third section, I explain some of the fundamental philosophical differences that Latina program participants and Latina program coordinators had with the agency about the purpose of the certification program and how to achieve those goals.

Finally, I conclude with recommendations for how an organization can be more culturally responsive to these philosophical differences between itself and the new Latino immigrant populations they serve.

Methods

The analysis developed in this chapter is an interpretive one grounded in workshop observations, a few interviews, and discussion meetings between myself, the program coordinator, and students who were working together to create a family childcare provider certification program in Spanish and conducting research to understand the experience of Latino immigrant families in the Midwest. The question that organizes the analysis in this chapter is not an empirical, descriptive phenomenological, or program evaluation. Instead, this analysis addresses an abstract conceptual idea and practical concern about how organizations that serve Spanish-speaking, new immigrant Latinos/as can be more responsive to the culturally specific philosophies that immigrants bring with them. The analysis is based on the first two years of the development of the Latino Family Childcare Project, a family childcare provider certification program in Spanish. The Latino Family Childcare Project was developed by a county level childcare resource and referral agency to increase the number of certified Spanish-speaking family childcare providers through certification. The program was a response to concerns about the accessibility and quality of childcare services for the growing Latino immigrant population in Madison, Wisconsin. Between 1990 and 2000, the Latino population almost tripled in this medium-sized, midwestern city. Official numbers stated that 15,000 live in Dane County (University of Wisconsin Extension & Applied Laboratory, 2001), whereas those working with Latinos assumed that this is a gross undercount. Social services agencies felt the increasing demand to serve Spanish-speaking immigrants and were developing their programs in Spanish.

The goal of the Latino Family Childcare Project was to certify Spanish-speaking family childcare providers. Family childcare providers typically care for their own children as well as other people's children in their own homes. By increasing the number of certified referrals, the agency hoped to increase the accessibility and quality of childcare available to Spanish-speaking immigrant families.

This program was the first one to be offered in Spanish by this particular agency. First, they hired a bilingual program coordinator to be the director of the project and provide workshops in Spanish. Over the course of two years, the project had two bilingual/bicultural program coordinators. The first step was to translate the existing certification program and materials into Spanish. By the end of the first year, a basic program was successfully established. The application and training materials were translated into Spanish, and arrangements were made for the early childhood education courses to be offered in Spanish through the local community college and training workshops. The program coordinator also removed obstacles and encouraged participation by holding workshops on weekends, providing transportation, and having childcare during workshops. She also offered incentives for participation such as providing meals and raffles of childcare equipment, children's books, and toys.

The Latino Family Childcare Project quickly moved forward in many applaudable ways. Attendance increased steadily, with as many as seventy participants at a workshop at its peak. The program was being attended by Spanish-speaking immigrants, representing women of diverse ages and countries of origin, and a few men. At the end of the second year, the program had successfully certified thirty-two Spanish-speaking family childcare providers.

The first program coordinator invited me, a university researcher, to work with her because I had been attending the citywide committee where the idea for a Spanish certification program was hatched. At each workshop, the bilingual program coordinator introduced me as a researcher from the university and participants were told that this information would be used to both improve the workshops as well as to learn more about the experience of Latino immigrants in the Midwest. I attended every workshop that was offered by the program in its first two years. I assisted with set-up and clean-up, and participated as an observer during the workshops, since I do not speak Spanish fluently enough to facilitate a workshop. All of my observations of the workshops were done with a translator by my side who not only translated the discussion, but also explained things to me that she thought I would need to understand about the culture because I am not of Latino heritage. In addition, three to five Spanish-speaking Latina graduate and undergraduate students were positioned at different places in the room and observed the workshops. They also collected topics and comments from side conversations that were frequently going on during the workshop.

The interpretive analysis written in this chapter is constructed by myself primarily from post-workshop dialogues between myself, the program coordinators, and student observers. This dialogical approach combines the dual focus approach used by Erkut et al. (1999) to determine the accurate meaning of translated terms, and the consensual qualitative analysis team approach used by Hill, Thompson, and Williams (1997) to arrive at consensual agreement about the themes found in ethnographic data (see Erkut et al., 1999, for how this is applied to research instrument development). However, it diverges from these two approaches in that this paper applies a solo-authored Heideggerian hermeneutical approach that acknowledges that every researcher could develop their own interpretation. The purpose of my analysis in this chapter is to extrapolate what can be learned from this particular case study about organizational cultural responsiveness to the values and practices of Latino immigrants.

In our post-workshop discussions, we focused on how to improve the certification program. Many materials were being developed for the first time at the same time that the program was being implemented. Changes were made, often in response to things that were not working well. Often, there was not enough time or staff support to plan the program, translate the materials, and organize workshops in a smooth manner. Furthermore, workshops were constantly experiences of the unanticipated. For example, the Spanish-dubbed videos of American family childcare homes showed practices that the program coordinator had not anticipated would capture the attention of the Latina women and need to be discussed at great length. These required on-the-spot transformations of the individual workshop curricula as well as post-workshop discussions that were often about how to introduce ideas so they would be better received and the program would go more smoothly.

These planning discussions were primarily conducted in English. However, they switched into Spanish when the meaning needed to be more carefully articulated, and then translated back into English. Members of the planning team spoke several different dialects and levels of Spanish.

Another ongoing level of discussion between myself and the two successive coordinators centered around how the larger agency was responding to their modifications to the certification program. Both program coordinators were constantly struggling with explaining the logic of their changes to the agency. The agency questioned their actions and decisions, such as why the program coordinators needed more time with each participant before and after the workshops. The coordinator explained to the agency how family childcare and government regulation of care were new ideas to Latino immigrants. She also explained how the application process required more hours per client than the agency budgeted for its English-speaking applicants. The official process to become a certified provider begins with filling out an application, submitting names of all persons living in their residence for background checks, and tuberculin tests required of all persons living in the home. The potential childcare provider must also submit the names and addresses of two unrelated individuals that will serve as references to her or his character. Additionally, many of the applicants lacked the formal education about how to fill out applications and this required more individual attention than what most English-speaking applicants required. Every step required the coordinators to walk with the participants and provide explanations. The program coordinator also had to justify the importance of the meal as an incentive and the necessity of providing childcare if Latina women were to be able to leave their homes for a meeting. Explanations to the agency about these differences were just as time-consuming as explanations of the new ideas to the participants.

A final source of data comes from written comments on the workshop evaluation forms, three focus groups with certified and uncertified Latino family childcare providers, and seven individual in-depth interviews with certified Latino family childcare providers. Bilingual graduate students conducted the focus groups and four of the interviews in Spanish. I conducted three in-depth interviews in English with bilingual speakers. The interviews and focus groups were organized for a separate project to ask participants why they thought so many people who did not plan to become family childcare providers were attending the workshops. In addition to these questions, we also asked participants to evaluate the usefulness and organization of the workshops. Oral consent only was obtained at the interviews because my institutional review board deemed it a risk to immigrants, some of whom may be undocumented, to ask them to identify themselves in writing on consent forms.

Taking the Context of Latina Immigrant Lives into Account

Many of the cultural discontinuities that occurred are typical encounters that arise when an agency develops a new program with a culturally unique population. To deliver a culturally adapted program, the program coordinator made several program modifications to the program curriculum. Another less well understood dimension of the extra adaptations is how the social context of the Latina immigrants' lives also needs to be taken into account if the program messages are to be received. According to Kumpfer, Alvarado, Smith, and Bellamy (2002), cultural adaptations have to go beyond adapting program materials or changing recruitment methods.

They also recommend taking into account the structural context of where the population has migrated to (rural, suburban, urban), educational and economic backgrounds, acculturation level, and self-identification (both individually and as a subgroup). To this list, I would also add how the participants' view themselves in relationship to the larger society around them. In this case study, acknowledging themselves as a Pan-Latino group that stood apart from mainstream U.S. society and culture created a collective identity that glued this diverse group together. These different aspects of the context of the lives of clients affect the effectiveness of programs (Harvard Family Research Project, 1996).

However, most programs do not consider these material conditions or identity issues in the core formulation of their programs, even though these are important aspects that shape human development (Garcia Coll, Meyer & Brillon, 1995). For example, one of the most pressing contextual issues for Latino immigrants is the legality of immigration status. Not only were many of the basic steps of the certification process new to the Latina immigrants, but they also created new steps for the agency. For example, the increasing number of undocumented applicants meant that the question arose about whether they could participate without social security numbers. The agency did not anticipate that they would need to broaden their services to include dealing with immigration policies and trying to determine if their publicly funded programs could be used to recruit, train, and certify undocumented Latino immigrants. (When the program started, the agency could substitute taxpayer identification numbers for social security numbers. This has recently changed and the agency is now requiring social security numbers from all applicants.)

Because of this legal context, Latino participants were also wary of engagement in any relationship with the government, even if they were documented. Both undocumented and documented women worried that background checks might lead to being deported. They objected to requests to conduct background checks on their household members, and these were even more threatening if some of their household members were undocumented. To address this concern, the program coordinator added information about immigration policy and processes to the workshops, and the agency had to investigate the legal ramifications of certifying undocumented workers. This change was necessary to ensure Latinos that they were not putting themselves or their families at risk when they engaged in the certification process and to also protect the agency.

Programs are also typically not prepared to address the racism that their participants experience. This issue came up when Latino participants tried to fulfill the requirement to obtain landlord consent. Although the requirements were the same for the English-speaking providers, the Spanish-speaking population had heightened difficulty with this program requirement because this target population is culturally and racially distinct. Participants reported that landlords were resistant to the establishment of family childcare homes in their rentals. They reported that some landlords made pejorative comments about overcrowded Latino housing conditions and how many children Latino families have.

Another impact on the program was that participants' information needs were never limited to the specific service (in this case, the certification program) being provided. Participants were often also dealing with an array of pressing, basic life-support issues, such as trying to find stable jobs, food, healthcare, housing needs, how to use the transportation systems, and school issues, as well as culturally specific issues such as citizenship status, discrimination, learning English, and bicultural parenting issues. They brought these concerns with them to the workshops and they were different from English-speaking applicants in that they expected the bilingual program coordinator to be an information resource for their general life needs. Often times, the bilingual program coordinator was their only point of contact with someone who could translate and explain to them how to navigate social services in the United States. Thus, it is not surprising that the certification workshops also became a site of community education around issues pertaining to the well-being of children and families.

To the outsider who is only familiar with the conventional English certification program, this attention to other issues in the Spanish workshops may have seemed chaotic or appeared as if the program was getting off track of the certification objectives. For example, an outsider might wonder what do conversations about using canned goods versus cooking from scratch have anything to do with certification? And yet, in the workshop about the food program for family childcare providers, this was a major discussion because many of the participants were not familiar with cooking with canned goods.

This expectation changed the nature of the job that the program coordinator had been originally hired to do. The coordinators found that when working with a population from a non-American culture and whose primary language is Spanish, it required them to respond to all kinds of information needs. This put a high demand on the program coordinator to know the full range of services and resources in the community as well as to act as a translator. Working beyond the official expectations of one's job duties was a common experience. Providing services to non-English-speaking immigrants also required a much broader integration and referral to several organizational social services as well as a deep understanding of the cultural differences that confuse communication and understanding.

Many of the services being provided by the program coordinator were not fully acknowledged or recognized in the agency's formal structure and expectations of the bilingual certification program. This difference suggests how cultural competency is more than a set of skills that individual staff acquire to work with clients. How staff in the same agency work with one another in response to serving a new population is transformed. This in turn can also have a transformative effect on how the goals of an organization are defined and achieved.

Organizational cultural competency is developed as a matter of the daily workings of the staff in the agency. Achieving this kind of organizational cultural competency will also become a more common challenge as agencies increasingly hire staff that are members of the culture they serve, such as hiring a Spanish or Hmong speaker to deliver a program in their mother tongue. In the past, the staff and agency stood on common ground as professionals, working with the client as "*other*." Now, not only is the client the *other*, but some staff can also be the *other* in an organization that views them more like the clients they serve than the original members of the agency. It also calls for additional attention to the role of newly hired bicultural program staff who may be culturally closer to their clients than their coworkers in the agency.

In sum, workshop participants requested information and training in topics that were not part of the certification requirements. Although the program coordinator understood this request and made accommodations, the agency had more difficulty taking into account these contextual and structural factors. Understanding would have required changing and making programmatic shifts in job descriptions and program delivery.

In the next section, I examine how the coordinators' program transformations challenged the agency to develop a more culturally specific program philosophy. Although this transformation was not successfully implemented into practice, many lessons can be learned about how to achieve this kind of philosophical cultural specificity from what did not happen.

Beyond Translation and Program Adaptations to Culturally Specific Organizational Responses

For the agency to be responsive to this Latino immigrant population would have required a major change in the philosophical assumption about whom the agency was supposed to serve and how they would do this. The agency approached the original certification program with a client-centered approach and it viewed its role as screening and providing training for individuals to open family childcare homes.

Yet, as the program developed, the program coordinator realized that in order to develop a local system of Latino-regulated childcare, the Latino community at large had to be educated about the legitimacy of regulating childcare services and general education was needed about family childcare homes. If Latinos were going to embrace the idea of regulated childcare, the program coordinator knew she needed to allow a broader scope of participants at workshops than just those who wanted to become family childcare providers. In addition to those who knew they wanted to become family childcare providers, parents and grandparents who wanted to learn about child rearing in the United States were also present at workshops. She also allowed workshops to be more open to questions and discussions about bicultural child rearing in the United States in order to encourage them to understand certified childcare standards. These open discussions broadened the focus of workshops away from the certification curriculum and invited in a more general population. These practices were more labor-intensive and far-reaching than the intentions of the agency when it embarked on translating its certification program into Spanish.

Similarly, the Spanish workshop participants told the bilingual program coordinator that they wanted a culturally specific program that addressed their interests holistically and as a community instead of just addressing their individual development as family childcare providers. The Spanish program participants embraced an alternative philosophy that viewed the program as serving the larger Latino community, not just individual providers and children. Although the program coordinator embraced these new directions, the agency was less responsive to this newly introduced community orientation.

The key cultural transformation needed in this case would have required rethinking who the *client* is—an individual person or the whole community of which the client is a member. Educational programs typically target individual-level behaviors because they are easier to change than the values and cultural practices of an entire ethnic group. Even though most social-service programs acknowledge the context and social ills that created the individual circumstances of their clients, the conventional agency approach is typically designed to work through a dyadic relationship between the social-service worker and an individual client. They often still relegate contextual factors and communalistic values to the background and focus the intervention on what the individual can do to strengthen and improve her or his life (Moos, 2003). The underlying philosophy of such client-centered programs emphasizes the importance of personal independence, individual competence, and autonomy of the individual. They rely heavily on treatment methods where the goal is to transform the life of an individual and to empower the individual to improve her or his personal circumstances. Even when social support is included as part of the intervention or treatment, social support is often viewed only as a wrap-around service to the client, and the importance of contexts and social relationships between the client and others are not viewed as the target of treatment or intervention. However, focusing on individual behavioral change is a color-blind approach that sidesteps attention to the culturally specific community-based orientation of Latino immigrants.

In this case, part of the reason that a philosophical shift was needed to account for more than individual development was that the needs of the individual were greater than what individual education alone could provide. Latino immigrant participants needed to know more about bicultural child rearing because the larger social context, American society, did not support their communalistic practices of child rearing. Workshop participants wanted more education in child growth and development training because they felt it would benefit the community and would help them understand better how to raise children biculturally in the United States.

This case suggests that organizational cultural competency—reshaping the philosophy of program delivery and organizational assumptions—may require a shift from the more typical individualistic, client-centered perspective to a holistic, community-based orientation if they are going to work in a culturally competent way with Latino immigrant populations. Because the way Spanish-speaking clients and program coordinators perceived, conceived of, and used this particular certification program was different from the original objectives defined by the agency, they asked the agency to reconsider how it conceived of, delivered, and viewed their services. They wanted the agency to embrace a more community-based philosophy. For them, community development and social support could not be disentangled from individual development.

Agency philosophies that do not understand an "ethos of community spirit" (Wandesman, 2003) will have a hard time understanding what appears to be a lack of efficiency, the inappropriate participation of non-targeted populations, and the misuse of their resources. Weaver (2005) argues that agencies might achieve a community-driven perspective by giving more attention to empowerment and developing the advocacy skills of their clients, especially if clients come from a community that has a community-based worldview. Weaver also recommends that problem identification, assessment, planning, goal setting, and implementation should all be done with community members as cultural guides and mentors. In addition, I would add that the authority to make changes needs to be given to the bilingual/bicultural program coordinators who have been hired to develop new culturally specific programs.

This example is instructive of the need for an organization to shift from client-centered programs to a community-based orientation in order to achieve organizational cultural competency. In this case, the agency did not change to develop this kind of organizational cultural competency, but the points of difference are informative about what changes might have been made.

Implications for Organizational Cultural Competency

Another measure of organizational cultural competency is whether new programs and methods suggested by new staff or clients are integrated into the agency rather than marginalized or rejected. Instead of conceiving cultural competency as a process in which newcomers' views and practices are selectively added onto the existing organizational philosophy, an organization that has achieved an integrated organizational cultural competency would reflect how the organization is able to knit together new and old approaches, developing transformed modes of operation and practices into a new organizational culture. Moos (2003) refers to this aspect of organizational culture as the importance of considering suprapersonal factors, that acknowledge that "when individuals come together in a social group, they bring with them social resources, abilities, and preferences. The aggregate of the members' attributes, or suprapersonal environment, in part defines the subculture that forms in a group, and in turn, its members' values and behaviors" (p. 3). This notion of a suprapersonal environment is useful to apply here to assess whether an organization is integrating the new ideas that come from the new bicultural staff. Not all members in any organization have the same power and influence to shape and define the dominant practices and values of the group, thus making it even more important for existing organizations to be hyper-attentive and responsive to the ideas proposed by new members, especially those who have been hired to culturally adapt programs to serve a new population. As the bilingual coordinator redesigned the program to take this into account, she also asked the agency to change some of its assumptions. This perspective brought to the agency new knowledge about Latino immigrants and how to incorporate their values and considerations into the agency's existing philosophy.

The agency was partially responsive to Latinos in the following ways:

- The agency hired a bilingual/bicultural staff person who was initially given full autonomy to redesign the certification program so that it would encourage the participation of Latino immigrants. The program coordinator provided the certification program in Spanish and allowed room for free-ranging discussions that gave new immigrants a deeper understanding of how things work in the United States.
- The program provided resources that addressed some of the culturally specific obstacles to participation, such as transportation (many of the women did not drive), and childcare (many of the women would not leave their children at home with others).
- The program was organized around a meal and encouraged social networking which was an incentive to participate for new immigrants who were socially isolated and looking for information from others about making the transition into U.S. society.
- The program content was redesigned and time was given to begin the curriculum where the target population was in order to ensure that they understood the program guidelines and assumptions (e.g., explaining what family childcare is and government regulation of care).
- The program coordinator allowed topics that initially appeared to be extraneous to the program objectives to be added to the curriculum (e.g., adding immigration information).
- The process at workshops was fluid, allowing many opportunities for participants to voice their opinions and question the program expectations. This questioning was used by the program coordinator to better understand their worldview and change fundamental assumptions about what the program was trying to achieve.
- The content and organizing philosophy of the program shifted from a client-centered, individual development approach to a broader purpose that embraced a community-based ethos.

Most of these changes were at the program level and were dependent upon the program coordinator's willingness to support the participants to go in the direction most meaningful to them.

Where the program ran into limits in achieving organizational cultural competency was when some of the changes driven by the program participants and the bilingual program coordinators were disallowed by the larger umbrella agency. For example, in the second year, the agency saw the attendance of people not directly seeking certification as an unnecessary expense rather than recognizing it as part of a larger Latino worldview that the program served Latino community education and development. Also in the second year, the second coordinator was given much less autonomy to design the program and was held more accountable to a supervisor in the agency before taking action. The agency was more resistant to continuing these program changes, especially moving from a client-centered to a community-centered approach.

What all this suggests is that an iterative process at all levels (between the clients and the program coordinator, between the program coordinators and their supervisors, and between staff and agency directors) is also needed to achieve cultural competency. One way that the agency might have adjusted to this broader purpose would have been to step back and see a larger vision of what they were trying to accomplish. Instead of making certification the primary goal of the program, certification could be reconceived as a community-based strategy used to move toward the greater goal of higher quality childcare and better knowledge about child rearing in the community.

Some of the questions that an agency trying to achieve organizational cultural competency with Latino immigrant populations might ask itself are:

- What practices do agencies have in place to learn about the worldview and expectations of Latino immigrants?
- How can agencies who understand that their outcome objective is individual development change to see the importance and success of their program in larger community-based terms?
- How can agencies implement a process that incorporates the new ideas brought by their bicultural program coordinators and clients to impact on the philosophy of the organization?

Cultural competency goes deeper than translation and adapting the components of an existing program. It also calls for organizations to re-think their operating assumptions and find authentic ways to incorporate the hopes, values, and beliefs of the target population and newly hired bilingual/bicultural staff. Making an authentic move from culturally adapted programming toward culturally specific organizational cultural competency depends on whether the organization will share leadership and authority so that the participants and program coordinators truly impact upon the operating assumptions of the organization.

Acknowledgments

Special thanks to Leticia Frausto, Lilliana Saldaña, Ane Marinez Lora, and Theresa Segura, who participated in the data collection that supported this analysis and Laura Pinsoneault for her careful reading and suggestions.

References

Bernard, J. A. (1998). Cultural competence plans: A strategy for the creation of a culturally competent system of care. In M. Hernandez & M. R. Isaacs (Eds.), *Promoting cultural competence in children's mental health services* (pp. 29–45). Baltimore: Paul Brookes Publishing.

Cheng Gorman, J. (1996). *Culturally-sensitive parent education programs for ethnic minorities.* No. PC Reports 7-96-26. New York University.

Cheng Gorman, J., & Balter, L. (1997). Culturally sensitive parent education: A critical review of quantitative research. *Review of Educational Research, 67*(3), 339–369.

Erkut, S., Alarcon, O., Garcia Coll, C., Tropp, L. R., & Vazquez Garcia, H. (1999). The dual-focus approach to creating bilingual measures. *Journal of Cross-Cultural Psychology, 30,* 206–218.

Garcia Coll, C., Meyer, E. C., & Brillon, L. (1995). Ethnic and minority parenting. In M. H. Bornstein (Ed.), *Handbook of parenting* (Vol. 2, pp. 189–209). Mahwah, NJ: Erlbaum.

Geron, S. M. (2002). Cultural competency: How is it measured? Does it make a difference? *Generations, 26*(3), 39–45.

Gross, D., Julion, W., & Fogg, L. (2000). What motivates participation and drop-out among low-income urban families of color in a prevention intervention? *Family Relations, 50*(3), 246–254.

Harvard Family Research Project. (1996). *Supporting Latino families: Lessons from exemplary programs.* Cambridge, MA: Harvard Family Research Project, 38 Concord Avenue.

Hill, C. E., Thompson, B. J., & Williams, E. N. (1997). A guide to conducting consensual qualitative research. *The Counseling Psychologist, 25*(4), 517–572.

Kumpfer, K. L., Alvarado, R., Smith, P., & Bellamy, N. (2002). Cultural sensitivity and adaptation in family-based prevention interventions. *Prevention Science, 3*(3), 241–246.

Malley-Morrison, K., & Hines, D. A. (2004). *Family violence in a cultural perspective.* Thousand Oaks, CA: Sage.

Moos, R. H. (2003). Social context: transcending their power and their fragility. *American Journal of Community Psychology, 31*(1/2), 1–14.

University of Wisconsin Extension & Applied Laboratory. (2001). *Wisconsin's Hispanic or Latino population: Census 2000 population and trends.* Madison, WI: Applied Population Laboratory.

Wandesman, A. (2003). Community science: Bridging the gap between science and practice with community-centered models. *American Journal of Community Psychology, 31*(2/4), 227–242.

Weaver, H. (2005). *Explorations in Cultural Competency: Journeys to the Four Directions.* Belmont, CA: Thomson Brooks/Cole.

About the Author

Lynet Uttal, Ph.D., is an associate professor in the Department of Human Development and Family Studies, University of Wisconsin–Madison, 1430 Linden Drive, #202, Madison, WI 53706. Phone: 608-263-4026. E-mail: luttal@wisc.edu.

Epilogue

ROCHELLE L. DALLA, JOHN DeFRAIN, JULIE JOHNSON,
AND DOUGLAS A. ABBOTT

THIS BOOK ABOUT immigrant family strengths was conceived as a means to articulate the unique factors, processes, and worldviews that help shape and mold the immigrant experience in America. So, what has been learned? And, more importantly, what does this knowledge mean for continued research, education, service provision, and policy formation? In writing this epilogue, we revisited each of the nineteen well-crafted chapters, looking for gaps that still might exist in the literature and questions that remain unanswered. In our closing comments below these gaps are addressed and questions for continued consideration are posed.

How Immigration Changes Immigrants and How Immigrants Change America

Knight, Jacobson, Gonzales, Roosa, and Saenz describe the reciprocal dual-cultural adaptation processes of acculturation (i.e., adaptation to the mainstream or host culture) and enculturation (i.e., adaptation by the larger society to the ethnic culture). These socialization processes are described as "multidimensional and multi-axial" and greatly influenced by the developmental state of each individual and experiences acquired over a lifetime. Yet, Knight et al. contend that our measurement instruments, research designs and analytic strategies are severely limited: they have not "kept pace" with the theoretical literature and thus, fail to capture the essence of these socialization processes both within and between immigrant groups.

To address gaps in the literature, the authors contend that recognition of and attention to *sub-group* variations within ethnic groups are critical, as are the use of longitudinal studies for deciphering individual and group change processes. We agree with these suggestions while noting that longitudinal studies are difficult because immigrants move frequently, thus rendering longitudinal assessments time-consuming and costly. Given time and resource constraints, one might ask how researchers can best leverage their resources in order to create successful longitudinal studies? What strategies can be used to maintain contact with immigrant families, across time and often geographic distance, so longitudinal research is feasible?

Complementing the work of Knight and colleagues, Leakhena Nou examined psychosocial adaptation (i.e., emotional well-being) of Cambodian adult refugees in three Massachusetts communities. She discovered that *daily hassles* and *unresolved post-traumatic stress disorder* (PTSD) were related to scores on the Brief Symptoms Inventory and psychological and somatic symptoms nearly thirty years after experiencing the brutality of the Khmer Rouge regime. Linking her research to that of Knight et al., one might ask the extent to which individual acculturation and enculturation processes lead to differential outcomes in mental health among those who have experienced psychological and physical trauma prior to immigration. Further questions arise from Nou's work as well. For instance, to what extent are *daily hassles* (e.g., use of public transportation, reading signs, and spoken English language skills acquisition) perceived differently given differential adaptation experiences and community resources? To what extent do these differences influence ongoing adaptation processes? Nou's work suggests additional questions for continued scholarship, such as: To what extent are mental health service providers culturally sensitive to psychosocial adaptation factors and traditional healthcare belief systems of immigrant and refugee populations within their communities? How can counselors, mental health experts, and other service providers destigmatize the use of mental health services for immigrant newcomers? Finally, but of equal significance, how can mental health service providers most effectively reach out to immigrant and refugee populations—groups notorious for underutilizing mental health services?

The chapter written by Trask, Brady, Qiu, and Radnai-Griffin *personalizes* the immigration experience and poignantly testifies to how a myriad of factors—from broad sociocultural structures (i.e., culture and ethnicity, country of origin, sociohistorical time of arrival) to unique individual demographic variables (e.g., age of arrival, marital status, education level, family connections)—significantly impact individual and familial adaption across the lifecourse. Clearly, there is immense variation in the immigration experience, yet individual differences are often overlooked when immigrants, as *collective bodies*, are the unit of analysis for our research. .

The work of Trask et al. clearly piques our interest, largely because of the micro-level perspective (four individual case histories) and the host of questions raised by such an approach. For instance, how can human service providers equip themselves to best recognize and respond to unique individual and familial-level factors, without losing sight of broader sociocultural and historical immigration issues? To what extent are members of the host country impacted by the unique values, belief systems, talents, skills, and resilience of their immigrant neighbors, coworkers, and friends—and how do these bidirectional influences further shape and mold the immigration experience? Finally, to what extent can U.S. social and immigration policy be flexible enough to allow for individual variability, yet inclusive enough to resonate with the needs and experiences of all immigrants?

In their chapter "Transnational Families and the Social Construction of Identity: Whiteness Matters," Libby Balter Blume and Lee Ann De Reus explore the complicated meanings of *ethnicity* for new immigrant families—many of whom maintain social relationships and family links across borders. Intersectionality, a term used by the authors, describes the multiple identities that people hold simultaneously, and highlights the complex and fluid nature of personal identifications that are often contextually embedded. Blume and De Reus argue that whiteness is not only a social construction that "confounds our understanding of ethnicity" but also a "privileging mechanism" in American society for immigrant newcomers and the service providers, educators, and researchers in which they come into contact. The multiple intersections of nationality, ethnicity, and social constructions of race thereby shape and mold the immigration experience of new immigrants in ways rarely examined by family scholars. This chapter raises important questions, including: To what extent are family practitioners and service providers aware of their own ethnicity? To what extent does ethnic self-awareness impact ongoing interactions between service providers, educators, scholars, and the new immigrants with whom they work? Finally, to what extent does *whiteness* as a social construct and privileging factor in American society differentially influence within- and between-group adaptation experiences for immigrant newcomers and their families?

Marriages and Families

East Indians are often considered one of the most "successful immigrant minorities" in America. Despite sociocultural and religious differences, they tend to "assimilate well into American society." It is surprising then that few studies have sought to explore changes in East Indian individual and familial adaptation processes. Abbott and Moulik Gupta address this gap in the literature by examining changes in marital interactions, parenting behaviors, and personal identity among recently immigrated East Indian couples with children. Results indicate that exposure to American society exerts substantial influence on both the spousal and parent-child subsystems that reflect "American values of individualism and autonomy" as opposed to the "values of a collectivistic society like India."

Given the results of this investigation, coupled with Knight et al.'s recommendation to identify and acknowledge *sub-group* differences in acculturation and enculturation, examination of similar processes among demographically diverse (e.g., different educational/economic resources) Indian immigrants is warranted. Moreover, some of the participants in the Abbott and Moulik Gupta study indicated that familial change was largely related to the *absence* of in-laws and to the successful integration into Indian communities in America. Incorporating the work of Blume and De Reus, future research is needed to examine individual and familial acculturation processes in conjunction with the multiplicity of ethnic identities experienced among *transnational* Indian immigrants or those whose extended kin have also immigrated to the United States.

Detzner, Şenyürekli, Yang, and Sheikh examined intergenerational perceptions of family strengths in Hmong and Somali refugees in Minnesota. Their research, coupled with the investigation of strong marriages within Latino culture by Skogrand, Hatch, and Singh, provide insight into familial resources that promote individual well-being among distinct populations of immigrant newcomers. Somali participants identified respect, communication, unity, and religion as prominent family strengths, while Hmong informants mentioned love, communication, role modeling, and religion. Latino immigrants identified children, communication, and religion as components necessary for maintaining strong marriages. Despite vastly different religious beliefs, countries of origin, and cultural backgrounds, strong similarities emerged among the three immigrants in the strengths they possessed. Communication and religion, in particular, were mentioned frequently by participants in both studies as critical for maintaining strong kin ties. These studies raise many questions. For example, how can service providers build upon and enhance family communication skills and religious beliefs and practices within families struggling with the acculturation process? In a related vein, how can educators and service providers help immigrant families *maintain* strong communication and religious commitment over time? Longitudinal work would be informative in this regard. Finally, to what extent do policies enacted at the local, state, and federal levels promote and/or erode these immigrant family strengths?

As evident in many chapters in this book, individual characteristics significantly impact the immigration experience and subsequent adaptation to a new country and sociocultural landscape. Gender is one of these significant characteristics. In chapter 8 by Miller and González, the grief process among migrating Latinas is examined while chapter 9 by Oksana Yakushko turns our attention to career and employment concerns of immigrant women. These two issues are likely to influence immigrant family adaptation and well-being in many important ways. Applying a theoretical model of the grieving process, Miller and González conclude the grieving process from immigration is similar to that experienced upon the loss of a loved one.

Numerous questions for continued reflection and research come to mind. Specifically, to what extent do immigrant women's experiences with grief and loss impact familial-level dynamics? Are women's experiences with grief different from those of their male partners? Do children and youth grieve differently than adult immigrants and, more importantly, what are the long-term impacts of such for their psychosocial well-being? Finally, to what extent are educators and service providers trained to identify and respond to symptoms of *grief and grieving* among immigrants in order to help ease feelings of loss?

In relation to employment and career advancement, results of Yakushko's study are similar to other studies in the extant literature indicating that immigrant women are more likely than their male counterparts to find jobs, yet their employment tends to be in low-level positions requiring few skills and offering little room for advancement. Broad, sociocultural issues (e.g., racism, sexism, discrimination, and poverty) complicate employment options for immigrant women, and these have significant implications for individual and family well-being. Connecting Yakushko's work with that of Blume and De Reus discussed earlier, future work examining the "multiple intersecting identities" (e.g., race, class, gender, age) of immigrant women and the implications of such for workplace oppression and discrimination would inform theory, research, and practice.

Parents and Children

Decisions regarding childcare (e.g., early childhood education, affordability, child rearing beliefs, transportation) and child rearing practices (e.g., feeding routines, toilet training, discipline) are often difficult for many parents—made even more so when one is simultaneously struggling with language barriers, employment, limited social support, and other acculturative stressors associated with immigration. Although their sample was small (seven families), Amarapurkar and Hogan conclude their investigation of African (i.e., Congolese, Ethiopian, and Nigerian) immigrant parents' childcare decisions by offering valuable theoretical and research implications for continued scholarship in this area. They also pose a series of practitioner recommendations relevant for any service provider working with immigrant parents of young children, regardless of country of origin.

This research is complemented by that of Londhe who found that Indian immigrant parents often struggle with *identity issues* (e.g., "What does it mean to raise an Indian child?") when making critical child rearing decisions. Consideration of the myriad challenges associated with parenting in a new sociocultural environment raises several questions. For instance, to what extent can immigrant parents' cultural beliefs, values, and child rearing practices (e.g., baby massage) be integrated into American parent-education curricula aimed at immigrant newcomers? How can teachers and service providers assist immigrant parents in making child rearing decisions that are respectful of unique *cultural* beliefs and values, and that simultaneously enhance children's socialization into American society? Do parenting *styles* differ appreciably between East Indian immigrant parents of variable socioeconomic and educational backgrounds? And further, what are the implications of such for long-term developmental outcomes and parent-child relationships? Finally, connecting Londhe's research with that of Abbott and Moulik Gupta, the implications of child rearing decisions on *marital relationships and subsequent familial dynamics* must be considered—particularly if the rate and magnitude of acculturation *differs* between parents and between parents and children.

The complexity of the immigration experience and its impact within families is further examined in the work of Hofstetter and colleagues. According to Hofstetter et al., differential change in attitudes, beliefs, and behaviors are important sources of intergenerational differences: youth acculturate more quickly than their immigrant parents. In this study, family conflict was reportedly low by both Korean youth and their parents, yet intergenerational acculturation differences were associated with family conflict. Dating, culture, and grades in school created the greatest conflict—issues similar to those reported in studies of other immigrant groups as well. Moreover, that youth become acculturated more quickly than their parents is not unique to this study of Koreans; such findings are consistent with research on other immigrant groups as well. According to Hofstetter et al., continued work is warranted in order to better understand unique familial dynamics and "larger societal contingencies that support low or high levels of family conflict." From an ecological and systems perspective, comparisons across immigrant groups within the same communities would be informative, as would those of immigrants from the same countries of origin residing in different geographical areas (e.g., rural versus urban) offering vastly different types and sources of formal and informal support.

What happens to adolescents and young adults who must adapt to a new culture and country without the support and guidance of their parents? This question is addressed by Luster, Johnson, and Bates in their investigation of the "Lost Boys" (and girls) of Sudan who lived in peer groups, lacking parental and often adult supervision for many years before they were resettled in Michigan. Challenges of adapting to American culture differed appreciably between the youth, largely based on age of resettlement and gender. Once again, the "intersectionality" of multiple identities—and the challenges of identity consolidation and integration—come to the fore. That is, the developmental stage of adolescence is typically characterized as a time of identity exploration. Thus, not only were these Sudanese youth and young adults confronted with "sorting out their cultural identity," but other identities as well that are typical of their developmental stage (e.g., education, career/employment, and personal values and belief systems), often in the *absence* of parental or other adult role models.

It was interesting to learn that many of the youth reported their strong religious beliefs helped them "interpret their experiences and find reasons to go on struggling" while in the Sudanese displacement camps. We see direct linkages between this and the research of others discussed in this book. Recall the work of Detzner et al. (who studied Hmong and Somali refugees) and Skogrand et al. (who studied Latino families): in both investigations, *religion* was one of the most frequently identified *family strengths*. Among the Sudanese youth, religion was paramount for maintaining resilience in the face of horrific atrocities and trauma. Continued work examining how children and youth define and characterize *family strengths*, in comparison to their parents or other adult role models, would be informative for directing service provision.

Finally, two additional chapters in this edited book further our under-standing of immigrant parent-child relationships. The chapters comple-ment one another in that both focus on adult children and their elderly parents. Panda and Sanders examine relationships between migrant adult children (from thirty-five different countries) living in the United States and their parents who remain in the home country; Xie and Xia focus on co-residence among Chinese immigrants and their adult children. From each study, we are able to glean a new and more informed understand-ing of immigrant parent-child relationship dynamics across the lifecourse. Continued work in this area is needed, as research on these unique dimen-sions of parenting are exceedingly uncommon.

For instance, the bidirectional influences of acculturation and encultura-tion socialization processes *between* adult immigrant children and their el-derly parents who co-reside have not yet been examined. Such work would provide valuable insight into familial dynamics across multiple generations of immigrant families. Further, exploration of the grandparent-grandchild relationships, in both transnational families and extended kin immigrant families co-residing in the United States, would be valuable for service providers as well as academicians. Finally, to what extent are formal service providers (e.g., health care) equipped to address the needs of elderly im-migrants, particularly given divergent (and often opposing) cultural values and belief systems?

Community and Programmatic Issues

From an ecological systems perspective, community level resources (e.g., formal and informal supports and infrastructure) can profoundly influence immigrant family adaptation. Yet, few have examined immigrant adapta-tion within *rural* communities. Two studies described in this book pres-ent data which begin to fill this gap in the literature. Potter, Cantarero, and Boren examine predictors of residential satisfaction among newly arrived Latino immigrants (NAR) and long-term, non-Latino Caucasian residents (LTR) of a rural Nebraska community, while Greder, Cook, Garasky, Sano, and Randall examine food security, housing, and social support among Latino immigrant mothers in three rural communities located in Iowa and Oregon. In the first study, both NAR and LTR reported stress as the most critical issue influencing residential satisfaction and quality of life. Among NAR, issues concerning family and friends created the greatest stress.

In the second study, immigrants' perceived social support was also significant in that it "contributed substantially to the economic and social well-being" of the families. For immigrant newcomers, the presence of a rich and multilayered formal and informal network structure from which to draw upon in time of need and in navigating unfamiliar social, cultural, and contextual territory is paramount to short-term adaptation and long-term well-being. To what extent do contextual conditions in rural versus urban areas (e.g., local assistance programs, outreach efforts, labor markets, housing conditions) promote and challenge immigrant family adaptation, despite available informal supports? To what extent can educators and service providers help build relationship bridges between new immigrants and their neighbors as a means of strengthening informal networks across cultural boundaries? Finally, the economic base of many rural communities would falter if not for the labor of immigrant newcomers. With this in mind, how can local and state policies be shaped in order to help rural immigrant families maintain and strengthen kin connections so that their presence in rural geographies continues across generations?

This book concludes with two chapters dedicated to programmatic issues relevant to those working in direct service to new immigrant families. Recognizing the unique stresses faced by immigrant parents, Radina, Wilson, and Hennon make significant recommendations for culturally relevant family life education "intended to meet the needs of Mexican heritage parents." Their recommendations are empirically grounded and based on the creation of a new model which presents factors that both precipitate and diffuse parenting stress. In her chapter, Lynet Uttal discusses the challenges to "achieving full organizational responsiveness to Latino world views and organizational cultural competency." Although both Radina et al. and Uttal focused on a particular group of immigrants (i.e., Mexican heritage and Spanish-speaking Latinos, respectively), we believe their recommendations for achieving cultural competence are relevant to organizations and agencies serving any immigrant group. In addition to providing valuable service, education, and policy recommendations, both chapters emphasize that strong, culturally relevant practice is research based. Following from this, a question worthy of further consideration is, to what extent do academicians and scientists purposely disseminate their research for use in an applied manner? In a related vein, how can policy makers, researchers, educators, and practitioners create and maintain stronger working relationships so the needs of immigrant families are addressed on multiple levels?

Conclusion

As we conclude work on *Strengths and Challenges of New Immigrant Families: Implications for Research, Education, Policy, and Service*, we would be remiss if we did not invest some time and thought in an effort to synthesize what we have seen into a meaningful conceptual framework for the reader. In this effort to put the nineteen chapters of this book into a broader context, we will not only rely upon a previously developed model of family strengths, community strengths, and cultural strengths, but we will also add new thoughts on immigrant family challenges and how communities can respond from a strengths orientation. For an in-depth perspective on these issues, see *Strong Families Around the World: Strengths-Based Research and Perspectives*, edited by John DeFrain and Sylvia M. Asay. This book presents studies of family strengths and challenges conducted by forty-three family specialists working in teams in eighteen countries around the world, representing all seven major geocultural areas of the earth.

Family Strengths Worldwide

The International Family Strengths Model has evolved out of research stretching back over four decades. Family strengths studies have been conducted involving more than 24,000 family members in 35 countries around the world. The International Family Strengths Model is a useful template for discussing family strengths from a global perspective. It posits that the qualities that define a strong, happy, highly satisfied, emotionally healthy, and loving family can be divided into six broad and overlapping clusters:

- Appreciation and affection for each other
- Positive communication
- Commitment to the family
- Enjoyable time together
- A sense of spiritual well-being, and
- The ability to manage stress and crisis effectively (DeFrain & Asay, p. 452)

As we think back on what we have seen in this book, the six family strengths in the International Family Strengths Model work well in describing what immigrant family members do to strengthen the bonds they have with each other and make it possible to work together in meeting the challenges they face. The research presented by Abbott and Moulik Gupta is illustrative. The East Indian couples in their investigation described how, after immigrating to America, spouses *spent more time together as a couple*, reported greater *communication*, and began to *appreciate one another* in new and different ways. Likewise, Hmong and Somali (see Detzner et al.) immigrants identified *communication* and *religion* (interpreted as *spiritual well-being*) as their greatest family strengths; and Skogrand et al. noted that "spending time together and talking often" were critical to maintaining strong marriages among their Latino participants. Further, research examining the grief process among migrating Latinas (see Miller and González) demonstrates that the *ability to manage stress and crises effectively* is particularly critical for immigrant families adapting to new cultural, political, and social landscapes. Examined in concert, these examples provide compelling evidence for the applicability of the International Family Strengths Model to *immigrant families in America*, as we would predict.

Community Strengths Worldwide

It is clear that strong families contribute to the well-being of communities, and strong communities enhance the development of strong families. A number of important *community* strengths were also described by the international team of investigators coordinated by DeFrain and Asay:

- A supportive environment that genuinely values families, and a general willingness and natural generosity infused in the culture to help when families are in need
- An effective educational delivery system
- Religious communities for families seeking this kind of support
- Family-service programs developed by government and nongovernmental organizations for families who cannot find the help they need from their own extended family, friends, and neighbors, and
- A safe, secure, and healthful environment (DeFrain & Asay, p. 454)

The work of Luster, Johnson, and Bates is particularly illustrative of the importance of these specific community strengths for *immigrants* in America. The successful adaptation of the "Lost Boys" (and girls) of Sudan was dependent upon the cooperation and collaboration of *family service programs* (i.e., St. Vincent Catholic Charities, Inc., and Lutheran Social Services), an *educational system* willing to adapt to the special needs of the youth, a *supportive environment* (including volunteer mentors and foster families), and *a safe and secure environment* free of violence and genocide experienced by the youth in their homeland. Various community strengths were also noted in

Amarapurkar and Hogan's research with African immigrant parents with preschool aged children and in Xie and Xia's study of multigenerational, co-residing Chinese immigrant families. In both investigations, *effective educational delivery systems* (especially those that are flexible and adaptable given unique cultural values, and which disseminate information about community-based resources), *supportive environments* (i.e., where families obtain assistance through a comprehensive coordination of services), and *communities that value safety and security* for all members regardless of age, educational level, or income were noted as particularly conducive to the successful adaptation of immigrant newcomers. Finally, both Radina et al. and Uttal note that, despite the challenges to creating *culturally relevant family service programs*, the short- and long-term investment in the success-ful adaptation of new cultural groups results in significant and positive community-wide outcomes.

Cultural Strengths Worldwide

Family strengths and community strengths reinforce each other, as we have seen so far. There is a third level or dimension that needs to be included in the discussion, called cultural strengths. These include:

- A rich cultural history
- Shared cultural meanings
- A stable political process
- A viable economy, and
- An understanding of the global society (DeFrain & Asay, pp. 456–57)

As part of the International Family Strengths Model, these five *cultural strengths* were clearly identified in the qualitative analysis conducted dur-ing the development of the *Strong Families Around the World* book. It is important to consider how these particular cultural strengths become *chal-lenged* or *tested* when families leave their homelands and immigrate to new environmental, sociopolitical, and cultural contexts.

When adult children and their elderly parents do not immigrate to-gether, for instance, fulfilling roles and expectations embedded within a family's unique *cultural history* and *shared cultural meanings* may become se-verely challenged, leading to conflict, stress, and tension. Such was evident in the work of Panda and Sanders. They describe how adult immigrant children experience difficulty in supporting elderly parents living within their home cultures because the *meaning* of adult child and caregiver roles is strongly influenced by the social and cultural context of the individual. "Efforts to fulfill these roles while living far away and in a different culture could be especially challenging if these roles are considered of great importance in the individual's culture and if the person's family standing (such as first-born son) gives even greater meaning to the role."

Likewise, even when parents and children immigrate together, these same cultural strengths (e.g., *cultural history* and *shared cultural meaning*) may weaken due to differential acculturation processes. This was noted by Hofstetter et al. who examined conflict between Korean parents and their adolescent children. "The forces of mandatory free public schooling, mass media, peer pressure, and trying to get along in American society may lead children to learn the language, folkways, and mores of this society more quickly than their parents. This process also may reflect the degree to which parents have experienced many years of the traditional culture, compared to fewer (and qualitatively different) traditional influences on their children." Parents may, in effect, become resistant to change resulting in greater intrafamilial conflict. Insight into how differences in rate and magnitude of acculturation change challenges immigrant family *cultural strengths* was also evident in the work of other authors as well, including Trask et al., Abbott and Moulik Gupta, and Blume and De Reus.

Likewise, Potter, Cantarero, and Boren also refer to the importance of *shared cultural meanings*—but from a slightly different point of view—one that incorporates cultural understanding between members of both sending and receiving communities. For Latino immigrant newcomers to a small rural community, "Tension with neighbors appeared to be the most stressful aspect of life" exacerbated "by the cultural dissimilarity between the long-term residents and newly arrived residents, resulting in racial tensions." Similar results have been reported in numerous other studies as well. To address this significant source of tension and strain, they recommend the following: for both newcomers and long-term residents, there need to be programs to help break down barriers created by the fear and mistrust arising from mutual cultural unfamiliarity.

We would be remiss if we neglected to address how the *cultural strengths* of immigrant newcomers are challenged by macro-level structures, including economic and sociopolitical forces. This is particularly evident in the work of Yakushko. She describes how xenophobia, racism, sexism, and poverty are often interconnected; each systematically contributes to the oppression and discrimination toward immigrant newcomers, generally speaking, and immigrant women in particular. "Economic discrimination and poverty, as well as employment discrimination, have the most impact

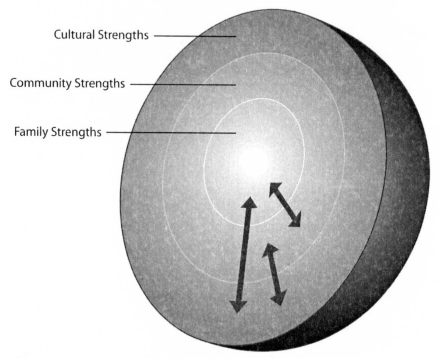

Cultural Strengths

Community Strengths

Family Strengths

The Interaction of Family Strengths, Community Strengths, and Cultural Strengths
Source: DeFrain & Asay (2007), p. 461. Reprinted with permission.

on immigrant women's well being in the U.S." Yet, employment is *central* not only for economic survival, but also for cultural integration. To address the intersection of multiple macro-systemic factors that challenge immigrant newcomers' successful adaptation, Yakushko recommends that "We step out from the U.S.-centric scholarly focus toward a more *global perspective.*"

For a very simplified view of how family, community, and cultural strengths interact with each other, see the model in the figure above.

The study of family strengths is not new. In fact, three decades ago they were defined by Nick Stinnett as:

> Those relationship patterns, interpersonal skills and competencies, and social and psychological characteristics which create a sense of positive family identity, promote satisfying and fulfilling interaction among family members, encourage the development of the potential of the family group and individual family members, and contribute to the family's ability to deal effectively with stress and crises. (Stinnett, 1979, p. 2)

Since then, interest in *strong families* and the study of family strengths has grown exponentially. Application of a family strengths framework from which to appreciate immigrant families in America, however, is cutting edge and utterly unique. We, as the editors of this book, feel fortunate for the opportunity to share the work, ideas, and experiences of so many experts on two topics that we care about deeply—family strengths and immigrant newcomers. Now that the book has been written, and the journey complete, we are convinced more than ever that families regardless of cultural reference, ethnic identity, or geographic birth place, share more similarities than differences. Further, it is our hope that the readers of this book will come to a similar conclusion, and, in doing so, will be able to identify with their immigrant neighbors with a new sense of commonality and a shared sense of humanity and respect.

References

DeFrain, J., & Asay, S. M. (2007). *Strong families around the world: Strengths-based research and perspectives.* New York and London: Haworth Press / Taylor & Francis Group.

Stinnett, N. (1979). Introduction. In N. Stinnett, B. Chesser & J. DeFrain, *Building family strengths: Blueprints for action* (p. 3). Lincoln: University of Nebraska Press.

Appendix A: Editorial Board

Rich Bischoff, Ph.D., associate professor, Child, Youth and Family Studies, University of Nebraska–Lincoln

Kathy Bosch, Ph.D., assistant professor, Panhandle Research and Extension Center, Department of Child, Youth and Family Studies, University of Nebraska–Lincoln

Leon Caldwell, Ph.D., research associate professor, Department of Psychology, University of Memphis, Tennessee

Nina Chen, Ph.D., human development specialist, University of Missouri Extension, Lee's Summit, Missouri

Sue Couch, Ph.D., professor and program director, Family and Consumer Sciences Education, Texas Tech University

Cherry de Guzman, Ph.D., assistant professor, Department of Child, Youth and Family Studies, University of Nebraska–Lincoln

Ruth Dohner, Ph.D., associate professor, Workforce Development and Education, College of Education and Human Ecology, Ohio State University

Arlin Etling, Ph.D., professor, College of Agriculture Sciences and Natural Resources, University of Nebraska–Lincoln

Tina Fitchett, M.Ed. (Hons), head of Department of Social Sciences, Manukau Institute of Technology, Auckland, New Zealand

Mary Gabriel, M.P.S., lecturer, Department of Child, Youth and Family Studies, University of Nebraska–Lincoln

Wendy Gamble, Ph.D., professor, Norton School of Family and Consumer Sciences, University of Arizona

Toni Hill-Menson, doctoral student, Department of Child, Youth and Family Studies, University of Nebraska-Lincoln

Cody Hollist, Ph.D., assistant professor, Child, Youth and Family Studies, University of Nebraska–Lincoln

Catherine Huddleston-Casas, Ph.D., assistant professor, Child, Youth and Family Studies, University of Nebraska–Lincoln

Genc Janaqi, doctoral student, Department of Child, Youth and Family Studies, University of Nebraska–Lincoln

Wenli Liu, Ph.D., assistant professor, Center for Science Education, Beijing Normal University, Beijing, People's Republic of China

Busisiwe Nkosi, Ph.D., senior researcher, Health Economics and HIV/AIDS Research Division, University of KwaZulu-Natal, Newcastle, South Africa

Carolyn Slotten, lecturer, Department of Family Studies and Social Work, Miami University of Ohio, Oxford, Ohio

Georgia Stevens, Ph.D., professor emeritus, Department of Child, Youth and Family Studies, University of Nebraska-Lincoln

Joseph Stimpfl, Ph.D., associate professor and department chair, Department of Religious Studies, Webster University, St. Louis, Missouri

Julia Torquati, Ph.D., associate professor, Child, Youth and Family Studies, University of Nebraska–Lincoln

Chico Villarruel, Ph.D., University Outreach and Engagement Senior Fellow and professor, Family & Child Ecology, Michigan State University

Virginia Vincenti, Ph.D., professor, Family and Consumer Sciences, University of Wyoming

Gyesook Yoo, Ph.D., assistant professor, Department of Child and Family Studies, Kyung Hee University, Seoul, Korea

Appendix B: The Kur Family and the Noe Bay Family

The Kur Family

JOSEPH WAS BORN IN THE SUDAN. Their father and mother were killed during the civil war between the Arab Muslims in the north and the Black African Christians in the south. Joseph was one of seven children. Two brothers were also killed. Joseph was captured by the Muslims when he was sixteen-years-old and forced to convert to Islam. He escaped three years later in 1991 and joined the rebels in the south. In one battle he was shot in the leg, received medical treatment in Kenya, and then ended up in a refugee camp on the Sudan-Uganda border. He and other family members finally escaped to Egypt and received a visa to America in 1999. He first settled in Pennsylvania but then moved to Nebraska. His family in Sudan arranged his marriage to Anyath. In 2003 he traveled to Egypt and married her. He returned to Nebraska alone and it took another three years before Anyath could join him in Lincoln. Their baby Aker is five months old.

The Noe Bay Family

Noe Bay, his wife, Pa Saw, and their six children arrived in Lincoln, Nebraska on July 3, 2007. Noe Bay and Pa Saw escaped separately from

---

The Kur family and the Noe Bay family are both featured on the cover of this book.

Myanmar in 1985 and 1987 respectively. They were part of the Karen minority group that has been persecuted by the Burmese military government for over forty years. Burmese troops have forced many Karen civilians to relocate to villages under their control. Old villages are burnt down and landmined to stop villagers from returning. Forced labor is demanded for months at a time. Sometimes Burmese soldiers would capture and enslave the older boys and younger men. Noe Bay and Pa Saw met and married in a refugee camp in Thailand named "Mae La." Their six children were all born in the camp. After living there for twenty-one years, Noe Bay finally received visas for his family to come to the United States.

Index

About the Editors

Douglas A. Abbott, Ph.D., is a professor of Child, Youth and Family Studies at the University of Nebraska–Lincoln. He received a doctorate in child and family studies from the University of Georgia. A primary research interest has been cross-cultural family studies and he has completed two U.S. Fulbrights to India in 1996 and to Israel and Palestine in 2006. He is currently working on a project regarding dating and sexual decision making in Muslim adolescents who are recent immigrants to America.

Rochelle L. Dalla, Ph.D., is an associate professor in the Department of Child, Youth and Family Studies at the University of Nebraska–Lincoln. She received a doctorate in family studies from the University of Arizona, with a minor in Native American studies. Her research is family-centered and developmental, with attention to change through time. She is currently studying gendered marital and family dynamics among rural-residing Latino immigrants.

John DeFrain, Ph.D., is an extension professor of family and community development in the Department of Child, Youth and Family Studies, University of Nebraska–Lincoln. His research over three decades has focused on family strengths and challenges around the world. He believes that, "New immigrant families remake America in countless positive ways, and America offers wonderful opportunities for newcomers."

Julie Johnson, Ph.D., is chair of the Department of Child, Youth and Family Studies, University of Nebraska–Lincoln. She is also professor of family and consumer science education. As the chair of the department, she is concerned about helping students and faculty embrace new immigrants and their cultures as they enrich our community. As a teacher educator, she is interested in helping prepare teachers to work effectively with all students.